A Future for Policing in and Wales

A Future for Policing in England and Wales

Timothy Brain

OXFORD
UNIVERSITY PRESS

OXFORD

UNIVERSITY PRESS

Great Clarendon Street, Oxford, OX2 6DP,
United Kingdom

Oxford University Press is a department of the University of Oxford.
It furthers the University's objective of excellence in research, scholarship,
and education by publishing worldwide. Oxford is a registered trade mark of
Oxford University Press in the UK and in certain other countries

© Timothy Brain 2013

The moral rights of the author have been asserted

First Edition published in 2013

Impression: 1

Published in the United States of America by Oxford University Press
198 Madison Avenue, New York, NY 10016, United States of America

British Library Cataloguing in Publication Data

Data available

Library of Congress Control Number: 2013940569

ISBN 978–0–19–968445–8

Printed and bound in Great Britain by
CPI Group (UK) Ltd, Croydon, CR0 4YY

Links to third party websites are provided by Oxford in good faith and
for information only. Oxford disclaims any responsibility for the materials
contained in any third party website referenced in this work.

To Elisabeth and Richard

Contents

Abbreviations

ACC	Assistant Chief Constable
ACPO	Association of Chief Police Officers
ANPR	Automatic Number Plate Recognition
APA	Association of Police Authorities
ASBO	Anti-social Behaviour Order
BCS	British Crime Survey
BCU	Basic Command Unit
CCTV	Closed Circuit Television
CEOP	Child Exploitation and Online Protection Centre
CFF	Crime Fighting Fund
Cipfa	Chartered Institute of Public Finance and Accountancy
CPS	Crown Prosecution Service
CRASBO	Criminal Anti-social Behaviour Order
CSEW	Crime Survey for England and Wales
CSR	Comprehensive Spending Review
DCLG	Department for Communities and Local Government
DNA	Deoxyribonucleic Acid
DTTO	Drug Treatment and Testing Order
EAW	European Arrest Warrant
EU	European Union
FBI	Federal Bureau of Investigation
FTA	Fixed Term Appointment
FTE	Full Time Equivalent
GDP	Gross Domestic Product
GLC	Greater London Council
HMI	Her Majesty's Inspector of Constabulary
HMIC	Her Majesty's Inspectorate of Constabulary
HOLMES	Home Office Large Major Enquiry System
HPDS	Higher Potential Development Scheme
HRA	Human Rights Act 1998
ICT	Information and Communications Technology
IFS	Institute for Fiscal Studies
IPCC	Independent Police Complaints Commission
ISIS	Information Systems Improvement Strategy
IT	Information Technology
LGA	Local Government Association
MPS	Metropolitan Police Service
NCA	National Crime Agency
NCIS	National Criminal Intelligence Service

NCRS	National Crime Recording Standard
NCS	National Crime Squad
NHS	National Health Service
NIM	National Intelligence Model
NNDR	National Non-Domestic Rates
NPIA	National Policing Improvement Agency
OBTJ	Offences Brought to Justice
OPR	*Operational Policing Review*
OUP	Oxford University Press
PAB	Police Advisory Board
PACE	Police and Criminal Evidence Act 1984
PAT	Police Arbitration Tribunal
PCC	Police and Crime Commissioner
PCP	Police and Crime Panel
PCSO	Police Community Support Officer
PFI	Public Finance Initiative
PITO	Police Information Technology Organisation
PNB	Police Negotiating Board
PNC	Police National Computer
PNICC	Police National Information and Co-ordination Centre
PPOP	Priority and Prolific Offender Programme
PPS	Police Pension Scheme
PR	Police Review
PRCS	Police recorded crime statistics
PSU	Police Standards Unit
RIPA	Regulation of Investigatory Powers Act 2000
RSG	Rate Support Grant
SAP	Senior Appointments Panel
SCC	Strategic Command Course
SOCA	Serious and Organised Crime Agency
SPP	Special Priority Payment
SSRB	Senior Salaries Review Body
UKIP	United Kingdom Independence Party
WAG	Welsh Assembly Government
WG	Welsh Government
YOT	Youth Offending Team

Introduction

The road from Dalston

Dalston, in the London Borough of Hackney, may not be the most obvious place from which to launch a revolution, especially one in policing, but that is what happened on Monday 16 January 2006.

David Cameron, a 30-year-old Old Etonian and Oxford Politics, Philosophy, and Economics graduate, had been elected Conservative leader only the previous December, and he had chosen Dalston to make one of his earliest policy announcements, on police and law and order. Dalston forms part of the London Borough of Hackney, an ethnically diverse area and, although experiencing along with other inner-London boroughs the phenomenon of 'gentrification', it was ranked high on the list of London districts denoting deprivation.[1] It is, furthermore, part of Labour's inner-London heartland, with a rock-solid Labour majority council, and returning two Labour MPs. It was not, therefore, an obvious location for a Conservative politician, particularly one with such a patrician background.

Nor was the precise venue of the policy announcement an obvious choice. He had chosen the Dalston Youth Project, an interventionist scheme, supported by the borough council, focusing on improving the social and educational skills of 11- to 14-year-olds in the area who were at risk of dropping out of school and of becoming involved in offending behaviour. Crucially, local volunteers, supported by professionals from within the project, provided the interventions. Over many years it had proved successful and had been subject to an encouraging Home Office study in 2001.[2] It was, in short, a scheme just about as far removed from the Conservatives' early 1980s method of addressing juvenile crime—the 'short, sharp shock'—as it was possible to get.

---

[1] Hackney Borough Council, *A Ward Profile of Dalston* (<http://www.hackney.gov.uk/Assets/Dalston/dalston-ward-profile.pdf> [accessed 25 April 2012]).

[2] R Tarling, J Burrows, and A Clarke, *Dalston Youth Project Part II, An Evaluation* (Home Office Research Study 232, Home Office Research, Development and Statistics Directorate, November 2001, <http://library.npia.police.uk/docs/hors/hors232.pdf> [accessed 25 April 2012]).

But David Cameron had not come to criticize the scheme. True, he had come to carry his political war to the enemy by speaking in a Labour stronghold, but he had chosen a successful youth-intervention scheme in inner London to symbolize a clean break with the recent Tory past.

In January 2006 Cameron was in the process of developing a new brand of 'compassionate' Conservatism, and Dalston marked an important staging post on the journey. His election had been a surprise. The successor to Michael Howard, doyenne of the old Right, was expected to be the experienced right-winger, Shadow Home Secretary David Davis, a self-made man from the wrong side of the tracks, but a combination of factors had eventually swung Cameron's way. There was a feeling abroad in the party that something had to change, and that a campaign based on such principles as Davis's might rally the core Conservative vote but make little impression on many in the aspirational professional classes who so far identified with Tony Blair's 'New Labour'. That Blair and his followers had largely forged their form of Labour principles on the groundwork of Thatcherism was to miss the point. It was Labour that was getting the votes and the Conservatives who remained in opposition. Without fundamentally repositioning, the party seemed likely to face another electoral defeat some time in 2008–9.

The key moment in Cameron's election campaign came with his speech to the October party conference. Speaking without notes, he passionately argued that Conservatism would have to be 'comfortable with modern Britain'. He promised to 'share' the benefits of economic growth between tax cuts and public services, to turn deprived areas around by setting voluntary sector leaders 'free'. His speech was necessarily light on detail, but he concluded in ringing tones: 'So let the message go out from this conference: a modern, compassionate conservatism is right for our times, right for our party, and right for our country.'[3] His visionary tone struck the right note and was sufficient to sway both Conservative MPs and the party at large his way.

Once elected, Cameron and his team sought to give the impression of 'not simply hitting the ground running but to hit it sprinting' but without actually saying anything very specific.[4] To beat Labour he knew that the party had to fundamentally reposition itself to attract new voters but not at the same time put off the traditional Conservative core. It would not be sufficient simply to reiterate old mantras around taxation, immigration, and Europe, and for that matter law and order; it had to divest itself of the image of being the 'nasty' party.[5] So he adopted a strategy of gradual expansion. First there would be some very general ideas; then some expanded statements, and finally detailed policies following the work of policy review teams.

---

[3] 'Full text: David Cameron's speech to the Conservative Party Conference 2005', guardian.co.uk, 4 October 2005 (<http://www.guardian.co.uk/politics/2005/oct/04/conservatives2005.conservatives3> [accessed 25 April 2012]).

[4] T Bale, *The Conservative Party: from Thatcher to Cameron* (Polity Press, Cambridge, 2010), 284.

[5] Bale, *The Conservative Party*, 285.

His first sprint came auspiciously on 1 January 2006 when he took out an advertisement in the *Sunday Telegraph* itemizing a six-point 'mini-manifesto', with strong statements on the environment, global poverty, and the NHS. He also had something to say about the police, but it was not the old Conservative traits of more officers and tougher laws: 'We shouldn't treat them with kid gloves just because officers do a brave job: we need radical police reform to help cut crime.' He further described the police as 'Britain's last great unreformed public service'.[6] It was a clear warning of what was to come.

At Dalston on 16 January, he did not mince his words but challenged both the police service and Labour's record directly. He condemned Labour's record on crime, for despite high levels of spending on the police Britain had the second-highest level of crime in Europe. But he focused not on crime but on 'the police', for the 'truth is that we won't deal with crime until we reform the police.'[7] This was an extraordinary way to begin his speech in two respects. First, because he focused on the police being the problem, not the solution; second, because the police had been subject to almost continuous 'reform' since Michael Howard, as Home Secretary, had first coined the term with the 1993 white paper.[8] Nevertheless, this was not enough: 'My view is clear: it's time for a fundamental shake-up of policing in this country. You can't be tough on crime unless you're tough on police reform.'[9] He did not at this stage actually point the finger of blame at the police themselves, rather the problem was Labour's massive centralization programme and its attendant excessive bureaucracy. His answer was to trust the people and share responsibility. At this point there was, however, a degree of equivocation about the precise method to be used to deliver increased police accountability; it could be through the medium of a directly elected individual 'like a police commissioner' or 'elected mayors'. It would not, however, be through the existing police authorities. The new elected officials would not interfere in operations but would set strategy and have the power 'to hire and fire the chief constable'.

The second tier of reform would be through 'real modernisation' of the police. Police officers would remain 'well rewarded' but in the context of creating 'workforces which are professional, flexible, and incentivised to their job'. This would be delivered through pay which focused on what officers did rather than how long they had served, more flexible pensions, powers to sack 'bad' officers, and ending the regulations that permitted officers to simultaneously hold down a second job. The role of the Home Secretary would be rolled back, although some residual powers would remain. Chief constables would be given the freedom to

---

[6] F Elliott, 'Cameron says police service must be reformed', 1 January 2006, (<http://www.independent.co.uk/news/uk/politics/cameron-says-police-service-must-be-radically-reformed-521288.html>).

[7] 'David Cameron's speech on police reform', guardian.co.uk, 16 January 2006 (<http://www.guardian.co.uk/politics/2006/jan/16/conservatives.ukcrime1> [accessed 25 April 2012]).

[8] Home Office, *Police Reform: A Police Service for the Twenty-first Century* (HMSO, London, 1993), *passim*.

[9] David Cameron's speech on police reform (n 7).

determine the structure of their forces, maximizing civilian support staff and community wardens in policing local neighbourhoods. A more flexible entry system would be introduced 'to make it possible for talented people and professionals to join the police later in their careers and at all ranks'. There would be change at the national level too. There would be 'a national border force' and 'support' for the 'serious and organised crime agency'. Finally, there would be reform to limit the impact of bureaucracy, particularly stop and search and Regulation of Investigatory Powers Act (RIPA) procedures. Only after all this could the real problem—crime—be tackled.

Something was also significant by its absence. Since Mrs Thatcher it had been the hallmark of Conservative policies to increase or, at the very least, maintain, police numbers, and that meant guaranteeing inflation-indexed pay settlements based on the Edmund-Davies pay formula. Tony Blair from 1994, first as Shadow Home Secretary, then as Labour leader, and finally as Prime Minister, challenged the assumption that 'law and order' was the natural preserve of the Conservative Party. He sought to turn his famous aphorism 'tough on crime, tough on the causes of crime' into reality through a series of simultaneous criminal justice, local authority, and police initiatives, which included, surprisingly for a Labour prime minister, a substantial increase in the prison population and in police numbers. Between 1997 and 2010 total police numbers—police officers and civilian personnel[10]—had increased by over 68,000, with over 18,000 of them being police officers and some 17,000 a new class of police personnel, the 'Police Community Support Officer' (PCSO).[11] It was an impressive record which the Conservatives tried to match in their 2005 election manifesto.[12] Significantly, in his Dalston speech Cameron now made no commitment to further increase police numbers.

Cameron's speech, while dutifully reported in mainstream and professional journals, did not at the time catch the popular imagination.[13] However, it was not David Cameron's last word on the matter in 2006. A few weeks later he published a major policy statement, *Built to Last*.[14] The sixth strategic aim 'To protect the country we love' dealt further with police reform. Top-down centralization would end, bureaucracy would be cut and 'direct local accountability, modern management, and a single-minded focus on fighting crime' introduced. In July he repeated his message at the annual Police Foundation lecture. The audience of police leaders and academics should have paid close attention to what he said

---

[10] The terms 'police civilian' or 'civilian' will be used in this work rather than 'Police staff', the term preferred by the principal staff union Unison. 'Police staff', while accepted in internal police usage, is often found to be confusing given its wider connotations.

[11] Chartered Institute of Public Finance and Accountancy (Cipfa) Police Statistics 1997–2010 (<http://www.cipfastats.net/publicprotection/> [accessed 5 April 2013]).

[12] Conservative Party, *Are You Thinking what We're Thinking?* (<http://www.conservatives.com/pdf/manifesto-uk-2005.pdf>, [accessed 21 August 2012]).

[13] Police Review (PR) 20 January 2006, 6.

[14] Conservative Party, *Built to Last: the Aims and Values of the Conservative Party* (<http://www.conservatives.com/pdf/BuiltToLast-AimsandValues.pdf> [accessed 25 April 2012]) 9 and David Cameron, Police Foundation lecture, July 2006, *passim*.

because Cameron's latest speech contained all the essential elements of what would become Conservative policing policy for the next general election. In fairness many were probably distracted dealing with Labour Home Secretary Charles Clarke's ill-considered plans for force amalgamations.

Politicians are often portrayed in popular imagination as cynically failing to keep their pre-election promises when in power. The generalization is often unfair as changing circumstances are normally the root cause of a deviation from any declared policy. However, in the case of policing policies no one could accuse David Cameron of failing to keep his pre-election intentions. By mid 2012, two years after he had become leader of a Coalition government, with the passing of the Police Reform and Social Responsibility Act 2011 the legal basis for his principal reform measures, notably elected Police and Crime Commissioners (PCCs), was in place.[15] With the publication of both parts of the *Winsor Review* of pay and conditions of service he possessed the detailed rationale to deliver radical change to police regulations to bring about his flexible and incentivized modern workforce.[16] It was a remarkable political achievement, especially given the distractions of a shaky economy and the mechanics of running a disparate coalition. Whether this political achievement could be turned into operational and community benefit remained the acid test as the Coalition government moved from policy development to implementation.

A 'revolution' in policing?

David Cameron's 2006 vision for policing was certainly bold, but did it amount to a 'revolution'? He has never claimed it to be so, at least not in public. The term he preferred was 'police reform', and as such laid claim to a nomenclature that had been common to both main political parties since 1993, when Conservative Home Secretary Michael Howard launched the *Police Reform* white paper. This was the basis for streamlined, less political police authorities, and new powers for the Home Secretary to set national objectives and targets. Labour leader Tony Blair simply annexed the 'police reform' label for his own purposes when in power. He was to outdo the Conservatives in terms of spending, controls, targets, and inspection regimes.

It is perhaps surprising that Labour did not seek some form of distinctive branding for their programme. Perhaps it was laziness, lack of imagination, the absence of an historical perspective, or simply because the Home Office saw 'reform' as a continuing process that was far from completion, and successive Labour home

---

[15] Police Reform and Social Responsibility Act 2011 (<http://services.parliament.uk/bills/2010-12/policereformandsocialresponsibility.html> [accessed 26 April 2012]).

[16] *Independent Review of Police Officer Staff Remuneration and Conditions, Part 1 Report* (<http://review.police.uk/publications/945287?view=Binary> [accessed 21 April 2013], cited as *Winsor 1*) and *Final Report*, volumes 1 and 2, <http://review.police.uk/publications/part-2-report/> [accessed 26 April 2012], cited as *Winsor 2*).

secretaries were not disposed to disagree. It is less surprising that David Cameron reappropriated the term when he made his Dalston speech. He certainly believed that much needed to change in policing. It was after all a Conservative term in its origin. He did not seem to pause to consider that after thirteen years of continual 'reform' perhaps the process had come to a natural end or at least it was time for a break to allow for consolidation. For him there was first unfinished business from the 1990s, and second Labour's own reform programme had taken the police down a spectacularly wrong course of easy growth and over-centralization. Third, he had to find something distinctive to say on policing that was not simply 'more of the same'. So, conceptually it was relatively simple; more but different reform was what was required.

But Cameron's programme amounts to more than mere reform. The programme he launched at Dalston amounts to a genuine 'revolution'. 'Reform' implies change within a structure; 'revolution', something cataclysmic. The *Concise Oxford English Dictionary* defines revolution as the 'forcible overthrow of a government or social order', and additionally as any 'dramatic and far reaching change'.[17] Cameron's police programme would certainly qualify under the second definition, 'dramatic and far reaching', but with some modification for police-related circumstances it also does so under the first. Of course, Cameron was not proposing the end of policing any more than French revolutionaries were seeking the end of France in 1789, but he was seeking such a radical change in police governance, leadership, structure, and conditions of service as to make the service's relationship with its old self recognizable in only its most superficial of forms.

The change he seeks is certainly rapid. Two years after his progress to the premiership on the back of a partially successful 2010 general election, which required him to form a coalition with the Liberal Democrats, he had fundamentally altered police governance, completed a controversial review of pay and conditions, and deconstructed much of Labour's centralized regime of targets, bureaucracy, and inspection. Cuts in police numbers were well advanced, reversing the growth of recent years, while the private sector was posed to extend its reach into more core police activities. In terms of content, speed, and extent Cameron's police programme amounts to a 'revolution'. To achieve his revolution he appears ready to face down opposition from the Police Federation, eliminate much local authority influence by abolishing police authorities, and diminish the power and status of chief constables and their representative organization, the Association of Chief Police Officers (ACPO). Yet Cameron himself appears wary of labelling his programme 'revolutionary'. This is understandable. Conservative leaders normally present themselves as restrained, rational modifiers of the status quo. 'Radical' might do, 'reformer' certainly, but 'revolutionary' would be a title they might enjoy near-contemporary history bestowing on them,

---

[17] *Concise Oxford English Dictionary* (12th edn, OUP, Oxford, 2011), 1,232.

but one which in real time might be thought too risky. That should not, however, prevent others from recognizing the programme for what it is. His programme is experimental, confrontational, iconoclastic, and high risk. It may not prove practical, durable, or successful. Only history will be able to judge its success or otherwise. Turning ideas into reality is the ultimate test of a politician, be they revolutionary or of a more conventional mould. As one would-be revolutionary once famously said, 'The first duty of a revolutionary is to get away with it.'[18]

As with all revolutions, furthermore, its initiators are not in control of the forces they unleash. Left to his own devices Cameron might have halted the growth in police resources; he might even have engaged in some retrenchment, but economic forces largely beyond his control required him to cut far, deep, and fast. This cut in absolute and relative terms may aid the course of his revolution as it adds leverage to the changes in working practices, and pay and conditions of service that he wishes to bring about. On the other hand, these economic forces substantially increase the risk not only to the achievement of his 'police reform' programme but also to the stability of his Coalition government, its wider programme, and to social stability in general. It was clear at the time and in retrospect that for the Coalition 2012 would be a critical year, as financial cuts deepened and the government sought to move across the board from policy development to implementation, and grass-roots opposition grew.[19] The indications by mid 2013, having seen off the Federation's challenge to the *Winsor Report*, implemented PCCs, reconstituted strategic leadership under the College of Policing, and survived the August 2011 riots, were that he was succeeding.

Police futures

It is the purpose of this book to describe, analyse, and explain the motivations, course, and likely outcomes of David Cameron's policing revolution. In doing so, it will make connections across external and internal policy fields to estimate the sum total of that revolution. It is self-evidently impossible by mortal means to 'predict' the future, and those authors who seek to do so must either be extremely opaque in their forecasts or be prepared for a retrospective rebuff from history. In 1989 Paul Kennedy's forecast of the demise of the Soviet Union was somewhat sceptically received at the time but proved to be accurate within two years.[20] On the other hand, Francis Fukuyama's 1991 confident conclusion that the triumph of liberal democracy and capitalism had led to the 'end of history' was widely accepted until the economic collapse of 2008 cast doubt on the ultimate survival

---

[18] A Hoffman quoted in N Comfort (ed), *The Politics Book: A Lexicon of Political Facts from Abu Ghraib to Zippergate* (Politico, London, 2005), 683.

[19] As exemplified by local authority election results May 2012; P Wintour and N Watt, 'Election drubbing piles pressure on Cameron', *Guardian* iPad edition, 5 May 2012.

[20] P Kennedy, *The Rise and Fall of the Great Powers* (Fontana Press, London, 1989), 565–692.

of both systems.[21] The odds are that both will eventually survive but will be sorely tested in the process. There certainly is a good deal more 'history' yet to be written.

This book will make no such claim of certainty, but it will seek to explore the possibilities, potentials, and pitfalls of the Cameron revolution. In doing so use will be made of the technique of 'environmental scanning', reviewing the political, economic, social, technical, legal, and organizational trends which will affect the police service and David Cameron's intentions for it. It is not an exact science, for if it were those governments and organizations which invest substantial resources in 'future proofing' would not be so routinely surprised or disappointed. But it does represent the only rational means available of comprehensively assessing what the future might hold.

It is this sense of fallibility that dictates this book's title. It is 'A future for policing', not 'The future of policing'. It is also recognition that others will see the same evidence and draw different conclusions about both the present and the future. The book's title is also a corollary to my earlier work A History of Policing in England and Wales from 1974. The use of the indefinite article in that work's title sought to imply no monopoly of either narrative or analysis of developments in policing since 1974. The current work similarly implies or infers no certainty of forecast or prediction. It offers a view of the future, one that has been informed by over thirty years of police service and a background in police futures since 1986, when I became the 'Policy Support Inspector' in the Avon and Somerset Constabulary, a job I was given by the then chief constable, Ron Broome, with the express intention of providing him with future policing scenarios at both the local and national level. It was a far-seeing move by Mr Broome, but one his staff had some difficulty in appreciating, and his senior staff soon found a series of 'just jobs' for me to perform when no one in their own teams seemed to have the research and analytical skills required for their purposes. Inevitably, this caused time-management problems but proved useful in other respects as my range of analytical skills expanded. However, it was not this multi-seated tasking that proved the biggest problem. The problem which confronted Mr Broome and his top team was what to do with the 'futures' I produced? My analysis of the outcome of the 1987 general election was deemed of such accuracy that all copies (there were only five) were shredded. My paper on what the populations of Avon, Somerset, and beyond might do in the event of a Chernobyl-style accident happening at a local nuclear power station, while well received, produced puzzlement on the part of emergency planners.

My earlier background in police futures made possible my selection in 1989 for the national review of policing jointly sponsored by ACPO, the Superintendents' Association and Police Federation, the Operational Policing Review (OPR). It was a remarkable and, so far, unique joint enterprise based on the assumption that the reforms widely anticipated from Mrs Thatcher's government at the end of the

---

[21] F Fukayama, The End of History and the Last Man (Penguin Books, London, 1992), ix.

1980s would be innately harmful to the service, forcing it into too narrow a focus on crime at the expense of wider social engagement and confidence-building measures. Most of the review was a survey of the current concerns, notably civilianization, but the final chapter, of which I was the principal author, was entitled 'Policing in the 1990s', attempting the fraught task of policy forecasting in such a way as to be both accurate and not to offend the sensitivities of police and the wider political audience. It is interesting, with the benefit of over twenty years' hindsight, to look back and see just how many of the projections came close to happening. It turns out to be a reasonable track record. We forecast accurately the advent of an intense performance regime; a narrowing focus on 'crime' at the expense of 'service', the diminishing influence of chief constables on policy making and the growing power of the Home Office, the growth of private sector involvement in policing, significant changes in conditions of service, merger of forces, and the end of the single point of entry at constable rank. Externally, we forecast the growing intrusion of Middle-Eastern terrorism and new technologies which would transform the workplace. Many of the forecasts came to pass in the 1990s; a few did not, although even these, such as direct officer entry, it might be argued, have simply been delayed in their implementation and one day, perhaps soon, their time will come.[22]

The *OPR* was well received at the time and led directly to such outcomes as the ACPO 'Quality of Service Initiative' and the 'Statement of Common Purpose and Values', but the futures section produced a polite but puzzled response. No one questioned the conclusions, but no one seemed to know quite what to do with it either. And herein lies the rub; even if the policy forecast is accurate, what do policy-makers do with it? Are the recipients of the message predisposed to believe and act upon it? Nor is this a problem of the past; it is one very much of the present. In July 2010, three months before the publication of the 2010 Comprehensive Spending Review (CSR 2010), I accurately forecast, based on economic analysis and a study of what the new Coalition minsters were saying, that the police could expect, in a worst-case scenario, cuts of 60,000 Full Time Equivalent (FTE) posts.[23] The data was easily available; the subsequent analysis was time-consuming but not difficult. No one else had bothered to look, not even the three police staff associations. The government condemned the forecast as 'speculative'; police leaders responded with indifference, denial, or a confidence that the cuts could be absorbed by 'efficiencies'. Two years later the loss of 30,000 posts and the prospect of more to follow had become accepted. The service itself appeared cowed and reconciled to the loss, with only minimal voices raised in opposition. To forecast accurately and yet be disbelieved has been the risk that all policy forecasters have faced since Cassandra first suggested to King Priam that Troy might have a few upcoming problems with the Greek city-states.

---

[22] See 'Policing in the 1990s', Joint Consultative Committee, *The Operational Policing Review* (Joint Consultative Committee, Surbiton, 1990), *passim*.

[23] BBC News, 'Budget cuts "threaten 60,000 police jobs"'.

Because of such scepticism it might be argued that there is no purpose in forecasting. That would be a fallacy. If based on rational criteria and progressed without bias or favour, it is a worthwhile endeavour. Forecasting can encourage debate and reflection; it can expose flaws in time for their correction; it can provide time for those affected to prepare and respond appropriately. Perversely, the consequences of a well-founded forecast might be so undesirable that it induces a change of policy, thereby negating its accuracy but not its value. If the forecasting elements of this book induce reflection and preparation as well as interest, the outcomes will have been worthwhile. For my part, I shall seek to forecast, as well as to describe, explain, and analyse, without bias or favour, although I cannot help but write from the perspective of someone who served as a police officer for over thirty-one years, with over fifteen of those years spent at chief officer rank.

'Police' or 'policing'?

One last consideration; should the title of this book be 'a future for *police*' or '*policing*'? The attempt to distinguish between the two has bedevilled many a debate about 'the police' or 'policing', and at least delayed consideration of what should be the focus of the discussion. I have on this occasion favoured 'policing'. The distinction between 'police' and 'policing' is a fine one, but broadly the use of 'police' focuses primarily on the institution of 'the police', whereas 'policing' includes not only that institution but what it does and its effect. It is also possible to argue that historically, even since 1829 and the advent of Peel's 'New Police', policing has never simply been about 'the police'; it has always involved the community, either actively or passively. In what David Cameron intends to be the era of the 'Big Society' this has never been more true. So 'A future for policing' it is.

Acknowledgements

Writing a book is an intensely personal experience yet it would not be possible without the advice and support of family and friends. As with *A History of Policing* I have been marvellously supported by my wife Elisabeth, who has critically read every word and offered critique, criticism, insight, and encouragement in equal measure. Similarly, my long-standing friend the Reverend Colin Smith has once again offered similar support, and as always my history graduate son Richard has offered his own informed view of contemporary political and policing developments, particularly from the consumer's perspective of both in London.

I am also grateful to academic colleagues who have assisted with their valuable insights and observations, although not necessarily in agreement with my conclusions, including Professor Martin Innes of the Universities' Police Science

Institute, Cardiff, Professor Marian Fitzgerald, Kent Crime and Justice Centre, the University of Kent, and Dr David Turner of the University of Gloucestershire. My thanks also to those professional colleagues who have found time to answer questions and provide information on the current scene, especially Sir Hugh Orde, President of ACPO, Tom Flaherty, Chief Executive ACPO, Peter Vaughan, chief constable of South Wales, Umar Hussain, chief financial officer South Wales Police, Chief Superintendent Irene Curtis, President of the Police Superintendents' Association of England and Wales, and Tony Dawson, assistant chief constable NPIA.

No scholarly book can be written without the resources and help of libraries and librarians, and once again I am grateful for the assistance of the College of Police Library at Bramshill. That library represents a unique resource and long may it continue to do so.

Finally, my thanks to Peter Daniell, Lucy Alexander, and the editorial team at Oxford University Press for their advice and support in the preparation and publication of this book.

Policing 2010—Labour's legacy

The general election 2010

Much had been expected of Gordon Brown as Prime Minister when he succeeded Tony Blair in June 2007. A potential leader in 1994, he stood aside to let Tony Blair succeed John Smith, whose sudden death had precipitated an early leadership election. He had proved a competent Chancellor of the Exchequer, and although a 'modernizer' was seen as more of a Labour traditionalist than the outsider Blair. Brown's reputation stood high, especially as he avoided the fallout from the Iraq War, the close alliance with the USA in the 'War Against Terrorism' and the 'cash for honours' scandal. At first he appeared authoritative rather than aloof, although that would change once in office. By 2007 Blair was damaged goods but there was much hope for a Labour renaissance under Brown. He thought about calling a snap election in October 2007, gaining an advantage from his 'honeymoon period' as Prime Minister, but, following a Conservative surge in the opinion polls, he hesitated at the last. Although not apparent at the time, Labour's best chance of gaining a fourth term in office had passed. From that time until the general election in May 2010 Brown's personal standing sagged.[1] The 2008 financial crisis wrecked his credibility as a sound manager of the nation's finances, and dissension grew within the party and even the Cabinet. Furthermore, he faced a credible alternative Prime Minister in David Cameron. Labour's response to the financial crisis of propping up failing banks and modest public sector efficiencies seemed indecisive compared to the Conservative alternative of simply eliminating the public sector debt.[2]

[1] R Worcester, R Mortimore, P Baines, and M Gill, *Explaining Cameron's Coalition: An Analysis of the 2010 British General Election* (Biteback, London, 2011), 71.

[2] George Osborne, 'We will lead the economy out of crisis', 8 October 2009 (<http://www.conservatives.com/News/Speeches/2009/10/George_Osborne_We_will_lead_the_economy_out_of_crisis.aspx> [accessed 14 July 2012]).

In the face of dwindling electoral support Brown clung on. By April 2010, just one month away from when an election had to be held, only 30 per cent of those surveyed in an Ipsos MORI poll were satisfied with the way the government was running the country, with 66 per cent dissatisfied. When it came to key issues there was more of a spread of preferences, with Labour leading the Conservatives on health, unemployment, benefits, and climate change. The Conservatives led on asylum and immigration, the economy, education, taxation (both narrowly), defence, and reforming MPs' expenses. However, the Conservatives' greatest lead was in crime and anti-social behaviour, where 33 per cent of those surveyed thought they had the best policies, a full ten percentage points advantage over Labour.[3] Given that Labour had massively invested in the police, prisons, and partnership interventions, and that recorded crime levels were at an historic low, the question was what had gone so badly wrong?

The answer lies deep within Labour's crime and police polices.

The Blair factor

For a leader of the opposition Tony Blair had an unusual background—he had been Shadow Home Secretary (1992–4), a post held by no previous twentieth-century Prime Minister or leader of the opposition. But where others might have feared a backwater Blair saw an opportunity. Blair had been an MP since 1983 and had witnessed the electoral destruction from within of the Labour Party as it lurched leftwards under the distracted leadership of Michael Foot. He is not recorded as saying 'never again', but he might well have thought it and certainly acted as if he had come to that conclusion, and when he became Labour leader he consciously repositioned the party to appeal to the electoral middle ground, in what was to be known as 'the third way'. He began that process while Shadow Home Secretary. Early in his tenure he recognized that crime and 'anti-social behaviour' were blighting the lives of many people, particularly in the inner cities and estates that constituted core Labour voting areas. In the 1980s Labour, influenced by municipal left-wingers such as Ken Livingstone and Paul Boateng, held the view that gaining political control of the police was the essential prerequisite to reducing crime and disorder. This cut little ice with most voters who preferred the Conservatives' simple approach of providing more police officers and tougher sentences.[4]

Blair determined to wrest the initiative from the Conservatives by a twin-track approach which would secure genuine social benefit and electoral advantage. He

---

[3] Ipsos MORI, *Best Parties on Key Issues—March 2010* (<http://www.ipsos-mori.com/research-publications/researcharchive/2569/Best-Parties-on-Key-Issues-March-2010.aspx> [accessed 14 July 2012]).

[4] See Ipsos MORI, *Best Party on Key Issues: Crime/Law & Order* (<http://www.ipsos-mori.com/researchpublications/researcharchive/poll.aspx?oItemID=29> [accessed 14 July 2012]).

began to talk about being 'tough on crime and tough on the causes of crime'.[5] This was an early example of the kind of sound bite for which 'New Labour' would become famous, and it made a profound impact. Ambiguous enough to attract wide-ranging support, the message could simultaneously appeal to those who favoured firm measures and those who sought social amelioration as the answer to crime and disorder. Although indelibly associated with Tony Blair, ironically Gordon Brown may have originally thought of the term first.[6] More than just a good turn of phrase, it came to define Labour's policing and crime policy. In a July 1993 BBC interview Blair gave his clearest exposition yet of his intentions:

> What I mean by being tough on the causes of crime is to say that the problem that we've had in this area is that people have felt they have to choose between punishment and prevention, between, if you like, personal and social responsibility. What I'm trying to say is if you want a hard-headed approach to law and order in the modern world, you require a thought-out strategy that deals with the underlying causes of crime as well as those that are committing crimes and should be brought to justice within the criminal justice system.

He also, almost surreptitiously, committed Labour to increasing the prison population:

> There's no doubt at all to my mind, you don't judge your prison population, you don't pluck a figure out of the air and say that's the, you know, that's the prison population we want, you've got to have a criminal justice system that deals with people in a fair, but firm way. And that is what produces your prison population or not.[7]

Once he had become leader in 1994 he began to fully develop his policing and crime polices. There were four evolutionary stages. First, the broad ideas were set out in Blair's 1993 Police Foundation lecture, in which he committed Labour (now increasingly linked with the prefix 'New') to a local problem-solving partnership approach to reducing crime, contrasting this with what he saw as the Conservatives' increasing centralism as evidenced by the Home Secretary's new powers contained in the Police and Magistrates' Courts Bill then going through Parliament.[8] The commitment to crime reduction through multiagency partnerships was not a new idea, it having been argued for by James Morgan in a Home Office report published under the Conservatives in 1992, but the critical difference was that the Conservatives preferred voluntary schemes while Labour would make them mandatory. The second phase came in the autumn of 1994 when

---

[5] BBC *On the Record*, Interview with Tony Blair 4 July 1993 (http://www.bbc.co.uk/otr/intext92-93/Blair4.7.93.html [accessed 12 April 2013]).

[6] T Newburn and R Reiner, 'Crime and penal policy' in A Seldon (ed), *Blair's Britain 1997–2007* (Cambridge University Press, Cambridge, 2007), 319.

[7] BBC *On the Record* (n 5).

[8] T Blair, 'Modern policing for safer communities' (Police Foundation Lecture, 14 June 1994, Labour Party Campaigns and Communication Directorate, London), *passim*.

more detail was added with the publication of a policy document, *Partners Against Crime*, which developed the partnership agenda allied to 'community policing', but which also emphasized that 'individual responsibility' was as important a cause of crime as social factors. Consequently, the criminal justice system must be speeded up with greater focus on victims.[9] In the third phase Jack Straw, Blair's successor as Shadow Home Secretary, adopted the 'broken windows' theory of crime reduction. Developed by American criminologists Kelling and Wilson, this argued that the outward signs of urban degeneration, such as graffiti, vandalism, damage (eg 'broken windows'), litter, and prostitution, if left unaddressed, would lead to further signs of degeneration and hence crime. Conversely, if these outward signs were quickly remedied then crime would fall.[10] It was argued that this was an essentially oversimplistic approach, but that did not deter Straw who now committed New Labour to a war on the blights on modern urban life—aggressive beggars, street drinkers, 'squeegee merchants, feral children roaming estates'.[11] The final phase was a piece of pure opportunism; Blair endorsed 'zero tolerance', a crackdown on minor offending in the expectation that this would inhibit and then reduce major crime. Originating in New York from Mayor Rudy Giuliani and Police Commissioner Bill Bratton, it was applied to the streets of Middlesbrough by high-profile Superintendent Ray Mallon.[12] It did not matter that neither Giuliani nor Bratton officially used the term, it was too good a sound bite for New Labour to miss. Wrong footed, Conservative Home Secretary Michael Howard lamely followed suit in saying that Ray Mallon was his 'kind of policeman'.[13] It was a measure of how far Labour had travelled. A few years earlier it would have been inconceivable that Labour would expect the police to target 'beggars, vagrants and people sleeping rough', but by 1997 it had become the norm.[14] Equally, a few years earlier it would have been inconceivable that they would have outdone the Conservatives talking tough on law and order.

All these elements came together in Labour's 1997 election manifesto. There would be support for the police, although no specific commitment to more officers. 'Crime' was now indivisibly linked to 'disorder'. 'Zero tolerance' would ensure that 'petty criminality among young offenders is seriously addressed'. New 'community safety orders' would deal with 'threatening and disruptive criminal neighbours'. Borrowing another Americanism, a 'drug czar' would be appointed to 'co-ordinate the battle against drugs'; drug treatment and testing orders would reduce individual drug misuse. Victims were to be informed of the progress in their cases and there would be greater protection for victims of racism and sexual crimes. Local authorities would be mandated to develop 'statutory partnerships to help prevent crimes' and 'set targets for the reduction of crime and disorder in their area'. Confirming Labour's 'third way' approach, the

---

[9] Labour [Party], *Partners Against Crime: Labour's Approach to Tackling Crime and Creating Safer Communities* (Labour Party, London, 1994), *passim*.

[10] See GM Kelling and CM Coles, *Fixing Broken Windows* (Free Press, New York, 1996), xv.

[11] *The Times*, 6 September 1995.   [12] PR 7 January 1997, 1.

[13] PR 21 March 1997, 4.   [14] *The Times*, 7 January 1997, 1.

European Convention on Human Rights would be incorporated into British law and there would be a freedom of information act, previously a Liberal Democrat flagship policy. Of the constitutional reforms of police governance that had so preoccupied Labour in the 1980s there was not a sign. There was, however, a significant limit to New Labour's policies—there was as yet no new money. In fact Labour intended to keep to the Major government's spending limits, which meant real term cuts, while once in power ministers would have to demonstrate 'value for money' and that they could 'save before they could spend'.[15]

In political terms Blair's achievement was remarkable. Between 1992 and 1997 he had completely reorientated Labour's crime, policing, and penal policies. Moreover, he had made them convincing and electorally popular, ensuring that on crime, and law and order, Labour led the Conservatives at the time of the 1997 general election.[16] He had stolen what should have been the Conservatives' flagship issue from their own dockyard.

Labour in power: partnerships, criminal justice, and the police

Having convincingly won the 1997 general election New Labour set about delivering on its promises. The Crime and Disorder Act 1998, embodying the 'third way', was a key first term measure. Following the logic of 'broken windows' the great underlying theme was crime reduction linked through disorder reduction, both of which would be achieved through various mandatory partnerships between the police, local authorities, and other specified agencies. There would be a range of behavioural orders—'Anti-social Behaviour Orders' (ASBOs), 'Drug Treatment and Testing Orders' (DTTOs), and 'Sex Offenders Order' and 'Parenting Orders'. In a measure at odds with the Act's otherwise prevalent localism, a National Youth Justice Board would be created to oversee local Youth Offending Teams (YOTs).[17]

The act in sum represented a radical approach which should have achieved the concentration of local resources to deliver sustained crime reduction, but there were problems almost from the start.[18] There was no new money, no clear leadership in the local partnerships, while uncertainty over data protection issues, real or perceived, inhibited the flow of information between partner agencies. Inherent cultural differences between the partners strained relationships. Using a method that soon became typical, the government began to make specific grants available for priority projects. It seemed a good idea, but access to the grant was

---

[15] Labour Party, *New Labour Because Britain Deserves Better* (<http://www.labour-party.org.uk/manifestos/1997/1997-labour-manifesto.shtml/> [accessed 18 July 2012]), *passim.*

[16] Ipsos MORI (n 3).

[17] Crime and Disorder Act 1998.

[18] C Phillips, J Jacobson, R Prime, M Carter, and M Considine, *Crime and Disorder Reduction Partnerships: Round One Progress* (Home Office Police Research Series Paper 151, London, 2002), xi.

often through arcane bidding processes. Lack of coterminous boundaries between police Basic Command Units (BCUs) and other partners created anomalies, but by the time the government stepped in to do something about it in 2006 most of the problems had been resolved locally and their intervention seemed heavy handed, adding to its growing reputation for micromanagement.[19] There was also a perception of what might be termed 'partnership fatigue', with the same individuals turning up in differing guises at different partnership bodies.

Then there was the bureaucracy. Targets necessitated records, records generated bureaucracy, as did the numerous guidelines and protocols that government issued or required. ASBOs were a case in point. Much was expected of them but excessive central guidance inhibited early progress; joint units between police and local authorities had to be created to manage the excessive processes involved in successfully obtaining one. Their impact was controversial, being simultaneously criticized from different quarters for being both too draconian in their restrictions and too easily breached.[20]

There was a constant restlessness about the government's whole approach to partnerships. The government followed the Crime and Disorder Act with a national crime reduction strategy, setting 'clear targets', and offering partnerships training, seminars, and consultancy but again with no new money.[21] New Acts followed in rapid succession, as did a five-year plan in 2003 and more targets, all monitored by increasingly burdensome inspection regimes. It all seemed rather frenetic with little time being allowed for one initiative to be absorbed before the next was on its way. As one distinguished academic has observed:

> Local partnerships need to be given space and authority, and encouraged to focus on local priorities. New Labour, in its drive to ensure effective delivery, has adopted a much too heavy handed centralised approach. Impatience at the pace of change has resulted in an over-bureaucratised delivery framework characterised by regular performance review cycles and stringent reporting frameworks. A much lighter touch from the centre is far preferable.[22]

Finding the 'lighter touch' was a quality that eluded New Labour.

Drugs policy

Labour came to power in 1997 with grand ideas about its drugs policy. It would not be 'soft' on drugs; it would, however, be pragmatic. It would reduce the harm

---

[19] T Newburn and P Neyroud (eds), *Dictionary of Policing* (Willan, Cullompton, 2008), 12.

[20] See BBC News, 'Rise in Asbos prompts criticism' (<http://news.bbc.co.uk/1/hi/4860384.stm> [accessed 18 July 2012]), and R Cowan, 'Asbo use doubles despite criticism', guardian.co.uk, 30 June 2005 (<http://www.guardian.co.uk/uk/2005/jun/30/ukcrime.prisonsandprobation> [accessed 18 July 2012]).

[21] Home Office, *The Government's Crime Reduction Rtrategy* (Home Office Communications Directorate, London, 1999), *passim*.

[22] E Solomon, 'New Labour and crime prevention in England and Wales: what worked?', *IPC Review*, vol 3, March 2009 (<http://www.sciencessociales.uottawa.ca/ipc/fra/documents/ipcr3solomon.pdf> [accessed 8 April 2013]), 56.

drugs could do to individuals and communities. Individual offenders would be compelled to undergo treatment regimes with breaches theoretically backed up with prison sentences. A 'Drugs Czar' would coordinate a national strategy. The problem was that it did not seem at first to be working, with numerous breaches of DTTOs and no noticeable inhibition on drug abuse and related crime. In 2003 a different tack was tried by reducing cannabis from a class 'B' to class 'C' drug, prompting the resignation of the Drugs Czar Keith Halliwell who, in tacit recognition of policy failure, was not replaced. In 2008 Gordon Brown launched a new drugs strategy, stressing enforcement against dealers. In 2009, following media pressure, the cannabis downgrade was reversed. It was all symbolic of a confused and ultimately unsuccessful policy, which ultimately allowed Labour to be criticized by both hardliners and liberals.[23] The irony was that there was progress in reducing all forms of drug misuse, although class 'A' use, seemingly impervious to any form of policy intervention, remained constant.[24] In the end perhaps it did not matter whether the culmination of Labour's drug policies was successful or not, it was simply that there was such a degree of equivocation that Labour could not claim any form of policy success.

Victims

At several points in the development of its crime and justice policies New Labour pledged to put victims and their needs at the centre of the criminal justice system. Over its thirteen years in power it could point to some notable achievements, setting standards which a victim of crime could expect from the criminal justice agencies, although that principally meant the police, providing victims with opportunities to have their views presented in trials, and introducing greater elements of 'restorative justice'. The problem was that it never seemed to be enough, and victims seemed to be as dissatisfied with the totality of their experience at the end of Labour's time in office as at the beginning. In December 2011 Sadiq Khan, Labour's Shadow Minister of Justice wrote: 'Victims are too frequently kept in the dark about the details of a trial, access to court papers are often difficult to obtain and complex legal processes difficult to understand, all of which can and should be remedied quickly and at little cost.'[25] Given that this was written some eighteen months after Labour had left

---

[23] See J Buchanan, 'Drug and alcohol policy under New Labour: pandering to populism?' in A Silvestri (ed), *Lessons for the Coalition: An End of Term Report on New Labour and Criminal Justice* (Centre for Crime and Justice Studies, London, 2011), 48–51, and K Gyngell, *The phoney war on drug* (Centre for Policy Studies, 2009, <http://www.cps.org.uk/files/reports/original/111026175647-thephoneywarondrugs.pdf> [accessed 8 April 2013]), i–iv.

[24] Home Office, 'Extent and trends in illicit drug use among adults aged 16 to 59' (<http://www.homeoffice.gov.uk/publications/science-research-statistics/research-statistics/crime-research/drugs-misuse-dec-1112/extent-adults> [accessed 4 August 2012]).

[25] LabourList, '"Put victims at the heart if criminal justice policy" experts tell Labour policy review', 14 December 2011 (<http://www.labourlist.org/2011/12/'put-victims-at-heart-of-criminal-justice-policy'-experts-tell-labour-policy-review/> [accessed 25 July 2012]).

office it must be considered as much an indictment of his own party's record as that of the Coalition.

Criminal justice

Addressing what was termed the 'criminal justice gap', that is the gap between crimes recorded and convictions, had been a concern of Labour since *Partners Against Crime*, but it remained largely unaddressed in Labour's first term (1997–2001). Those agencies involved in the criminal justice process, principally the police, the courts (Crown and Magistrates'), the Crown Prosecution Service (CPS), the Probation Service, and the Prison Service, although possessed of notionally similar purposes, in practice worked largely in isolation from each other, with mutual simmering frustration and irritation for each other's working practices and cultures often characterizing their relationships. Problems abounded, with the police often producing poor quality and late files, enabling some of the other agencies involved to pass off their own inefficiencies onto the police.

Labour first attempted to paper over the cracks in the fractured relationship between the police and the CPS. The Conservatives had made an initial attempt to do so with the 1995 Masefield Scrutiny which had promoted the use of standardized national files and the greater use of civilian support staff in police 'Administrative Support Units' to improve file quality and timeliness. However, the 'reforms' created more not less bureaucracy. Labour sought to solve the problem through enhanced joint CPS-Police units, but these did not address the criminal justice system's systemic problems. Labour pushed ahead early in its second term with a white paper *Justice for All* which promised to rebalance 'the criminal justice system in favour of the victim' and to give 'the police and prosecution the tools to bring more criminals to justice'.[26] Local Criminal Justice Boards would be formed in all police force areas requiring the key agencies to collaborate and produce meaningful local plans to deliver mandated national targets for improving file timeliness and quality and, ultimately, convictions. The strategic object was still to reduce crime and disorder, but it seemed to focus on the 'tough' rather than the 'causes' part of Labour's historic promise.

There were improvements as a result of the joint working, but problems remained. A key feature for delivering improved services was colocation of key agencies, but apart from a few flagship schemes there was never enough investment to make this sufficiently widespread to be effective. New technology was also needed, but this was slow in coming and inadequate when it arrived.[27] Similarly, the creation of a plethora of national forms intended to facilitate joint working simply produced a nightmare of bureaucracy. In 2005 the CPS assumed

---

[26] CPS, *Justice for All* (<http://www.cps.gov.uk/publications/docs/jfawhitepaper.pdf> [accessed 12 April 2013]), 11.

[27] 'MoJ plans to "exploit IT investments" to join up service delivery' (<http://www.guardian.co.uk/government-computing-network/2012/jul/13/ministry-of-justice-white-paper?newsfeed=true> [accessed 20 July 2012]).

full responsibility for the initial charging of suspects, a move intended to ensure that only those prosecutions would proceed where there was unequivocally sufficient evidence to ensure a reasonable chance of success at a later trial. In reality it meant an increase in the evidence being gathered by the police to provide sufficient information for the CPS to make a decision. In an attempt to speed the system up 'CPS Direct' was introduced to ensure that advice to officers was available twenty-four hours a day, and while on the whole the system was an improvement on what went before, its represented yet another twist in the bureaucratic ratchet.

At the same time as it was trying to simplify the practice of the law Labour seemed to make the law itself more complicated. The Human Rights Act 1998 (HRA) had been an election commitment and offered to bring the United Kingdom into line with most states in Europe in mainstreaming the principles of the European Convention into domestic law. The full impact took some time to be felt, but ensuring that plans, policies, and processes were 'Human Rights Act compliant' became a common feature of police plans and operations, and added more bureaucracy without seeming to increase any greater concept of fundamental 'rights'.[28] The same might be said of much of Labour's legislative effort over thirteen years. RIPA placed police surveillance procedures on a statutory footing, and met the requirements of the HRA, but it generated a host of new forms and procedures yet still failed to satisfy many civil libertarians, who focused on the additional powers it gave the police rather than the new restrictions under which they operated. Labour attempted to introduce effective counter terrorism legislation which simultaneously met HRA requirements, but the extension of police powers, especially stop and search powers, generated extensive and, through the civil courts, effective opposition. The extension of the DNA database and CCTV in public spaces gave the government an increasingly authoritarian and sinister air which alienated many of Labour's natural supporters amongst the liberal elite that dominated much academic thinking on crime and criminal justice policy.[29] In all Labour is estimated to have introduced over 3,600 new criminal offences, although no one seems quite sure of the exact number.[30]

Labour could at least over its time in office point to an increase in the number of 'offences brought to justice' (OBTJ), a key pledge and a supposed important step in closing the justice gap. Labour set a target of delivering 1.2 million offences brought to justice by 2005–6, which it exceeded. By 2010 almost 1.4 million offences had been brought to justice, compared to little over 0.9 million in 2001. It would appear to have been a case of a stiff target unequivocally attained, but closer inspection revealed a more problematic analysis. The target had not been straightforwardly attained by an increase in convictions before courts but

---

[28] See K Bullock and P Johnson, 'The Impact of the Human Rights Act 1998 on Policing in England and Wales', *British Journal of Criminology* (October 2009), *passim*.

[29] For example see Silvestri, *Lessons for the Coalition, passim*.

[30] R Morgan, 'Austerity, subsidiarity and parsimony: offending behaviour and criminalisation', in Silvestri, *Lessons for the Coalition*, 18.

principally by an increase in cautions and, a Labour innovation, fixed penalty notices for disorder.[31] There was a sense that although Labour had reached its own target it had made little positive social impact and, by formally introducing more first-time offenders, especially young people, to criminal justice processes may even have perpetrated a greater social harm.[32]

Regardless of what happened to convictions, the prison population increased substantially under Labour. Despite the rhetoric, under Mrs Thatcher the prison population remained relatively static. This changed in 1993 when then Home Secretary, Michael Howard, initiated a profound change in British penal policy, summarized in his sound bite 'prison works'. Automatic life sentences were introduced for a range of violent and sex crimes; judges were given greater licence to impose more and longer custodial sentences; the use of short sentences tripled; those convicted of burglary for the third time were given mandatory three-year sentences. Labour reinforced these measures, with the result that by 2010 the prison population exceeded 84,000, making the UK's the second highest in Western Europe.[33] While this was an achievement of sorts, it was hard to present as a positive one. That this increase coincided with the sustained reduction in recorded crime over almost exactly the same period was a link that Labour, or for that matter anyone else, seemed reluctant or unable to make.[34] The result was that Labour gained more criticism than credit from its investment in sentencing.[35] More to the point, by constantly introducing innovation Labour created the sense that what it had done for criminal justice had not worked.

The police: Straw's pragmatism

Labour ought to have received acclamation from both the public and professionals for the summation of its policing policies. Between 1997 and 2010 it increased police numbers to a degree that made Mrs Thatcher's efforts look positively incremental; it increased police powers, created a range of national institutions, kept faith with the Edmund-Davies pay formula, and formed an effective partnership with ACPO, its bête noire during the 1980s. That political opponents might criticize this could be expected; that the public and police professionals might also frequently criticize them was something they probably had not anticipated.

---

[31] Number of offences brought to justice (notifiable) over a twelve-month period by outcome and numbers of recorded crime (<http://www.justice.gov.uk/uploads/...data/.../offences-tables.xls.xls> [accessed 30 June 2013]).

[32] Morgan, 'Austerity', *passim*.

[33] House of Commons Library, *Prison Population Statistics* (<http://www.parliament.uk/briefing-papers/SN04334.pdf> [accessed 23 July 2012]).

[34] Prison Reform Trust, *Prison Briefing May 2010* (<http://www.prisonreformtrust.org.uk/uploads/documents/prisonbriefingsmall.pdf> [accessed 23 July 2012]).

[35] Prison Reform Trust, *Bromley Briefing Fact File April 2006* (<http://www.prisonreformtrust> [accessed 23 July 2012]) and A Sanders, 'What was New Labour thinking? New Labour's approach to criminal justice' in Silvestri, *Lessons for the Coalition*, 12–13.

Jack Straw, New Labour's first Home Secretary, formed an unspoken pragmatic alliance with the police. This was perhaps a strange position for one who had been early in his career an advocate of municipal control of police.[36] However, Straw it appears convinced not only himself but Tony Blair as well that initially there was more to be gained by working with the police than confronting them. This was a shrewd move, as there was every indication that the senior police leadership was willing to cooperate in implementing Labour's agenda. Straw was equally pragmatic when it came to the legislative tools he had inherited from the Conservatives; Blair had opposed the introduction of the Police and Magistrates' Courts Act, condemning its centralization, but Straw sought neither to repeal nor moderate it. New Labour did deliver its long-standing promise to repeal the Prevention of Terrorism Act, but only to replace it with an updated and more powerful version which did not require annual renewal. Straw even kept the Police Federation on side by persuading Chancellor of the Exchequer, Gordon Brown, to permit a 4 per cent pay increase in 2001 when other public sector workers had to make do with 2.5 per cent. More pragmatism was evident with the reinstatement of the ranks of deputy chief constable and chief superintendent, both needlessly abolished by the Conservatives after the *Sheehy Report*'s recommendations. For its part, ACPO implemented an internal reorganization, strengthening the central presidency and committee structure, which, although not its purpose, facilitated Labour's centralism. Straw also gently allowed HMIC (Her Majesty's Inspectorate of Constabulary) to return to prominence as principal assessor of police performance, displacing the Audit Commission. In return Straw was to find HMIC a willing accomplice in implementing Labour's agenda.

By later standards Straw's centralization and standardization was modest. In this it is important to emphasize that he was doing very much what the ACPO leadership, most chief constables and even the staff associations, saw as sensible, even valuable. Indeed, in most cases the service itself had proposed the change and was anxious for the Home Office, which tended to be cautious if not actually obstructive, to get on with it. ACPO itself drove through the introduction of the 'National Intelligence Model' (NIM), standardizing and improving the gathering, analysis, and retention of criminal intelligence, although its standardization inevitably increased bureaucracy in an already bureaucratic system. A 'National Crime Squad' (NCS) and a 'National Crime Faculty' were established with the intention of increasing capability to deal with serious and organized crime.

What Straw did not at first provide was more resources. He inherited declining police numbers, a result of Conservative cutbacks in the face of an earlier economic recession. By sticking to the Conservatives' spending plans officer numbers declined still further in the first two years of the Blair government, dipping to 122,000 by 2000.[37] The police were also required, with other public services, to

---

[36] The author recalls one such exposition of this position in an address he gave to the Police Staff, College, Bramshill in 1982.

[37] Cipfa Police Actuals 2000–1 (<http://www.cipfastats.net/>).

demonstrate 'best value' in the use of their resources; a reasonable requirement but, as this had to be inspected and evidenced, a new notch on the bureaucracy ratchet.

In the end Straw recognized that Labour would not be able to make the kind of progress it wanted to make in reducing crime and disorder and gaining credibility as an effective 'law and order' party without reversing the decline in police numbers. This was achieved to an initially modest extent in 1999 with the introduction of the 'Crime Fighting Fund' (CFF). This would deliver an increase of 5,000 officers over four years, but the money came with strings attached. First, it could only be spent on extra police officers and not on equipment or infrastructure developments, thereby negating the managerial freedoms given to chief constables by the Police and Magistrates' Courts Act. Second, central funding had to be matched by police authorities delivering a share through council tax. Third, it came with an inspection regime, which meant more bureaucracy. Despite this injection of numbers, Labour still fought the 2001 general election with fewer officers than it inherited in 1997.[38]

Labour's second term and beyond: 'police reform' revived

It was under Straw's second-term successor David Blunkett that developments in police policy really began to accelerate. The 2001 manifesto committed Labour to increasing police spending by £1.6 billion by 2003–4, and thereby increasing police officer numbers by 6,000.[39] This was part of a general drive to increase spending on the public services, with more doctors, nurses, and teachers pledged. Devolvement to the frontline was promised along with pay increases for frontline staff, but it would come at the price of 'reform' of working practices. It seems that Blair was already committed to a more radical 'reform' of the public sector than he was prepared to state in the manifesto. There would be a Prime Minister's 'Delivery Unit' to make sure he got what he wanted.[40] The police would be no exception and in David Blunkett he had chosen someone who was prepared to fight the police's corner, but also someone who was intolerant of opposition to his plans.

Resources

Labour had every intention of delivering on its election pledge of police officers, its policy-makers no doubt aware of the practical and electoral advantage increas-

---

[38] Cipfa Police Actuals 1997–8 and 2000–1.

[39] Labour Party, 2001 Labour Party General Election Manifesto: *Ambitions for Britain* (<http://www.labour-party.org.uk/manifestos/2001/2001-labour-manifesto.shtml> [accessed 28 July 2012]).

[40] A Seldon, P Snowdon, and A Collings, *Blair Unbound* (Pocket Books, London, 2007), 20–1.

ing police numbers had achieved for the Clinton administration in the United States.[41] Indeed, within a year of coming to power it set a new target of increasing officer numbers to 130,000 by 2003, although that meant police authorities underwriting with an increase in council tax. There was probably not much science behind the numbers, but the increase was not only achieved in time but also exceeded.[42] At the end of Labour's time in office in 2010 there were 144,000 officers and 79,000 civilian staff, including 17,000 Police Community Support Officers, a new type of police personnel providing visible police-uniformed presence without police powers, an increase of 33 per cent in total personnel.[43] Within that overall increase civilian numbers had grown by 69 per cent, a deliberate consequence of the government policy of 'civilianization', with civilians replacing police officers in such core tasks as custody supervision, scenes of crime, and control rooms.[44]

PCSOs were introduced under a legal platform provided by the Police Reform Act 2002, itself presaged by a 2001 white paper, *Policing a New Century*. It was a far-reaching measure, but not its least significant feature was its title. 'Police Reform' had been a term first used by Conservative Home Secretary Michael Howard in the mid 1990s but had been used sparingly in Labour's first term. Now it was back with a vengeance, inferring that things were not good enough and needed radical change (incidentally, an implicit criticism of Straw).[45] To government insiders the pressures for fundamental change appeared numerous. The police seemed tardy in responding to demands for gender and racial equal opportunities; management was cautious and insular; the rank and file appeared protected from the rigours of modern management by a system of inflexible 'regulations'; there remained the hangover from the 'miscarriages of justice' scandals of the 1980s and early 1990s; and, despite the post-Scarman report increased emphasis on consultation, community-police relations had barely improved and there remained a lack of what in the commercial sector would be termed 'customer focus'. The United States seemed to offer examples of success in terms of community policing (Chicago) and management ('Compstat' in New York), to which British police were slow to respond. That crime had continued to fall in Labour's first term, that many of the central programmes were ones initiated or strongly influenced by the police, that the service had already positively responded to an

---

[41] Community Oriented Policing Services, *The Impact of the Economic Downturn on American Police Agencies* (US Department of Justice, Washington DC, 2011), iv.

[42] Home Office, The National Policing Plan 2003–2006 (<http://webarchive.nationalarchives. gov.uk/20100413151441/ http://police.homeoffice.gov.uk/publications/national-policing-plan/ nat_police_plan022835.pdf?view=Binary> [accessed 29 July 2012]), 22.

[43] Cipfa Police Actuals 1997–8 and 2009–10.

[44] HMIC, *Modernising the Police Service: A Thematic Inspection of Workforce Modernization—The Role, Management and Development of Police Staff in the Police Service of England and Wales* (HMIC, London, 2004), *passim*.

[45] See S Savage, *Police Reform: Forces for Change* (OUP, Oxford, 2007), 11–45.

extensive change agenda despite the government's own slow release of additional resources and that Police Regulations had ultimately been approved by successive home secretaries were not deemed sufficient mitigation to the prevailing assumption that radical change was needed. Possibly Labour losing its hard-won opinion poll advantage over the Conservatives on law and order in the lead-up to the general election may have prompted the course of action, although the sense that Blair wanted to deliver a radical agenda during the second term to cement his place in history may have been equally important.[46] If Labour appeared restless in its first term it would be positively frenetic in its second.

Centralization

Labour's police reform programme was expansive. It had always been less inhibited about centralization than the Conservatives, and when in opposition in the early 1980s it had wanted to introduce a 'National Police Agency' to take over some of the national functions performed by the Metropolitan Police. It also wanted an independent organization to investigate complaints against police. In power it created a whole series of national organizations and agencies. These included the Serious and Organised Crime Agency (SOCA), the Independent Police Complaints Commission (IPCC), the National Policing Board, and the National Policing Improvement Agency (NPIA), the last subsuming the Police Information Technology Organisation (PITO) and a range of existing national functions, such as higher level training, which had hitherto existed under Home Office Common Police Services or possessed ad hoc forms of governance. There was also investment in national technology programmes, notably a national radio network ('Airwave') and fingerprints (National Automated Fingerprint Identification System), Automatic Number Plate Recognition (ANPR), and, eventually, a new national intelligence system. Labour continued to support ACPO's national coordinating and policy-making role, the latter reinforced by the creation of the NPIA. Further concentration of resources and power was prevented, however, by the failure of their planned amalgamation of forces in 2005–6. Somewhat perversely counter terrorism remained to one side of Labour's centralization drive, although the mechanism of specific grants ensured that the increased funding available after the 2005 terrorist attacks was spent in the way it wanted, creating a series of regional counter-terrorist 'hubs' and intelligence units. However, notwithstanding its fractured nature and dubious value for money, adherents of the arrangements could point to its success as demonstrated by its successful negation of the Islamic terrorist threat after 2005. The same could not be said of the

---

[46] Ipsos MORI, *Best Parties on Key Issues—March 2010* (n 3), and Seldon, *Blair Unbound*, 24.

policing of serious and organized crime in general, which remained under-resourced compared to the size of the problem.[47]

The pace of centralization notably quickened after the appointment of the assertive David Blunkett as Home Secretary (2001), with the publication of the white paper *Policing a New Century* (2001), and the passing of the Police Reform Act 2002. Home secretaries could set national objectives through a series of 'National Policing Plans', with monitoring through first 'performance radars', then the 'Police Performance Assessment Framework' (PPAF), which in turn developed into 'Assessments of Policing and Community Safety' (APACS). All was monitored by a new, and highly intrusive, inspection body, the 'Police Standards Unit' (PSU) which operated in addition to HMIC, the Audit Commission, and the inspectorates of other departmental bodies which became involved through partnership working.[48] The inspectorate bodies could make use of new, powerful data-gathering technology, 'iQuanta', which gave them near 'real-time' access to force data. Although forces were never, as other public services, compared through 'league tables', forces and BCUs were grouped into 'similar families' for comparative purposes, and the lack of official tables did not stop the media creating unofficial ones of their own. Forces or BCUs which slipped sufficiently behind their family average could expect a warning letter and then a PSU intervention, which effectively meant chief constables would be told how to run their forces by a panel of specialists. David Blunkett also ensured, through the medium of the Police Reform Act 2002, that he acquired new powers to suspend chief constables. These tendencies were accentuated by the Home Secretary's highly didactic personal style.

It is important to set Labour's centralization in some context. In Blair's second term Labour was prepared to invest not simply in policing but all public services, but the deal was increased speed, conformity, accountability, and adoption of new public management techniques. Policing was, however, problematic. Its devolved constitution risked too much variation, and the evidence was that given the chance chief constables would exercise any management freedom given to them. For Labour this was too loose an arrangement in which the consequences of individual or corporate failure would rebound on them. Consequently, Labour was prepared to invest heavily in police numbers and new technology, but only so long as these were used precisely in the way the government wanted. That might seem reasonable, as government stumped up much of the bill, but as they were required to raise a greater share of the costs through

---

[47] The cost of serious and organized crime in 2012 was estimated to be between £20 and £40 billion. In 2012 SOCA's core budget was £417 million (parliament.uk, Home Affairs Committee, 17 January 2012, oral evidence by Keith Bristow <http://www.publications.parliament.uk/pa/cm201012/cmselect/cmhaff/uc1553-i/uc155301.htm>, [accessed 11 January 2013]) and Home Office, 'New appointment to National Crime Agency', 11 January 2013 (<http://www.homeoffice.gov.uk/media-centre/news/gordon-meldrum-nca> [accessed 11 January 2013]).

[48] National Policing Plan 2003–2006, 42–51 and Government News, 'Removing barriers to success', 21 November 2002 (<http://www.gov-news.org/gov/uk/news/removing_barriers_success_police_standards/5878.html> [accessed 4 August 2012]).

council tax, many police authorities felt that they should receive less proscription about how they used it. Also too much central proscription stifled local initiative and enthusiasm. It is also important to emphasize, however, that Labour did not pursue centralization in isolation from or, for much of the time, in opposition to the service's leadership as represented by ACPO. Several of the key centralizing measures—the National Intelligence Model, the National Crime Recording Standard (NCRS), and the Neighbourhood Policing Programme, even the introduction of PCSOs—were all police-led initiatives with the Home Office lending subsequent agreement, support, and enforcement. Sometimes that support was less than wholehearted, as for example was David Blunkett's support for the NCRS.[49] Many of the polices and guidance introduced under Labour were in fact generated by ACPO or, after 2007, jointly by ACPO and the NPIA, although these might to some degree, as with the stop and search, reflect government wishes or expectations.

The sum of Labour's programme represented a very substantial growth in the amount of finance and resources allocated to central police services, growing by 30 per cent between 2003–4 and 2009–10. It also represented a substantial growth in the proportion of national spending allocated to central services. In 2003–4 it amounted to £0.6 billion, or 6 per cent of total police spending; by 2009–10 it amounted to £1.2 billion, or 14 per cent.[50] Even excluding the counter terrorism budget, which had understandably increased after the attacks of July 2005, growth in the remaining central agencies and institutions amounted to 43 per cent. This growth would give grist to the Conservative mill that Labour was pursuing too much centralization. What was less clear was exactly what success could be directly attributed to this growth. The problem with this arrangement, however, was that much of this was at the expense of regional or individual force capability to address serious and organized crime, while some of its flagship schemes, notably SOCA, failed to deliver as much as expected.[51]

However matters might appear to outsiders, especially the Conservative opposition, the relationship between the police leadership and the government was never comfortable. True, Ian Blair, Metropolitan Police Commissioner 2005–8, seemed to be very much 'on message' with the Labour version of 'police reform', but his adherence to what might be termed 'progressive' police initiatives pre-dated his accession to high office or even Labour coming to power. For example, his advocacy of what would become PCSOs was launched at the 1994 ACPO autumn conference, almost three years before 'New' Labour won the 1997 general

---

[49] D Blunkett, *The Blunkett Tapes: My Life in the Bear Pit* (Bloomsbury Publishing, London, 2006), 432.

[50] Home Office, *Departmental Report 2009* (London, The Stationery Office, 2009 <http://www.official-documents.gov.uk/document/cm75/7592/7592.pdf> [accessed 21 April 2013]), 106 and Cipfa Police Actuals 2003–4 and Estimates 2009–10; authors' extrapolations.

[51] Home Affairs Committee, New landscape of policing, National Crime Agency (<http://www.publications.parliament.uk/pa/cm201012/cmselect/cmhaff/939/93905.htm> [accessed 1 August 2012]).

election and eight years before Blunkett adopted the initiative as government policy.[52] Blunkett might have been grateful for Blair's support, but he held in near contempt some of the great police centralizers, for example Sir David Phillips (ACPO President 2001–3).[53] However, there were moments when at least the leadership appeared too close to the Labour government, notably in 2005 when, at the initiative of the Prime Minister himself, the Home Office induced the ACPO leadership to seek an extension of detention without trial for terrorist suspects from fourteen to ninety days. The extension was defeated in a Commons vote but not before damage had been done to the police's reputation for political impartiality.[54] ACPO was found to be a valuable tool in delivering a degree of unity across the otherwise disparate forty-three forces, and accordingly it was rewarded in the Police Reform Act by the official recognition of its 'President' as a salaried post independent of any individual force, while the ACPO organization itself became a surrogate national police policy-making and oversight body, although that had not stopped Labour creating a National Policing Board as well in 2006. ACPO retained a high degree of independence and could, and would, openly disagree with the Home Secretary, but the new arrangements still represented a fundamental gain for the government which could now focus its influence on a single individual.

However, in other respects Labour, and Blunkett in particular, showed less sympathy for senior police leadership. Police leadership remained too disparate, too variable in its effectiveness for such a dominant personality. The Police Leadership Development Board, another national body, produced a report *Getting the Best Leaders to Take on the Most Demanding Challenges* arguing that police leadership would be improved if there was greater competition for the top jobs through shorter fixed term appointments, enhanced payments for chief officers of the larger forces, and bonuses of up to 10 per cent of salary for 'exceptional' performance.[55] A 'Senior Appointments Panel', run by the Chief Inspector of Constabulary, theoretically targeted individuals to the most suitable chief officer jobs, but it was not clear what improvement had been made in the overall suitability of appointments. Blunkett also introduced a protocol which gave greater power to the Home Secretary to initiate the suspension of chief officers for reasons not merely of misconduct but the more nebulous concepts of efficiency, effectiveness, and public confidence, although his high-profile attempt to remove the chief constable of Humberside following the Soham tragedy (2002) and Bichard inquiry (2004) ultimately failed.[56]

Even so, to the Conservative opposition it all looked a bit too cosy, especially when in 2008 the Metropolitan Police arrested Conservative immigration

---

[52] T Brain, *A History of Policing in England and* Wales (OUP, Oxford, 2010), 236 and Blunkett, *The Blunkett Tapes*, 377.

[53] Blunkett, *The Blunkett Tapes*, 377.

[54] Brain, *A History of Policing*, 360–3.

[55] Police Leadership Development Board, *Getting the Best Leaders to Take on the Most Demanding Challenges* (Home Office, London, 2004), *passim*.

[56] See Brain, *A History of Policing*, 325 and 336.

spokesman Damian Green for alleged involvement in the leaking of material highlighting government immigration failures. The Metropolitan Police were simply following through a complaint received from the Home Office Permanent Secretary, but it looked like the police were attempting to join with the government in suppressing politically embarrassing information. The principle of MPs not being above the law seemed to be lost in the furore that followed the search of his office in the Houses of Parliament. Even with considerable retrospection it is difficult to see how the Metropolitan Police could have done other than investigate the affair and when the evidence was sufficient arrest Green, but handing the matter to the Counter Terrorist Branch looked unnecessarily heavy handed, with a Conservative source labelling it 'Stalinesque'.[57] It could not have done other than sour the perception the Conservatives held of the police.

Pay and conditions of service: *Sheehy* continued?

In line with its policy across the public services Labour also instituted 'reform' of police pay and conditions. Straw had not ventured close to the Edmund-Davies formula in Labour's first term and even Blunkett was prepared to stick with it for the annual uplift of basic pay, but in other respects he wanted radical change. *Policing a New Century* outlined plans for priority payments for specialist duties, bonuses for exceptional performance, and restrictions in overtime compensation. To the Federated ranks it looked a bit too much like a reprise of the detested *Sheehy Report*, and it duly provoked a mass protest. It was enough to provoke the normally assertive Blunkett to compromise on overtime but in other respects he got his way.[58] He also managed to introduce a new process for dismissing inefficient officers, although in practice it was so bureaucratic that it was never successfully implemented. Blunkett's changes to pay and conditions were supposed to reflect modern management practices for incentivizing the workforce, but he misread police culture. Bonuses and specialist payments proved unpopular, bureaucratic, and cumbersome while delivering no identifiable improvement in performance. Instead it would leave the service a hostage to fortune when the financial crash of 2008 turned the media and general popular esteem against the whole bonus culture.

Blunkett may not have changed the Edmund-Davies pay formula, but that did not stop his successor, Charles Clarke, attempting to do so. In 2006 he publically said that it had 'had its day', and was showing impatience with the police pay negotiating machinery. He initiated a fundamental pay review under Sir Clive Booth, who recommended retaining an index as the basis of awarding an annual uplift in police pay but on the basis of a new, less generous 'public sector facing' index and opening up the possibility of different increases for different sections of the service. In December 2007 the staff associations reluctantly accepted a delayed 2.5 per cent increase, below the Edmund-Davies calculation, but the

[57] BBC News, 'Senior Tory arrested over leaks' (<http://news.bbc.co.uk/1/hi/uk_politics/7753557.stm> [accessed 16 September 2012]).

[58] Brain, *A History of Policing*, 316.

then Home Secretary, Jacqui Smith, declined to backdate it until September, the usual month when pay settlements took effect. It was a petty decision which provoked another protest march of 20,000 off-duty officers in early 2008, but in technical terms the Home Office had followed the required procedures and the decision stuck, thereby successfully creating antipathy amongst the rank and file towards a government which over its lifetime had substantially invested in policing. It was, however, by then typical of the antipathy that Labour had engendered across the whole public sector, whose workers, for all the investment, felt increasingly undervalued.[59]

Neighbourhood policing

The Neighbourhood Policing Programme exemplifies the best and the worst of Labour's police reform programme. Labour invested heavily in police numbers but did not seem at first to have a game plan as to how to use them. Crime was continuing to decrease but the public did not appear to actually feel safer. 'Neighbourhood Policing' was supposed to provide the answer.

The theory of 'Community Policing' had been developed by John Alderson, the chief constable of Devon and Cornwall, in the late 1970s, but it was out of step with the then prevailing professional attitudes, which tended to favour detection and response over prevention and patrol. Outside Devon and Cornwall the resources allocated to community forms of policing were minimal, but the philosophy and practice was endorsed in the 1981 Scarman Report and over the next two decades its presence was at least sustained at a minimum level. 'Total Geographic Policing' as developed during the late 1980s and early 1990s in some areas of the Metropolitan Police and Surrey, and adopted in modifications elsewhere, was a variant, and John Major endorsed the principle of 'Community Policing' in the 1992 Conservative manifesto. The problem was that there were never quite enough personnel to deliver the concept satisfactorily. While all forces allocated officers to community duties, amounting to 18 per cent of the total, there was considerable variation between forces and abstraction to other duties was common.[60] Then there was the effect of the drop in police numbers after the 1992 recession. In 1995 Major sought to redress the balance by making money available for 5,000 officers, but as this was never 'ring fenced' chiefs and police authorities tended to exercise the management freedoms granted by the Police and Magistrates' Courts Act 1994 and spend it on other priorities.

---

[59] To some extent Labour had never recovered from Blair's 1999 off-the-cuff remark that bore 'the scars' on his back of trying to reform the public sector. See N Assinder, 'UK Politics: Blair risks row over public sector', BBC News, 7 July 1999 (<http://news.bbc.co.uk/1/hi/uk_politics/388528.stm> [accessed 30 July 2012]) and B Page, 'Culture and attitudes', in *Blair Unbound*, 458–9.

[60] T Bennett and R Lupton, 'A survey of the allocation and use of community constables in England and Wales', *British Journal of Criminology* (vol 32, no 2, Spring 1992), 167–82 and Conservative Party, 1992 *Conservative Party General Election Manifesto: The Best Future for Britain* (<http://www.conservativemanifesto.com/1992/1992-conservativemanifesto.shtml#law> [accessed 1 October 2012]).

However, community policing experienced a revival in the early 2000s when an HMIC report *Open all Hours* posed the question of why, if crime was falling, the public did not actually feel safer? It concluded that the police could only make the public feel safer if they were 'visible, accessible and familiar'.[61] Surrey Police, a then successful force in performance terms, recognized the problem and began work with the University of Surrey to find solutions. The answers included not only basic work on visibility and accessibility, but also engaging with communities in finding and implementing solutions to their problems, and concentrating on the crimes and issues ('signal crimes') of greatest concern to *them*. 'Reassurance policing' teams were established in several pilot sites and after close evaluation deemed a success. Even so, this may not have been sufficient to convince the sceptics who preferred the 'Kent model' of local intelligence-led policing. In the event a choice was unnecessary as Labour almost simultaneously embarked on its police expansion programme, including the introduction of PCSOs, meaning it would be possible to deliver response, investigative, and reassurance policing. In many respects the initiative looked like John Major's 1992 election manifesto version for 'Community Policing', but he made the mistake of giving chiefs a choice about introducing it. Labour did not make that mistake. From 2005 chief constables were mandated to introduce the 'National Neighbourhood Policing Project'.[62] Even that was not enough; forces received detailed guidance on how it was to be uniformly introduced. Logic should have dictated that this, of all Labour's initiatives, required a high degree of local flexibility. It was, of course, backed up with an intensive inspection regime. It may have been over-prescriptive, driving out the local customization, but with growth in police numbers, especially PCSOs, Labour succeeded in delivering a viable scheme of community policing for the modern era. It ought to have brought goodwill and delivered electoral advantage. It did not.

Labour's record: crime, confidence, competence, and cuts

During its thirteen years in office Labour had invested material, intellectual, and political capital in policing. Total public spending (central and local government) on 'public protection' had more than doubled during Labour's thirteen years in power, although as a proportion of public spending it had increased only slightly from 4.1 to 4.8 per cent.[63] It achieved a radical shift in culture and management

---

[61] M Innes, 'The reassurance function', *Policing* (vol 1, no 2, 2007), 135.

[62] Home Office, *Neighbourhood Policing: Your Police; Your Community; Our Commitment* (Home Office Communications Directorate, London, 2005), *passim*.

[63] ukpublicspending.co.uk, United Kingdom Central Government and Local Authority Spending Fiscal Year 1997 (<http://www.ukpublicspending.co.uk/year_download_1997UKbn_12bc1n#usgs302> [accessed 4 August 2012]), and United Kingdom Central Government and Local Authority Spending Fiscal Year 2010 (<http://www.ukpublicspending.co.uk/year_download_2010UKbn_12bc1n#usgs302> [accessed 4 August 2012]).

style, even if it had wanted more. There was a plethora of new laws and policies, and record high numbers of police officers and support staff. Where previously there had been much talk of new national bodies to meet the challenges of the twenty-first century, Labour had created them, albeit often using the intellectual energy of the service. It had even changed police terms and conditions of service. It had provided a credible system of community policing and backed it up with more personnel. But in the prevailing management jargon these had all been 'inputs'; what genuine 'outcomes' had been delivered?

First and foremost, recorded crime was down. In 1997 nearly 4.6 million crimes had been recorded; by 2009–10 the number was 4.3 million, a drop of almost 6 per cent.[64] That in itself might not seem a huge reduction, but the distance was greater in reality because Labour had introduced a series of changes in the way crime was recorded, principally through the introduction of the National Crime Recording Standard in 2002, which aimed at more fully reflecting crimes *reported to* rather than those simply *recorded by* the police after an assessment of the evidence of whether a crime had been committed. The cumulative impact of the changes was principally to increase the number of sexual offences, minor assaults, and harassments recorded. Changes in recording practice contributed to but did not entirely explain an increase in violent crimes and this proved to be a particularly difficult public relations issue for both the service and the government, and protestations that the underlying trend in the British Crime Survey (BCS), a measure of public perceptions and experience rather than official records, was down cut little ice with a critical media and a public increasingly sceptical of Labour's adroit use of presentational 'spin'.[65] Nor could Labour avoid criticism over its support to victims in general, and to vulnerable groups in particular, especially violence against women.[66] The government's record on anti-social behaviour also suffered when news broke of a Leicestershire mother driven to unlawfully kill her daughter and take her own life after years of abuse from her neighbours and apparent insufficient action by Leicestershire police. Although the coroner criticized the police, it was apparent that the 'partnership' approach to crime and disorder also permitted uncertainty between the police and the local authority as to whom actually possessed ultimate responsibility for dealing with

---

[64] Home Office, Recorded crime statistics 1898 to 2001/2 (<http://www.gov.uk/government/publications/recorded-crime-statistics-1898-to-2001-02> [accessed 8 April 2013]), and Data.gov.uk, Crime in England and Wales 2009/10 (<http://data.gov.uk/dataset/crime-in-england-and-wales-bcs> [accessed 8 April 2013]).

[65] For contrasting interpretations see for example Datablog, 'Crime rates where you live', guardian.co.uk (<http://www.guardian.co.uk/news/datablog/2010/apr/22/uk-crime-rates-police-force> [accessed 31 July 2012]), and G Wilson, 'Crime up 44% under Labour', *The Sun*, 9 March 2010 (<http://www.thesun.co.uk/sol/homepage/news/2884595/Crime-up-44-under-Labour.html> [accessed 31 July 2012]).

[66] See for example House of Commons Library, *Labour Policy on Domestic Violence—1999–2010* (Standard note SN/HA/3989, 22 May 2010, Home Affairs section, <http://www.parliament.uk/briefing-papers/SN03989.pdf> [accessed 30 June 2013]) and A Ballinger, 'New Labour and responses to violence against women' (in Silvestri, *Lessons for the Coalition*), 38–41.

anti-social behaviour, and that was a problem which reflected badly on the whole of the government's approach.[67] It was unsurprising, therefore, that Labour found that it was losing the battle for people's hearts and minds, with most believing that crime was still rising and that confidence in the police while still higher than for politicians, lawyers, and journalists fared less well in comparison with doctors, nurses, and teachers.[68]

Brown's government thought it had the answer to what was now labelled 'the confidence gap': more standardization and central direction. Louise Casey, in charge of the 'task force' to improve police performance, recommended in her report of June 2008 less local discretion and greater national conformity. A didactic 'green paper' *From the Neighbourhood to the National*, published a month later by new Home Secretary Jacqui Smith, outlined a series of measures intended to close the gap, but many of them were simply recycled from earlier initiatives or borrowed. So there would be a 'policing pledge' (a recycled idea from the early 1990s), online local crime maps (borrowed from Chicago, but thought of first in this country by new London Mayor, the Conservative Boris Johnson), new target response times (in existence since the early 1990s), and an offer to victims of crime to keep them informed (recycled from the recently revamped 'Victim's Charter').[69] To put it simply it looked like after ten years in office Labour, now led by Gordon Brown, had not only failed in its key policy areas but it had also run out of new ideas. True to form, the Policing Pledge was backed up by an inspection which found that most forces were already at or near the standard required, which in turn emphasized that Labour had not understood that technically meeting targets did not necessarily equate to satisfying people's needs and expectations. The attempted solution was, typically, a new target intended to measure 'confidence'. Amongst the problems associated with this measure was that the initial measurement revealed that many forces had below 50 per cent confidence ratings, with a national average of only 46 per cent, suggesting again that for all its investment in policing Labour had made little beneficial impact on how people felt.[70]

By the 2010 general election Labour also looked like it had lost its reputation for competence when it came to handling home affairs issues. Straw's time at the Home Office had been relatively uneventful. He had been handed something of a bonus with the end of Irish-related terrorism on the British mainland following the Good Friday Agreement, while the new threat of Islamic-based terrorism did not emerge until after Britain's intervention in the 2003 Iraq War. There had been

---

[67] 'Mother and daughter who burned to death: "no excuses" says Alan Johnson', *The Telegraph*, 29 September 2009 (<http://www.telegraph.co.uk/news/uknews/6241791/Mother-and-daughter-who-burned-to-death-no-excuses-says-Alan-Johnson.html> [accessed 1 August 2012]).

[68] B Duffy, R Wake, T Burrows, and P Bremner, *Closing the Gaps: Crime & Public Perception* (Ipsos-MORI, London, 2008), 1–10.

[69] See Brain, *A History of Policing*, 396–7.

[70] National Statistics, Statistical new release: Public confidence in the Police and their local partners: results from the British Crime Survey year ending September 2008 (<http://webarchive. nationalarchives.gov.uk/20110218135832/rds.homeoffice.gov.uk/rds/pdfs09/pubcon-bcs-snr. pdf> [accessed 1 August 2012]).

a moment of concern over deficiencies in rural policing in 1999, when the Norfolk farmer Tony Martin was found guilty of murdering an intruder at his remote farm. Popularly the verdict seemed perverse but it also summed up the perceived neglect of rural policing under Labour. The problem was largely addressed in the short term by a series of rural policing initiatives and in the longer term by the increase in police numbers. Straw also gained credit for initiating the Macpherson Inquiry into the murder of Stephen Lawrence, which resulted in a major overhaul of police culture, training, and investigative practices concerning minority ethnic communities and victims. Blunkett proved particularly adept at turning crises to long-term advantage, gripping events such as the Soham tragedy and the 9/11 terrorist attack in New York to introduce major changes to police practice, technology, and strategy. But under his successor Charles Clarke the aura of omnicompetence began to diminish. Tony Blair, Clarke, and senior ACPO leadership, seriously miscalculated the political opposition over the 2005 attempted increase in detention without trial. Clarke also badly miscalculated over his 2005–6 attempt to reduce the number of forces from forty-three to around sixteen to eighteen, underestimating community and professional opposition, failing to identify the financial implications and secure the necessary resources, and even to ensure that he had the backing he needed from Cabinet colleagues. The attempt ended in utter failure and was made to look all the more damaging as Clarke, implicated in a failure of immigration policy, was sacked in a Cabinet reshuffle following poor local election results in May 2006.

John Reid, Clarke's successor, concentrated on breaking up the Home Office, hiving off a new Ministry of Justice, although few noticed at the time that was simply a revival of an old Liberal Democrat idea. His successor Jacqui Smith was beset by a series of problems, including losing her Metropolitan Police Commissioner, Sir Ian Blair, after a series of mishaps and mistakes, notably the fall-out from statements he made following the shooting by his officers of Jean Charles de Menezes, an innocent inadvertently caught up in the aftermath of the 7/7 terror bombing of central London in 2005. She also felt the full force of the reaction against the growth in administrative and bureaucratic procedures which had accrued under New Labour. A Channel 4 television documentary and a popular blog by a patrol officer writing under the pseudonym 'David Copperfield' brought the problem to public attention, with especial focus on the lengthy 'stop and search' form, a requirement of the Macpherson Report intended to improve the managerial monitoring of stops and searches of minority ethnic people. Inquiries and reports into bureaucracy followed, but while these made sound if hardly revolutionary recommendations about reducing police paperwork, in practice little progress was made before the sands of time ran out on Brown's administration.[71]

---

[71] D Normington, *Reducing the Data Burden on Police Forces in England and Wales* (Home Office, London, 2009), *passim* and J Berry, *Reducing Bureaucracy in Policing: Final Report* (<http://www.homeoffice.gov.uk/publications/police/reducing-bureaucracy/reduce-bureaucracy-police?view=Binary> [accessed 4 August 2012]), *passim*.

In a largely meaningless gesture of submission the Police Standards Unit was subsumed within the mainstream Home Office. In theory the number of targets was consolidated into the single confidence target but as many measures and priorities remained it too made little practical impact.

In the end not even the massive increase in police numbers was safe. The banking crisis of 2008 may have actually triggered cuts in police funding and thence in police numbers, but Sir Ronnie Flanagan, then Chief Inspector of Constabulary, had already warned in 2007 that in future resources would be 'tight', implying that the current high numbers were unsustainable.[72] He suggested more collaboration and technology to mitigate the effects of funding restraint, but neither he nor anyone else foresaw the financial crash of late 2008. By 2009 general cuts were anticipated regardless of which party might win the next general election.[73] By the time of the May 2010 general election no one was in any doubt that there would be cuts in public spending, the questions were only how big would they be and would there be any exceptions?

The state of policing in 2010

A credit and debit account of policing under the Labour government from 1997 to 2010 would technically be in credit. The achievements were significant and impressive—lower levels of crime, more police officers, a credible system of neighbourhood policing, a range of national agencies consolidating hitherto disparate functions, reform of police regulations, and, for better or worse, a change to the underlying calculation of increases in police pay, the first since 1978. There had been a mass of new legislation, some of which, despite negative reporting and comment, had been necessary and timely. The collective shock to the system of the Macpherson Report had been necessary and well managed. The 7/7 attack on the London transport network had been a surprise but after that measures had been put in place sufficient to prevent or disrupt major attacks.

There were, however, genuine, and not merely perceived, debits. Initial underinvestment meant that the great partnership initiative of the late 1990s suffered a faltering start from which it took several years to recover. Labour appeared never to have fully trusted the core of professionals who ran their public services, including the police, and had subsumed personal initiative, competence, and loyalty with excessive central direction and inappropriate incentives. For the police there was over legislation, over measurement, and over centralization. There was too much bureaucracy and the attempts to redress the balance were at best superficial. Above all, launching and then constantly relaunching

---

[72] R Flanagan, *The Review of Policing: Final Report* (Sir R Flanagan, London, 2008), 45.

[73] George Osborne, 'We will lead the economy out of crisis' (n 2).

'police reform', backed up with a succession of white or green papers, plans, and initiatives, Labour gave the impression that what it had been doing was not working. By March 2010, just two months before the general election was due, the Conservatives had a 31-point lead over Labour on crime and law and order.[74] This was an incredibly poor political return on Labour's investment, one which the Conservatives ruthlessly exploited.

---

[74] Ipsos MORI, *Best Party on Key Issues: Crime/Law & Order* (n 4).

2

The 'Big Society'

Conservative political philosophy and its implications for policing

The 'Big Society': big idea or aspirational waffle?

By the time David Cameron formally launched his flagship 'Big Society' policy at the Hugo Young Memorial Lecture in November 2009, he had been party leader for four years.[1] This might seem a lengthy gestation for such an important concept, especially as it was launched at a time which could be no more than six months away from the next general election. In reality, however, the launch was the logical cumulation of work on repositioning the Conservative Party which had been the defining feature of Cameron's leadership, the intellectual origins of which can be traced back to at least the leadership of Iain Duncan Smith at the beginning of the decade. The term 'Big Society' itself came very late in the day, in fact in November 2009. That it failed to ignite much interest, much less passion, when launched (in fact so little of either that it had to be relaunched the following year), and that it has attracted political and intellectual criticism, not to say derision, should not diminish the importance of the political philosophy which underlies it. For Labour Chancellor of the Exchequer Alistair Darling it was a return to 'the politics of the poor house'. For TUC policy officer Richard Excell it was 'the closest any Conservative has come to explaining how they expect reactionary methods to achieve progressive ends'. Three years later the retiring Archbishop of Canterbury, Rowan Williams, thought it no more than 'aspirational waffle designed to conceal a

---

[1] D Cameron, *The Big Society*, 10 November 2009 (<http://www.conservatives.com/news/speeches/2009/11/david_cameron_the_big_society.aspx> [accessed 16 August 2012]).

deeply damaging withdrawal of the state from its responsibilities to the most vulnerable'.[2]

What exactly the 'Big Society' amounts to has taken a lot of explaining. Books have been written about it, arguably adding to, not resolving, confusion.[3] In December 2011 a report published by the Public Affairs Committee concluded that there was 'little clear understanding of the Big Society project among the public', coupled with 'confusion over the Government's proposals to reform public services'. Yet that same committee recognized that Cameron 'placed the Big Society project at the centre of his political agenda, and in turn, it occupies a central place in the Coalition Agreement.'[4] The committee had grasped the significance of the 'Big Society'. It does not really matter that it has intellectual weaknesses, or that it has failed to excite much public imagination, much less buy-in. What counts is that it is an intellectual stimulus for the leaders of the party. That the term itself by mid 2013 had almost dropped out of use is equally unimportant. The underlying ideas were still the driving force behind the Conservative element of the Coalition government. Understanding the Big Society is, therefore, the key to understanding what the Coalition government is about. This is as true for policing as for any other aspect of the government's business, and police officers, of whatever rank or calling, who think that the Big Society is a remote and meaningless concept had, in popular parlance, simply better 'wake up and smell the coffee'.

'New Conservatism'

'New Conservatism' is not a term which many members of the Conservative Party will use, it being too close to Tony Blair's 'New Labour' project which led to the 'modernization' of the Labour Party in the early 1990s. It is nevertheless a realistic description of the Conservatism that David Cameron has created since becoming leader. That it has no official sanction means that in this work 'new' when it precedes 'Conservatism' will be in the lower case, but when it precedes 'Labour' it will be in the upper. Blair's 'New Labour' (a term he deliberately used) was a renewal of philosophy and organization with three primary intentions—to renew the fundamental doctrines of the party, making them fit for purpose in the

[2] P Wintour and A Stratton, 'I'll need volunteers to make the big society work, says David Cameron', guardian.co.uk, 10 November 2009 (<http://www.guardian.co.uk/politics/2009/nov/10/david-cameron-big-society-speech> [accessed 16 August 2012]) and R Excell, 'David Cameron's Big Society Speech' Touch Stone, 11 November 2009 (<http://www.touchstoneblog.org.uk/2009/11/david-cameron's-big-society-speech/> [accessed 16 August 2012]), and quoted in T Helm and J Coman, 'Rowan Williams pours scorn on David Cameron's "big society"', guardian.co.uk, 24 June 2012 (<http://www.guardian.co.uk/uk/2012/jun/23/rowan-williams-big-society-cameron> [accessed 16 August 2012]).

[3] For example J Norman, *The Big Society: The Anatomy of the New Politics* (University of Buckingham Press, Buckingham, 2010).

[4] Public Administration Select Committee, The Big Society (<http://www.publications.parliament.uk/pa/cm201012/cmselect/cmpubadm/902/90203.htm> [accessed 17 August 2012]).

late twentieth–early twenty-first centuries; to conspicuously move the party to the centre ground of British politics; and, to make the party electable again. Blair was brilliantly successful in electoral terms but left the impression to party traditionalists that he had betrayed basic Labour values.

By the mid 2000s the Conservatives found themselves in a similar territory to Labour in the early 1990s. Following their defeat in 1997 and failing to make progress at the 2001 election they pushed themselves further to the right to appeal to their core voters. They were successful in this but in doing so continued to make no headway in regaining the central ground where elections are won. They also had an image problem. For many they had become, as one party chairman warned, 'the nasty party'.[5] By 2005 it was easier for the electorate to determine what the party was against—immigration, Europe, the Human Rights Act—rather than what it was for. In the words of one right-wing political consultant, the party had 'switched from policy making to position taking'.[6] The party had begun 'modernization' under Iain Duncan Smith (2001–3), but his lack of charisma was amongst the reasons he was ousted well before the next general election. His successor, Michael Howard, principally sought to consolidate around traditional polices but made little progress in the 2005 general election. After his defeat he realized there had to be fundamental change and he precipitated this with his early resignation. Before he stood down, however, he appointed some key modernizers to the Shadow Cabinet, including George Osborne (chancellor) and David Cameron (education).

David Cameron had not previously been branded as a conspicuous modernizer, but he began to position himself as such in the late summer of 2005 with a series of speeches on social enterprise, constitutional reform, community relations, and improving the quality of life. He began to effectively develop a 'Cameron manifesto', the theme of which was 'modern compassionate Conservatism'.[7] In purely political terms he made the running while the principal leadership contender David Davis retained 'a magisterial silence'. This may still not have been enough for Cameron to displace Davis but what probably clinched it for him was a charismatic speech at the 2005 Conservative conference.[8] Ostensibly speaking about education he turned the occasion round to become effectively his vision for a new Conservatism and a new Britain. The party must stop its rightward drift: 'I say that will turn us into a fringe party, never able to challenge for government again. I don't want to let that happen to this party. Do you?'

---

[5] M White and A Perkins, '"Nasty party" warning to Tories', *The Guardian*, 8 October 2002 (<http://www.guardian.co.uk/politics/2002/oct/08/uk.conservatives2002> [accessed 18 August 2012]).

[6] J Tate, 'Preface' in J Tate (ed), *What's Right Now: Conservative Essays on the Role of Civil Society, Markets and the State* (Social Market Foundation, London, 2005), 10.

[7] F Elliott and J Hanning, *Cameron: the Rise of the New Conservative* (Harper Perennial, London, 2009), 276.

[8] D Cameron, 'Full text: David Cameron's speech to the Conservative conference 2005', guardian.co.uk, 4 October 2005 (<http://www.guardian.co.uk/politics/2005/oct/04/conservatives2005.conservatives3> [accessed 17 August 2012]).

We have to change and modernise our culture and attitudes and identity. When I say change, I'm not talking about some slick rebranding exercise: what I'm talking about is fundamental change, so that when we fight the next election, street by street, house by house, flat by flat, we have a message that is relevant to people's lives today, that shows we're comfortable with modern Britain and that we believe our best days lie ahead.[9]

Under his vision of new Conservatism the benefits of economic growth would be shared between tax reduction and better public services; the benefit system would be changed to enable families to stay together; taxes would be simplified; foreign policy would be ethical and compassionate; there would be support for business and social entrepreneurs. He concluded: 'So let the message go out from this conference: a modern, compassionate conservatism is right for our times, right for our party and right for our country.'[10] In comparison, Davis's speech fell flat, and it was the beginning of the end of his leadership bid.

Cameron still had an election to win, however, and an agenda to set out. In this it is interesting to consider the extent to which he was leading the development of 'new Conservatism' and the extent to which he was responding to the intellectual forces around him. A snapshot of those forces can be seen in *What's Right Now*, a series of papers by leading Conservatives, some already MPs, some to be in the not-too-distant future, published in the autumn of 2005, immediately before the leadership election. The contributions were not all from 'modernizers' but they were all by those at the centre of policy development, including Oliver Letwin, Michael Gove, John Redwood, Shadow Chancellor George Osborne, and future Big Society guru Jesse Norman. The two leadership contenders were amongst the contributors, Cameron restricting himself to his education brief, David Davis roaming into more conceptual territory with a paper on 'The consequences of state failure and the modern Conservative response', a paper which, despite his more traditional right-wing credentials, actually put him amongst the modernizers when it came to the emerging Conservative view of the role of the state. While each contributor had something distinctive to say from their own perspective, the sum total of what emerged was a challenge to New Labour's expanding and intrusive 'entrepreneurial state', replacing it with a rebalanced relationship between the people and the state which would affect every aspect of public policy.

There were five main building blocks to the emerging vision of new Conservatism. The first was the rebalancing of the state, and that (ironically given what was about to happen to him in the leadership election) was most clearly stated in the article by David Davis. He saw himself applying 'the timeless Tory values of personal freedom and smaller government'. This was, of course, a necessary fiction, given that all post-war Conservative governments, including Mrs Thatcher's, had,

---

[9] Cameron, Speech to the Conservative conference 2005 (n 8).
[10] Cameron, Speech to the Conservative conference 2005 (n 8).

in one way or another, presided over an accretion of centralized power. Davis was serious in wanting to do something about the plight of the poor and disadvantaged, but Labour's state intervention and more money had failed. The new Conservative way would be better because there would be 'a new political settlement' between politicians and the people which acknowledged that 'people know better than politicians do about how to improve their own lives'. It would not be enough to 'roll back the frontiers of the state': a modern Conservative government would change the very way power is wielded in Britain, committing itself 'to a genuine transfer of power from the political elites to the people'. It would do this by ending 'government monopolies' and valuing 'the expertise and dynamism of the independent and voluntary sectors'. There would be 'a fundamental shift in the balance of power between the state and the citizen, putting the state's spending power in the hands of patients, parents and other public service users'. In education it would mean more schools free from state control; in health the NHS would become a 'provider of personal healthcare rather than national healthcare', admitting a greater role for the private sector. In policing it would not 'obviously' be possible to give individuals direct control of the police, but it would be possible to 'empower' them by 'allowing them to elect local police boards which would set the priorities and the direction for policing in their areas.' He summarized the new people–government relationship: 'Where we cannot empower people directly, we should empower communities instead. It is the job of central government to set a new framework and to give individuals the opportunity to wield power within in it.'[11]

Other contributors to *What's Right Now* identified the benefits of this rebalanced state. It would allow a flourishing free market which would be to everyone's advantage, through greater, shared prosperity, greater social mobility, and more choice, especially in health care and education. The state would retain an essential regulatory role—independent courts, domestic and international security, honest tax collection—while individuals and businesses need to operate according to basic core values to protect the environment and family life, but after that it would be up to the markets to regulate not just the economy but society in general. In this utopia businesses would pursue 'socially valuable ends' and therefore would be ideally placed to run public services. Certain policies would flow naturally from this rebalanced state: a restriction on the growing power of the European Union, a restatement of national over international rights (specifically replacing the Human Rights Act with a UK 'Bill of Rights'), a recommitment to local government at the expense of central state power, 'decentralized' public services, a greater role for independent and voluntary organizations in delivering welfare, an elected House of Lords, equalized parliamentary constituencies, and a codified constitution.[12]

---

[11] D Davis, 'The consequences of state failure and the modern Conservative response' in Tate, *What's Right Now*, 52–8.

[12] Tate, *What's Right Now, passim.*

The second building block was the new Conservative vision for the economy. The new Conservatives had a fundamental problem here, in that in 2005 New Labour seemed to be using Mrs Thatcher's economic policies rather well to deliver a sustained period of economic growth. Shadow Chancellor George Osborne recognized the absolute centrality of creating a credible alternative economic vision to the New Labour success story: 'However interesting our social policies may be, we will not have the chance to implement them until we gain public confidence in our economic policies.' He thought he had the answer in four 'economic principles'—'macroeconomic stability; increased productivity; reduced long-term demands on the state and lower taxes.'[13]

In macroeconomics he started from the assumption that the principles of Thatcherite economic policy—control of inflation, eliminating union militancy, privatization, enhanced competition, and freedom from exchange control—had been correct, so much so that the unprecedented fifty-two quarters of economic growth experienced under New Labour was entirely attributable to Blair and Brown assimilating the economic principles of Thatcherism. However, these principles had now run their course: 'This framework now needs revitalising to make it credible again.'[14] However, at this point in the evolution of his economic policies Osborne became extraordinarily circumspect. In macroeconomic policy he would maintain the Bank of England's 'independence' established by Brown, but he would create an independent statistical service to bring credibility to the government's figures.[15] It was no more than a minimalist revision of the continuum of government economic policy since the 1980s and reflected the difficulty the Conservatives had in coming up with a credible macroeconomic alternative to Brown before the full effects of the banking crisis, which was beyond the planning horizon in autumn 2005.

When it came to increasing productivity he was on surer ground. The US economy was at the time a paragon of performance and enjoyed less regulation and lower taxes for businesses. Britain should therefore ape America. A smaller public sector, again on the American model, would also be essential: 'Tackling the growth of the public sector is also crucial for improving productivity, for it crowds out the rest of the economy. Public sector employment has risen by over half a million. Those people are no longer available to work in the private sector.'[16] Decreasing the size of the public sector would free up employment resources—numbers, skills, and innovation—for the private sector to expand. A smaller public sector would be crucial to delivering his third economic principle—reducing the long-term demands of the state, which would necessitate an increased role in private sector providers of health care, education, and childcare, and reducing the demand for public sector pensions. A smaller public sector would make possible his fourth principle—a system of simpler and lower taxes,

---

[13] G Osborne, 'Principles of a Conservative economic policy' in Tate, *What's Right Now*, 141.
[14] Tate, *What's Right Now*, 143.   [15] Tate, *What's Right Now*, 145.
[16] Tate, *What's Right Now*, 146.

although he clearly had in mind principally lower business taxes so that businesses would be attracted to relocate, or simply stay, in Britain. By adopting his economic principles Britain could continue to 'create wealth through the private sector, provide security through public service reform, and raise living standards in an increasingly competitive and mobile business market.'[17] For Osborne, and all the Conservative modernizers, a smaller state and all it entailed was axiomatic with continued economic growth.

The third key building block of new Conservatism was public service reform. Weaning the public off state help was in itself essential to delivering the revitalized Britain. It was not that Britain's 'new Conservatives' wished to go as far as some of the American radical Right, which saw virtually all public services as not simply unnecessary but actually damaging to the very fabric of society. For Osborne and his colleagues the 'government can and should provide a safety net below which none can fall'.[18] However, they were equally dissatisfied 'with a situation where the public sector takes an increasing share of our national income. It damages economic dynamism and undermines the civic society that underpins our freedom.'[19] So a smaller public sector was essential, but how could this be reconciled with providing 'a safety net below which none can fall'? The answer would lie in more effective public services. 'Wider social goals would be more efficiently achieved through the use of market mechanism'; private sector monopolies would be broken up, allowing 'for greater competition and pluralism' in service delivery.[20] Private enterprise would be encouraged in the state sector, particularly as these providers were increasingly demonstrating the 'development and deepening of a culture of social responsibility in business'.[21] Increased political control of public services, rested from the professionals in health, education, and the police who ran services according to their sense of priorities, would ensure that the public services would be better focused on what the public actually wanted. This was especially so for the police, where it was chief constables who had the power 'to determine how police officers are used'.[22] It was the state's duty to provide universal access to public services, not necessarily provide the services themselves. Thus there would be a plurality of provision with public services provided by government, private sector, and voluntary sectors, with distinctions between the three sectors being broken down. There would be less prescription about the way of delivering a service, as long as the outcomes were satisfactory. Individuals would be given more choice about where they would receive their public services.[23]

---

[17] Tate, *What's Right Now*, 149.   [18] Tate, *What's Right Now*, 147.

[19] Tate, *What's Right Now*, 147.

[20] M Gove, 'Putting the "social" back into markets' in Tate, *What's Right Now*, 25.

[21] M Gove, 'Putting the "social" back into markets' (n 20), 25.

[22] N Gibb, 'A new theory of the state and a new agenda for public services' in Tate, *What's Right Now*, 98.

[23] Tate, *What's Right Now*: D Green, 'Better public services the modern Conservative way', 103, Davis (n 11), 56, and D Krueger, 'Love, money and time: how to grow a civil society', 157.

If the provision of public services was to be refounded, if those services were to become more responsive to what the public wanted, then there had to be a democratic renewal, and this formed the fourth building block of new Conservatism. Power had to be put back into the hands of the people. This would have the parallel advantage of ending popular alienation from the political process, as evidenced by the low esteem politicians were held in and declining turnouts at elections. For MP Douglas Carswell this would be achieved first by decentralizing power to local councils. With this would come increased powers to raise local taxes (on goods and services), eliminating national VAT. Police authorities would be replaced by 'directly elected sheriffs, with real power to direct local police forces' priorities'. Schools would become 'independent, freestanding institutions'. In health the patient would be empowered 'to purchase health care from the provider of their choice'. The power of the judiciary to effectively make new laws and thwart the will of Parliament would be proscribed, with a degree of democratic appointment of judges being introduced. The House of Lords would be a properly elected upper house; constituencies would be equalized; 'quangos' abolished; the power of the European Union curtailed. In sum: 'Direct Democracy and localism offer the British centre-right an answer to their greatest strategic problem: namely, the fact that a left-leaning liberal elite has successfully taken control of those institutions responsible for almost every aspect of life in Britain today.'[24]

The fifth building block of new Conservatism was to foster 'civil society'. It would be tempting to dismiss 'civil society' as part of Rowan Williams's 'aspirational waffle', but again it would be wrong to do so. One of the first acts of the Coalition government was to create an 'Office for Civil Society' within the Cabinet Office. Defining exactly what 'civil society' is, however, is more difficult. The BBC World Service has made an effort: 'A civil society is a public space between the state, the market and the ordinary household, in which people can debate and take action.' It could therefore 'include any voluntary collective activity in which people combine to achieve change on a particular issue—but not political parties, even though civil society has a political dimension.' As a concept it long predated new Conservatism, with arguably its foundations originating in the city-states of ancient Greece. In the USA the administration of George W Bush thought it the correct path to 'the third way'.[25] At one level it might simply be described as voluntary or charitable activity, and it certainly included that, but in modern politics it means more. It means all citizens expanding their contribution to their neighbourhood and community. 'Civil society' becomes terrifically important if at the same time the role of the state

---

[24] D Carswell, 'Direct democracy: a radical agenda for change' in Tate, *What's Right Now*, 109–18.
[25] BBC World Service, What is civil society?, 5 July 2001 (<http://www.bbc.co.uk/worldservice/people/highlights/010705_civil.shtml> [accessed 20 August 2012]).

is retreating, as envisaged by the new Conservatives. But it is not simply about filling the void left by the state; civil society, by being quite literally 'of the people', will do a better job than traditional public services, even those fuelled by the techniques of 'new public management' and public service targets of the 1990s and 2000s.

Consequently, for the new Conservatives of 2005, 'government's first priority is indeed to get out of the way'. Its second priority is to create 'a level playing field' with the state when it comes to providing services by incentivizing individuals through tax breaks to give more of their income to charities and to spend time in support of voluntary activity ('altruism responds to incentives'). The then director of studies at the Centre for Policy Studies Danny Krueger summarized the primary duties of new Conservatism thus:

> The two political imperatives for the Tories, therefore, are to moralise and to localise. 'Moralising', of course, does not mean preaching from on high: it means imbuing the Party's message with a moral motif, and celebrating the compassionate instincts of the public. 'Localising' does not mean government abandoning its responsibilities: it means taking direct action to restore to the public their rightful power over the institutions which affect them.[26]

There was little that was entirely original in *What's Right Now*, with its drawing intellectual antecedents from many sources, including traditional nineteenth-century liberalism, Von Hayek's defence of liberal capitalism, Schumacher's 'small is beautiful' philosophy, George W Bush's presidential vision of compassionate conservatism, and even aspects of Tony Blair's 'new localism', as well as examples of Iain Duncan Smith's stalled attempt at party modernization.[27] What was original, however, was drawing all these strands together in a single coherent source, and presenting it definitively as the way forward for both the country and the Conservative Party. By contributing to it, even if in a relatively small and indistinct way, David Cameron indelibly associated himself with the modernizers. It was bold but it was also shrewd; he understood that the party not only needed to rebrand after three defeats, it was ready for it, and he presented himself as the man to deliver it. It can also be assumed that this was a critical point in his own intellectual development. No real-world politician can be entirely philosophical; there are simply too many compromises which have to be made because of force of circumstance. However, as a student of political and moral philosophy Cameron clearly understood the importance of core 'values' in politics, providing a moral compass amid the chancing and changing scenes of life. By his association with *What's Right Now* he publically signalled his personal acceptance of the principal values of new Conservatism.

---

[26] D Kruger (n 19).

[27] Conservative Party, *Are You Thinking what We're Thinking?* (<http://www.conservatives.com/pdf/manifesto-uk-2005.pdf> [accessed 21 August 2012]).

Refining and developing new Conservatism

Once safely elected as leader in December 2005 there was much work for Cameron to do in refining the new Conservative message. He had an advantage in that a general election was unlikely before 2009 and not legally due until 2010. He could therefore avoid being trapped into providing too much detail early in his tenure. He even took his time before initiating a series of key policy reviews. Instead he first established a set of core values, published in August 2006 under the title *Built to Last*. The links with *What's Right Now* were clear. He called for a 'revolution' in 'personal', 'professional', 'civic', and 'corporate' responsibility. The party's 'mission' was to deliver 'a responsibility revolution to create an opportunity society in which everybody is a somebody, a doer not a done-for.' This would be delivered through eight principal values: encouraging enterprise; fighting social injustice; meeting environmental threats; providing 'first class healthcare, education and housing'; taking a lead in 'ending global poverty'; protecting the country; giving 'power to people and communities, and to recognise the limitations of government', with political power being 'exercised as close to people and communities as possible'; and, being 'an open, meritocratic and forward-looking party'.

The eight values may have been principally intended to be inspirational, but even at this stage they beget some emerging policy principles. Encouraging enterprise would mean sharing economic growth between investment in public services *and* tax reduction. Competitiveness would be encouraged by 'fairer, flatter and simpler taxes', and less regulation. Saving for a pension would be incentivized but ultimately paid for by raising the retirement age. Social injustice would be fought by 'setting social enterprises and the voluntary sector free to tackle multiple deprivation'. First class health care would be provided by ending top-down targets and increasing patient choice; first class education by giving schools greater freedom over their own affairs. Some old policy favourites were given a new rationale by associating them with core values. Thus working towards a target of 0.7 per cent of national income given in international aid by 2013 was allied to ending global poverty by reforming the Common Agricultural Policy and promoting international free trade. Protecting the country would mean a single UK border force, abolishing police targets, and replacing them with 'a single-minded focus on fighting crime', and replacing the Human Rights Act with a new Bill of Rights. People would be empowered by abolishing regional assemblies, giving 'local communities greater control over local services', and 'welcoming directly elected mayors in cities where they have public backing'. The party would be 'open, meritocratic and forward-looking' by encouraging more women and minority ethnic candidates, and 'undertaking more social action in our communities to help improve people's well-being and quality of life'.[28] Although

---

[28] Conservative Party, *Built to Last* (Conservative Party, London, 2006), *passim*.

the term was not used in the pamphlet itself, *Built to Last* was intended to be representative of what was becoming known as 'compassionate Conservatism'.[29]

Cameron then initiated six major policy reviews—social justice, national and international security, quality of life, public service reform, overseas aid, and economic competitiveness. These reviews were intended to mount 'a real intellectual revival of Conservatism' but with the practical intention of 're-establishing contact with the people'.[30] To this list could have been added *Policing for the People*, a so-styled 'mid-term report' of the 'Police Reform Taskforce', work led by shadow 'police reform minister' Nick Herbert, which reported in April 2007.[31] For some reason this was not included in the formal policy review structure, but it was, nevertheless, very much part of the fundamental review process initiated by Cameron. It will be reviewed in detail in the next chapter but it will suffice to observe here that it was already imbued with the emerging fundamental principles of 'new Conservatism'. Following the reviews came a series of policy green papers, generally developing the discursive views of the reviews into more specific policies which were intended to form the basis of the next manifesto. These collectively, together with a series of effectively policy-making speeches, represented an intellectual repository of new Conservatism, and hence what would drive the thinking of the leading members of a future Conservative government. Understanding what these policy-makers thought between 2005 and 2010 is the key to understanding how they would approach the next general election, and what they would do in power.

The review on schools, *Raising the Bar, Closing the Gap*, is one of the most interesting, not principally because of what it says about education and choice, but of what it says about the philosophy of new Conservatism. Its first eight pages are an exposition of the new conservative view of what's wrong with society and politics, what's changing, and what the Conservatives would do to put matters right. Labour was 'stuck in the past' with a culture of '"we know best" top-down centralisation', stripping individuals of 'autonomy', sapping 'us of our instinct to make the best of ourselves', fostering a culture of 'apathy and disengagement'. The Conservatives, in contrast, understood the new world order, which 'is one where people demand more power and control over their own lives', and one 'where people expect to make more and more decisions for themselves'. One of the key enablers of this new world was 'the democratisation of information' through technology which 'has put the facts, and the power to use them, at the disposal of everyone'. Consequently we 'are entering a new era of personal responsibility, choice, and local control. People power replacing state power. Democracy replacing bureaucracy. This is the post-bureaucratic age.' People

---

[29] See J Norman and J Ganesh, *Compassionate Conservatism* [sic] (Policy Exchange, London, 2006), [1].

[30] T Bale, *The Conservative Party: From Thatcher to Cameron* (Polity Press, Cambridge, 2010), 288.

[31] Police Reform Taskforce, *Policing for the People: Interim Report of the Police Reform Taskforce* (Conservative Party, London, 2007), *passim*.

power would be based on trust: 'Conservatives have always believed that if you trust people, they will tend to do the right thing. That if you give people more responsibility, they will behave more responsibly. That if you give people more power and control over their lives, they will make better decisions than those the state would make on their behalf.' The state would continue to have a role, providing security, 'high quality, efficient public services, and to work tirelessly for social justice and a responsible society.' However, 'politicians should stop pretending they can fix every problem, and start trusting people, families, businesses, communities and all the myriad institutions of civil society more.'[32]

Returning power to communities was further developed in policy green paper number 9, *Control Shift*. This would be essentially a two-stage process. First power would be devolved from central to local government, and then the people would be given a greater say in local priorities and spending. Central targets would be scrapped, bureaucratic burdens reduced, ring fenced funding (a favourite Labour device) phased out, and council tax capping abolished. Instead local people would be empowered to veto high council tax rises, elect mayors (only 'in all large cities') and police commissioners, permit further devolution of spending to ward level, and gain more say over how central funds would be spent in their area. The regional tier of government, much beloved by Labour, would be abolished.[33] 'Localism' was theoretically a common agenda of all three main parties, and Tony Blair, recognizing and seeking to redress the problem of disassociation between local communities and government, had made what became known as 'new localism' a key feature of his second term. But the problem was that Labour could never quite let go.[34] Just as with Scottish and Welsh devolution, under Labour central government might devolve responsibility for delivery but it would seek to maintain control over all the levers of power. Labour, haunted by the fear of unequal delivery of key services (the so-called 'postcode lottery') to the neglect of deprived areas (and therefore an element of its electoral base), hedged its version of localism with central directives and targets. It appeared that the Conservatives were prepared to tough that problem out. Councils would be given 'a general power of competence', summarized by Cameron as 'councils can do whatever they want so long as it's legal'.[35] The Conservative version of localism was, therefore, intended to be the real thing, although from the beginning Cameron made it clear that while there might be more power there would also be less money to spend.[36]

---

[32] Conservative Party, *Raising the bar, closing the gap: an action plan for schools to raise standards, create more good school places and make opportunity more equal* (Conservative Party, London, 2007), 3.

[33] Conservative Party, *Control Shift: Returning Power to Local Communities* (Conservative Party, London, 2009), 2–3.

[34] T Travers, 'Local government' in *Blair's Britain*, 78.

[35] Conservative Party, *Control Shift*, 3, and D Cameron, 'Speech to the LGA Conference', 2 July 2009 (<http://www.conservatives.com/News/Speeches/2009/07/David_Cameron_Speech_to_the_LGA_Conference.aspx> [accessed 28 August 2012]).

[36] Cameron, Speech to the LGA Conference.

Commensurate with localism was a vision for 'a stronger civil society' in which the voluntary sector would play a significantly increased role in delivering what had hitherto been seen as core public, or state provided services. For the Conservatives 'charities, social enterprises, co-operatives, and community groups' were not 'the third sector' but 'the first', delivering solutions which neither the state nor the market could provide. The Conservatives would support the voluntary sector through grants, reducing bureaucracy, incentivizing private giving, and creating 'a level playing field' on which voluntary sector organizations could compete fairly with state providers to deliver services. Crucially, voluntary organizations would be able to receive 'a competitive return on investment'. In addition to traditional voluntary organizations, 'social enterprises' ('a business trading for social purpose') would be encouraged to take up more state sector work, supported by a 'Social Investment Bank', and permitted to earn a 'competitive return'. In case this was not enough, a future Conservative government would introduce 'a National Citizen Scheme, available to all 16-year-olds' which would provide 'a compelling and challenging programme that will help teach young people about their responsibilities in society and provide a focus for participating in community service.'[37] Increased support for civil society would take place in the context of support for individuals delivering welfare in the home, increased access to good education and skills, and incentives to work rather than live off welfare.[38]

In the Conservative vision of the rebalanced state there would still be a role for the public services, even if a reduced one, but those services would become more efficient. The plan for the NHS typified the new approach. Labour had let down the NHS; despite massive investment its productivity was actually declining and its staff had become demoralized. The Conservatives, working with health care professionals, would turn this round. The NHS would, through 'the collection, collation and publication of data on health experiences and outcomes', become accountable to patients 'not the whims of politicians'. The Conservatives would scrap top-down 'process-driven' targets, replacing them with information about 'the results of people's treatment' ('Patient Reported Outcome Measures'), introduce patient choice and 'payments by results', rewarding 'those doctors and hospitals that achieve good results and to incentivise improvement amongst those whose standards are falling behind.'[39] The message was that the NHS, and by implication other public services, would not only be safe, they would actually be better off in Conservative hands.

There was a further aspect to the rebalanced state, and perhaps a curious one for those who had witnessed the accretion of authority for the police and other

---

[37] Conservative Party, *Repair Plan for Social Reform: Plan for Change* (Conservative Party, London, 2009), 44–50.

[38] Conservative Party, *Repair Plan* (n 33), 4–7.

[39] Conservative Party, *Delivering Some of the Best Health in Europe: Outcomes not Targets* (Conservative Party, London, 2008), 15.

agencies when the Conservatives were last in power. In opposition the party's position became more equivocal. Under Michael Howard the party had supported Labour measures such as the extension of the DNA database and the proposed introduction of identification cards, but in 2005 it opposed Labour's ill-conceived attempt to extend detention without charge up to ninety days. Cameron was prepared to go even further. He thought the Human Rights Act should be repealed, because it failed to protect such fundamental British liberties as trial by jury, and because it was indicative of a whole justice system tilted in favour of the criminal. However, he would instead replace it with a British 'Bill of Rights' that would both protect fundamental British liberties and emphasize individual responsibilities.[40] New Shadow Home Secretary Dominic Grieve's policy review of surveillance and privacy, reporting in September 2009, took the commitment further. This policy promised to roll back 'the mammoth data bases and wide powers of data sharing' created by the Labour government. Specifically this would involve scrapping Labour's ill-fated identity card scheme, 'establishing clear principles' for the use and retention of DNA, while supporting its use, 'ending the permanent or prolonged retention of innocent people's DNA', and strengthening the audit powers of the Information Commissioner. As a point of principle, government was to be guided by 'proportionality', meaning that personal details would be held by public authorities on a 'need-to-know basis', and then only for limited periods.[41]

The sum total of Cameron's analysis was that British society was 'broken'. The evidence for him was pervasive: crime (especially knife crime), family breakdown, disincentives to work, even 'a denial of personal responsibility and the concept of moral choice'. The 'mission' of the Conservative Party was to 'heal the wounds of poverty, crime, social disorder and deprivation that are steadily making this country a grim and joyless place to live.'[42] No matter that it could be contested that Britain was broken, there was enough of a perception to make it a realistic concept and worthwhile to find political solutions. In the new Conservative analysis the manifestations of a broken society were linked. It followed that the solutions were linked: support for the family, ensuring that people who could work would work, better education and health, and effective crime fighting. In Cameron's world this meant allowing professionals to be professional; it also meant holding these professionals more effectively to account. There was a chain of connection between social problems, social responsibility, professionals being

---

[40] D Cameron, speech 'Balancing freedom and responsibility: a modern British bill of rights', quoted in House of Commons Library, Background proposals for a British bill of rights and duties (Standard Note SN/PC/04559, 3 February 2009 <http://www.parliament.uk/documents/commons/lib/research/briefings/snpc-04559.pdf> [accessed 31 August 2012]), 5.

[41] Conservatives, *Reversing the Rise of the Surveillance State: 11 Measures to Protect Privacy and Hold Government to Account* (<http://www.conservatives.com/News/News_stories/2009/09/~/media/Files/Policy%20Documents/Surveillance%20State.ashx> [accessed 30 August 2012]), 1–2, 9–11.

[42] D Cameron, speech 'Fixing our broken society', 7 July 2008 (<http://www.conservatives.com/News/Speeches/2008/07/David_Cameron_Fixing_our_Broken_Society.aspx> [accessed 31 August 2012]).

allowed to do their job but being held accountable, and the increased profitability of business. One feature of the broken state could not be fixed without fixing the others.

> Saying to parents, your responsibility and your commitment matters, so we will give a tax break for marriage and end the couple penalty. Saying to head teachers you are responsible and if you want enforceable home school contracts and the freedom to exclude you can have it and we will judge you on your results. Saying to police officers you are responsible and the targets and bureaucracy are going but you must account to an elected individual who will want answers if you fail. Saying to business, if you take responsibility you can help change culture and we will help you with deregulation and tax cuts...but in the long run they depend on the steps you take to help tackle the costs of social failure that have driven your costs up and up.
>
> It is the responsibility agenda and it will be the defining thread of any government I lead.[43]

These ideas were expanded in the policy green paper *Repair* published in 2009, which it has already been noted previously provided detail concerning the extended roles for charities, voluntary organizations, and social enterprises. It also provided extra detail of new Conservative views on crime and punishment. On the police they would cut bureaucracy, including reform of the Regulation of Investigatory Powers Act and scrapping the lengthy stop and search form, which to police officers and many Conservative politicians was the symbol of all that was bad with Labour's bureaucracy and centralism.[44] The commitment to make the police accountable to an elected individual was reiterated, but rationalized as a crime reduction measure. Local crime maps would be made available, presumably as an example of the democratization of information. On sentencing and punishment, a 'rehabilitation revolution' was promised, with increased transparency in sentencing, earned rather automatic release, and 'tough and effective' community sentences. Interestingly for the future, 'Prison and Rehabilitation Trusts and private sector prisons will be paid by results—with a premium awarded if the offender is not reconvicted within two years.'[45]

The sum of the new Conservative policies may have been to 'repair our broken society', but there was a necessary requisite: 'A strong economy is the foundation of everything we want to achieve, so we will reconstruct it after years of spending and borrowing, taxing and regulating.'[46] By 2009 Cameron and his Shadow Chancellor George Osborne had travelled something of an economic Damascene road. They had started with the assumption that in economics Blair and Brown had simply taken up Thatcherite doctrine and effectively applied it. There was, therefore, nothing fundamentally wrong with Labour's approach, it was just that

---

[43] D Cameron, 'Fixing our broken society' (n 37).

[44] D Copperfield (pseud S Davidson), *Wasting Police Time* (Monday Books, Cheltenham, revised 2007), 119–21.

[45] Conservative Party, *Repair Plan* (n 33), 6.   [46] Conservative Party, *Repair Plan* (n 33), 1.

the Conservatives, by applying the principles set out in Osborne's contribution to *What's Right Now* would do it so much better. This view changed fundamentally after the publication of the report of John Redwood's 'Economic Competiveness Policy Group' in August 2007, published about the time the Northern Rock bank collapsed, and a full year in advance of the banking crisis that affected the world economy. His group argued that while Britain was wealthy it was not as wealthy as it should be and was, unless drastic action was taken, likely to lose out to the rising Asian economies. They concluded, rightly in retrospect, that the factors that had temporarily facilitated Britain riding the crest of a global economic wave could not last and because of underperformance the UK economy was not well placed to adapt to new circumstances.

Less presciently they argued 'that countries which choose the lowest tax rates, and which have the least oppressive but effective regulatory regimes, are the ones that grow the fastest and become the richest.' A Conservative chancellor should therefore 'set businesses free to compete, by a simpler and more competitive tax and regulatory framework'. Specific measures would include setting an 'annual regulatory budget...setting out how much cost government will impose on business in the following year, and ensuring that in each year of Conservative government the costs imposed will be reduced.' Deregulation would be accompanied by improvements to Britain's 'ageing infrastructure', particularly in transport. Crucially, the report also considered 'the way in which so much money has been absorbed by the public sector in the last few years, with so little expansion of output. We propose a new approach to public sector management, releasing the talents of public officials, and incentivizing them to achieve higher quality and more output for the money the government will be spending.' This would be achieved by reducing the number of 'quangos' and civil servants (through natural wastage), and by changing 'the culture of public sector management'.[47]

The Economic Competitiveness Policy Group report only edged Cameron and Osborne closer towards a US style of economic balance, that is lower taxes and a smaller percentage of GDP spent on public services. What fully committed Cameron and Osborne to a macroeconomic policy which reduced the proportion of GDP spent on public services was the debt crisis consequent upon the banking crisis of 2008. In response to the international banking crisis, which threatened to destabilize the global economy, the Brown government supported British banks by over £800 billion.[48] While it is possible to argue that since British taxpayers have not received good value in terms of the way the banks in general have subsequently used the public funds they have been given, it is difficult to see what else the Brown administration could have done at the

---

[47] Economic Competiveness Policy Group, *Freeing Britain to Compete: Equipping the UK for Globalisation* (Conservative Party, London, 2007), 2–4 and 72.
[48] A Grice, '£850bn: official cost of the bank bailout', *Independent*, 4 December 2009 (<http://www.independent.co.uk/news/uk/politics/163850bn-official-cost-of-the-bank-bailout-1833830.html> [accessed 29 August 2012]).

time. The problem was that this 'bailout' left the British government with a residual deficit of fearsome proportions, which the Conservatives attributed to Brown's economic mismanagement, both as Chancellor and Prime Minister. In attributing blame the Conservatives did not at first cite overspending on public services, more that Labour had allowed personal debt to balloon and had not controlled public debt. In a pamphlet entitled *Labour's Debt Crisis* the Conservatives argued that the debt must be eliminated before economic prosperity could return. They did not in this publication suggest *how* the debt might be eliminated.[49]

In fact both Cameron and Osborne remained coy about exactly to what degree, by what means, and how quickly the structural deficit would be eliminated until the publication of the 2010 general election manifesto.[50] There were, however, hints. At the 2009 party conference, Osborne expected to deliver savings through cutting ministerial salaries, 'getting more for less' in the public services, freezing public sector pay in 2011, and increasing the state pension age.[51] It was not until the 2010 election campaign that the Conservatives committed themselves to eliminating the deficit in one parliament, but even then they expected to do so without adversely affecting frontline delivery by the public services.[52]

The 2010 Conservative manifesto

The election manifesto launched by the Conservatives on 13 April 2010 reflected the philosophical road which the party and its leader had travelled since the defeat of 2005. It achieved what the authors of *What's Right Now* had sought: a presentation of policies based on fundamental values. Those values had themselves been defined and refined in the interceding years. It did not matter that the sum was far from truly original thinking, showing influences and borrowings from a variety of sources, nor that those values and policies could be hotly contested; what mattered was that the values and policies which flowed therefrom were deposited in a single document which would and could be presented to the electorate and provide a programme for action when in government. It was, however, also of necessity the product of practical politics. In *What's Right*

---

[49] Conservative Party, *Labour's Debt Crisis* (<http://conservatives.com/News/News_stories/2009/01/~/media/81BBD85197AB4CC89A5C0DB67F92BB8F.ashx> [accessed 29 August 2012]), *passim*.

[50] A Neil, 'Confusion over Tory budget cuts', 3 February 2010 (<http://www.bbc.co.uk/blogs/dailypolitics/andrewneil/2010/02/confusion_over_tory_budget_cut.html> [accessed 29 August 2012]).

[51] G Osborne, 'We will lead the economy out of crisis', 6 October 2009 (<http://www.conservatives.com/News/Speeches/2009/10/George_Osborne_We_will_lead_the_economy_out_of_crisis.aspx> [accessed 29 August 2012]).

[52] G Osborne, 'Stopping Labour's tax rise on working people', 29 March 2010 (<http://www.conservatives.com/News/Speeches/2010/03/George_Osborne_Stopping_Labours_tax_rise_on_working_people.aspx> [accessed 29 August 2012]).

Now the underlying assumption was that economic growth would continue and that the British public could have its cake and eat it. The 2008 banking crisis, leading to a credit crunch and thence periods of recession or indifferent growth, altered realities. By the spring of 2010 cuts to public service funding had moved from being a political and/or economic preference to being an essential element in first reducing, then eliminating, the UK's structural deficit, ie that part of the deficit run up in keeping the banks solvent and the economy functioning which would remain after the assumed return to economic growth. Labour and the Liberal Democrats equally recognized that cuts were necessary, but Labour intended to delay making cuts, while the Liberal Democrats intended that closing tax loopholes should provide a larger share of deficit reduction. Some experts assessed that none of the parties' election policies were sufficient for the scale of the problem.[53]

Despite the scale of the deficit providing a harder edge to public service spending policy, the other elements of new Conservative views on civil society, the voluntary sector, the future scale and role of the public services, localism, a repaired society, and a rebalanced democracy were all there. The transformation would be from 'big government' to 'the Big Society'. Public service reform would not be simply about making state services more efficient or responsive, it would 'enable social enterprises, charities and voluntary groups to play a leading role in delivering public services and tackling deep-rooted social problems.' A 'new agenda for a new politics', using 'decentralisation, accountability and transparency', would 'weaken old political elites, give people power, fix our broken politics and restore people's faith that if we act together things can change.' The localism agenda was there in its entirety, plus commitments to reform the Lords and electoral boundaries. The police did not escape attention. 'Police reform' was repatriated as a Conservative policy, with less bureaucracy and more collaboration, but also with more democracy and more localism. The police would be obliged to give local people more information, while elected commissioners, reinforcing the principle of policing by consent, would replace 'invisible and unaccountable' police authorities.[54]

The 2010 Conservative manifesto had been almost five years in the making. People might disagree with it; people might even be puzzled by it, but no one could realistically argue that it had not been the product of a radical philosophical reappraisal of what modern Conservatism was all about. It reflected the principal intellectual concerns of the new Conservatives—repairing a broken society, a broken polity, and a broken economy. In May 2010 the new Conservative project was put to its ultimate test.

---

[53] C Giles, 'UK economy: drenched in debt', ft.com, 14 April 2010 (<http://www.ft.com/cms/s/0/6b3cd9d2-47f6-11df-b998-00144feab49a.html#axzz24w6HDQqt> [accessed 29 August 2012]).

[54] Conservative Party, *Invitation to Join the Government of Britain* (<http://media.conservatives.s3.amazonaws.com/manifesto/cpmanifesto2010_lowres.pdf> [accessed 29 August 2012]), *passim.*

The 2010 general election

The Conservative manifesto might have been the product of considerable intellectual endeavour but in the end it did not convince sufficient of the British electorate to return a Conservative government with an outright majority. There may have been several reasons for this, but not least among them may have been a natural caution creeping into the electorate as the election approached, an uncertainty about Conservative public spending plans, and a sudden stalling in the popularity of David Cameron consequent upon a good showing from Liberal Democrat leader Nick Clegg in the televised election debates.[55] Very probably most voters were less excited about ideas of civil society and 'the Big Society' than their protagonists. Whatever the precise reasons, their culmination was sufficient for Labour to lose its overall parliamentary majority and sufficient to make the Conservatives the largest single party, but insufficient to give them the number of seats they needed for an outright majority. They chose to treat with the Liberal Democrats to form a coalition which would provide a government, under David Cameron, with an absolute majority over Labour and the other parties. Ruling as the single largest party in the Commons was a theoretical alternative but, with international credit agencies paused to downgrade the UK's 'AAA' rating should a satisfactory political settlement not be found, formal coalition was the only realistic choice. There was, furthermore, sufficient philosophical alignment between the Conservatives and the Liberal Democrats, as evidenced by their election manifestos, for them to form a working policy union to present a joint programme of government for the next parliament.[56]

The final version of the Coalition's programme for government included some important Liberal Democrat policies, notably in areas of constitutional reform where five-year fixed terms were to be established for parliaments, a referendum of electoral reform, and the prospect of a 'wholly or mainly elected upper chamber'. The reality was, however, much as individual protagonists might not wish to acknowledge it, that there had been a process towards intellectual convergence between the two parties over several years, and certainly between the front benches, making coalition agreement relatively easy.[57] If there were areas of doubt they were normally resolved in favour of the Conservatives. Thus both parties were agreed on eliminating the deficit and cutting public spending to do so. The Liberal Democrats would not begin to cut until 2011–12; the Conservatives would start in 2010–11 and would aim to eliminate the deficit in the parliament. It was the Conservative view which prevailed in the agreement. In policing,

---

[55] R Worcester, R Mortimore, P Baines, and M Gill, *Explaining Cameron's Coalition: An Analysis of the 2010 British General Election* (Biteback, London, 2011), 5–27.

[56] cf Conservative Manifesto 2010 with Liberal Democrats, *Our Manifesto* (<http://www.libdems.org.uk/our_manifesto.aspx> [accessed 30 August 2012]).

[57] M Stuart, 'The formation of the Coalition' in S Lee and M Beech (eds), *The Cameron–Clegg Government: Coalition Politics in an Age of Austerity* (Palgrave Macmillan, Basingstoke, 2010), 38–48 and 51.

the Liberal Democrats wanted to democratize police authorities by making them wholly electable; the Conservatives wanted a single elected commissioner. Again it was the Conservative view which prevailed. But in many other policy areas, particularly when it came to the centrality of communities in social and political life, together with a rolled-back state, both parties had a similar worldview. The key concession to the Liberal Democrats over allowing a referendum on the alternative voting method was sufficient to clinch the deal.[58] The two leaders were not wide of the mark when they jointly signed the Coalition *Programme for Government*:

> We arrive at this programme for government a strong, progressive coalition inspired by the values of freedom, fairness and responsibility. This programme is for five years of partnership government driven by those values. We believe that it can deliver radical, reforming government, a stronger society, a smaller state, and power and responsibility in the hands of every citizen.[59]

As for the 'Big Society', it was specifically mentioned twice. In the foreword the language and thinking of the new Conservatives was unmistakably present:

> when you take Conservative plans to strengthen families and encourage social responsibility, and add to them the Liberal Democrat passion for protecting our civil liberties and stopping the relentless incursion of the state into the lives of individuals, you create a Big Society matched by big citizens.[60]

In the 'Social Action' section of the agreement, the new Conservative view of civil society was similarly present, with support for 'mutuals, co-operatives, charities and social enterprises' to have 'a much greater involvement in the running of public services', encouragement for charitable giving and volunteering, a National Citizen Service, and the establishment of a 'Big Society Bank' all listed as a joint programme. Taken together with the plans to deliver more socially responsible banking, reduced bureaucracy and regulation, a comprehensive civil liberties programme, and commitment to localism, the Coalition represented a high point for the new Conservatism nurtured into life after the 2005 election debacle. The 'Big Society' was its most convenient expression and the Coalition commenced its governance in deadly earnest. It pervaded every aspect of the Conservative element of the Coalition's approach. It would provide its intellectual map and compass. It did what the authors of *What's Right Now* intended: to transform the party from being issue-driven to being value-driven. It mattered not that the intellectual origins of those values might not be original to the politicians that now owned them, or that there might be powerful political and intellectual arguments ranged against new Conservatism. It was what the Conservative leaders of the Coalition believed in that counted, and they believed in this. The

---

[58] Stuart, 'The formation of the Coalition', in S Lee and M Beech (eds), *The Cameron-Clegg Government*, 51.

[59] HM Government, *The Coalition: Our Programme for Government* (Cabinet Office, London, 2010) cited as *Coalition Programme for Government*, 8.

[60] HM Government, *The Coalition Programme for Government*, 8.

response to the credit crunch and the subsequent recession was to add considerable leverage to the sum of policies which would shrink the state; it was not its prime mover. The Conservatives may not have won the 2010 election outright but because of the sufficiency of the common ground with the Liberal Democrats the Coalition created the opportunity for 'new Conservatism' to move from philosophy into policy into a programme for government.

The success of new Conservatism and its implications for policing

Almost every aspect of the Coalition Agreement, and by extension new Conservatism, had implications for the future of policing. Timing might obscure the common intellectual origins of Conservative policing policy and the fully developed ideas of new Conservatism, but they sprang from the same political, social, and economic environmental analysis and response. Smaller government, less regulation and bureaucracy, increased democratization, localism, increased public availability of data and information, the promotion of 'civil society' and volunteerism, the Coalition commitment to civil liberties (and specifically DNA retention), and, at least in the immediate term, the determination to eliminate the deficit in a single parliament through public spending cuts and such measures as increasing pension age—in fact the totality of the Coalition programme—would all have direct or indirect implications for policing. The questions were whether the police, its leadership, the rank and file, and its representatives would understand and willingly embrace the new political realities or whether they would simply oppose the radical programme the Coalition envisaged for the service, failing to grasp the enormity of what the Coalition was seeking to achieve. There was also, however, the question of whether the service could adapt to the new realities after thirteen years of Labour government and allay the apparent suspicions of leading Conservatives that the police had simply got too close to Labour.

The situation was in stark contrast to how the Conservatives viewed the police when taking office in 1979 under Mrs Thatcher. Just what had brought this to pass?

3

Where did it go wrong?

The police and the Conservatives

From consensus to conflict: 1964–1979

The 2010 Conservative election manifesto *An Invitation to Join the Government of Britain* was 118 pages long. Just two of them were devoted exclusively to policing.[1] This might seem brief, but it was considerably more than was contained in manifestos of an earlier political age. The 1964 Conservative manifesto was typical. It contained one brief sentence: 'We shall continue to build up the strength of the police forces, and see that they are equipped with every modern scientific aid.'[2] This approach typified the more discursive, less specific style of earlier manifestos. It also reflected the consensus approach that all three main parties had towards policing, exemplified in the way the Conservatives and Labour responded to the 1960–2 Royal Commission. The Conservatives initiated the commission in 1960 and presented its product, the Police Act 1964, to parliament. However, it was implemented by Harold Wilson's Labour administration (1964–70), which it did with enthusiasm, initiating the series of amalgamations that reduced 117 forces to just forty-nine in four years. It was Edward Heath's Conservative administration (1970–4), which completed the amalgamation process, further condensing the forty-nine to the current forty-three. As for more general policy the parties were saying more or less the same thing: increase or protect numbers, with the occasional variation about internal organization. If there was a difference between the parties it was about management rather than issues.

All this changed profoundly in 1979. The Conservatives made law, order, and policing, but especially policing, an issue of distinction between the parties.

---

[1] Conservative Party Manifesto 2010, 56–7.

[2] Conservative Party, *Prosperity with a Purpose* (<http://www.conservativemanifesto.com/1964/1964-conservative-manifesto.shtml> [accessed 4 September 2012]).

What was different about the Conservatives' 1979 manifesto was not the length of what they said about policing; it was what they promised and why. Labour had allowed crime to increase, respect for law to decline, and had kept police numbers below the official force establishment levels. By implication, Labour had, by failing to give police officers the pay increases immediately due under the new Edmund-Davies pay formula, contributed to poor police morale, and thereby facilitated the problem in retaining police officers in post. The Conservatives, in contrast, would prioritize 'fighting crime' even though 'we will economise elsewhere', allow chief constables to fill vacancies, and implement the Edmund-Davies pay formula in full and immediately. Juvenile offenders would experience 'the short, sharp shock'.[3] In contrast to Labour's general promises the Conservatives were specific and assertive.[4]

The relatively short statements contained in the manifestos marked a new and fundamental divergence between the parties over policing. The divergence was between the 'due process' model of policing and criminal justice, which stressed legal safeguards for individuals and social amelioration as the principal tools for combating crime, broadly adhered to by Labour and the Liberals, and the crime control model, which stressed strengthening police powers, increasing police numbers, and toughening penal policy, broadly adhered to by the Conservatives. The police themselves, as represented by many chief constables and the Police Federation, the staff association representing constables and junior managers, in the late 1970s increasingly aligned to the crime control model, thereby adding distance to the gap between them and Labour which already existed over pay.[5] For many in the Federation it appeared that Labour had gone 'soft' on law and order while, by failing to address pay, had allowed morale to plummet.[6] Matters reached a head in 1977 with vociferous agitation to allow officers the right to strike. A crisis was narrowly averted when Labour Home Secretary Merlyn Rees reluctantly set up the Edmund-Davies inquiry into pay. In a political sense it was too late because in the previous January Shadow Home Secretary William Whitelaw had already publically associated the Conservatives with the Federation's cause.[7] The convergence of interests between the Federation and the Conservatives appeared cemented in April 1979 when the Federation published an open letter in several newspapers addressed to prospective MPs, criticizing Labour's record on crime and failing to maintain a sufficient police

---

[3] Conservative Party, *1979 Conservative Party General Election Manifesto* (<http://www.conservative-party.net/manifestos/1979/1979-conservative-manifesto.shtml> [accessed 6 September 2012]).

[4] cf Labour Party, *The Labour Way is the Better Way* (<http://www.labour-party.org.uk/manifestos/1979/1979-labour-manifesto.shtml> [accessed 6 September 2012]).

[5] R Reiner, *The Politics of the Police* (4th edn, OUP, Oxford, 2010), 96–7. See contrasting examples of the approach in M Berlins, 'Police commissioner seeks more powers in war against crime', *The Times*, 3 August 1978, 1, and H Harman, 'Police powers: when one man's constraints need not be another man's safeguards', *The Times*, 9 August 1978, 12.

[6] In January 1974 PR reported that an officer resigned from the Durham Constabulary on average once every 48 hours. PR 11 January 1974, 29.

[7] T Brain, *A History of Policing in England and Wales* (OUP, Oxford, 2010), 49.

service.[8] The 1979 Conservative manifesto therefore marked a convergence of interest and principle between the party and at least the largest police representative body.

The Conservatives and the police: 1979–1990

As far as policing was concerned, both the police and the Conservatives had gained something from the 1979 general election. The police gained numbers and pay; the Conservatives had neutralized police discontent. The price for both had been the politicization of policing at the national level. The sight of police officers in riot gear confronting violent mobs in a series of urban riots or facing down the challenge of the year-long Miners' Strike (1984–5) seemed to reinforce that impression. It was a phenomenon that David Hall, then chief constable of Humberside and president of ACPO, recognized in June 1984, not long after the start of the Miners' Strike: 'Gone are the days when party politics and police remained apart. And we have great fears that the path we are treading will inevitably bring into question in the eyes of the general public one of the most essential pillars of our organisation—impartiality.' Both sides of the political spectrum sensed the danger. Shadow Home Secretary Gerald Kaufman warned that the police were 'being pushed unwillingly into a gap created by the failure of the Government's employment legislation'. Even Mrs Thatcher warned that there 'is no place for politics in policing'.[9] But it was too late; the genie was already out of the bottle. British politics was more polarized than it had been for a generation and the politics of the police simply reflected that.

However, in another respect policing was less politicized than it had been. The 1964 Police Act had established a single system of governance for provincial police forces. Previously there had been two systems; borough watch committees, comprised entirely of councillors and with considerable powers over the management of forces (including appointing and promoting officers), and joint standing committees for county forces, comprising councillors and magistrates, which had less direct control of their forces. Under the 1964 Act the county system prevailed, diminishing the role and number of councillors involved in police governance, a process accentuated by the reduction in forces between 1966 and 1974. It was Labour councillors who felt the loss most keenly. Not only were their numbers substantially diminished by the culling of borough forces (numerically the largest group of forces), but so was their role, with 'direction and control' of forces now firmly placed into the hands of chief constables.

This provoked a response from Margaret Simey, Labour chairman of the Merseyside Police Authority, in a 1976 article entitled 'All dressed up and nowhere to go?', in which she described police authorities as 'not very effective cogs in the

---

[8] *Daily Telegraph*, 20 April 1979, 8.   [9] PR 8 June 1984, 1112, and 18 October 1985, 2103.

administrative system of public service'. The irony that the largest swathe of mergers had been instigated by a Labour Home Secretary, Roy Jenkins, seemed to have been lost on her. Labour in opposition, however, was prepared to redress the balance. Recently elected Labour MP Jack Straw proposed a private members' bill which would have empowered police authorities to have 'some say in the way in which the area is to be policed', and be given some role in the appointment of superintendents and chief superintendents.[10] It had not the remotest chance of being passed, but it was a mark of Labour's discontent with its disenfranchisement in police governance, and another indication of the widening gulf between the main parties on policing. It is, however, important to note that Labour's concern about what might be termed the de-municipalization and the distancing of Labour councillors from police governance predated the disputes over operational control and accountability occasioned by issues like the Miners' Strike and the urban riots of the 1980s.

What could be said in terms of local councillor disenfranchisement in the provincial forces of England and Wales could be emphasized several times over in the Metropolitan Police area, where the Home Secretary fulfilled the function of the police authority. The arrangement, essentially unchanged since 1829, became the target of the radical Labour administration of the Greater London Council (GLC) elected under Ken Livingstone in 1981, one of whose manifesto commitments was to create a police authority for Greater London. He established a 'police committee' chaired by newly elected councillor Paul Boateng, a prominent civil rights lawyer, which in 1983 produced a radical plan for policing London. It proposed to replace the Home Secretary with a police authority composed entirely of GLC councillors, hive off the national functions of the Metropolitan to a 'National Police Agency', and create police committees for each London borough with considerable powers over local commanders. The role of Commissioner would be reduced to ensuring compliance with GLC polices. In a major leap, the office of constable would be reconstituted as a local authority employee rather than Crown office holder.[11] This might have remained of largely academic interest had it not exemplified the national Labour Party's approach to policing as a whole. The argument ran that the remoteness of police governance, accentuated under the Conservatives in power, had created alienation between the police and the people which prevented the police and community working together to reverse the continuing rise in recorded crime. By extension it was this alienation that had caused the riots that had afflicted inner-city England in the 1980s. It followed that political control of the police was the essential prerequisite to reversing trends in crime and establishing social stability. This philosophy, however, despite formal denials, often appeared as little more than 'police bashing'.

---

[10] M Simey, 'All dressed up and nowhere to go?', *Police*, August 1976, 14–15 and PR 23 November 1979, 1917.

[11] GLC Police Committee Support Unit, *A New Police Authority for London* (GLC, London, 1983), *passim*.

Conscious of its lack of appeal to mainstream voters, new leader Neil Kinnock and his Shadow Home Secretary Gerald Kaufman, as with much other Labour policy, began a process of conscious moderation. However, increased democratization of police governance was to remain an element of Labour police policy.

'Police reform' delayed: 1985–1990

Labour's enthusiasm for more democratic control ensured that the Conservative government resisted such demands. This did not, however, mean that the Conservatives were content with the status quo. On the contrary, both Mrs Thatcher and her successor John Major showed considerable impatience with the service and its leadership. Ideologically incapable of accepting that adverse social and economic conditions could be a principal cause of crime and disorder, the Conservatives under Mrs Thatcher pursued law enforcement and sentencing as the primary means of stemming the increase in recorded crime. However, these policies were, despite the accompanying rhetoric, surprisingly incremental. Change in sentencing policy was minimal and as prison overcrowding became a problem the government responded with various forms of early release. A rigorous regime of juvenile detention was briefly established (the 'short, sharp shock') but quietly abandoned when it proved ineffectual. The Police and Criminal Evidence Act (PACE) 1984 is often portrayed as a massive extension of police powers, but in reality it codified existing police practice or updated old laws, and was consequently an extreme example of 'due process' policing. The considerable powers granted under the Prevention of Terrorism Act were subject to annual renewal in parliament. The police were allowed to adopt more offensive equipment and develop more effective riot-suppression tactics in response to the urban riots of the early to mid 1980s, but simultaneously they were also required, after the Scarman Report (1981), to engage in more local consultation. The police were also required to engage in local crime reduction partnerships, although these were non-statutory and weighted towards private sector involvement.

However, increasing police numbers was seen as the primary means of delivering crime reduction, and here the Conservatives under Mrs Thatcher became increasingly frustrated with police performance. Despite more pay and increased numbers, crime rose, riots broke out, and a series of miscarriages of justice damaged the reputation of the police and by extension the government that backed them. The government's response was to subject the police to the techniques of what was becoming known as 'new public management', with the service being required to demonstrate increased 'effectiveness, efficiency and economy', and while never subject to the same degree as some other public services, the police were required to privatize some elements of their service. 'Civilianization' of many back office police functions was encouraged. HMIC adopted increasingly quantifiable inspection measures, and a new inspection body, the Audit Commission, introduced an additional level of intense scrutiny. The Audit

Commission and HMIC encouraged chief constables to abandon traditional divisions and sub-divisions and replace them with flatter hierarchies based on the BCU; those forces that tarried found themselves subject to censure.

Towards the end of the 1980s there was an expectation that the Conservatives would initiate a radical reconstruction of the service, creating a 'British FBI', merging forces into bigger units and, a particular favourite of Mrs Thatcher (who eventually lost confidence in senior police leadership), appointing senior military officers directly to chief officer rank, and focusing increasingly on crime-related measurable results. Such was the concern amongst leading police representatives that the three staff associations (ACPO, the Superintendents' Association, and the Police Federation) jointly concluded that 'traditional policing was under threat' and that an antidote was needed. The result was the *Operational Policing Review* (*OPR*), a substantial survey of the service and assessment of its future options.[12] It recommended several new initiatives, including central information technology procurement and what became the ACPO 'Quality of Service' programme. This, combined with Home Secretary Douglas Hurd's innate pragmatism, resulted in an incremental rather than radical approach to what would soon become known as 'police reform'. Instead of creating central institutions and agencies, Hurd favoured the less disruptive policy of empowering ACPO to assume a wider range of national functions and allowing the quality of service programme to address issues of performance and public confidence. For the time being it was sufficient. Thought of more radical reorganization went into abeyance with the political distractions that pervaded Mrs Thatcher's final years in office.

'Police reform': 1990–1997

At the end of her eleven years Mrs Thatcher could point to one solid achievement: police numbers had increased by over 13,000 officers to number over 127,000 by 1990.[13] However, over the same period recorded crime had increased by over two million offences, or 80 per cent.[14] There was a feeling that the police had failed to deliver a return on the investment in them. Many had begun to empathize with David Mellor, then Chief Secretary to the Treasury, who privately asserted that the police were 'overpaid; we've thrown money at them, and we have the highest level of crime in our history'. It seemed that the new Prime Minister, himself recently Chief Secretary and Chancellor of the Exchequer, shared this opinion.[15]

John Major might not have seemed an obvious leader of a radical phase of British Conservatism, but that was how it turned out. He had been elected essentially

---

[12] Joint Consultative Committee, *Operational Policing Review* (Joint Consultative Committee, Surbiton, 1990), *passim*.

[13] HMIC, *Annual Reports 1979–1990* (HMSO, London, 1979–90).

[14] Home Office historical crime data: A summary of recorded crime from 1898 to 2001/2 (<http://www.homeoffice.gov.uk/publications/science-research-statistics/research-statistics/crime-research/historical-crime-data/> [accessed 8 March 2013]).

[15] K Baker, *The Turbulent Years: My Life in Politics* (Faber and Faber, London, 1993), 451.

because of what he was not; he was not strident like Mrs Thatcher, or assertive like Michael Heseltine, or patrician like Douglas Hurd. He was expected to be more corporate and consultative, even clubbable, and more 'one nation' than his predecessor.[16] However, he had a big idea—reform of the public services. His approach marked the high point of new public management delivered through the medium of the 'Citizens' Charter'. Public services were to become more sensitive to the requirements of the public they served; those requirements would be represented by a series of targets, which theoretically reflected public demands, expectations, and priorities, although in practice it was not always clear that they did. Regulators would be appointed as surrogate customers, who would set the targets and measure performance. The police had the benefit of two inspection bodies— HMIC and the Audit Commission. The Citizens' Charter delivered seventeen 'quality standards' and forty-five 'key performance indicators' for the police nationally. 'Matrix tables' were compiled for each force allowing comparison between forces.[17] Although in contrast to other public services formal league tables were never compiled for the police, this did not stop the media using the publicly available data to compile ones of their own.

Major vigorously pursued his vision after his unexpected 1992 general election victory. The 1992 manifesto dispelled any doubt that the police might be exempt from his public service reform programme. There would be money for more officers but in return there would be more neighbourhood policing, more civilianization, and Charter standards would have to be met.[18] A new broom was appointed as Home Secretary in the form of new public management enthusiast Kenneth Clarke. Clarke increased privatization, notably of prison escort services, introduced performance measures and comparisons, and through the Sheehy inquiry and report, made a controversial attempt at changing police pay and conditions of service.[19] If accepted Sheehy would have introduced fixed term appointments for all ranks, dismissal for poor performance, and reduced pension benefits in exchange for bonus payments for specialists (eg firearms officers) and outstanding performance. It provoked general opposition from within the service, including some chief constables, but direct confrontation was avoided when, in response to a political crisis, Clarke was moved to the Exchequer and replaced by Michael Howard. Howard temporized over Sheehy but pressed ahead with his own radical reforms of governance and finance, using for the first time the generic label of 'Police Reform'.[20]

---

[16] R Taylor, Major (Haus Publishing, London, 2006), 23–34.

[17] See HMIC, Report of Her Majesty's Chief Inspector of Constabulary for the year 1991 (HMSO, London, 1991).

[18] Conservative Party, 1992 Conservative Party General Election Manifesto: The Best Future for Britain (<http://www.conservativemanifesto.com/1992/1992-conservative-manifesto.shtml#law> [accessed 1 October 2012]).

[19] Sir Patrick Sheehy, Inquiry into Police Responsibilities & Rewards, vol I (HMSO, London, 1993), passim.

[20] Home Office, Police Reform: A Police Service for the Twenty-first Century (HMSO, London, 1993), passim.

Under his reform programme the police were to focus on 'fighting crime', shedding many of the administrative tasks they had accrued over the years (such as licensing, escorting abnormal loads, and dealing with stray dogs). They received new powers under the Criminal Justice and Public Order Act 1994, extending stop and search powers, and modifying (not abolishing) the suspect's so-called 'right of silence' in line with the earlier Philips' commission recommendation. In return police governance and management were to become more streamlined and businesslike, so the remaining management functions of police authorities, principally budget micromanagement, would be transferred to chief constables. In compensation police authorities would become more strategic, akin to a board of directors, setting the budget and holding the chief constable (post-Sheehy on a fixed term appointment) to account for performance against the key indicators. To reflect their new role, police authority membership would reduce (from between thirty to sixty, depending on area, to sixteen) and change in composition; only half the members would be councillors with the remainder to be split between three magistrates and five independent members appointed by the Home Secretary. There were also new powers for the Home Secretary, who was empowered to set general objectives for the service. Such a radical package provoked opposition at both the consultative and legislative stages, but although Howard was forced to make some minor changes over police authority membership (such as agreeing that there would be seventeen police authority members, nine of whom would be councillors), he got most of his measures through, and the resultant Police and Magistrates' Courts Act 1994 (later consolidated in the Police Act 1996) became the most radical shift in police governance since the Metropolitan Police Act 1829. Howard backed his legislation up with an enhanced inspection regime from HMIC and the Audit Commission which increasingly focused on delivery against the performance indicators ('effectiveness') and value for money (redefined 'efficiency'), and with a range of new national organizations including those for technology (PITO), and a national crime squad (although this did not actually form until April 1998). ACPO was to continue to provide other national functions.

While strategic objectives and performance measures increased police focus on 'fighting crime', the near exclusive attention that Howard seemed to want never came about, principally because the public continued to seek assistance from the police across a wide range of problems, of which crime was merely one. However, the 'Posen Review' (1994–5) provided a vehicle for the police shedding some extraneous tasks (lost property, stray dogs, liquor licensing, etc), more interagency working, increased civilianization, and greater specialization.[21] Less ostensibly controversial than Sheehy, it was more pervasive, effectively setting the template for the service's composition and primary purposes for the next twenty-five years and beyond. The exclusive focus on 'fighting crime', however, remained elusive, although the development of 'intelligence-led policing', championed by

---

[21] Home Office, *Review of Core and Ancillary Tasks* (HMSO, London, 1995), *passim*.

Sir David Phillips in Kent, and which in turn led to the National Intelligence Model, represented a considerable shift in that direction.

Conservative police reform in abeyance: 1997–2010

It might have seemed that Howard had been immediately rewarded for his efforts, as crime fell by 18 per cent between 1992 and 1997. However, such attribution is doubtful as the effect of many of Howard's police reforms post-dated the decline in crime.[22] His parallel policy of 'prison works', which resulted in a rapid increase in the prison population, may have played a bigger part.[23] Whatever its cause, the drop in recorded crime availed the Conservatives little in terms of political advantage. For many people anti-social behaviour, which barely featured in the official crime figures, was of much greater concern and it was Tony Blair's rejuvenated Labour Party which more effectively tapped in to this mass of public opinion. Labour's 'third way' in economic, social, policing, and crime policies saw them rewarded with three successive election victories, and at first the Conservatives had no effective counter to Labour's populist brand. During Labour's first term, Conservative criticism of falling police numbers was neutralized by the government pointing out that they had fallen because they were implementing the Conservatives' own spending plans.[24] Nor could they criticize centralization as the Conservatives in government had increased both the Home Secretary's powers and the number of central institutions. An attempt by new Conservative leader William Hague to accuse Labour of political correctness at the expense of police morale over the Macpherson Report backfired, as did the attempt to generally link law and order with immigration.[25] Lack of imagination characterized Conservative police policy during its first term of opposition and this was duly reflected in the 2001 election manifesto which presented a highly conventional law and order ticket—more officers, less bureaucracy, secure training centres for persistent young offenders, and new (unspecified) powers to combat drugs.[26] Along with much else in the 2001 manifesto, this did not excite the electorate sufficiently to convince them to transfer their confidence in Labour and hand it back to the Conservatives.[27]

Oliver Letwin

After the defeat Hague quickly resigned to be replaced by Iain Duncan Smith, seen by many as the compromise candidate between the extremes of Michael

---

[22] Home Office, historical crime data: A summary of recorded crime from 1898 to 2001/2.

[23] G Berman, *Prison population statistics* (House of Commons Library, London, 2012), 2.

[24] PR 7 January 2000, 8.

[25] T Bale, *The Conservative Party from Thatcher to Cameron* (Polity Press, Cambridge, 2010), 122.

[26] Conservative Party, *Election Manifesto: Time for Common Sense* (<http://www.conservative-party.net/manifestos/2001/2001-conservative-manifesto.shtml> [accessed 16 September 2012]).

[27] Ipsos MORI, *Best Party on Key Issues: Crime/Law & Order* (<http://www.ipsos-mori.com/researchpublications/researcharchive/poll.aspx?oItemID=29> [accessed 16 September 2012]).

Portillo and Kenneth Clarke. Although he lacked the charisma to sustain his leadership he did begin the process of policy reorientation, and, because such heavyweights as Portillo and Clarke declined to serve, he perforce made some imaginative Shadow Cabinet appointments. One such was erstwhile Shadow Home Secretary Oliver Letwin. An old Etonian, with a Cambridge PhD entitled 'Emotion and Emotions', he brought intellectual rigour to policy making. Home affairs and policing had not previously been amongst the topics that obviously excited his considerable imagination, but this meant he was prepared to challenge accepted norms and develop new concepts. Quite when he became intellectually convinced of the philosophical merits of 'civil society' is not entirely clear but he certainly used the term in a speech entitled 'Beyond the causes of crime' in January 2002. Here he presented a radical repositioning of the Conservative law and order policy. His starting point was that current social and crime reduction policies were not working, evidenced by social breakdown in Britain's most deprived estates. His answer was to re-establish the 'neighbourly society', but that necessitated some essential policing prerequisites:

> So this is our approach: to break the vicious circle that destroys community through a proper combination of sophisticated high-level policing and highly active community policing, drawing on all the agencies of the state and of local government; to remove the barriers that stop the community from supporting the individual; and, by these means, to facilitate the re-establishment of the neighbourly society where it has broken down, in order to restore the cycle of responsibility. This does not necessarily involve more police. It does involve more effective use of existing police resources. It will also require the active co-operation of local inhabitants and of voluntary agencies.[28]

In this paragraph, although few, if any, recognized it at the time, he effectively rewrote Conservative law, order, and policing policy, and set it on the course it was to follow up to and beyond the 2010 Coalition Agreement. The intellectual link with *What's Right Now* is obvious, but it is important to note that it predated the latter's publication by over three years.

Letwin also predated another policy initiative: he aligned himself to the emerging service-led refined concept of neighbourhood policing, trialled in Surrey and the Metropolitan, before either ACPO or the Home Office so enthusiastically took it up. But there was a nuance: 'Neighbourhood policing can only be restored to its rightful position through fundamental reforms that transform the police service from top to bottom. What I am proposing is the biggest change to policing since the foundation of the police service by Robert Peel.'[29] In his speech 'The front line against fear', delivered in March 2002, he, by then somewhat conventionally, registered his support for what Giuliani had achieved in New York. In particular he picked out intensive, crime-focused beat patrol, targeted through

---

[28] O Letwin, *The Neighbourly Society: Collected Speeches 2001–2003* (Centre for Policy Studies, London, 2003), 12.

[29] Letwin, *The Neighbourly Society*, 'The front line against fear', 31.

crime mapping on 'hot-spots', and subject to the rigorous 'Compstat' process; a single non-emergency number (again before adopted as government party policy); and, the connection between 'low-level disorder' and all forms of crime, which he declined to label as 'aggressive "zero tolerance"'. Significantly he also suggested that police governance would have to change: 'Very possibly, we may need to look again at the internal structure of our Police Authorities to see how they can be provided with the means to hold Chief Constables to account.' Crucially, he was prepared to see an end to central proscription and the probability that different models of policing would emerge between forces: 'In the United States, there are about 20,000 police forces. We have less than 50. There is every reason to suppose that we shall see 50 different models emerging—and every reason to suppose that the virtual revolution will be best achieved in 50 different ways, each responsive to the differing configuration of the area and population served by the police forces in question.'[30] This, as he would in a speech delivered later in 2002 explain, was all to take place in the context of a radically smaller system of state governance.

> So we have a massive opportunity and one which, at this conference, we are grasping. It is the opportunity to argue, not that we stress liberty at the expense of civil society or civil society at the expense of liberty, but that we can rescue both individual liberty and civil society. We can set people free without setting them adrift, but if, and only if, we are willing to tame the State: to seek to improve the quality of people's lives, as we once sought to improve their standard of living, by diminishing the role of the State as the comprehensive provider of all, the comprehensive regulator of all, the setter of every target and the monitor of every performance. We are seeking—and we will go on seeking as we go through the next few years—device after device, fitting into a single pattern of thought, to give back to the people of Britain, individually and collectively, the power to change their own lives for the better, to make Britain a better society and to do that without excessive interference from the bureaucracy.[31]

Letwin was prepared to be more specific the following year. He had always recognized that his vision of neighbourhood policing was in addition to, and not instead of, response and investigative policing. He therefore proposed creating 40,000 additional police posts specifically for neighbourhood policing. He estimated it would cost £280 million a year building up over eight years. It all seemed far-fetched in 2003, and Home Office Minister Bob Ainsworth immediately condemned the figures. Ironically, Labour itself was to create over 50,000 police posts (police and civilian) in the next five years, 10,000 of which were police officers and 16,000 PCSOs, so Letwin was not so wide of the mark and he may well have stimulated Labour's own dash for growth.[32] However, in proposing such a large

---

[30] Letwin, *The Neighbourly Society*, 'The front line...', 32–4 and 37.
[31] Letwin, *The Neighbourly Society*, 'The moral market', 46, (on the role of the state) delivered at a Conservative Party conference fringe meeting, 2 October 2002.
[32] PR 14 March 2003, 7, and 21 March 2003, 8, and Cipfa police statistics 2003–10.

increase in police numbers and specifically for neighbourhood police purposes, he was not being original in his thought. US President Clinton had, since 1994, centrally provided over 500,000 additional 'law enforcement personnel' for neighbourhood policing, but then many other aspects of the Conservative concept of civil society owed much to American influences.[33] The key, however, was not the originality of Letwin's thinking but his adaptation of developing US political and policing philosophies to UK circumstances in general, and those of policing in particular. How Letwin intended to find the money for such expansion, when he had been, and was to be again, so conspicuously associated with cutting government expenditure was, however, another matter.

'Elect the Sheriff'

That Letwin was not alone in his thinking was illustrated by the appearance shortly after his 2002 series of speeches of a pamphlet written by Douglas Carswell, an aspiring Conservative candidate, and published by the right-of-centre think tank 'Cchange' (sic). His argument was that power in Britain was not in the hands of the people's elected representatives but 'a combination of unaccountable central government institutions, an ever more assertive judiciary, and unelected supranational authorities', a consequence of which was 'electoral apathy'. His strategic answers to these problems were 'localism', with the shift of power and accountability to the most local level feasible, and, where that was not possible, direct accountability at the national level. To achieve localism 'responsibility for the delivery of key public services should be transferred from unaccountable central government bodies, to either individuals who local voters are able to hold directly to account, or directly to the people themselves.'

His proposals ranged across all public services. There would be elected health officials; a parliamentary committee would appoint judges; 'elected Parliamentarians' would appoint the heads of public bodies.

> Responsibility for policing and for prosecuting criminals would be handed to a directly elected Sheriff representing each county, city or large town. Elected for a fixed-term mandate of perhaps three or four years, each Sheriff would be held directly accountable by local people for how effectively the law was upheld, the effectiveness with which suspected criminals were prosecuted, and the extent to which police and prosecutors worked together to reduce crime.

To remove any doubt, 'The Sheriff would replace the role of chief constables as head of each local police force', although it was envisaged that the forces would be much smaller than most of the current forty-three forces. Inevitably, the success of Giuliani in New York was cited as the exemplar. In policy terms this 'might mean that the police and prosecutors adopt a "zero-tolerance" attitude to street

---

[33] Office of Community Oriented Policing Services, *The Impact of the Economic Downturn on American Police Agencies* (US Department of Justice, Washington DC, 2011), 8.

crime, a more robust approach to burglary, yet a less aggressive stance towards motorists'. The elections 'would ideally coincide with other local elections'.[34] Flawed it may have been in its analysis, particularly in using the New York example, but influential it was. Not initially with the public, but with Conservative politicians looking for new ideas with which to counter Labour and with some academics prepared to challenge prevailing received wisdom.

Carswell's ideas were not developed in precise detail. That fell to two academics writing for another right-of-centre think tank, Policy Exchange. *Going Local: Who should Run Britain's Police?* Its authors were Barry Loveday, an experienced Portsmouth University academic, and Anna Reid, director of Policy Exchange's 'Local Choices' programme. The pamphlet's conclusions were highly critical of the centralization of successive Labour and Conservative governments. Labour's recently expanded centralization, however, had neither delivered greater efficiency nor generated more public confidence. Police authorities, deemed 'invisible and irrelevant', were part of the problem, as they did not possess sufficient control and influence over senior officers or budgets. The report argued that smaller forces 'with a strong commitment to visible policing' were more successful than larger ones, while the US model of local political control had 'chalked up some remarkable achievement'. Central to their case was local political control over chief constables, the foundations of whose independence they concluded were 'ancient and mysterious', and by implication unjustified. The authors placed much reliance on an ICM survey which found that 68 per cent of 'the British population' ('of those surveyed' would have been a more accurate description) believed they had little or no impact on setting police priorities, 80 per cent would like to have 'more input', and 48 per cent would be more likely to vote in a local election if input into police services was an issue.

From these conclusions the authors set out a series of radical recommendations. Rejecting directly elected police authorities principally on the grounds that this would dilute local accountability and resources, they recommended that the chief constable should report to the mayor 'or the leader of a unitary authority' (unitary authorities being their preferred model of local government). Large police force areas encompassing 'more than one county' were to be split up into county or district forces 'as decided by local referenda', in effect reversing the amalgamations initiated after the 1964 Act and returning forces to municipal control. The mayors were themselves to be subject to scrutiny 'by a police committee', while the elected local assemblies would approve the police budget. Police forces would be 'funded out of local taxation', although in 'deprived areas' it was accepted that there would need to be continued central government grant, even if a substantial amount of money was still to be raised locally. Police chiefs were to be put on short-term contracts, the up to seven-year contracts currently available to chiefs being presumed to be too long. The 'convention' of constabulary

---

[34] D Carswell, 'Direct democracy: empowering people to make their own decisions' (<http://www.douglascarswell.com/downloads/upload12.pdf> [accessed 13 December 2012]), 8–13 and 40–2.

independence was to exclude the 'direction of strategy and operational priorities'. National and international level crime would be transferred to a 'National Crime Agency' (NCA), from which local forces would be encouraged to seek assistance when they needed specialist support. A 'National Police Holding Body' would be set up to handle residual national assets, although it was expected to dispose of these within five years, either selling them to local forces, floating them 'as self-financing stand alone institutions', or, if no longer useful, shutting them down.[35]

Although the authors presented their case with considerable confidence and plausibility, from ACPO President Sir David Phillips, whose intelligence-led policing in Kent was singled out for particular criticism, it received but a terse dismissal: 'That the report eschews intelligence is a stunning revelation of its ineptitude. The opposite to intelligence-led policing is unintelligent policing.'[36] However, the presentation of a contrary case would probably not have made much difference to the pamphlet's impact. Policy Exchange presented a credible and detailed argument to support a thorough repositioning of police organization based on the emerging principles of civil society and localism, which in due course would come to dominate Conservative Party policy. The pamphlet was to prove highly influential and contained many of the antecedents of what would become the Cameron–Clegg Coalition government's police programme. It may also mark the point at which the police service and the Conservatives parted company. There may have been occasional dissenters but the ACPO leadership remained locked into its own vision of an increasingly centralized service based on fewer, larger forces; the Conservatives were henceforth bound on a divergent course.

Policing for the People

In the meantime there were more elections to fight and more angst for the Conservatives. Uncertainty and disunity characterized the party under Duncan Smith's leadership and he lost a vote of confidence in November 2003. He was instantly replaced by Michael Howard, who moved Letwin to Shadow Chancellor and replaced him with David Davis, a heavyweight right-winger, who was to hold the post for the next six years. Civil liberties and immigration seemed to receive more of his attention than policing, but he kept the Conservatives on their decentralization path. There was one key modification, however. In February 2005, with the possibility of a general election later in the year, Howard announced that the next Conservative government would replace police authorities not with elected mayors or sheriffs but with a directly elected 'Commissioner'.[37] This also meant, implicitly, that the Conservatives would not be following the Policy Exchange recommendation of re-municipalizing the police structure in England and Wales. However, while much of the 2005 manifesto marked

---

[35] B Loveday and A Reid, *Going Local: Who should Run Britain's Police* (Policy Exchange, London, 2003), *passim*.

[36] PR 10 January 2003, 10.   [37] PR 18 February 2005, 6, and 25 February, 13.

something of a pause in the Conservatives' path to modernization, the policing section was heavily influenced by the ideas of Letwin and Policy Exchange. The forty-three forces might be retained and elected commissioners would be the preferred mode of governance, but there was a commitment to neighbourhood policing, with '5,000 new police officers each year' (although it did not say for how many years), and, crucially, people would be given 'a say over police priorities'.[38] Voters seemed to prefer the Conservatives to Labour when it came to law and order, although the commitment to 'zero-tolerance' methods may have had more to do with that than somewhat arcane arguments over police governance.[39] However, law and order was peripheral to voter preferences in 2005 and Labour duly won the election with its majority barely dented.

The lack of electoral success, even lack of progress, for the Conservatives, evident in the 2005 results, precipitated the chain of events that led to David Cameron becoming leader, the adoption of the modernization programme, and the inclusion of policing within it, as announced in the Dalston Youth Project speech. Once in post Cameron initiated several major policy reviews, including one for the police led by Nick Herbert, whom he appointed to the new position of 'Shadow Minister for Police Reform'. Herbert had no previous home affairs or policing background, but as a director of the 'Reform' think tank he possessed the right kind of experience when it came to the emerging new Conservative view of the state and civil society. In his work he was supported by an able team of similarly minded researchers and analysts—Blair Gibbs, previously of the Tax Payers' Alliance and 'Reform', Oscar Keeble, also with a background in 'Reform', and Aidan Burley, a management consultant whose clients had included the Home Office and the Metropolitan Police.[40] They were styled 'the Police Reform Taskforce', thus consciously reclaiming the police reform label for the Conservatives following its sojourn with Labour.

It was never likely that a group so composed would have delivered a report that defended the status quo, and in their 2007 report *Policing for the People* they did not. Their work was no mere desk-top review, but, based on a series of visits to selected forces and a Tax Payers' Alliance survey, their conclusions were not dissimilar to those already reached by Letwin and Policy Exchange, and to some extent already, if briefly, reflected in the 2005 manifesto. Many of the ideas were not original and it was possible to challenge some of the report's key assumptions, but this would be to miss the point. The report presented an alternative to the current Labour model of growth and centralization, which was both intellectually coherent and potentially popular, although, in a conspicuous break with the past, there was no commitment to increasing police numbers. It was, furthermore, fully in accordance with the principles of civil society and localism that were being developed simultaneously under Cameron's modernization programme.

---

[38] Conservative Manifesto 2005.   [39] Ipsos MORI, *Best Party on Key Issues* (n 27).
[40] Police Reform Taskforce, *Policing for the People: Interim Report of the Police Reform Taskforce* (Conservative Party, London, 2007), 7.

The report concluded that crime was too high, the police themselves over-burdened by bureaucracy and constrained by inflexible working practices, while police authorities were too anonymous and remote. People trusted their police but only 50 per cent thought they were doing a good job. The answers were sim-ple: introduce the New York model of more officers on the streets and reduce crime, together with proper management accountability at force and beat level. The key, in an echo of Labour in the 1980s, was proper democratic control through directly elected 'commissioners', the name retained from the 2005 man-ifesto. There would be checks and balances. 'Operational independence' for the police would be guaranteed, although chief constables would no longer possess 'direction and control' authority over their forces but the more nebulous 'opera-tional responsibility', as favoured by Policy Exchange and the recent Patten report on policing in Northern Ireland. The elected commissioner's role would be strictly defined, but it would include appointing and dismissing chief constables, setting targets, drawing up the policing plan for their area (removing that role from the chief constable), and setting the force budget. It was envisaged they would chair 'police boards' on which would sit 'non-executive directors' who would play 'an important role in exercising scrutiny'. Councillors and magis-trates might be members of such boards, but 'automatic mandate of these posi-tions should be avoided'. In keeping with the principles of localism, the role of the Home Secretary would be 'reduced and refocused onto areas of national policing and security'.

Chief constables might lose some of their influence and power in relation to the elected commissioner but it was intended to give them more managerial authority over their forces, reducing the bureaucratic burden imposed by central targets, laws, guidance, and regulations. PACE would be reviewed and the role of the CPS limited. The inhibitions arising from political correctness and health and safety legislation would be removed in favour of a 'common sense' approach. Workforce efficiency would be achieved through better management of over-time, and pay reflecting skills rather than seniority. Pensions would become more 'flexible'. A staff college would be established (more strictly re-established) to train higher ranks. 'The old-fashioned model of the omni-competent officer should give way to, through workforce modernisation and extending the police family, forces consisting of teams with diverse specialist skills.' Following the example of chief officers, BCU commanders would be placed on fixed term con-tracts. Reviving an idea promoted by some chief officers in the late 1980s, chief officers would be placed on a 'national cadre' and deployed 'across forces and responsibilities'. There would be direct entry at senior officer level from other professions.

This was, however, all to take place in the context of what was presented as a new national structure, capable of meeting the challenges of terrorism and seri-ous and organized crime, simultaneously with delivering increased value for money. Here the report, so confident elsewhere, curiously temporized, recogniz-ing that two viable models existed: one in which forty-three forces with 'effective leadership from the centre' drove through collaboration, ensuring both the development of community policing and an enhanced ability to deal with 'serious crime', and the other in which 'approximately' forty-three forces focused on local crime, while major crime became the responsibility of a 'Serious Crime Force' answerable to the Home Secretary. In an unacknowledged debt to *Going Local*, this second model would allow for 'smaller' forces to be created where there was a local demand.[41]

The report was a powerful exposition of coherent policy, and it would be immensely influential on the next Conservative government, as it was presumably intended to be. There was, however, a substantial unresolved issue. What exactly was the primary purpose of police work? The report focused on 'crime', and primarily divided it between local crime and serious and organized crime. In 1993 Howard had wanted the police to concentrate almost exclusively on 'fighting crime' and had initiated the process by which the police would be stripped of distracting administrative tasks better performed by other agencies. But under Labour and its preference for a 'broken windows' approach to crime reduction, 'crime' had become inextricably linked to 'disorder', which in turn had been expanded in definition to include most forms of 'anti-social behaviour'. Where did the Police Reform Taskforce sit on this issue? The answer had to be inferred. When it talked 'crime', it also meant 'anti-social behaviour', and therefore 'broken windows' and 'zero tolerance' remained acceptable principles. Bratton, New York, and Middlesbrough remained icons of successful policing.[42]

Policing and the 2010 Conservative manifesto

The Police Reform Taskforce may have presented a brave new vision for the police under the Conservatives but Labour was still in government, and it was to remain so for the next three years. However, Cameron appeared to touch a raw nerve in Labour policy-making circles. While the fundamental centralizing tendencies were never fully reversed, a succession of policy reviews and a highly didactic green paper *From the Neighbourhood to the National* attempted to roll back some of the bureaucracy and make conscious concessions to localism. Neighbourhood officers were to spend 'at least 80 per cent of their time' visibly working in their areas; crime maps would be introduced; there would be a 'policing pledge'. Once again there would be a light-touch inspection regime; targets would be reduced. Labour even contemplated an increased democratic element in the composition of police authorities by replacing nominated councillors with directly elected members, but it was quickly dropped.[43] Somehow it now all seemed tired and derivative, a fact that is possibly reflected in opinion poll data

---

[41] Police Reform Taskforce, *Policing for the People, passim*.
[42] Police Reform Taskforce, *Policing for the People*, 6, 7, 13, 24, 39, 45–66, 73–81, 214, and elsewhere.
[43] Brain, *A History of Policing*, 396–400.

that from 2007 onwards gave the Conservatives a double-digit lead over Labour on law and order.[44]

Was this the time for the police service to beat a collective path to the Conservatives' door and establish some kind of common ground? From late 2007 when the Conservatives led in opinion polls it seemed inevitable that the Conservatives would win the next general election; it also seemed likely that the Conservatives would radically refashion their relationship with the police. Then in September 2009 the then new Shadow Home Secretary Chris Grayling, described as David Cameron's 'attack dog', said what many Conservatives had been thinking: 'Individual officers have been politically too close to the government.' Setting aside whether it was a generalization which withstood close scrutiny, and the fact that there were several chief officers[45] who had openly challenged some of Labour's less practical or more inappropriate schemes, he went on to draw a significant policy implication from his assessment: ACPO would no longer have a place of primacy amongst police representative bodies when it came to making policy. 'No particular representative organisation should have a privileged position,' he said. 'You talk to everyone but you listen with a sceptical ear.'[46] Such attitudes meant that if there was an opportunity for the police to build a positive relationship with the Conservatives it was a difficult one to take. However, Labour was still the government, and showed every intention of clinging on to the last moment. Furthermore, by late 2009 it was no longer a foregone conclusion that the Conservatives would win the next election. If the police leadership moved too soon to establish a new relationship with the Conservatives it would look like blatant politicking. This, of course, had not inhibited the Police Federation in 1979 in sending its open letter to MPs, but there was a critical difference; then it was a political party, the Conservatives, that chose to identify themselves with the police and not the other way round. Even so, such incidents as the Damian Green affair simply seemed to confirm the distance between the police and the party. In any case, by the last years of the Labour administration the Conservatives were sufficiently set in their policing policy as to admit little in the way of amendment.

The 2010 election manifesto was the culmination of the process of policing policy repositioning set in train by Oliver Letwin in 2002. 'The fight back against crime' was the purpose of Conservative policy, but 'crime', by inference, was not the narrow definitions imposed by Home Office crime statistics. The Conservatives pledged to 'fight back against crime', but to that was instantly added 'and anti-social behaviour'. 'Broken windows' was very much the underlying concept when it came to crime and disorder, although neither that term nor 'zero tolerance' featured in the manifesto. 'Reform the police', however, certainly did. Some

---

[44] Ipsos MORI, Best Party on Key Issues.   [45] The author for one.

[46] J Oliver, 'Tories will rein in new Labour police', timesonline, 25 January 2009 (<http://www.timesonline.co.uk/tol/news/politics/article5581736.ece> [accessed 12 September 2009]).

of the itemized reform programme was in a strict sense 'tactical', such as scrapping the 'stop form entirely', but behind these lay wider strategic intentions of reducing central targets, controls, bureaucracy, and inspection. Communities would be 'empowered', by being supplied with more information, to enable them to 'challenge their neighbourhood police teams to cut crime'. At the national level a 'Border Police Force' would be created as part of 'a refocused Serious and Organised Crime Agency, to enhance national security, improve immigration controls, and crack down on the trafficking of people, weapons, and drugs.' More vaguely they would 'work with police forces to strengthen the arrangements to deal with serious crime and other cross-boundary policing challenges, and extend collaboration between forces to deliver better value for money.'[47]

However, the flagship policy was the explicit commitment to replace 'invisible and unaccountable police authorities' and with 'a directly elected individual who will set policing priorities for local communities'. The evidence that the majority of electors actually wanted such a policy was slight and based on no more than a series of public opinion surveys which alluded to more democratic arrangements for local police governance.[48] But the policy had been around for too long now to stop the bandwagon from rolling; the only thing that might prevent directly elected commissioners being introduced would be if the Conservatives were denied an outright Commons majority.

The Coalition Agreement

In the event the electorate denied the Conservatives a majority. In the negotiations between the Conservatives and the Liberal Democrats over the detail of the Coalition Agreement it was uncertain what would emerge as the combined policing policy. Would the 'elected individual' policy survive? On policing policy in general the two parties used similar language, but on the matter of police governance they differed. The Conservatives wanted a directly elected individual, the Liberal Democrats a directly elected police authority.[49]

The Coalition Agreement was formed following a two-stage process. An initial agreement was secured in a few days following the election result. It was a short document, almost a 'heads of agreement', covering the major issues of deficit reduction, a public spending review, education, political reform (a five-year parliament and bringing forward proposals to replace the House of Lords with an elected chamber), the EU, and civil liberties. Policing did not feature in this first document and was left for a second, more detailed 'programme for

---

[47] Conservative Manifesto 2010, 55–8.
[48] Police Reform Task Force, *Policing for the People*, 185–6.
[49] Liberal Democrat Party, Manifesto 2010 (<http://www.network.libdems.org.uk/manifesto2010/libdem_manifesto_2010.pdf> [accessed 21 September 2012]), 71–2.

government'.[50] There was much common ground between the two partners in government, but when it came to police governance it was the Conservative policy of the 'elected individual' that prevailed. There was, however, some acknowledgment of the Liberal Democrat position, so the individual was to 'be subject to strict checks and balances by locally elected representatives.' If there was any lingering doubt that the Conservatives meant business in delivering their long-term commitment to increased democratic control of policing it was removed by the appointment of Nick Herbert as Police and Justice Minister. He was there to drive through delivery of the new reform programme.

Policing in the 21st Century

There remained one final piece in the jigsaw to place before the legislative programme commenced. Even in its second, extended form the Coalition Agreement lacked sufficient detail to form a legislative programme, particularly one as radical as the Coalition intended. Normally, a white paper and, possibly, also a green paper, would have preceded such an extensive programme. The Coalition did not have time for such formalities and in July 2010 it published a policy paper, *Policing in the 21st Century*, setting out more detail of the programme. A period of consultation was allowed but there were clear limits to the extent of this exercise: the new Home Secretary, Theresa May, wanted to only hear views 'about how we can best make the reforms work.' The principles of the measures themselves were not up for discussion.[51]

These principles by then were familiar. An increased focus on reducing crime; cutting bureaucracy and targets; more cross-border collaboration; neighbourhood scrutiny; 'a new National Crime Agency'; better value for money; a review of 'remuneration and conditions of service' and pensions; increased central procurement for information technology. This much was familiar territory, but the language and the detail provided were important. In her foreword the Home Secretary made explicit the link between the Coalition's police programme and 'the Big Society', just as Letwin had made the link eight years previously with 'the neighbourly society'. In policing it was the Coalition's intention to 'transfer power away from government—trusting police professionals. We will do away with central targets. Frontline staff will no longer be form writers but crime fighters: freed up from bureaucracy and central guidance and trusted to use their professionalism to get on with their jobs.' But the transfer of power was not simply to professionals; it was to the people through the medium of the elected individuals, now termed as 'Police and Crime Commissioners' (PCCs). Chief constables would have 'operational

---

[50] Conservatives, 'Conservative and Liberal Democrat coalition negotiations: agreements reached', 11 May 2010 (<http://www.conservatives.com/News/News_stories/2010/05/Coalition_Agreement_published.aspx> [accessed 21 September 2012], cited as *Coalition Agreement*) and HM Government, *Coalition Programme for Government*, 13–14.

[51] Home Office, *Policing in the 21st Century* (TSO, London, 2010), *passim*.

responsibility' and 'day to day' control, but it was emphasized that the strategic power would shift to the PCCs.

The police were now to focus on 'crime' but, in keeping with the 'broken windows' theory, and indeed the practical politics of dealing with what affected most people in their everyday lives, this was not narrowly defined; the intention was to keep people safe 'from the harm caused by everything from ASB [anti-social behaviour] to serious crime and terrorism'. This was an extremely wide brief. There would be no centrally mandated priorities; these would be set by the PCC, who would also drive through regional and national collaboration. Localism there might be, but it would have to be within existing force boundaries; gone was the suggestion present in *Policing for the People* that local views might drive the re-creation of smaller forces. The PCC would appoint and 'where necessary' remove the chief constable. In a concession, and in keeping with the philosophy of greater professional discretion, chiefs would appoint their own top management team. In contrast to Labour's neighbourhood policing model, there would be no central template for local policing: 'policing must vary according to the characteristics of different neighbourhoods'.

Each area would have a 'Police and Crime Panel' (PCP), comprising elected councillors and 'independent and lay members'. The panel was to hold the commissioner to account, not the chief constable, whose relationship was directly with the commissioner. The panel would consider progress against the policing plan and could require the commissioner to give evidence on his work. They would hold 'confirmation hearings' on the commissioner's choice for chief constable, but would not possess a veto. They would, however, be able to 'trigger a referendum' on the commissioner's proposed council tax. It was some way short of the elected police authorities desired by the Liberal Democrats in their manifesto, but neither was it the 'police boards' envisaged in *Policing for the People*. That Police and Crime Panels featured at all was, therefore, a slight concession to the Liberal Democrats.

On coming to power the Coalition scrapped Labour's misconceived 'public confidence' target but their intention was to go further. Data management requirements would be reviewed, as would be the NCRS, RIPA, and even PACE. Charging decisions for less serious offences would be returned to the police. ACPO was expected to lead the reduction in its own bureaucracy and risk averse policing. The NPIA would be phased out, with some of its functions being possibly taken up by the 'new National Crime Agency that will lead the fight against organised crime, protect our borders, and provide services best delivered at national level.' Compulsory force mergers were dead: 'Big is not necessarily beautiful or better value for money. British policing at its best is strongly grounded in local communities. The Government does not support the imposition of structural changes on local forces which will be seen by the public as creating vast and distant conglomerations, weakening their capacity to influence and hold to account those who keep them safe.' However, the National Crime Agency would also have an as yet nebulously outlined responsibility for 'providing effective national tasking and coordination of police assets'.

By the time *Policing in the 21st Century* had been published the Coalition had already agreed to a comprehensive public spending review intended to eliminate the UK's structural deficit by 2014–15. There was no strong expectation that the police service would be protected, and it was not, but *Policing in the 21st Century* went further; there might be cuts but these were not expected to affect the frontline. Cuts to the frontline would be avoided by forces driving out value for money through such initiatives as adopting flexible shift rosters, privatization, and the increased use of volunteers. Proximation in the text implicitly linked the reviews of pay, conditions of service, and pensions with general cost reductions. Previous home secretaries had hesitated to mandate information technology collaboration between forces; now the Coalition would 'legislate at an early opportunity to ensure a coherent basis for the Home Secretary to specify procurement arrangements to be used by the police service, and to drive the convergence of IT systems.' There was an exception, however, to the localism of the programme; forces would be mandated to introduce a single non-emergency telephone contact number.

In opposition in the 1980s, Labour had targeted ACPO; in government it had come not simply to accept it but to value it and use it as a partner in delivering its

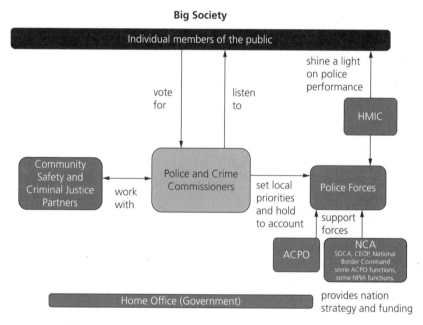

Figure 3.1: 'What the policing landscape will look like in future'
Home Office, *Policing in the 21st Century*[52]

---

[52] TSO, London, 2010.

agenda. Now the Coalition was set to diminish it, in size, role, and status. ACPO's future role would not be as a surrogate national service but simply to provide leadership in delivering value for money and in 'advising' government, PCCs, and the service. It would also have to admit PCC and government representatives into its governance structure.

If there was any doubt about how the new policing landscape would look, about the significance of 'the Big Society', and about the reversal of the place of communities and national bodies, then the diagram on page 43 of the document was intended to dispel them. Some might say it was literally the world turned upside down. Figure 3.1 is a representation of the diagram.

Summation

Publication of *Policing in the 21st Century* marked a remarkable achievement for the Conservative Party. It was the culmination of a philosophical journey that commenced in 2002 with Oliver Letwin's speech 'Beyond the causes of crime' when he first linked policing with the concept of the 'neighbourly society'. As a term, the 'neighbourly society' might morph into the 'Big Society' but as a concept it was to be a consistent theme throughout the next eight years of policy development. Over the eight years between Letwin's speeches and the Coalition Agreement, policing became a key exemplar of their intentions to roll back the centralizing state, assert localism, and promote civil society. Practicalities required some modification of detail: mayors had to be abandoned in favour of elected commissioners; there could be no return to small municipal forces. But the key principles of increased political control vested in a single individual, more involvement by neighbourhoods in policing, and a significantly diminished role for the national institutions, be they the Home Secretary, ACPO, or quangos, remained.

But for all its intellectualism, this still amounted to a leap of faith. The elected individual model was untried and untested. PCCs were not elected mayors; they would be separate from local authorities and therefore could not ensure the delivery of the synergies that were seen as essential by Policy Exchange in 2003. In fact Policy Exchange rejected directly elected police authorities because they could not command the concentration of resources across local agencies, while mayors could. What, might well be asked, was now the advantage of a single elected individual over a police board? But it was too late for such considerations. The policy juggernaut was rolling. The key question was would it work? Above all, would it reignite the public's interest in the political process as the enthusiasts of localism envisaged?

4

Armageddon or necessary readjustment?

Police finances and the Coalition

Introduction

> *No historical event is better calculated than the French Revolution to teach political writers and statesmen to be cautious in their speculations; for never was any such event, stemming from factors so far back in the past, so inevitable yet so completely unforeseen.*[1]

So wrote the French historian and political analyst Alexis de Tocqueville in 1856 of the cataclysmic revolution that erupted in his country some sixty-seven years previously. He might easily have been writing about the credit crunch of 2008. No contemporary spotted the French Revolution coming, not Frederick the Great, not William Pitt the Younger, certainly not the hapless Louis XVI, and not even the revolutionaries. The same might also be said of the great economists and statesmen of the early twenty-first century. There were some who had been concerned about the accumulation of debt, principally personal and household, which had accelerated from the 1990s, and there were some who were concerned about the increase in public spending on the back of an increase in government debt, but none of the principal commentators predicted the scale and speed of the economic crash that overwhelmed the Western economies between 2007 and 2009 and its enduring consequences.[2]

---

[1] A de Tocqueville, *The Ancien Regime and the French Revolution* (translated S Gilbert, Fontana, London, 1971), 33.

[2] As an example see S Briscoe, *Britain in Numbers: The Essential Statistics* (Politico, London, 2005), 198–247.

The 'credit crunch' of 2007 and the recession that followed were to business and commerce severe and dislocating. For a short while the public services were protected, but this could not last. The Labour government guaranteed to protect levels of public spending only as far as the general election of 2010; the Conservatives and Liberal Democrats to differing degrees made it clear that, if elected, tackling the public debt that had accrued from 2007 onwards would be their urgent priority. From 2008 through to the general election of May 2010 the public services necessarily inhabited a kind of policy limbo; everyone knew the spending axe would fall, but no one knew exactly when and by how much. The police were not to be, unlike in previous recessions, an exception. In the event the Conservative–Liberal Democrat Coalition agreed within a few days of formation to deliver an emergency budget and commission a Comprehensive Spending Review (CSR) to report in the autumn of 2010. That review when completed initiated a programme of general cuts in public service spending, both in 'real' (relative to general inflation and GDP) and absolute (less cash) terms. In the specific case of the police this first halted and then reversed the long-historic increase in police resources most conspicuously expressed as police officer numbers. It is the purpose of this chapter to trace the general economic and political factors which created these circumstances and identify the effects—short and long term—on the police.

From credit crunch to recession

There remains debate about the causes of the banking crisis and general recession that followed, but not much about its timings, course, and consequences. The credit crunch is recognized as beginning in late 2007 and affected all Western economies. Confidence withered and liquidity began to dry up as banks and other financial institutions stopped lending to each other. This triggered a general recession as banks then stopped lending to businesses. The immediate cause of the crisis in liquidity was the overexposure of numerous banks and financial institutions to 'subprime' mortgages. These had been lent to high-risk individual borrowers, principally but not exclusively in the USA and Western Europe. The exposure of banks which promoted such high-risk loans was exacerbated by the practice of packaging subprime loans and selling them on, at a profit. All worked well as long as confidence was maintained in the institutions themselves and the value of property, upon which the values of the loans were fundamentally underwritten, kept going up. Some poor returns in European banks, however, damaged confidence in 2007, and began a process of rapid re-evaluation of the subprime market and those banks and institutions overexposed to it. Lenders became cautious, stopped lending to the at-risk banks, and the credit began to dry up. Suddenly several banks, including, because of interconnectivity, those not directly overexposed to subprime debt, were threatened with failure, prompting a world banking seizure. That led to global economic, not just banking, collapse. Governments, including the UK's, were forced to intervene by injecting capital into the banks most threatened with failure.

The rescue packages averted a general banking failure but were insufficient to prevent a loss of general confidence. Lending to even successful businesses dried up, and in the UK a general recession followed in early 2009. The Brown government had little option in the short term other than to extend its own borrowing to maintain public finances, support the banks, and to try and maintain a general degree of confidence. Its measures were sufficient to stop the 2009 recession deepening and extending, but it incurred a massive increase in public debt in doing so. This in itself became a problem, as doubts crept in amongst international creditors about the long-term prospects of Britain's economy, now recognized as overdependent on financial services, to recover and pay off the debts, even though the amount of public debt was small compared to the extent of household and financial sector debt.[3] Focus on the 'structural deficit', that part of the public debt that would remain after the hoped for general recovery occurred, became a political obsession in 2009. How and when the structural deficit, which reached 9.8 per cent of GDP in 2009–10, would be addressed now became a matter of political standpoint.[4]

The economic policies of the principal political parties in 2010

As Labour was in government when the financial crisis broke, it therefore was the first party to have to address the problem. It rescued the banks and hoped that would be enough. It was not; a recession followed in 2009. To kickstart growth the Bank of England created money in a process known as 'quantitative easing', but Labour accepted that it would have to address the structural deficit. However, it decided not to risk the fragile recovery with precipitate public sector cuts. The March 2009 budget was therefore cautious; public spending growth was pegged back at 1.1 per cent with a limitation of 0.7 per cent growth from 2011; £9 billion of 'efficiencies' would be found. For the rest, some of the deficit would be tackled through tax increases for those earning over £150,000, borrowing would increase, but the big hope was in the economy picking itself up to 3.5 per cent annual growth from 2011. In public service terms it meant an end to upward expansion.[5] It did not yet mean substantial cuts.

When it came to its 2010 election manifesto Labour did not avoid addressing the structural deficit through public spending cuts, and it acknowledged it would introduce a 1 per cent limit on public sector pay, make 'tough decisions' on public

---

[3] PwC, 'PwC projects total UK public debt and private debt to hit £10 trillion by 2015' (<http://www.ukmediacentre.pwc.com/News-Releases/PwC-projects-total-UK-public-and-private-debt-to-hit-10-trillion-by-2015-f84.aspx> [accessed 13 October 2012]).

[4] C Giles, 'Britain's "structural deficit" disease', ft.com, 4 March 2010 (<http://www.blogs.ft.com/money-supply/2010/03/04/britains-structural-deficits-disiease/> [accessed 30 June 2013]).

[5] BBC News, 'At-a-glance: budget 2009', 22 April 2009 (<http://www.news.bbc.co.uk/1/hi/uk_politics/8011882.stm> [accessed 11 October 2012]).

sector pensions, and make savings through a series of 'efficiencies' and 'reforms' which were presumably euphemisms for cuts. These savings would be balanced by tax increases for those earning over £150,000 and a penny on National Insurance, effectively a poll tax on those in work. However, Labour emphasized that it would do nothing to endanger the limited economic recovery that had taken place; therefore, these measures would not eliminate the structural deficit but simply reduce it by two-thirds over the lifetime of the next parliament; it was in fact Labour's intention to increase public spending in 2011–12.[6] The Liberal Democrats, while boldly stating that they would not flinch from identifying the measures necessary to reduce the deficit, largely did just that and broadly endorsed Labour's longer term approach with its greater emphasis on taxation.[7]

The Conservatives had no such inhibitions; it was their intention to 'eliminate the bulk of the structural deficit over a Parliament'. Until the effects of the economic crisis began to become apparent in 2008 it will be recalled from Chapter 2 that Cameron and Osborne had been rather cautious public sector reformers. That changed in 2008 with the banking crisis, the rescue package, and the increase in deficit. In *Labour's Debt Crisis* the Cameron–Osborne leadership became totally committed to identifying debt as the cause of Britain's economic crisis and elimination of it as the road to renewed growth, although they remained low on specifics in terms of timing and method until much closer to the election itself.[8]

The full Conservative macroeconomic policy was revealed in the party 2010 election manifesto. The Conservatives linked their economic intentions to their wider vision for society and politics with a smaller state, more engaged communities, and a rebalanced, revitalized economy. However, the first link in the chain of delivering this new vision was elimination of the 'bulk' of the structural deficit 'over a parliament', which presumably meant by 2015 at the latest. Amongst a package of other measures (a rebalanced, greener economy, and reformed banking system) the public services would be reformed to deliver better value for money. The Conservatives would ensure that most of the deficit reduction would be achieved through cuts in spending rather than increases in taxation. If elected there would be an emergency budget to cut £6 billion of waste across departments. Thereafter they would take the £12 billion of savings already identified in the Gershon review of the public sector, in the strong expectation that this could be achieved without adversely affecting the frontline. Some departments, health and overseas aid, would be spared, at least to a degree, while defence would be subject to a strategic review.[9] The billions of pounds identified as 'savings' sounded impressive but were in reality only a drop in the ocean. It was necessary to read between the lines. If the structural deficit was to be removed, or even largely reduced within five years, very extensive cuts would be required, well beyond those identified in the manifesto.

---

[6] Labour Party Manifesto 2010 (<http://www2.labour.org.uk/uploads/TheLabourPartyManifesto-2010.pdf> [accessed 11 October 2012]), 0:6–1:4.
[7] Liberal Democrat Manifesto 2010, 14–17.
[8] See Chapter 2.   [9] Conservative Manifesto 2010, 5–31.

While all three parties promised to reboot the economy and do something about the deficit through a combination of revenue raising and spending cuts, all three were detail light. It was left to an independent think tank, the Institute for Fiscal Studies (IFS) to work out what this really meant. Under Labour and the Liberal Democrats debt would return to 40 per cent of GDP in 2016–17, a year later than the Conservatives. The big difference would be in terms of public spending. With a greater proportion of the reduction to be achieved through taxation Labour and the Liberal Democrat cuts would restore public spending to the 2006–7 levels. The Conservatives would take the levels back to 2003–4, in other words practically eliminating the growth achieved under Labour.[10] For most departments this meant that spending levels would go back to before the era of Labour growth in the early and mid 2000s. Significantly, the police was not listed amongst the protected departments, entirely in line with the rhetoric and doctrine that David Cameron had espoused since his Dalston Youth Project speech in January 2006.

The growth in police resources under Labour, 1997–2010

Over the last four decades the police service in England and Wales experienced a prolonged period of general growth, most conveniently represented by the number of police, both officers and civilians. Taking 1967, the year when the first round of national amalgamations took effect, there were 89,660 officers and just 21,000 civilians of all grades and specialisms. In 1974, the year when the forty-three-force structure came into being as a consequence of local government reorganization, the numbers had increased to 102,467 officers and 39,557 civilians. Despite the economic stagnation and recession at the end of the 1970s, strength still increased to 113,309 and 39,810 respectively. The problem that the Callaghan Labour government faced in 1979 when confronted with these figures by a resurgent Conservative opposition was that numbers should have grown to approximately 120,000 for police officers, this being the official 'establishment' figure set by the Home Office. That the figure was below the establishment was because of the well-documented problem of low wages leading to difficulties in recruiting but above all retaining officers. The Thatcher government made the police a priority and recruited over 13,000 officers in the next eleven years, an increase of 12 per cent. Under the Major administration numbers at first continued to rise but then slowed and decreased as a consequence of the government response to the 1990–2 recession. However, over the remaining years of his administration the decrease was marginal, with officer numbers falling from 125,821 in 1992 to 125,058 in 1997. Numbers decreased in the first years of the Blair government, as it persisted with the Major government spending plans, to

---

[10] Institute for Fiscal Studies (IFS), *Election Briefing 2010 Summary* (<http://www.ifs.org.uk/election/ebn_summary.pdf> [accessed 23 April 2013]), 12–14.

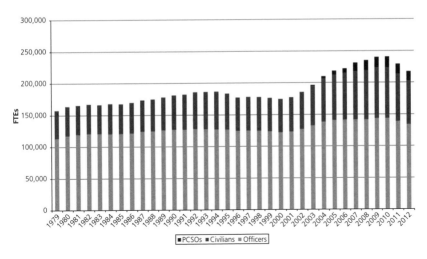

Figure 4.1: Growth in police personnel 1979–2012
Cipfa Police Actuals and HMIC 1979–2012

reach a low point in 2000 with 121,966 officers, although civilian employee numbers had remained more stable at 52,589. It was at this point that Labour decided to reverse the trend and increase numbers through the medium of the Crime Fighting Fund grant. The trend was reversed sufficiently in time to show an increase by the 2001 general election. After that Blair made the major policy decision to grow public service capacity, including that of the police service, with growth accelerating sharply until the first impact of the 2008–9 recessions.[11] The growth in police personnel from 1979, Mrs Thatcher's election, and the impact of the 2009 recession are illustrated in Figure 4.1.

There can be no doubt about the scale of Labour's growth, but it does require some explanation. Government grant is only one element of funding for the forty-three individual forces. A proportion is funded through council tax raised by the police authority for the area, and this in turn may or may not be subject to 'capping' by the central government department responsible for local authorities. Furthermore, government grant is made up of three main elements—Police Grant, National Non-Domestic Rates (NNDR), and Rate Support Grant (RSG). Police Grant is the responsibility of the Home Office and distributed by means of the Police Funding Formula, itself determined by a complex range of social and policing factors. It may also contain several elements of specific grants, ie grants set and distributed by the Home Office which are 'ring fenced' and may only be used for the purpose specified.

It was a device much favoured by Labour as it delivered a measure of central control over local budgets. The Crime Fighting Fund, to be used for the purpose of funding additional police officers, was simply the most significant of these

---

[11] HMIC, *Annual Reports* 1967–1995 (HMSO) and Chartered Institute of Public Finance and Accountancy (Cipfa), Police Actuals 1995–2011 (<http://www.cipfastats.net/publicprotection/policeactuals/> [accessed variously]).

grants. The NNDR and RSG were grants set by the department with responsibility for local authorities (variously the Office of the Deputy Prime Minister, the Department for Communities and Local Government (DCLG), or, for Wales, the Welsh Assembly Government (WAG), and more latterly the Welsh Government (WG)) and determined by local social and economic factors. There was significant growth during Labour's period in office, but as will be noted from Table 4.1, the growth in funding was not uniform across all categories. The baseline year is 1998–9, the first full year's funding for which the Labour government was responsible; 2009–10 was the last financial year for which it was fully responsible.

In 2009–10, 81 per cent of revenue was spent on personnel, with 19 per cent on goods and services, a general proportion that has remained relatively constant over many years. Capital expenditure amounted to £0.7 billion in 2009–10. This had similarly grown since 1998–9 (176 per cent), but inconsistently and, because of statistical changes, strict like-for-like comparison is difficult.

There were some significant shifts in resources under Labour. There had been an increase of 15 per cent in the number of police officers, but a 70 per cent increase in civilian employees, including over 16,000 PCSOs. The Rate Support Grant diminished as a proportion of central grants, but the National Non-Domestic Rate increased by 185 per cent. The consolidated Home Office grant increased by 26 per cent, while overall government grants increased by 33 per cent. However, the element of police funding paid for locally by council taxpayers increased by 193 per cent. As a proportion of funding for the forty-three forces it almost doubled

Table 4.1: Growth in resources, 43 forces England and Wales 1998–9 to 2009–10

	1998–9	2009–10	% change
Council tax (£000s)	1,027,153	3,014,628	193
NNDR (£000s)	1,011,760	2,880,135	185
RSG (£000s)	1,514,433	740,273	−51
Consolidated police grant (£000s)	3,655,796	4,606,269	26
Total grants (£000s)	6,181,989	8,233,677	33
Total funding (£000s)	7,209,142	11,248,305	56
Total funding per 1,000 population (£s)	137,505	205,228	49
Total grant funding per 1,000 population	117,914	150,225	27
Officers (FTE)	124,808	143,734	15
Civilians (FTE)	56,894	96,734	70
PCSOs (FTE)	0	16,918	n/a
Total police personnel (FTE)	181,702	240,468	32

Cipfa Police Actuals 1998/9–2009/10

during Labour's period in office, accounting for 14 per cent of police funding in 1998–9 and 27 per cent in 2009–10. This was despite the massive increase in central direction by the Home Office. Labour's growth in police funding was to a large extent underwritten by local council tax. It will also be observed that by 2009–10 the Department for Communities and Local Government and the Welsh Government were between them responsible for 32 per cent of police funding, despite having no statutory responsibility for policing, although the balance of their contribution shifted from Rate Support Grant to National Non-Domestic Rate.

Significant, even spectacular, as the growth had been in terms of the forty-three forces of England and Wales, Labour also substantially invested in national police agencies, a consequence of its centralizing policies. Spending figures are hard to obtain before 2003–4 but Table 4.2 is illustrative of the growth in central agency spending.

Table 4.2: National agency and forty-three-force expenditure and grants 2003–4 to 2009–10

Agency	2003–4 £000s	2009–10 £000s	Change £000s	% change
PCA (2003-for only) + IPCC	15,785	33,306	17,521	111
Centrex	93,246	–	–	–
PITO	121,295	–	–	–
Centex + PITO	214,541	–	–	–
NPIA	–	395,522	180,981	84
NCIS	82,432	–	–	–
NCS	162,541	–	–	–
SOCA	7380	424,699	179,726	73
NCIS + NCS + SOCA	244,973	–	–	–
OSCT	132,495	931,940	799,490	603
Total national agencies	615,174	1,785,441	1,170,267	190
Forty-three force grant	7,329,818	8,119,186	789,368	11
Total of grant from central government	7,944,922	9,904,627	1,959,635	25
National police budget (total grants + council tax and other income)	9,999,992	13,014,992	3,015,000	30

Cipfa Police Actuals 2003/4–2009/10 and Home Office Departmental Report 2009[12]

---

[12] NB Centrex (Central Police Training Executive) and PITO (Police Information Technology Organisation) merged to form the National Policing Improvement Agency; NCIS (National Criminal Intelligence Service) and NCS merged with SOCA (Serious and Organised Crime Agency).

In 2003–4 central agency budgets accounted for 6 per cent of the national police budget; by 2009–10 they accounted for 14 per cent. The 603 per cent growth in the Office for Security and Counter Terrorism (OSCT) budget after the 2005 7/7 terrorist attacks is understandable, but the growth in the remaining central agency budgets amounted to 80 per cent in five years. Combining the total funding of forty-three forces and the national police agencies gives a total funding, excluding police officer pensions, of approximately £13 billion in 2009–10, or 0.009 per cent of GDP for that year.

While the growth under Labour is an incontestable fact, some qualifications and observations are required. First there has been the effect of inflation, both general and specific to policing, the latter largely pay related. Second, from 2000 increasing amounts of grant came in the form of grants for specific purposes, such as the Crime Fighting Fund (police officers), PCSOs, and Airwave (new radio system). These specific grants did not generally cover all of the cost of the intended project but required matched funding by police authorities, fuelling increases in locally raised council tax. Third, the benefit or productivity of the growth was diminished in hard to quantify ways by the imposition of new overheads, such as the European Working Time Directive, new legislation, and additional bureaucracy. Finally, the amount of grant received by individual forces varied considerably because of the effect of the Police Funding Formula, which will be further discussed later. Even allowing for such qualifications, however, the growth in police resources under New Labour was significant and sufficient to allow for the simultaneous development of neighbourhood policing and national projects.

It is worth dwelling on the effects of the Police Funding Formula. It distributes the Home Office block grant by quantifying various social, economic, and police operational factors, weighting them, and then combining them in a single formula. The grant is then divided by the formula and distributed to the forty-three forces. It is not meant to do so equally, and consequently produces differences in distribution. The formula was first devised in the mid 1990s as part of Michael Howard's 'reforms'. However, it had never worked as intended. When first calculated it produced such wide variations in grant allocation from the existing norm that it would have cut the level in some forces to dangerously low amounts that either would have severely dislocated policing or required commensurately high levels of council tax to compensate. Neither option was realistic or politically acceptable, so a 'dampening' mechanism was introduced to even out the peaks and troughs. The problem was that this left some police authorities feeling aggrieved that they were not receiving their fair share of grant. The formula has been incrementally modified over the years but never fundamentally altered with the result that the differences have been magnified with increasing grant levels. Flanagan, in his *Review of Policing: Final Report*, recommended 'a fuller application of the funding formula', but had that occurred it would have produced severe financial and operational dislocation.[13] Even allowing for its unreformed

---

[13] R Flanagan, *The Review of Policing: Final Report* (Home Office, London, 2008), 29.

nature the formula produces a wide range of disparities, principally in terms of funding in relation to population and the degree to which local council taxpayers support their local forces. For example, the Metropolitan Police has a budget of £2.6 billion, combined grants of £255,536 per 1,000 population, and receives 25 per cent of its funding through council tax. Northumbria has a budget of £0.3 billion, combined grants of £176,321 per 1,000 population, and receives 12 per cent of its income in council tax. In contrast, Surrey has a budget of £0.2 billion, combined grants of £91,465, and receives 48 per cent of its income in council tax.[14] It consequently follows that any general cuts in government grants will have different effects in different forces dependent on the original level of grant funding and through the willingness or otherwise of local politicians to compensate for cuts through council tax.

CSR 2010

Even before the impact of the 2009 recession was felt on police spending there were already indications that expansion would at least slow down and possibly retrench. The attempted amalgamations programme of 2005–6, notwithstanding the financial weaknesses of the scheme, was intended to partly address the problem of meeting the challenge of serious and organized crime without increasing resources. By 2006 the Treasury was already making it plain that there would be 'slower funding growth', and that 'the pace of improvement in police resource management and operational productivity' needed to 'speed up significantly', with concomitant changes in culture and transformation in 'information, skills and incentives in the service'.[15] In 2007 Sir Ronnie Flanagan in the interim report of his *Review of Policing* recognized that future resources would be 'tight'.[16] The Treasury was already suspicious that it was difficult to prove police efficiency, much less productivity, and there was an increasing recognition that it was reluctant to continue underwriting index-linked police pay and pensions. With the collapse of the 2005–6 amalgamations the Home Office sought to close the funding gap through increased inter-force collaboration, but these have generally proved ineffective because the underlying financial assumptions of collaboration are often erroneous. The Home Office did take other steps to limit police spending increases, first by introducing new pension regulations in 2006, lengthening eligibility to thirty-five rather than thirty years, and by adopting a new index to determine the annual uplift in police pay, thus effectively ending the Edmund-Davies formula that had determined police pay since 1978. The DCLG reintroduced council tax capping for

---

[14] Cipfa Police Actuals 2009–10 and author's extrapolations.
[15] HM Treasury, *Delivering a Step Change in Police Productivity* (<http://www.openeyecommunications.com/agencyreports/delivering-a-step-change-in-police-productivity/> [accessed 20 October 2012]), [1].
[16] Flanagan, *Interim Report* (Home Office, London, 2007), 6–7.

the financial year 2007–8, although the Welsh Government did not follow suit. Thirty-three police authorities anticipated general cuts by introducing limits on council tax funding and increasing the use of reserves, a short-term measure which weakened their ability to invest in efficiency measures which might enable them to deal more effectively with general cuts.[17] However, these cost-saving measures were intended to deal with a *slowdown* in public spending growth, perhaps a moderate corrective, and not the deep and lasting cuts necessitated by severe and prolonged general recession. The measures taken before 2010 were, therefore, inadequate to deal with the post credit crunch world and, in particular, the political expectations of the Conservative opposition, but they were sufficient to already weaken the financial resilience of the service before the CSR 2010 cuts were even announced.

In their 2010 manifesto the Conservatives had promised to introduce an emergency budget within fifty days of taking office *and* to immediately cut £6 billion of 'wasteful departmental spending'.[18] This, together with the more general intention to complete a spending review in the autumn of 2010, featured in the first Coalition Agreement published on 12 May 2010.[19] The £6 billion cuts were announced on 24 May. As expected health, overseas aid, and defence were exempt; the police were not. The Home Office took £242 million in direct cuts, which fell on the central agencies. The forty-three-force share was £135 million, with £125 million to be found from the 'rule 2' specific grants and £10 million from counter terrorism allocations. There was also a £10 million cut in capital grant.[20] The cuts were inconvenient but 'doable', the sums being found principally by immediately suspending the unpopular and bureaucratic Special Priority Payments (SPPs) to staff, overtime reductions, and holding personnel vacancies. However, although the short-term impact was slight, the long-term impact was not without significance. The baseline from which future cuts would be calculated was not, therefore, a little over £13 billion, but £12.9 billion. It might not have sounded much but the effect would be cumulative and made the job of finding future savings just that bit harder.

The emergency budget on 22 June set out the parameters of the spending review. It specified that the structural deficit was to be eliminated *by* 2014–15, and required departments, other than health and overseas aid (defence would be subject to a separate review), to make 'average real cuts in real terms of around 25 per cent over four years'.[21] Real term cuts amounted to a combination of actual cash cuts and an estimation for what growth might have been allowing for inflation and anticipated growth in GDP. The police share of the cuts was revealed when

---

[17] Cipfa Police Actuals 2009–10.   [18] Conservative Manifesto 2010, 7–8.

[19] Coalition Agreement (<http://www.conservatives.com/News/News_stories/2010/05/Coalition_Agreement_published.aspx> [accessed 21 September 2012]), 1.

[20] Home Office, *Proposals for Revised Funding Allocations for Police Authorities in England and Wales* 2010/11, 27 May 2010 (<http://www.merpolfed.org.uk/homeoffice.pdf> [accessed 30 June 2013]).

[21] HM Treasury, *Budget 2010* (TSO, London, 2010), 17.

the CSR was published in October.[22] The Home Office received a 'real terms' cut of 23 per cent, so faring a little better than the 25 per cent average for unprotected departments, but neither did it fare as well as health and overseas aid.[23] Specifically, the police fared a little better, receiving a 20 per cent real cut. The Chancellor, speaking in the Commons on 20 October, thought that this would mean police spending would fall by '4 per cent each year', and that by 'cutting costs and scrapping bureaucracy...hundreds of police man hours' would be saved and thereby 'avoid any reduction in the visibility and availability of the police in our streets'.[24]

It was at the time a curious statement and with hindsight remains so. Presumably the Chancellor must have realized that, setting aside the use of non-inclusive terminology, saving the police 'hundreds of man hours' would not be enough to avoid any 'reduction'. 'Hundreds' would not do; saving many thousands might, but there was clearly going to be no attempt at adding any precision on 20 October. What was interesting was the priority attached to that part of policing which it was intended to avoid reducing—'visibility and availability of the police on our streets'. The Chancellor was setting out a very simplistic vision of policing for the future. Furthermore, the Chancellor's '4 per cent a year' cut was, arithmetically, not an easy figure to reconcile with the total 20 per cent real terms cut. This could only be achieved by estimating the effects of inflation and GDP growth (the Treasury's 'deflator' calculation) to be around 5 per cent, allowing council tax to rise in line with projections, and then round down from 4.6 per cent (actual) to 4 per cent, rather than round up to 5 per cent.

Police Grant Settlements

More detail was subsequently revealed in the published spending review document. From the new 2010–11 baseline of £12.9 billion, spending on the forty-three forces would fall to £12.1 billion in 2014–15, a cash cut of £0.8 billion or 6.2 per cent, with the effects being frontloaded in the first two years. However, this calculation included an estimate for the contribution to the total forty-three-force budget from council tax. This could only be an estimate as the level to be set was in the hands first of police authorities and later, although this was not certain in 2010, PCCs, and not the Chancellor. The cut in central grants

---

[22] The official title of the document published in October 2010 is simply '*Spending review*', however, general reference is almost universally to the 'Comprehensive Spending Review' (CSR) and that terminology is, therefore, used in this text.

[23] HM Treasury, *Spending Review 2010* (TSO, London, 2010), 10.

[24] parliament.uk, Parliamentary business, 20 October 2010, Comprehensive Spending Review (<http://www.publications.parliament.uk/pa/cm/cmhansard/cm101020/debatext/101020-0001. htm#10102049000003> [accessed 28 December 2010]).

amounted to £1.2 billion, cash, or 12.4 per cent. To arrive at the Chancellor's cash figures council tax had to rise £0.4 billion, or 12.5 per cent; anything less than that would leave the forces short. This would in turn mean that collectively council tax would account for 30 per cent of the total spend on the forty-three forces by 2014–15 compared to 24 per cent in 2010–11. This would represent a substantial shift from central to local spending, entirely consistent with the 'new Conservative' philosophy of localism that had been developing since the early 2000s.

The details of the effect on individual forces were not known until the police grant settlement was announced in December 2010. Even this was hard to determine as it came in four instalments—a statement by the Police Minister in the Commons, a Home Office written report, a statement by the DCLG setting out NNDR and RSG for England, and a statement by the Welsh Government setting out NNDR and RSG for Wales. While these majored on the settlement for 2011–12 they also provided indicative figures for the years up to 2014–15, although qualifying them to the extent that there would be a fundamental review of central government grants to local authorities (ie RSG and NNDR), another factor not apparently taken into account in the Chancellor's October projections. The proliferation of statements was complicated enough, but the government made matters more complicated by consolidating some of the specific grants with the general Home Office police grant. This gave forces more budgetary discretion but also less money with which to exercise it. The matter was complicated yet further by the Secretary of State for Communities and Local Government announcing the availability of a special grant for local authorities in England (including police authorities) which froze their council tax, although the Welsh Government did not follow suit. Furthermore, while the headline cut was 5.1 per cent this was only calculated by taking into account Public Finance Initiative (PFI) which only went to fifteen forces, and security grants, which were not distributed by means of the Police Funding Formula but according to a secret estimate of threat. There were further complications in the form of additional planned consolidations of specific grants into the main grant and the one-off availability of a £50 million grant to fund the anticipated 2012 PCC elections.[25] For a government supposedly committed to increasing participation in 'the government of Britain', by publishing

---

[25] Home Department, Police Authority Grants (England and Wales), 13 December 2010 (<http://www.theyworkforyou.com/wms/?id=2010-12-13a.72WS.4> [accessed 7 January 2011]), cited as Ministerial Statement; Home Office, Provisional Police Grant Report (England and Wales) 2011/12 (<http://www.homeoffice.gov.uk/publications/police/police-finance/provisional-grant-report-2011-12> [accessed 7 January 2011]); Communities and Local Government, Local Government Finance Settlement 2011/12 (<http://www.local.communities.gov.uk/finance/1112/grant.htm> [accessed 7 January 2011]); and Minister for Social Justice and Local Government, Welsh Assembly Government, Written Statement—Provisional Police Settlement 2011–12 (<http://wales.gov.uk/about/cabinet/cabinetstatements/2010/101213police/;jsessionid=nLQbNJLQSrTnjQrPBqhcnzqzQ2kTXtY2gXYpGxNlcVkc5b7QmlZ2!-1746883796?lang=en> [accessed 7 January 2011]), cited as WAG Statement; and author's extrapolations.

information in such a complex fashion it was making it remarkably hard for the public to do so. Table 4.3 seeks to track the changes and outcomes. The overall consolidation and then reduction in central government grants now became plain.

It will be observed that the Council Tax Freeze grant remains constant throughout the period, and consequently will lose value when allowing for inflation. Furthermore, it only replaces what might have been raised in council tax and therefore does not represent 'new money'. If the security and PFI elements are discounted, the amount of grant remaining for local policing is projected to decrease by £976 million, or 17 per cent. Over the same period capital grant is also set to fall, from £146.7 million in 2010–11 to £120 million by 2014–15, a cut of 18.2 per cent.

There remained considerable uncertainty over council tax. The council tax freeze grant amounted to the equivalent of a 2.5 per cent increase in council tax. The Chancellor had calculated on a 3 per cent increase, although that calculation is complicated by the projected increase in the 'council tax base' as properties increase in number in local authority areas. That might account for the difference. However, the council tax freeze grant is an annual grant and does not add to the authorities' base budgets. Should the grant cease without providing some funding to shore up the base budgets those forces whose governing bodies had availed themselves of the grant would face a severe financial dislocation. Notwithstanding this long-term uncertainty the offer was too big an incentive for the thirty-nine English police authorities to decline in 2011–12. As previously observed, the scheme did not apply to Wales; there the authorities increased council tax. The problems with the grant, however, were becoming apparent during its second year of operation and only twenty took the grant, the remaining increasing council tax to a limited degree.[26] In October 2012 Eric Pickles, Secretary of State for CLG, announced that the grant would continue for another year, but at the equivalent rate of a 2 per cent increase in council tax.[27] The Chancellor of the Exchequer in the 2013 spending review announced that it would continue for 2014–15 and 2015–16, but there remained the question of what would happen in future years.[28] If the council tax freeze grant is simply ended in theory most PCCs would have to calculate increases from the 2010–11 base, which will result in unacceptably high increases. PCCs must hope that some form of additional grant or dampening mechanism is introduced otherwise the effect will be highly disruptive. There is, in any case, the impact of the 2012 Treasury Autumn Statement to take into account. This will be considered in Chapter 8.

[26] CLG, Council tax levels set by local authorities in England—2012–13 (Revised), Table 6, 9 May 2012 (<http://www.communities.gov.uk/publications/corporate/statistics/counciltax201213update> [accessed 21 October 2012]).

[27] CLG, Third year of tax freeze announced, 8 October 2010 (<http://www.communities.gov.uk/news/corporate/2232092> [accessed 21 October 2012]).

[28] See Chapter 8, p. 167–72.

Table 4.3: Changes in police funding 2010–14

Funding source	2010–11 £m	2011–12 £m	2012–13 £m	2013–14 £m	2014–15 £m	% change 2010–14
Home Office main grant	4643	4579	4251	4515	4429	−4.6
Capital City (Metropolitan Police Service only)	?	200	189	185	183	−8.5
Security	490*	567	564	563	562	14.7*
Neighbourhood Policing Fund	346	340	338	0	0	−100
Crime Fighting Fund	278	0	0	0	0	−100
'Rule 2' (miscellaneous specific grants)	208	0	0	0	0	−100
Basic Command Unit grant	31	0	0	0	0	−100
Other specific grants	102	13	20	20	20	−80
PFI	41	54	54	60	79	95
PCC election fund	0	0	50	0	0	n/a
CLG and Welsh Government	3670	3506	3289	3242	3198	−12.9
Council tax freeze	0	75	75	75	75	n/a
Total government grants	9807	9334	8823	8660	8546	−12.9
Council tax (projection)	3200	3300	3400	3400	3600	12.5
Total spend	**13,007**	**12,634**	**12,223**	**12,060**	**12,146**	**−6.6**

* estimate
Home Office, CLG, and WG[29]

29 Sources as n 25, and also: Home Office, Police Grant Report 2013/14 (<http://www.homeoffice.gov.uk/publications/about-us/parliamentary-business/written-ministerial-statement/police-grant-report-201314-wms/police-grant-report-201314?view=Binary> [accessed 16 February 2013]). NB, there was some change in the 2013–14 presentation, principally in the distribution of the Welsh force grant (to the specific disadvantage of South Wales) and the non-rotation of the Council Ci...

The effect

From the start ministers expected the cuts to be delivered by 'driving out wasteful spending on support functions, reducing bureaucracy, and increasing efficiency in key functions—leaving the frontline of policing strong and secure.'[30] With over 80 per cent of revenue spent on personnel was this ever realistic? On 31 March 2010 there were 143,734 police officers, 80,015 civilian employees, and 17,032 PCSOs, a total of 240,667 FTEs. It was an historic highpoint and is unlikely to be surpassed for many years. It set the benchmark for cuts. Using 2010–11 as the baseline the average cost of each police FTE, police and civilian, amounted to £49,500 in 2010–11.[31] The cumulative effect of CSR 2010, the Police Grant Settlements, and the council tax freeze (which cannot be counted twice, as both a government grant and an increase in local funding) would be to reduce the amount spent on local policing by £1.3 billion. Using the average cost of £47,155 the projected loss would be 26,260 FTEs. This would take numbers back to levels last seen in 2004–5. However, this average projection is short of what the forces themselves were projecting. In July 2011 an HMIC survey, based on returns from the forty-three forces, estimated that the FTE losses would be 34,100 by 2015, with 11,000 already lost through a combination of redundancies, early retirements, holding posts vacant, and cancelling programmes. Significantly, HMIC estimated that the loss would be almost equally split between officers (16,200) and civilians (17,900).[32] The structure of CSR 2010 and the subsequent grant settlements required the bulk of the cuts to be achieved in the first two years, and this was duly reflected in the pace of staff reductions. By September 2012 almost 26,000 posts had already been lost, 10,000 of them police officers.[33] This produced a disproportionate impact. Because so much of New Labour's growth had been in civilian employees and PCSOs, the loss in police officer terms was marginally more severe, taking levels back to those in 2003–4, that is about the time the growth was beginning to support the burgeoning Neighbourhood Policing Programme. Consequently, most of the impact of the losses are being felt at the very local level. On average in England and Wales there is an 11 per cent loss in FTE police officers, a 16 per cent loss in civilian employees, and a 15 per cent loss in PCSOs.

There was, however, considerable variation between forces, determined by varying combinations of central grant distribution, local council tax, preferences

---

[30] N Herbert to House of Commons, 27 May 2010 (<http://www.publications.parliament.uk/pa/cm201011/cmhansrd/cm100527/wmstext/100527m0001.htm> [accessed 21 October 2012]).
[31] Cipfa Police Actuals 2010–11 and 2011–12.
[32] HMIC, *Adapting to Austerity: A Review of Police Force and Authority Preparedness for 2011/12–14/15 CSR period* (HMIC, London, 2011), 4.
[33] Home Office, *Police Service Strength England and Wales, 31 March 2010* (<https://www.gov.uk/government/uploads/system/uploads/attachment_data/file/115745/hosb1410.pdf> [accessed 3 July 2013]) and *Police Service Strength England and Wales, 30 September 2012* (<https://www.gov.uk/government/uploads/system/uploads/attachment_data/file/143957/hosb0113.pdf> [accessed 3 July 2013]), 6.

by police authorities concerning the combination of posts to be lost, and special factors such as the Welsh Government's decision to give the four Welsh forces a specific PCSO grant, or Surrey's high council tax. As Figure 4.2 shows, Greater Manchester is the force set to lose the greatest number of police officer posts at 1,510, a 19 per cent reduction compared to March 2010, but the greatest percentage reduction in a force is in Humberside, which loses 21 per cent by 2015. Only one force plans for a net increase in officers, Surrey, which intends a net increase of 50 officer posts by 2015. It is not a coincidence that Surrey is a force where nearly 50 per cent of its funds are raised by local council tax and it possesses a wealthy tax base. Civilian losses by force are harder to calculate because of the potential privatization, but Northumbria, for example, is scheduled to lose 47 per cent of its civilian employees excluding PCSOs. The Welsh forces are scheduled to increase PCSOs due to a specific Welsh Government grant. Cleveland is scheduled to lose 29 per cent of its overall workforce, but outsourcing complicates its position. Northumbria with no such complications is scheduled to lose 28 per cent of its total workforce. The Metropolitan Police is scheduled to lose 6 per cent, although the potential closing of New Scotland Yard and numerous other police

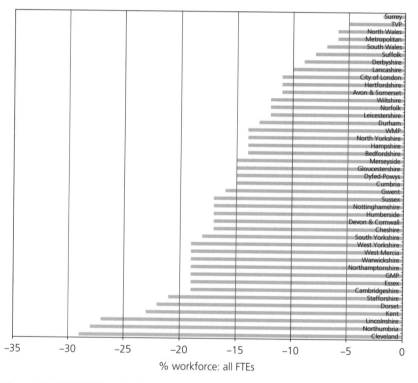

Figure 4.2: CSR 2010 reductions in all FTEs 2010–15, by force, as a percentage of the workforce

HMIC: *Policing in Austerity: One Year On*

stations in its area grabbed more headline attention when these cuts were announced in October 2010.[34]

In 2012 HMIC assessed how forces were adapting to the new financial realities. In *Policing in Austerity: One Year On*, a follow-up to a 2011 inspection report, it found that forces were 'balancing their books' by cutting the workforce and reducing spending on goods and services, but that the 'frontline' was, in a curious phrase, being 'protected, although not preserved', service to the public was being 'largely maintained', although the nature of the frontline 'was changing'. Neighbourhood policing had in many places become increasingly blurred with response and minor crime investigation work. Even allowing for this, the number of officers designated to response, the first line of public response to emergencies, had been reduced by 5,200 posts. HMIC pointed out that while the *proportion* of officers in the frontline might be increasing, the actual *number* was decreasing. The report also found that the 'spend' on public protection and investigation had increased between 2010/11 and 2011/12. All forces intended to increase the proportion of officers designated as frontline by 2015.[35]

The tone of the report sought to be reassuring. So too did the accompanying statement from Police Minister Nick Herbert: 'The proportion of officers on the front line is increasing, the number of neighbourhood officers has gone up, crime is down, victim satisfaction is improving and the response to emergency calls is being maintained.'[36] He could not be accused of seeking to spread alarm and despondency, but his statement tended to cover over the more disturbing picture revealed in the report itself. By March 2015 HMIC now estimated total FTE losses at 32,400, with 15,000 being police officers. That would still effectively wipe out the gains in personnel achieved under New Labour, gains which had made neighbourhood policing a realistic option without risking response or investigation. HMIC sought to offer some comfort by pointing out that the proportion of frontline officers had increased, but that was in proportional terms only, as there had in fact been a numerical reduction in frontline officers of 6 per cent. The report also observed that the nature of neighbourhood policing had changed, in the sense that it had been largely subsumed with response and some forms of investigative policing, and even then the number of response officers had reduced by 5,200 posts. The 'spend' on investigation and public protection had increased, but this did not necessarily mean that the number of officers available for such duties had increased. There were wide variations between forces, with Dyfed-Powys and the Metropolitan planning to cut staff by 6 per cent, compared to Cleveland which expected to lose 29 per cent of staff. Seventeen forces would still find it necessary to 'balance their books' in 2014–15 by using reserves. Crime had

---

[34] HMIC, *Policing in Austerity: One Year On* (<http://www.hmic.gov.uk/media[force]> [accessed 31 October 2012]) and Welsh Government, *Programme for Government* (<http://wales.gov.uk/about/programmeforgov/communities/keyactions?lang=en> [accessed 14 December 2012]).

[35] HMIC, *Policing in Austerity: One Year On*, passim.

[36] Home Office, 'Report says frontline policing is being protected', 2 July 2012 (<http://www.homeoffice.gov.uk/media-centre/news/frontline-policing> [accessed 21 October 2012]).

indeed fallen, but this might still have been connected with the continuing high prison population, while the public satisfaction figure quoted required some examination. The survey was not a straightforward police 'satisfaction' survey, but a victim survey, and the increase had been from 83.4 per cent to 83.9 per cent, which the report felt necessary to reassure its readers was statistically significant. Of most concern was that the survey had taken place in December 2011, so the full effects of the cuts had not yet been felt by those surveyed. Nevertheless, despite these qualifications the indications were that the service was generally coping with the rapid contraction required by CSR 2010. A new HMIC report published in July 2013 confirmed the decline in provision for neighbourhood policing and that in future more would be demanded from fewer personnel.[37]

Efficiencies

Ministers had high expectations that efficiencies, achieved principally through 'scrapping bureaucracy', would ensure that 'frontline' services could be maintained despite the unavoidable cuts in both personnel and materiel. There was, however, at first a distinct lack of precision about what savings these efficiencies might generate. In 2011 the Home Office thought that 'hundreds of millions of pounds and hundreds of thousands of man hours' might be saved, although the precise figures presented offered only minimal savings: 840,000 'man hours' by scrapping targets and the stop and search form; £380 million by joined-up IT procurement; £350 million by freezing pay.[38] These might sound impressive but did not bear closer scrutiny: 840,000 'man hours' amounted to no more than *the equivalent* 456 officers; £380 million savings on IT is a figure hard to compute as £277 million was spent on the forty-three force IT in 2009–10 alone;[39] £350 million might well be saved through freezing pay, but in making these projections to 2014–15 no pay increases have been presumed. The Home Secretary, in a speech on 9 May 2011, presented a series of measures that, once achieved, were intended to save 2.5 million police hours.[40] By 2012 this expectation had risen to 4.5 million hours, although it is not clear how that figure had been calculated.[41] These measures included returning police discretion for charging minor offences, new health and safety guidance, 'light touch' HMIC inspections, more complaints resolved by frontline supervisors, a review of ACPO's 600 doctrines, and a simplified crime recording process.

---

[37] See T Brain, 'Accentuate the positive', *Policing Today*, September 2012, 41, and HMIC, *Policing in Austerity: Rising to the Challenge* (<http://www.hmic.gov.uk/media/policing-in-austerity-rising-to-the-challenge.pdf> [accessed 18 July 2013]), 17 and 20.

[38] Home Office, *A New Approach to Fighting Crime* (<http://www.homeoffice.gov.uk/publications/crime/new-approach-fighting-crime?view=Binary> [accessed 21 October 2012]), 5–6.

[39] Cipfa Police Actuals 2009–10.

[40] Home Office, 'The Home Secretary's speech on police bureaucracy' (<http://www.homeoffice.gov.uk/media-centre/speeches/one-year-on> [accessed 30 June 2013]).

[41] Home Office, *Have You Got What it Takes? Working With the Reducing Bureaucracy Programme* (<https://www.gov.uk/government/uploads/system/uploads/attachment_data/file/117428/reducing-bureaucracy.pdf> [accessed 18 April 2013]), [2].

However, there remains a problem with these estimates. Even accepting the Home Office's optimistic projection, it was only the *equivalent* of 2,100 FTEs that were expected to be saved, which might be judged small compensation for the actual losses in FTEs.[42] Some of the measures, such as frontline supervisors resolving more complaints, will actually create more work for the frontline, not reduce it. Many of these measures remained promises for the future and had not stopped the loss of the 26,000 FTEs by September 2012. Finally, the effects of efficiencies fall variably on forces. Those forces which actively and progressively sought efficiencies before 2010, and there were several, had less room to manoeuvre once the spending cuts started, whereas those which were less active before 2010 perversely had more scope to find them in the CSR 2010 era.

The fundamental ministerial expectation was that the 'front line' would be preserved while the hit would be taken in the 'back office', which by implication was presumed to be largely wasteful and would be fulfilling no useful purpose once needless bureaucracy had been dispensed with. There were some problems attached to this approach, however. The first was defining 'front line' and 'back office'. A patrol or response officer might be easily recognized as 'front line', but how was the control room operator to be defined, who might have many more encounters with the public in a single day than a patrol officer, albeit through telephony rather than face to face? In its 2011 report *Demanding Times* HMIC felt constrained to introduce a third category of 'middle office', and found that about one-third of police personnel were involved in back or middle office work, but the questions still remained how much back office was intrinsically useless and could savings made there be transferred to the frontline? HMIC assessed that 24 per cent of personnel were engaged in 'middle office' work managing or supporting those in the frontline. Only 15 per cent were engaged in the 'back office', but categories of work here included finance, information technology, human resources, and vehicle workshop.[43] A detached observer might conclude that 15 per cent is not so very large an amount of a workforce and that the frontline might find it difficult to function efficiently without being effectively paid, managed, or having its vehicles serviced and IT maintained.

Considerable store was also placed in the efficiencies that might be achieved through collaboration in all its forms—between forces themselves, between forces and other public agencies, and between forces and the private sector. The previous Labour administration had been similarly convinced of the value of collaboration, especially as it offered a face-saving compromise following the amalgamation debacle of 2005–6. A 2012 HMIC report on collaboration, however, revealed some problems with relying on collaboration as a principal means of

---

[42] Conservatives, 'Reduction in crime shows police reform is working' (<http://www.conservatives.com/News/News_stories/2013/01/Reduction_in_crime_shows_police_reform_is_working.aspx> [accessed 18 April 2013]).

[43] HMIC, *Demanding Times: The Front Line And Police Visibility* (HMIC, London, 2011), 4–6 and 12.

delivering a significant proportion of the cash savings required under CSR 2010. It identified that police forces already had 543 collaboration schemes of one form or another, which intrinsically limited the scope for collaboration delivering further savings over the lifetime of CSR 2010. There was much variation between forces concerning the extent of their collaboration, an implied criticism but one which ignores that fact that much policing is operationally focused and locally delivered, and therefore not susceptible to the benefits or otherwise of collaboration. Furthermore, planned collaboration would only deliver £169 million, or 11 per cent of the savings required by 2015. That would be the *equivalent* of approximately 3,600 FTEs, another useful contribution but one which would only mitigate and not remove the necessity of reducing police numbers, not least because there is no guarantee that some of the efficiencies generated might be used for reinvestment in new, replacement, or maintenance of plant, building, and equipment. Most problematically, in terms of quantifying future cash savings, it was not clear if the savings identified by HMIC were in addition to or simply part of those speculated upon by the Home Secretary in her speech on police bureaucracy in May 2011. Further, it was not clear that cash savings generated through collaboration would be used to mitigate personnel losses, to reduce the cash requirements of budgets in the face of further grant cuts, or to use for new equipment and buildings.[44]

All this is to set aside the political enthusiasm for further collaboration. PCCs, with a precise remit to deliver for their local electorates, might have some misgivings in contributing to schemes whereby they would lose direct control over a portion of their resources. There was also by the end of 2012 the emergence of politicization of the issue of privatization or outsourcing following the G4S Olympic Games recruiting debacle, when this major private sector provider massively underestimated the challenge of the processes involved in recruiting the numbers of security guards it was contracted to deliver in time, and the Games organizers were rescued by the late engagement of the military. This high-profile failure brought into the open many hitherto suppressed doubts about the wisdom of the publicly unaccountable private sector providing increasing elements of police services. Some ambitious public–private partnership schemes were put on hold while several PCC candidates lined up to express their determination not to introduce further schemes in their areas should they be elected. This was an overreaction generated by political, not to say populist, considerations, but the episode did serve notice that political rather than policing considerations might be the driving forces behind some PCC decisions, and that privatization in itself was no panacea.

Aspects of collaboration that receive scant public attention are those of accountability and direction and control. Just who is in charge? To whom is that person accountable? Lead-force collaboration, where one force provides the service across force boundaries, receiving financial and support in kind from partner

---

[44] HMIC, *Increasing Efficiency in the Police Service: The Role of Collaboration* (HMIC, London, 2012), 5–9 and Home Office, 'Home Secretary's speech on police bureaucracy' (<https://www.gov.uk/government/speeches/home-secretarys-speech-on-police-bureaucracy> [accessed 25 August 2013]).

forces, is the clearest form of collaboration, but still blurs the issue of accountability. Police authorities have established joint boards to provide some accountability, but it is a tenuous form. The clearest form of accountability in outsourcing or privatization arrangements is the client/provider split, leaving the force client in a clear position of authority. Public–private partnerships, such as 'Southwest One' between Avon and Somerset Police, local councils, and IBM, however, blur accountability.[45]

Would the ultimate form of collaboration, force amalgamations, resurface? The Scottish Government had decided that it was an answer to what it presented as cuts forced on it by Westminster and pressed ahead with merging the eight local forces into a single national unit (Police Scotland) by April 2013. However, the business case was at best equivocal, with Cipfa Scotland voicing doubts about the attainability of a projected £1.7 billion of savings over *fifteen years*.[46] The business case for the 2005–6 New Labour planned mergers was woeful; there seemed in 2012 no reason to think it would be any stronger. This did not stop the chief constable of the new Scottish force, Sir Stephen House, arguing in October 2012 that mergers were 'inevitable' or ACPO President Sir Hugh Orde observing that the idea was 'gaining support' amongst chief constables. In fact, many chief constables were in favour of the idea in 2005–6, notwithstanding the absence of a conclusive business case. Meanwhile, in June 2013 Shadow Chancellor Ed Balls, by posing the question of whether it was necessary to have 'so many separate government departments, agencies, fire services and police forces', hinted that perhaps a future Labour government would reopen the issue.[47] In contrast, the Coalition government, with its enthusiasm for localism, showed no inclination to revitalize amalgamations, putting its faith instead in PCCs, collaboration, and new national agencies.[48]

There was, therefore, no efficiency 'magic bullet' that would enable ministers to have their cake and eat it. Efficiencies might mitigate but not eliminate the need for staff reductions. As for the ministerial expectation that frontline delivery would be unaffected by the losses in staff, there was some evidence by the end of 2012, halfway through the CSR 2010 period, that this had in fact happened. The service had succeeded in implementing severe staff losses in a remarkably short period of time with little evidence of short-term operational disruption. True, crime, the primary accountable measure for the government, has continued to fall despite the cuts, while HMIC had assessed that the frontline had been 'protected if not preserved', which,

[45] M Ballard, 'Southwest One is blocking Somerset cuts, says county councillor', 6 September 2012 (<http://www.computerweekly.com/news/2240162786/Southwest-One-is-blocking-Somerset-cuts-says-county-councillor> [accessed 27 October 2012]).

[46] K Aitken, 'Cipfa warns against rush to national police force', Public finance (<http://www.publicfinance.co.uk/news/2012/02/cipfa-warns-against-rush-to-national-police-force/> [accessed 27 October 2012]).

[47] E Balls, 'Striking the right balance for the British economy', 3 June 2013 (<http://www.labour.org.uk/striking-the-right-balance-for-the-british-economy> [accessed 30 June 2013]).

[48] N Dowling, 'Police force mergers in England and Wales "inevitable"', BBC News, 30 October 2012 (<http://www.bbc.co.uk/news/uk-20118194> [accessed 30 October 2012]).

despite the intrinsically contradictory nature of that phrase, was something of an achievement.

There are, however, two significant qualifications that must be added to that assessment. First, the frontline had been diminished and the effect had been most noticeably felt in neighbourhood policing, the nature of which had changed in at least some force areas by effectively merging with response and basic investigative functions. Second, the cuts had not reached their end point.

Summation and prognosis

The bottom line assessment of police finances at least until the end of the CSR 2010 period is that there will be much less cash, in absolute and relative terms, available to spend on any form of policing, but particularly at the forty-three-force level. All forces will to some degree suffer, but the effects will not be evenly distributed because of the effects of the Police Funding Formula, the degree to which forces had sought or not efficiencies before 2010, and the ability or willingness of PCCs to deliver mitigating increases in council tax. With over 80 per cent of funding spent on personnel, cuts in numbers have been and will be unavoidable. Ministers acknowledge this; what they do not acknowledge is the degree to which this cut in numbers will adversely affect policing delivery. By the end of 2012 the evidence that this was happening was equivocal. The service had lost nearly 26,000 posts in just two-and-a-half years. Even HMIC had been forced to acknowledge that the frontline had been 'protected' but not 'preserved', and, despite optimistic statements, there was scant evidence that many of the effects of the cuts in bureaucracy had reached the real frontline.[49] The problem for the future was that slashing bureaucracy in the way so favoured by the Coalition would be an absolute necessity that had to extend beyond reducing centrally driven targets and into the very sinews of the police organization if service levels to the public were not to regress to those of the late 1990s. Reducing targets, the principal activity of the Home Office in this field during the first years of the Coalition, would be insufficient compensation.

Aspects of police funding which are unlikely to change are the forty-three-force structure and the mechanisms by which forces are funded. There is little political appetite for changing either. Both are fraught with difficulties, but the latter more so than the former. There is no better than a highly equivocal case for amalgamations, but it could be achieved. There is, however, a pressing need to do something about the funding mechanism, which is complicated to the point of being chaotic, but it is so embedded that to do something, even incrementally, risks massive destabilization. With two governments involved (Westminster and

49 M Beckford, 'Recorded crime now at lowest level since 1986', *The Telegraph*, 18 October 2012 (<http://www.telegraph.co.uk/news/uknews/crime/9617967/Recorded-crime-now-at-lowest-level-since-1986.html> [accessed 27 October 2012]).

Wales), two government departments (Home Office, and Communities and Local Government), and four forms of local governance (PCCs, the Welsh Government, the London Mayor, and the City of London Common Council), it is hopelessly complicated. True accountability is obfuscated, with each party able to slip responsibility and blame another for whatever aspect they wish. This is before the effect of damping is considered. In theory this should be ended, but if it did the subsequent reallocation of central government funding would be dislocating. Two reforms, however, would be both practical and beneficial. First, in England the removal of the Department for Communities and Local Government from police funding and concentrating all grants into the Home Office. Second, wholly devolving funding to the Welsh Government for its four forces. This at least would clarify responsibility for central funding, but for that very reason it is unlikely that such a reform is likely. Removing 'damping', no matter how desirable in theory, would cause massive financial destabilization.

Forces and PCCs will pursue a range of efficiencies, including collaboration and reducing bureaucracy, but neither will deliver sufficient savings to compensate for the extreme losses in personnel consequent upon CSR 2010. All that both are offering are savings which *equate* to notional numbers of personnel; they are not offering to actually prevent those numbers being lost in the first place. Furthermore, CSR 2010 does not represent the end of the savings required. The June 2013 spending review, set in the context of the general economy continuing to 'flatline', suggests the likelihood is for further spending cuts and further losses in personnel, a prognosis to be explored in Chapter 8.

5

Reform or politicization?
The Coalition and police constitutional change

Introduction

The date 15 September 2011 became highly significant in the history of policing for England and Wales (conspicuously not for Scotland and Northern Ireland) for it was on that day that final parliamentary hurdles for the Police Reform and Social Responsibility Bill were overcome and it passed into law. The bill's passage had been a closer-run thing than the Coalition had bargained for, with the government having to use its Commons majority to overcome determined opposition in the Lords. A tied vote in the Lords defaulted in favour of the government and the bill became law. It was the end of a long process which, as we have seen in Chapter 3, began in 2002 with the Conservatives signalling their preference for a fusion in police governance of representative and executive elements in the form of a single elected individual. It was claimed to be the single biggest change in police governance since the creation by Peel of the 'New Police' in 1829. That was a historically dubious claim, but it undoubtedly was a big constitutional change. The new Act replaced local police authorities (collective boards which in one form or another had been ultimately responsible for local policing since the Municipal Corporations Act of 1835 and the County Police Act of 1839) with a single, elected, responsible individual. In doing so it put at risk the delicate constitutional balance so carefully crafted by the Royal Commission of 1960–2, which permitted politics to play but a limited role in local policing. This for the government, however, was not an unfortunate by-product of the Act but a defined benefit, entirely in accordance with the fundamental principles of the 'Big Society'. For its opponents, the Act risked upsetting the balance of the police constitution, risking 'politicization', a characteristic that was popularly presumed to have been excluded from British policing since time immemorial.

An apolitical police?

The idea of their police being independent of party politics seems to be deeply embedded in the collective psyche of the people in England and Wales. The history of policing in England, Wales, and Scotland would support the contention that policing has been broadly politically neutral. This is the result of a combination of factors—the uncoordinated development of policing in England, Wales, and Scotland in the nineteenth century, and a general sense by the leading politicians, starting with Peel, that politics and the police were best kept at arms' length. Neither the centre, in the form of the Home Secretary, nor the localities, in the form of borough watch committees and county joint standing committees, had total dominance in governance, while in matters of police management there was the slow development of police professionalism, led by chief constables and the Home Office, which by and large ensured appointments were made on professional merit and not political influence. There were occasions when the system threatened to tip out of balance, but several High Court decisions (notably *Fisher v Oldham*, 1930, and *R v Metropolitan Police Commissioner, ex parte Blackburn*, 1968) established professional primacy of direction and control of forces over political influence. The dispute between the chief constable of Nottingham City, Athelstan Popkess, and the Nottingham Watch Committee, in 1959, however, demonstrated that the conventions that were developing concerning the professional control of forces were still equivocal. Popkess investigated borough councillors for alleged corruption. When this did not result in a prosecution the watch committee demanded to see the investigators' report. Popkess refused to hand it over and was suspended. He was eventually reinstated when Conservative Home Secretary, 'Rab' Butler, threatened to withhold the Home Office block grant. The controversy revealed the potential for political interference in operational matters, a problem seemingly settled by the 1964 Police Act which finally established that the 'direction and control' of forces would be in the hands of the chief constable, while a chief constable would be protected from arbitrary dismissal by the requirement that both the Home Secretary and the police authority consent before the dismissal became effective.[1]

The 1964 Act created a dynamic tension between the three elements of police governance. The Home Secretary possessed powers to regulate, promote general efficiency, and protect chief constables from arbitrary dismissal. Police authorities, replacing both watch committees (boroughs) and joint standing committees (counties), were responsible for providing for an efficient force, which in practice meant ensuring there was enough money, while chief constables managed forces and made operational decisions free from political interference. That police authorities were composed of both councillors and magistrates further mitigated against political interference. It was not that there was no place for politics in policing, but it was 'boxed off' and made safe. Politics could operate at a national

---

[1] Police Act 1964, ss 5 and 29.

level in terms of policy, as Mrs Thatcher demonstrated in 1979, but it could not operate at a local level to distort operational or managerial decisions.

In the 1970s, '80s, and '90s this was a source of some dissatisfaction amongst principally local Labour politicians, who either felt they had lost control and influence through the abolition of watch committees, or that they needed it to complete their dominance of every aspect of local government. Attempts to reinstate local political power were, however, resisted by successive Conservative home secretaries, and distanced still further by the Police and Magistrates' Courts Act 1994, by which police authorities were reduced in size and independent members were appointed in addition to magistrates, making political control of individual authorities practically impossible. It was the highpoint of depoliticization. However, the corollary of this depoliticization was that it allowed the Home Office to assume a dominant position over police governance, which when exercised by New Labour was a considerable motivation in Conservative plans to emasculate both the police professional element (which they only partly correctly assessed had become too close to Labour) and the Home Office through the medium of the elected single responsible person. That the people of England and Wales preferred their policing to come without undue political influence and control at the local level was demonstrated in a 'YouGov' survey conducted in the late summer of 2012 in which 61 per cent of those polled disapproved of candidates being supported by a political party, while 21 per cent said they were 'absolutely certain not to vote'.[2] It was hardly an auspicious introduction for a flagship Conservative policy.

Policing in the 21st Century: the consultation phase

As charted in Chapter 3, from 2002 onwards the Conservative Party became committed to the idea of introducing a single elected person to become responsible for the governance of local policing. The commitment appeared in the 2005 and the 2010 election manifestos. What did not appear was any detail about what precisely this would mean, how it would be constructed, or how it would work in practice. A late addition to the scheme was that the single elected individual, termed in *Policing in the 21st Century* the 'Police and Crime Commissioner' (PCC), would be to a degree counterbalanced by a 'Police and Crime Panel' (PCP), comprising principally representative local councillors but aided by two independent members, which would publicly scrutinize the work of the PCC.[3] *Policing in the*

---

[2] Royal United Services Institute, 'Yougov-Cambridge/RUSI Poll' (<http://www.rusi.org/news/ref:N506DFE0DF3F56/#.UL4SmqUx_Hj> [accessed 4 December 2012]).

[3] *Going Local* had recommended that the mayors and council leaders responsible for policing would be themselves subject to scrutiny by 'a policing committee and seek approval by elected assemblies and councils for the police budget and strategy.' The Police and Crime Panel therefore represented a significant shift from the direct local democratic control and scrutiny envisaged in *Going Local* (*Going Local*, 8).

21st Century provided some detail about the nature and scope of the new role. The PCC was to represent and engage with those who lived and worked in force areas; set the 'priorities' for the force; hold the chief constable to account for achieving the priorities; set the force budget, including the council tax precept, although this was qualified by the stated intention to make 'precept raising subject to referendum'; and finally 'appointing—and, where necessary, removing— the Chief Constable'.[4] PCCs were empowered to appoint 'a team to support them', but the government, in line with their philosophy, declined to be proscriptive about the detail. PCCs would serve a four-year term, probably elected by 'a preferential voting system'. The government pledged to 'work closely with local government representatives and the Electoral Commission to ensure that these elections are coordinated effectively and represent good value for money.' It is possible that the latter consideration came to dominate over ensuring the actual effectiveness of the elections themselves. It was expected that candidates would come 'from a wide range of backgrounds, including both representatives of political parties and independents.'[5]

Policing in the 21st Century from hereon became increasingly vague on detail, possibly as befitted a consultation document, but probably because the detail was not there to give. The chief constable would be held to account but retain 'operational independence' (not, at this stage, it will be noted, the more encompassing 'direction and control'). Commissioners would need to provide for local policing but balance this with 'cross boundary action', as well as deliver value for money.[6] Interestingly PCCs would have a wider role, coordinating partnership within the local criminal justice system. All this would be set in a national context where performance indicators would be slashed, bureaucracy and central guidance reduced, and new agencies would take responsibility for crime and police technology.

The PCP was to have a vital role in scrutinizing the work of the PCC. It was, however, to be no mere replication of the police authority; its job was to scrutinize the work of the PCC, not the force. It would advise the commissioner on his plans and budget. They would be empowered to summon the commissioner to hearings, take evidence, issue reports, and see all but 'operationally sensitive' papers sent to the commissioner. They would hold confirmation hearings for the post of chief constable and the commissioner's staff, but, confusingly, 'without the power of veto'. In a strange negation of the representative principle this unelected panel would have the power to 'trigger a referendum on the precept recommended by the Commissioner'. However, the 'public at the ballot box will be the ultimate judge of the success or failure of each Commissioner'.[7]

---

[4] Home Office, *Policing in the 21st Century* (TSO, London, 2010), 11.
[5] Home Office, *Policing in the 21st Century*, 12.
[6] Home Office, *Policing in the 21st Century*, 13.
[7] Home Office, *Policing in the 21st Century*, 14–15.

The consultation produced a mixed response. ACPO carefully did not oppose the government directly over the principle of the single elected individual but rather sought to define the limits of that office's powers and safeguard the professionalism of chief constables. Consequently, they argued that chief constables not only possessed 'operational independence' but also required 'direction and control' to enable them to 'run a force'. It accepted that commissioners could dismiss chief constables but sought safeguards to ensure it was 'a step of last resort based on a clear, evidenced, defensible, and fair basis only.' Unsurprisingly, it welcomed the ability of chief constables to appoint their own deputies and assistants. It thought the proposed PCC precept-raising powers too limiting. It broadly supported the remainder of the agenda—cutting bureaucracy, becoming less risk averse, creating a national crime agency—if with some qualifications. Although not asked the question, it returned to its old theme from the 2000s and argued for amalgamations to deliver fewer but larger 'strategic forces', regarding the 2006 decision to abandon the proposals as simply the scheme becoming 'stalled'. Conscious that it was not the government's favourite professional association, it argued that it should retain 'the professional leadership of the Service and have overarching responsibility for doctrine in its revised format.'[8] This last point was to prove a vain hope, as was any expectation that the Coalition would revive the politically disastrous policy of amalgamations.

The other staff associations similarly did not challenge the government on the principle of PCCs, although both sought reassurances about political independence. Unison, the principal civilian employee union, was concerned about its members being employed by a 'corporation sole', whether by the PCC or chief constable, but otherwise did not object to the principle of the single elected individual. It is unlikely that the government would have been disturbed if all three associations had objected to the principle and practice, but it was useful, at least, to have no substantial objections from those sources. More serious were the objections to both principle and detail from the Labour-led coalition Welsh Government. Coming to an agreement with the Welsh Government was essential given that it had a distinct legal role in community safety partnerships, responsibility for which in England would devolve to the commissioner.[9] What should have been of equal concern was what lay behind an anecdote related by Carl Sergeant, the Minister for Social Justice and Local Government.

---

[8] ACPO, *Response to Policing in the 21st Century: Reconnecting Police and the Public* (<http://www.acpo.police.uk/documents/HO_Consultation_Response.pdf> [accessed 21 November 2012]), *passim*.

[9] Welsh Government, Oral statement—The Welsh Assembly Government's response to the Home Office consultation on the Police Reform and Social Responsibility Bill (<http://wales.gov.uk/about/cabinet/cabinetstatements/2010/101012police/?lang=en> [accessed 22 November 2012]).

We must ask who wants police commissioners. When I have spoken to residents in Flintshire, no-one has ever said to me, 'What we really need, Carl, is a police commissioner.' What they have said is that they want to see more bobbies on the beat. Therefore, I suggest that the Home Secretary would be better off spending her time trying to protect police numbers rather than dabbling with bureaucracy.[10]

The Association of Police Authorities (APA) rejected the logic behind the idea of being replaced by elected commissioners, providing evidence that most of the public knew about their police authority and understood its role, but, recognizing the way the wind was inevitably blowing, undertook to 'engage constructively with the Home Office over the coming months.' Nevertheless, it stated that its own consultation exercise had found that the public were concerned about the 'injection of overt party politics into policing—the election process of a single individual will mean a single party representative or individual interest taking decisions on policing. This will inevitably give rise to a short-term focus, local political conflict, and tensions with partners.'[11] The Local Government Association (LGA) had no problems with increased local accountability, it simply though that it should be local councillors who should provide it.[12] The civil liberty organization 'Liberty', while agreeing with the principle that the police governing body should be more visible and accountable, thought the current system could be adapted to provide it, and considered the proposed change to a single elected individual a step too far. The new post, furthermore, risked politicization, and that, even if only by perception, was a risk not worth taking.[13] There were other responses in similar vein, but in reality nothing was going to make any difference. The Home Office might tweak some detail, as it would over ensuring that 'direction and control' was retained rather than 'operational independence', in the subsequent draft bill, but it was never going to compromise on the principal issue of substance; there would be a single elected individual responsible for police governance, come what may.[14]

---

[10] Welsh Government, Oral statement (see n 9).

[11] APA, *Response to Policing in the 21st Century: Reconnecting Police and thePublic* (APA, London, 2001), 3, 10, and 11.

[12] LGA, *Local Government Association Response to Policing Consultation Paper* (<http://centrallobby.politicshome.com/members/member-press/member-press-details/newsarticle/local-government-association-response-to-policing-consultation-paper///sites/local-government-association/> [accessed 22 November 2012]).

[13] Liberty, *Liberty's Response to the Home Office Consultation Policing in the 21st Century: Reconnecting Police and the People* (<http://www.liberty-human-rights.org.uk/pdfs/policy10/policing-in-the-21stc-reconnecting-the-people-and-the-police-sept-2010.pdf> [accessed 22 November 2012]), 17 and 19.

[14] Home Office, *Policing in the 21st Century: Reconnecting Police and the People: Summary of Consultation Responses* (<http://www.homeoffice.gov.uk/publications/consultations/policing-21st-century/response-policing-21st?view=Binary> [accessed 22 November 2012]), 3.

The passage of the Police Reform and Social Responsibility Bill

The bill that was introduced into the Commons at the end of November 2010 comprised three principal parts. The first part contained the government's proposals for constitutional change to police governance; the second a series of measures to 'rebalance the Licensing Act 2003 in favour of local communities', including raising a 'late-night levy' to cover the cost of extra policing associated with the night-time economy; the third, miscellaneous measures including those to control Parliament Square. It is the first set of measures, concerning police governance that concerns us here.

The initial stages of the bill's progress in the Commons were completed without undue incident for the government. The Coalition was always likely to have a relatively easy passage in terms of votes at this stage but it was an opportunity for the Labour opposition to at least place on record some of its concerns in a coherent fashion. It failed to do this. Part of the problem for Labour is that it neither seemed certain of defending the status quo or presenting a practical alternative. Former police minster Hazel Blears came closest in presenting that alternative.

> I have real concerns, however, about the idea of electing a single individual who is not connected to the rest of the local governance arrangements for the provision of public service...One way of achieving the greater visibility for policing...would be having a directly elected person in each local authority area who would be responsible for local policing but would also have a duty to operate within the rest of the local public service framework to mobilise all those resources to make communities safer. Those directly elected local commissioners could act collectively at force level to hold chief constables to account and to provide direct, local links to their communities. I am genuinely concerned about the ability of a single police and crime commissioner to be visible and accountable to 2.5 million people across Greater Manchester in communities as diverse as those in Rochdale, Wigan, Stockport, Oldham, Manchester city centre and Salford. I wonder whether the Minister has considered having directly elected local commissioners. There is all the rhetoric about localism, but then this policy of having a single police and crime commissioner for millions of people. That is not localism.[15]

The weakness of her position was that she had not taken the opportunity to deliver such a change when in office. The reality was that the status quo, of a small police authority comprising councillors nominated by their party leaders from within the higher-tier constituent councils of the force area, and independent members selected essentially by the police authority itself, was difficult to defend. The struc-

---

[15] parliament.uk, Police Reform and Social Responsibility Bill—second reading, 13 December 2010, columns 748–9 (<http://www.publications.parliament.uk/pa/cm201011/cmhansrd/cm101213/debtext/101213-0002.htm> [accessed 22 November 2012]).

ture (ironically) established by Conservative Home Secretary Michael Howard had essentially worked well, but could make no claim to encapsulating the principles of local democracy and active citizenship now being championed by David Cameron's new Conservatives. Labour in government had brought forward plans to introduce a directly elected element into police authorities but had abandoned them when the difficulties seemed to outweigh the benefits. There was a democratic deficit in terms of police governance and the government had a clear plan to address it; at this stage the opposition did not. As expected, the government secured a comfortable majority.

The bill received intense scrutiny during its committee stage but only a small number of clauses were altered. One that was, however, was of critical importance in defining the new relationship between the new commissioner and the chief constable. Under the Police Act 1996, responsibility for drafting and preparing the authority's strategic plan rested with the chief constable. Although that still left the authority scope to alter it, in practice the guiding hand in preparing the plan was the chief constable's. Even then the chief constable needed only to 'have regard' for the plan, which meant that he was not required to implement the plan if circumstances or his judgement suggested otherwise. This was rarely the case, but the ability to veer from the plan was there if required. The new bill as originally drafted did not merely preserve that ability; it extended it. In the original wording of clause 5, the plan could not be accepted without the effective approval of the chief constable. Given the fundamental purpose of the bill—to extend the influence of the representative element of governance over the executive—it was an extraordinary inclusion, and must have been a drafting error. It was removed in the committee stage and the wording adjusted so that while the chief constable had to be consulted about the plan he could not exercise a veto. Moreover, the chief constable was no longer required to prepare the draft, although in practice the commissioner might invite him to do so. It was a subtle but important shift in influence away from the chief constable and towards the commissioner. However, the chief constable, legally at least, still need only 'have regard' for the plan, although the Home Secretary would be empowered to issue guidance 'about how that duty is to be complied with'. In the intricate wording of such clauses, however, the parties involved (ie the PCC and the chief constable) need only 'have regard' to that guidance.[16] Similar amendments were made for the Metropolitan Police, where the Mayor of London would fulfil the functions of the PCC but be enabled to delegate them to the 'Deputy Mayor for Policing and Crime', whom he would appoint.

Labour's attitude towards the bill in its early Commons stages was ineffective, presumably reflecting its intellectual uncertainty as to how to respond.

---

[16] parliament.uk, Police Reform and Social Responsibility Bill, Revised second marshaled list of amendments to be moved in committee (<http://www.publications.parliament.uk/pa/ld201011/ldbills/062/amend/ml062-iir.htm> [accessed 23 April 2013]).

The House of Lords, however, had more time to adjust to the process and to be lobbied by effective external organizations opposed to the principles of the bill.[17] Many peers were also acutely aware of their role as guardians of the unwritten constitution. In the debate on the bill's second reading in April 2011, the contributions from the peers were evenly matched between government supporters and those opposed, comprising a loose alignment of Labour, some Liberal Democrats, and cross-bench peers. For the government, Baroness Neville-Jones argued that the bill was about increased accountability and local control, but those opposed countered that the government had not established its case. As former Labour Home Office Minister, now cross-bench peer Lord Elystan-Morgan expressed:

> The problem is not what has been identified but the solutions that are now proposed. They are disastrous. The idea of introducing a civil commissar, for that is what it will be, into this situation will jeopardise the future of the police service—the best police service in the world. It is a police service whose development we have been very proud of over the last 175 years.[18]

The bill passed its formal second reading and proceeded to committee, but the government should have been wary that opposition might yet build. Normally, the government could have expected the Lords to observe the 'Salisbury Convention' by which they would not reject, although might amend in detail, a proposal contained in the government's general election manifesto; but did the convention apply in this case? It was doubtful because the government was a coalition and the manifesto commitment by the Conservatives was vague and devoid of detail. It gave the Upper House an opportunity to exercise considerable discretion in its observance of the government's democratic mandate.

The Lords considered the bill again in early May and on its presentation Liberal Democrat Baroness Harris of Richmond, a former chair of the APA, immediately proposed an 'amendment' which effectively wrecked the government's measure. Instead of being directly elected, the commissioner would be elected by the police and crime panel from amongst its members. It was not an ideal amendment, but that it was accepted at all was a measure of the Lords' concern. The scale of the defeat was 176 for the government and 188 against, but the latter total included thirteen Liberal Democrats, thirty-seven cross-benchers, and four bishops.[19] In the stages that followed, the Lords were far from cowed by the government's intention

---

[17] Including the 'Campaign Against Political Policing', of which I was a member and for which I prepared briefing papers.

[18] Police Reform and Social Responsibility Bill—second reading (<http://www.theyworkforyou.com/lords/?id=2011-04-27a.128.0> [accessed 28 November 2012]).

[19] 'Police commissioners plan has its "heart ripped out" by Lords', *The Telegraph*, 11 May 2011 (<http://www.telegraph.co.uk/news/uknews/law-and-order/8508212/Police-commissioners-plan-has-its-heart-ripped-out-by-Lords.html> [accessed 28 November 2012]) and University College, London, Constitution Unit, 'Government defeat in Lords on police reform and social responsibility bill' (<http://www.ucl.ac.uk/constitution-unit/research/parliament/house-of-lords/defeats_tabs/2011-defeat-16.pdf> [accessed 28 November 2012]).

to reassert the critical clauses and enforced their decision to create 'a police commission' rather than a single commissioner.

The government accepted some minor amendments but the biggest single effect of the Lords' tactics, however, was to provoke a rethink by the government of the timing of the elections. When the Home Secretary announced her intention to reinstate the bill's principal measures, she added that the elections would be delayed from May 2012, when they coincided with the routine local elections, until 15 November 2012. She informed the Home Affairs Committee that the new date was a direct consequence of the Lords' amendments, but the BBC reported that it was the result of lobbying from the Liberal Democrats, ostensibly because they wished to 'depoliticize' the vote. There was, however, the suggestion that the delay was to protect the Liberal Democrats as the coincidence of the local elections and the elections for PCCs would prove electorally disadvantageous for them. The delay was to prove a significantly negative factor when it came to the turnout for the new elections, and was to serve no useful purpose in protecting the Liberal Democrats.[20]

The government was clearly annoyed by the effectiveness of the Lords' opposition and determined to ensure that the principle of the single elected individual was ultimately carried. The bill came back to the Lords in September and after a three-hour debate, described by one participant as 'occasionally heated by House of Lords standards', the result was a tied vote. A tie meant a government victory. It was an unsatisfactory outcome in many respects, as Lord Harris of Haringey, an opponent of the bill, observed with resignation: 'My Lords, this Bill leaves a situation in which there are no proper governance arrangements around directly elected individuals with the most amazing and strong powers in respect of policing, one of the most vital services in our country. I am sorely tempted to divide the House again but I recognise that there are only so many times that a dead horse can be flogged.'[21] For better or worse, the government had succeeded in securing its prized principle of a single elected individual to be locally responsible for policing.

The Police Reform and Social Responsibility Act 2011

When the excitement of the Act's passing had died down, exactly what had the government succeeded in enacting?

---

[20] BBC News, 'Lib Dems urge police election delay to help councillors', 7 September 2011 (<http://www.bbc.co.uk/news/uk-politics-14819550> [accessed 29 November 2012]) and P Strickland, *Police Reform and Social Responsibility Bill—House of Lords Amendments* (House of Commons Library, Home Affairs Section, 8 September 2011 <http://www.parliament.uk/briefing-papers/SN06063.pdf> [accessed 29 November 2012]), 6–7.

[21] Lord Toby Harris, 'A tied vote means that the government's Police Reform and Social Responsibility Bill will get Royal Assent tomorrow and become law' (<http://www.lordtobyharris.org.uk/2011/09/> [accessed 29 November 2012]) and parliament.uk, 14 September 2011, Police reform and social responsibility bill, Commons amendments (<http://www.publications.parliament.uk/pa/ld201011/ldhansrd/text/110914-0002.htm> [accessed 29 November 2012]).

The first principal element was the replacement of the collective body responsible for the governance of provincial police forces, the police authority, with a single elected individual.[22] That in itself would have been a significant change, but it was not a like-for-like replacement; a commissioner would have more power than the police authority. Furthermore, it represented a fusion of executive and representative governance functions in way which was unique in the British constitution, at either the national or local level. Any comparison with the office of elected mayor in unitary local authorities was misplaced. A commissioner's statutory authority exceeded that of an elected mayor by some quantum. An elected mayor is not a corporation sole, does not directly appoint chief officers, must work with a cabinet, and must work with a council to decide where certain powers remain, including council tax and budget setting. The commissioner would, on the other hand, receive the Home Office main and other central grants and set the council tax, although that would be subject, as will be examined in more detail later, to a potential veto by the PCP, a potential referendum of local council taxpayers, and reserve powers to the Home Secretary to require a minimum budget if it was thought necessary 'to prevent the safety of people in that area from being put at risk'. The degree to which that budget was devolved to the chief constable to use for direct policing purposes, as opposed to the commissioner's own office and staff, was for the commissioner to determine, and opened up the possibility of a commissioner extending their direct control of police civilian staff beyond that strictly necessary to run their own arrangements. The commissioner would also be responsible for preparing and issuing a 'police and crime plan'. There remained the requirement for the commissioner to consult with the chief constable, but the balance of power had subtly but significantly tipped away from the professional towards the representative functions of police governance.

Chief constables were to remain responsible for the 'direction and control' of their forces, but the Act now sought to define and set limits to the extent of that direction and control. In future, chief constables would be required to exercise direction and control 'in such a way as is reasonable to assist the relevant police and crime commissioner to exercise the commissioner's functions.' The independence gained under the 1968 *Blackburn* judgment had not exactly been overturned but 'direction and control' powers had been set in new context. The commissioner was required to 'send' the plan to the PCP and to 'have regard to any report or recommendations' it made. The commissioner had to send a copy of the plan to 'responsible bodies', ie the statutory partners, under the Crime and Disorder Act 1998. There was no requirement to consult with them.

The plan was to contain the commissioner's objectives; the ambiguously worded 'policing of the area which the chief officer is to provide'; the 'financial

---

[22] Unless shown otherwise all references to the provisions of the Act in this section are to be found in the Police Reform and Social Responsibility Act 2011, *passim*, Statutory Instruments, Police, England and Wales, The Policing Protocol Order 2011, *passim*, and College of Policing, *Guidance for the Appointment of Chief Officers* (<http://www.acpo.police.uk/documents/reports/2012/201212 guid-appt-chief-off-cop.pdf> [accessed 6 August 2013]), *passim*.

and other' resources the commissioner intended to provide to the chief officer; the means by which the chief officer was to report to the commissioner; and the means by which the chief officer's performance would be measured. In another extension of role and power, the commissioner's plan would also include how crime and disorder grants would be allocated and any conditions that might be attached to them, such as, presumably, payment by results. This last was intended to place PCCs at the centre of what had hitherto often been a somewhat disparate crime and disorder partnership effort. In the legal intricacies of such legislation, the commissioner was to have 'regard' for their own plan, as was the chief constable, although that was presumably set in the overriding context of the duty to assist the commissioner in the discharge of their functions. In developing the plan the commissioner had, as with the requirements of the Police Act 1996, to obtain the views of the community, to which the new Act, in maybe a touch of populist politics, specifically added 'victims of crime'. The commissioner was to publish information about his and the chief constable's role, produce an annual report, and supply information to the PCP, save for that which might be against national security, jeopardize the safety of any person, or 'prejudice' the prevention or detection of crime.

On a more technical level, a commissioner was to be a 'corporation sole', which enabled them to employ staff and enter into contracts. So too was the chief constable. The commissioner could appoint one or more deputy commissioners, one of whom in extremis might become commissioner in the event of an unforeseen vacancy, there being no provision for interim elections outside the prescribed election schedules. It would only be possible to remove a commissioner between elections for misconduct or criminality. In the Metropolitan Police area the powers and responsibilities were assigned to the London Mayor who could, and did, delegate them to a 'Deputy Mayor for Policing and Crime'. In deference to the unstated power of the City of London Corporation, the Common Council would continue as the responsible body for the City Police.

The second key element was the shift in the balance of power from the professional element of police governance—the chief constable, to the representative— the commissioner. Much was made of the ability of the commissioner to appoint and dismiss the chief constable. No indication in the legislation was given as to the dynamics of the appointment process, but here again was a subtle but significant power shift from the professional to the local representative. Previously, under the 1964 Act, the Home Secretary had ultimately approved chief constable appointments, although this had been slightly modified after the Police Reform Act 2002, where the Home Secretary delegated power to the Senior Appointments Panel (SAP). In practice the interests of the Home Secretary and SAP were also overseen in the actual shortlisting and appointment process by the physical presence of a local HM Inspector of Constabulary (HMI) to advise the police authority. The final choice of a candidate was the authority's, but by that point their choice had been focused by the central powers. These provisions and practices had originally been introduced to ensure that chief officers were of a required standard of education, experience, and capability. Under the new Act these central powers, some might argue safeguards, were dispensed with.

However, the Home Office did not quite give the commissioners carte blanche to do as they pleased. The Home Secretary could still issue guidance, and what turned out to be the first under the new regime related to the appointment of chief officers. For a government supposedly committed to slashing bureaucracy and localism it was a remarkably detailed work. The guidance considerably restricted the ability of commissioners to choose whom they wished. Only those who had served as a 'constable' in the United Kingdom were eligible for selection, thus ruling out wild-card American appointments. Candidates had to have successfully completed extended assessment and attended the NPIA Strategic Command Course (SCC). PCCs were expected to convene a selection panel, with at least one an independent member. There was an expectation that they would also obtain the advice of a senior police professional via the newly established College of Policing (under the previous arrangements this would have had to have been an HMI; by now the choice was wider). In theory at least, the appointments had to be made on the principles of 'merit, fairness, and openness', and, of course, not even PCCs could escape the requirements of equal opportunities law. After the appointment the successful choice was subject to a confirmation hearing before the PCP, one of the tasks of which was to confirm that the process had been conducted in accordance with the principles of merit, openness, and fairness. The PCP could veto an appointment, but that would require a two-thirds majority. On the other hand, it could, with a lower voting threshold, make a recommendation, although the commissioner was only obliged to accept the veto. An interesting situation would occur if the PCP rejected a candidate by a majority but one of less than two-thirds. Would the commissioner proceed with the appointment, and what kind of mandate would the commissioner's appointee possess? Presumably to allow for such situations, reserve candidates were permitted. The guidance also applied to chief constables for their appointments of assistants and deputies, and, with suitable adjustments, applied to London. The sum total was that while in theory the commissioners had freedom of choice, and, indeed, they may have had the dominant role in the process, in practice their choice was hemmed in by a series of procedural restrictions, checks, and balances. It was as if the Home Office suddenly lost confidence in the underlying principle of localism.

The new Act appeared to give commissioners sweeping powers to dismiss chief constables. Under the 1964 Act chief constables could be retired by the Home Secretary in the interests of 'efficiency'. This was extended under the 1996 Police Act to 'efficiency and effectiveness', and the police authority could initiate the process, although final approval remained with the Home Secretary. There had, furthermore, to be a 'process' which required the initiating party to establish a case for inefficiency or ineffectiveness before a tribunal. It was a safeguard against arbitrary dismissal by political powers. That dismissing a chief constable for such equivocal reasons was hard to do was demonstrated by the failure of the assertive

David Blunkett while Home Secretary to dismiss the chief constable of Humberside, David Westwood, for failings in intelligence and record-keeping in the case of Ian Huntley, a school caretaker responsible for the murder of two young girls in 2002. Under section 38 of the new Act such inhibitions were swept aside. The commissioner could suspend (usually, but not invariably, an irrevocable step in itself) a chief constable and 'call upon' him to 'resign or retire'. If so called upon 'the chief constable must resign or retire'. Schedule 8 to the Act placed some restrictions on the commissioner. The PCP possessed a right of scrutiny, and until the scrutiny period of six weeks had elapsed the dismissal would not become effective. The commissioner was required to give the chief constable reasons in writing for requiring him to resign or retire, but no reasons, such as effectiveness or efficiency, need be specified. The chief constable could make representations to the panel, which *might* consult with the relevant HMI, but which must hold a hearing. However, at the end of the process the panel was only able to make a recommendation to the commissioner, which the commissioner might or might not accept. It was a thin thread by which to hang the continuation of a career, especially if the majority of the panel were of the same political allegiance as the commissioner. At the end of 2012, neither the Home Office nor the Police Advisory Board (PAB) had issued any additional guidance, so it appeared that PCCs had been given considerably more discretion when it came to dismissing chief constables than when appointing them.

This was not the end of the chief constable's vulnerability to local political whim. Since 1995 all chief officer appointments had been made subject to fixed term appointments (FTAs). These were abandoned for assistant chief constables when it was found they were a disincentive to leaving the security of the superintending ranks, but they remained for chief and deputy chief constables. Now the authority for extending appointments for chief constables devolved to the commissioners, and nor was this subject to PCP veto. A chief constable needing an extension to achieve pension eligibility was highly vulnerable to the power of the PCC. It was not even necessary for the PCC to formally refuse an extension request; a mere threat of termination might be sufficient to induce more compliant behaviour in the chief constable's exercise of their direction and control powers. As some compensation, chief constables for the first time possessed authority to appoint their assistants and deputies, and gained similar powers as commissioners to dismiss and extend FTAs. It was, however, small compensation for the diminished independence of the office of chief constable.

In another accretion of executive power which exceeded police authorities, commissioners possessed authority to distribute 'crime and disorder reduction grants'. This gave them considerable influence over partner bodies in their area. Also PCCs and 'criminal justice bodies' (which included the chief constable, the CPS, the courts, youth offending teams, and contractors) in the area were required, 'so far as it is appropriate to do so', to make arrangements for 'the exercise of functions so as to provide an efficient and effective criminal justice system for the police area'. In theory at least the Police and Crime Commissioner was given a role that could, if working well, increase effective cooperation between crime and disorder reduction partners and the criminal justice agencies. The extent to which this would occur would not, however, be attributable to legislation but to individual personalities and organizational culture. This was the closest the legislation came to achieving the synergies of governance between the police and local government that Loveday and Reid saw as so important in *Going Local* in 2003. Whatever the merits of that idea, the 2012 Act fell some way short of it.

The third key element in the Act was the creation of the PCP. As has been seen, it possessed important scrutinizing roles and certain reserve powers of veto. However, the functions of the panel were set in the context under section 28 of 'supporting the effective exercise of the functions of the police and crime commissioner'. It was the job of the constituent local authorities of the police area (including district authorities) to establish the PCP, which was to comprise one representative from each constituent local authority up to a theoretical maximum of ten. The councillor members were then to co-opt two independent members (more if the Home Secretary permitted and as long as the overall size of the panel did not exceed twenty). The representation of political parties was left very much to the constituent local authorities to sort out, although if agreement could not be reached the Home Secretary could make a determination. In theory there was no obligation for local authorities in Wales to participate because responsibility for local government there rested with the devolved government, but in the end the Welsh Government voluntarily conformed.

The panel had the power to review the plan and decisions made by the commissioner, require information, and question the commissioner about it, hold advise and consent-style scrutiny hearings over chief constable appointments by the commissioner, and potentially veto the appointment subject to a two-thirds majority, and similarly veto the council tax precept. The relationship was principally with the commissioner, but the PCP could require members of his staff to attend, but only invite the chief constable. The business of the panel would be principally conducted in public. While the panel had considerable reserve powers, in theory, the question as to how they might be used in practice remained the unknown factor. With the threshold set at a two-thirds majority to veto either a budget or appointment of a chief constable, in most cases a commissioner should get their way. The business of the commissioner would be considerably aided if the majority of panel members were of the same political party as the commissioner; conversely it could be commensurately hindered if the commissioner was of a different party, or none. Ultimately, the PCP might scrutinize and criticize, but it had no power to 'recall' a commissioner and instigate a mid-term election for poor decisions. The only grounds for dismissing a PCC were if the commissioner had been convicted of an 'imprisonable' offence.

Crucially, the routine decision-making of the governing body would not neccessarily be conducted in public, as was the case with police authorities. Panels might scrutinize, and in doing so facilitate or present difficulties for the commissioner, but in the preceding decision-making deliberation would not be subject to the natural scrutiny of the public conduct of principal business. Furthermore, while the commissioner could hold the chief constable to account for the force's conduct and performance, it was not specified how he would do so.

In sum, the Police Reform and Social Responsibility Act 2011 represented a massive constitutional shift—from the professional to the representative; from the apolitical to the political; and from the centre to the local. But there was an irony in this. Much of the foundation of the very idea of elected commissioners was based upon the ideas developed by Loveday and Reid in *Going Local*. Their rationale stemmed largely from the supposed success of US models of police governance. In the run up to the elections of November 2012, frequent reference was made to 'US-style elected commissioners'. Only in its vaguest outlines could the system of governance developed in the Police Reform and Social Responsibility Act be described as 'US'. As far as it is possible to generalize about US police governance, local police chiefs are either directly elected sheriffs, or commissioners holding direction and control powers similar to those of British chief constables, accountable either to a mayor or a police board appointed by the mayor. The appointment of Bill Bratton by Mayor Giuliani was frequently hailed as the near apotheosis of the arrangement. It might have come as a shock to some, had they been ready to listen, when in November 2010 Bratton gave evidence to the Home Affairs Committee that with 17,000 police departments in the USA 'there is no generic American police system', and the system being developed in England and Wales did not conform to any of them. Such was the esteem in which elected Westminster politicians held him, barely a year later he was back giving evidence again. This time they should certainly have been listening. When asked 'what kind of turnout of the electorate would show that the Commissioner is credible', he ominously replied:

> I know in my country unfortunately it is abysmally low. I think it will come to the idea of how aggressive the campaigning is for the positions, how much they are publicised and then certainly, because it is going to be something that is so significant, the issue of public safety, the first obligation of government and the first thing that the public expects of government, that I would hope that the turnout would be very large to basically determine who was going to be guiding public safety in any one of your communities.[23]

In the event England and Wales would definitely copy the US style in at least one respect.

---

[23] Home Affairs Committee, Examination of witnesses, 30 November 2010 (<http://www.publications.parliament.uk/pa/cm201011/cmselect/cmhaff/645/10113002.htm> [accessed 29 November 2012]) and 11 October 2011 (<http://www.publications.parliament.uk/pa/cm201012/cmselect/cmhaff/1456/11101101.htm> [accessed 29 November 2012]).

PCC elections, November 2012

Officially the Home Office wished to encourage a wide variety of candidates to stand for election as PCCs, and their pre-election publicity suggested that the essential qualities for candidates were to want to 'play a leading role in how crime is tackled in your area', 'bring the voice of the people into policing and bring the community together to tackle crime', and 'hold the Chief Constable and police force to account for reducing crime'. Additionally it was necessary 'to have a commitment to public service and the skills to be a good leader'. Little was said about the executive requirements to handle large budgets, build complex alliances, absorb personal and political criticism, and make senior appointments. Mention was made of the statutory restrictions—candidates must be British, Commonwealth, or EU citizens (thereby eliminating Bratton or other US possibilities), not convicted of an imprisonable offence, or holding certain public offices and employment, including police officers and the judiciary. Sitting MPs could stand but would resign before accepting appointment as PCC.[24] Presumably mindful of the commitment in *Policing in the 21st Century* to deliver elections which represented 'value for money', in framing the regulations under which the November elections would take place the Home Secretary declined to provide financial support for printed publicity to be distributed to each elector's address, leaving the principle means of electoral information to be found on the Internet. In theory this restriction should have benefitted candidates representing the main political parties. The Home Office would provide a website where candidates could place election statements ('choosemypcc.com'), but this was not sufficient to prevent criticism from the Electoral Commission, the official body charged with overseeing the fairness of elections. The criticism later extended to a publicity campaign (notably a series of embarrassing television advertisements) mounted by the Home Office to increase awareness of the elections themselves.[25] Notwithstanding this late publicity campaign and behind–the-scenes, high-level government encouragement of mainstream media to increase its pre-election coverage (to which only the BBC of the broadcast media seriously responded), it became a matter of growing concern that the turnout would be as low as 18 per cent, which would make it easily the worst turnout for any election. Not least amongst its concerns was the decision to restrict publicity and hold the election in November.[26] A low turnout was likely to create a series of volatile results, as would the large size of the electoral areas (far larger than

---

[24] Home Office, *Have You Got What it Takes?* (<http://www.homeoffice.gov.uk/publications/police/pcc/have-got-what-takes/got-what-it-takes?view=Binary> [accessed 30 November 2012]).

[25] Election Commission, Media briefing (<http://www.electoralcommission.org.uk/__data/assets/pdf_file/0011/151769/PCC-Media-Briefing-Nov-2012-FINAL-2.pdf> [accessed 30 November 2012]).

[26] C Urquhart, 'Police commissioner polls could have "record low" turnout', guardian.co.uk, 18 August 2012 (<http://www.guardian.co.uk/uk/2012/aug/18/police-commissioner-elections-low-turnout> [accessed 30 November 2012]).

Westminster Parliament constituencies) and the use of the supplementary vote system.

Such concerns did not, however, ultimately restrict the number of independent candidates, which despite having to largely fund themselves, in the end totalled fifty-four, with all but seven areas having at least one standing. The Conservative and Labour Parties fielded candidates in each area, but the Liberal Democrats, expecting poor results, fielded candidates in only twenty-three areas, one less than UKIP. Over half the total candidates were or had been elected politicians in one form or another, while thirty-two had had some form of police service, although only two had served at chief officer rank (an assistant and a deputy); sixteen had served in the armed services.[27] Regardless of political alignment, there was a degree of blandness about the candidates' statements contained on the website, with generalizations about 'community', 'engagement', 'victims', 'cutting crime', and 'bobbies on the beat' prevailing. Some Labour candidates were specific about rejecting the more extreme forms of outsourcing or privatization and fighting government cuts (over which they would have practically no influence), but very few of any party or alignment were specific about budgets or council tax. Some independents simply asked voters to support them because of their independence from political parties. It was to prove a relatively successful tactic.[28]

In the event, concerns about a low turnout were more than justified, with a national average of 15 per cent, the worst in British electoral history.[29] Retrospectively, the Electoral Reform Society produced a damning report, listing failures largely attributable to the government. It summarized:

> From the start, the PCC elections looked set to be an exercise in how not to run an election. The date of the election was moved from May to November creating the first barrier to voters turning out. Voters were then left in the dark about who they could vote for with a lack of centrally provided candidate information. Candidates were kept away by huge deposits, unclear eligibility rules, vast electoral districts and high campaign costs.[30]

To that litany might have been added a growing disillusionment with politics and the quality of some of candidates. For example, Lord Prescott for Labour in

---

[27] Association of Police and Crime Commissioners (APCC), Police and crime commissioners (<http://www.apccs.police.uk/page/pcc-candidates> [accessed 30 November 2012]); Mailonline, 19 November 2012 (<http://www.dailymail.co.uk/news/article-2233386/Landslide-victory-voter-apathy-The-nations-crushing-verdict-elections-police-chiefs--turnout-14.html> [accessed 16 December 2012]); and J Garland and C Terry, *How Not to Run an Election: The Police & Crime Commissioner Election* (<http://www.electoral-reform.org.uk/images/dynamicImages/How%20not%20to%20run%20an%20election.pdf>, [accessed 18 April 2013]), 22.

[28] APCC, 'What might police and crime commissioners do?' (<http://www.apccs.police.uk/fileUploads/PCC_election_results_2012/APCC_analysis_of_PCCs_priorities_201112.pdf> [accessed 30 November 2012]).

[29] N Walayat, 'All PCC election results', Election Oracle, 15 November 2012 (<http://www.marketoracle.co.uk/Topic21.html> [accessed 18 November 2012]).

[30] Garland and Terry, *How Not to Run an Election* (n 27), 5.

Humberside and Michael Mates for the Conservatives in Hampshire were always going to be controversial choices, and both lost on second preference votes; the Conservative and Labour candidates in Gloucestershire lacked any conspicuous relevant qualification or experience for their projected role; the defeated Labour candidate in Dyfed-Powys had been an unpopular Welsh Government agricultural minister. The number of candidates who were former MPs or councillors ('retreads' as they became known) and who were otherwise seeking to enter into a second political career via the PCC route, appeared as another contributory factor to low turnout.[31] Voter antipathy to the principle of elected commissioners appeared as another (if unquantifiable) factor, itself linked to deep-rooted rejection of potential politicization of the police.[32] Whatever the cause or causes, the low turnout brought into question the validity of even the successful candidates' mandate. The largest percentage of the electorate voting for a successful candidate was for Christopher Salmon in Dyfed-Powys but that represented only 8.3 per cent of those entitled to vote. At the other extreme Simon Hayes, the successful independent in Hampshire, secured only 3.26 per cent. Eight candidates, six of them independent, were returned as a result of the reallocation of second preference votes.[33]

Apart from the low turnout the 'big story' was the unexpected success of independent candidates, which were returned in twelve areas, including such a Labour stronghold as Gwent, and Conservative Gloucestershire.[34] The Conservatives were successful in sixteen areas, Labour in thirteen. No other party or alignment came close to success. In vote terms, however, it was Labour that polled best, with 1.6 million, the Conservatives second with 1.3 million, and then the independents with 1.1 million. The Liberal Democrats were beaten into fifth place by UKIP, although one independent, Winston Roderick in North Wales, was a member of the Liberal Democrats. As a Welsh-speaking Welshman in an area with high concentrations of Welsh speakers and Plaid Cymru voters there may, however, have been other contributory factors to his success. The use of the supplementary vote system probably cost the Conservatives seven successes and Labour two. The greatest successes for the independent cause were Ann Barnes in Kent, a high-profile chair of the police authority, Martin Underhill in Dorset, and Sue Mountstevens in Avon and Somerset. Ian Johnston's win in Gwent, although narrow, was remarkable given the inherent strength of Labour in the area.

---

[31] K Buchan, 'Labour wants "retreads" in top police jobs', express.co.uk, 11 November 2012 (<http://www.express.co.uk/posts/view/357400/Labour-wants-retreads-in-top-police-jobs/> [accessed 1 December 2012]). The term was coined by police minister Damian Green to describe several Labour candidates, but it could have applied to many others.

[32] Garland and Terry, *How Not to Run an Election* (n 27), 9.

[33] N Walayat, 'All PCC elections results, record low turnouts, birth of illegitimate police and crime commissioners', Election Oracle, 16 November 2012 (<http://www.marketoracle.co.uk/Article37567.html> [accessed 16 December 2012]) and Datablog, theguardian (<http://www.guardian.co.uk/news/datablog/2012/nov/16/pcc-election-results-police-crime-commissioners> [accessed 16 December 2012]).

[34] Guardian, Datablog and Walayat (see n 33).

There would be a dearth of professional expertise amongst the successful candidates, however. Twelve were former councillors, four former (or about to be) MPs. Twelve had served on police authorities. There were six successful candidates who had served at middle or junior police ranks, but only two had been chief officers (John Dwyer for the Conservatives in Cheshire and Ron Hogg for Labour in Durham). Five had a military background.[35] It would remain to be seen how all the non-politicians would deal with the rough-and-tumble world of local politics which they had now entered.

In pure electoral terms, both main parties had failed to motivate voters to vote in the first place, and then to vote for them. The Electoral Commission laid the blame for the fiasco firmly at the door of the government; impervious, the government blamed an allegedly disinterested media, although that appeared to be clutching at straws. In reality it was simply that the government and main parties had failed to tactically deliver the right ingredients for success in terms of turnout, and, strategically, the Conservative element of the Coalition had put great store in a policy to which the electoral public was either opposed in principle or entirely apathetic. The government should have initiated a fundamental review of both its strategy and tactics; convinced of its own correctness, it did neither.

Prognosis: towards a political police?

There was only a week between the elections and the PCCs replacing police authorities. There were already decisions to be made and policies which would have to be set in motion. Many already had to consider chief constable appointments. Such a degree of 'churn' at the highest ranks was unprecedented since the 1974 amalgamations, and was entirely the result of the advent of PCCs. Where vacancies had naturally occurred because of chief constables retiring or moving on, vacancies had been kept pending the outcome of the elections. With some the link was more direct. One chief constable, Tony Melville of Gloucestershire, cited the prospects of commissioners as his reason for precipitously retiring in May 2012. Another, Simon Ash of Suffolk, announced his intention to retire immediately after the results were known. In perhaps the shape of things to come, Colin Port of Avon and Somerset announced his retirement when his commissioner made it clear his FTA would not be automatically renewed, and then failed in his belated use of the judicial process to gain an extension.[36] The most high-profile 'casualty' of the new regime, however, occurred even before the elections, when some of the PCC candidates in West Yorkshire made it clear that, as a result of the

[35] Choose My PCC (<http://www.choosemypcc.org.uk/election-results> [accessed 1 December 2012]).
[36] E Koch, 'Avon and Somerset chief constable Colin Port "loses court action"' (<http://www.thisisbristol.co.uk/Avon-Somerset-Chief-Constable-Colin-Port-loses/story-17792208-detail/story.html#axzz2QqDSGi1v> [accessed 18 April 2013]).

chief constable Sir Norman Bettison's controversial association with the Hillsborough tragedy of 1989, he might be called upon to resign or retire. Sir Norman did not stay to find out which.[37]

This was only the start of the process. Because a moratorium had been placed on vacancies occurring in the months before the PCC elections, sixteen appointments were waiting to be made by early 2013. Others occurred in the months following, notably in Gwent where the independent PCC, Ian Johnston, called on his chief constable, Carmel Napier, to retire or resign, citing managerial reasons. Mrs Napier went but publically defended her managerial reputation, prompting a hearing before the Home Affairs Committee in June 2013. Although the affair was controversial, PCC Johnston had demonstrated the practical power and constitutional authority of the new post. Mrs Napier could have resisted the call to resign or retire and sought a hearing before the Police and Crime Panel. She did not.[38]

The new realities were plain. A chief constable was unlikely to survive long without the unequivocal support of their PCC, provided the PCC had the evidence and was procedurally correct. The case of the suspension of Lincolnshire's chief constable by the PCC, however, demonstrated that there were limits. In February the Lincolnshire PCC suspended the temporary chief constable pending an investigation into the chief constable's alleged involvement in 'an employment issue'. The chief constable, Neil Rhodes, did not take the matter lying down and appealed the suspension before the High Court. The result was his reinstatement after the High Court ruled the suspension was 'irrational and perverse'.[39] In the short term the matter was resolved in favour of the chief constable, but the question remained over the long-term sustainability of their working relationship.

Since the elections, more chief constable posts fell vacant with the result that by July 2013 twenty-two appointments had been made or were still pending.[40] As each chief constable vacancy was filled so more opened up in the subordinate management chain. Such senior managerial turnover could not but add to the general atmosphere of organizational uncertainty created since May 2010. On the other hand, it presented an opportunity for PCCs to appoint their own

---

[37] The West Yorkshire Police Authority also indicated that it wanted him to go. J Hall, 'West Yorkshire chief constable Sir Norman Bettison resigns following criticism of his conduct after the Hillsborough disaster', *The Independent*, 24 October 2012 (<http://www.independent.co.uk/news/uk/home-news/west-yorkshire-chief-constable-sir-norman-bettison-resigns-following-criticism-of-his-conduct-after-the-hillsborough-disaster-8224659.html> [accessed 16 December 2012]).

[38] BBC News, 2 July 2013, 'Ian Johnston: Carmel Napier "did not accept PCC's role"' (<http://www.bbc.co.uk/news/uk-wales-23147339> [accessed 4 July 2013], and 'Carmel Napier says she was "bullied" into leaving Gwent Police' (<http://www.bbc.co.uk/news/uk-wales-23154307> [accessed 4 July 2013]).

[39] BBC News, 29 March 2013, 'Chief Constable Neil Rhodes' suspension "irrational"' (<http://www.bbc.co.uk/news/uk-england-lincolnshire-21964844> [accessed 4 July 2013]).

[40] B Rix, 'Which Chief Constables were recruited by PCCs? And more...', 14 June 2013 (<http://www.bernardrix.com/2013/06/14/chief-constables/> [accessed 4 July 2013]).

choice chief constables. Of course, this opened up the prospect of different PCCs wanting to replace them with their own choices after the next scheduled PCC elections in 2016.

The newly elected commissioners were soon to find out what political world they had entered when, less than a month after the elections, criticism began to surface over the appointments that several had made as deputy commissioner or to their own personal staff. Examples were cited of Adam Simmonds, the successful Conservative in Northamptonshire, appointing seventeen staff, including four 'assistant' commissioners, for which there was no provision in the Act; the West Midlands Labour PCC, Bob Jones, appointing a sitting Birmingham city councillor; and Conservative Matthew Gore in Humberside appointing an East Riding councillor as his deputy. All these appointments were entirely legitimate, but that did not stop accusations of 'cronyism and empire-building' being levelled.[41]

The requirement to appoint a new chief constable would, of course, pitch the relationship between the PCC and the PCP into high profile, as would the other big decision pending in the autumn of 2012—what to do about council tax and the precept, particularly in the light of the Chancellor's Autumn Statement, which required further cuts in public spending. Bob Jones, the successful Labour PCC in the West Midlands, might have been predicted to have had a slightly easier time with the PCP there, with its fourteen members, eight of whom were Labour councillors, than Martin Surl, the independent PCC for Gloucestershire facing a twelve-strong PCP, seven of whom were Conservatives—the party that had so narrowly lost the PCC election. It was to turn out that the PCCs would get their choices for both, although not necessarily without adverse comment from the PCPs.[42]

Would future chief constables be appointed on the basis of political allegiance, actual or supposed? It would be a possibility. It would, of course, be against the sweep of police history since 1829, and it cannot be supposed that even those commissioners returned with party backing would always behave in a party political way, or, as the example of Gwent demonstrated, that commissioners with a police background would not be prepared to have a robust relationship with their chiefs; but this does not mean that the party allegiance of chief constable candidates would not play some part in some future appointments. It would be strange if PCCs were not to look for indications that a chief constable would not, as required by the 2011 Act and attendant protocol, support him in his role. That could include at least being 'on message' with the PCC's broad

---

[41] A Travis, 'Police and crime commissioners accused of power grab', the Guardian, 6 December 2012 (<http://www.guardian.co.uk/uk/2012/dec/06/police-commissioners-accused-of-power-grab> [accessed 18 April 2013]).

[42] For example see BBC News, 'New Gloucestershire chief constable appointment approved', 14 January 2013 (<http://www.bbc.co.uk/news/uk-england-gloucestershire-21019085> [accessed 18 April 2013]).

political standpoint. Besides, how, with minimal external supervision, would anyone outside a narrow circle find out what part party politics played?

Would chief constables be induced to direct and control their force in ways which would support the political ambitions of their PCCs, particularly near re-election times? Commissioners are required to take an oath of impartiality and cannot interfere operationally, but these factors are unlikely to be sufficient to prevent political influence in local policing. This would normally be done in subtle, behind-the-scenes ways, and it is difficult to see how at least the attempt could be prevented. A chief constable could always refuse to act or be influenced, but that might initiate either a dismissal process, which, while ultimately successful for the PCC, could be publically messy, or, more likely, a refusal to renew an FTA when the time came. Commissioners had, furthermore, fought elections on the basis of certain promises, often to ensure a more high-visibility police presence. The police protocol required chief constables to support commissioners in the attainment of their plan. By such incremental means could politicization be institutionalized.

Would the PCC stand by the chief constable after a controversial operation went wrong, even if the chief constable was in no way personally culpable? This could go either way, as commissioners might be reluctant to let their own appointees go in circumstances which might adversely reflect on their own judgement. The evidence of past events is that the chief constable could not rely on political backing going all the way if the going got really tough. A similar question might arise in the case of such controversial deployments as were seen in the Miners' Strike of 1984–5. Then, several Labour-dominated police authorities made their opposition plain to their chief constables either seeking or sending mutual aid, and the use to which it was put in negating the effects of secondary picketing. The chief constables were then able to shelter under the protective umbrella of the Home Secretary, who held an effective veto over an unreasonable dismissal, although this was insufficient to protect Alf Parrish, the chief constable of Derbyshire, who was suspended for alleged financial irregularities. The case was never established against him, but it was a prolonged suspension and he was eventually 'retired' by the Home Secretary in the 'interests of efficiency'. A chief constable might now have the ultimate right to deploy officers in politically sensitive circumstances, but would that be sufficient to protect him from a subsequent call to resign or retire, or the quiet failure to extend an FTA? On the balance of probabilities it would seem not, unless the Home Secretary threatened to withhold the main grant, as happened in the Popkess case of 1959. That would be, to say the least, a blunt instrument, and possibly in itself illegal, as the commissioner would not have exceeded their own powers, merely exercised them in a way that might be inconvenient to government.

Might the chief constable be invited to resign or retire for being too successful? This seems an unlikely outcome, but that, ironically, is exactly what happened to Bratton in New York when his profile began to exceed that of his boss, Mayor Giuliani. Chief constables in future would have to tread the delicate line between being powerful leaders of their own organizations to get the job done and deal with operational crises, and yet giving enough deference to allow the PCC to bask in success. The evidence from local government is that chief constables will have to spend more time than they have been used to in looking after their PCCs, even if this does not extend to overt political allegiance.

Will these worst cases happen in every PCC/chief constable relationship? That, on the balance of probabilities, is unlikely, and in many cases commissioners and chief constables will work harmoniously and successfully, but the early evidence is that considerations other than right, wrong, or competence will determine the attitude of at least some commissioners.

How effective will commissioners be and what will happen in the mid to long term? The principle behind introducing commissioners in the first place was, according to Conservative thinking, to reconnect the police and the public. This presupposed that the relationship needed reconnecting—for the evidence was, at best, scant—and that elected commissioners were the best way of reconnecting it if it did. While the focus may be on how the politics, both big and small, of the new arrangements work, the real test of success will be how the commissioners address the concerns of the public in their areas. In some cases that will be physically difficult. In Dyfed–Powys the commissioner has over 4,000 square miles to cover; the West Midlands commissioner must address, not merely represent, the needs of over 2.5 million people. Mrs May has said that the test for commissioners is by how much they reduce crime. With recorded crime at a twenty-year low that may not be how the electorate choose to assess the effectiveness of their commissioners, but simply how they feel they are being looked after. That requires addressing anti-social behaviour, and that in turn requires neighbourhood policing, the very sector of policing under most pressure as a result of the spending cuts. To be truly successful commissioners must also address the more difficult crime problems, such as serious and organized crime, sexual offences, and cyber bullying; issues that rarely surfaced in candidates' statements.

This leaves the question of what will happen to the police constitution after the next general election, theoretically due in 2015. It may be presumed that if the Conservatives remain in government the system will continue, at least in its principal features. However, that the Conservatives would remain in power after 2015 is at best doubtful given opinion poll evidence in late 2012.[43] However, if elected, either in a majority administration or coalition, Labour would be faced with a difficult challenge. It had opposed, if not very effectively, the idea of PCCs in principle. It might have been predisposed to continue with the system if it had been successful in the 2012 elections, but while it had polled best in terms of total vote, it lost in some areas where it could have been expected to win and gained a meagre total of only thirteen, one better than the independents. But if Labour wished to change the system, then to what? Going back to representative police

---

[43] YouGov, 'UKpollingreport', 16 December 2012 (<http://www.ukpollingreport.co.uk> [accessed 16 December 2012]).

authorities seems unlikely but could not be ruled out; altering to multi-member, directly elected police authorities would result in a structure that would be difficult to control and influence from the centre, which had been Labour's hallmark when last in power. For the time being that question had been outsourced to an 'Independent Police Commission' chaired by former Metropolitan Commissioner Lord Stevens, but with a general election due no later than May 2015 the answer was not one which could be long delayed.

However, whatever the long-term outcome, the sum total of the Coalition's policies in its first three years in office was to ensure that the police service would enter the next phase of its development with a weakened professional leadership and was more vulnerable to local political influence than at any time in its history. It also marked the beginning of a massive experiment in policing, which in terms of scale and speed was without precedent in British history. With the Scottish Government implementing a single Scottish force under effective central control and the Westminster government fusing executive and representative functions of governance in the single elected individual, the 'Tripartite System' was effectively dead in the Island of Great Britain. Only a residue remained, somewhat ironically given its chequered history, in Northern Ireland.

6

The new police landscape
Pay, conditions, and pensions

Introduction

Although constitutional 'reform', principally through directly elected individuals, lay at the heart of the Coalition's approach to policing, it was not the only
item of police reform on its agenda. In addition there was intended to be significant change to the national policing institutions, as well as to pay, pensions,
general conditions of service, policy-making, training, the investigation of serious and organized crime, and technology. As with other aspects of the Conservative element of the Coalition's police agenda, no one could say that they had not
been warned of what was coming; the changes had been well trailed, first in
David Cameron's Dalston Youth Project speech of January 2006, and then in the
interim report of the party's Police Reform Taskforce, *Policing for the People*, in
2008. By 2010 and *Policing in the 21st Century* the changes had become collectively known as 'the new police landscape'. This chapter will map its contours.
The sum total represents a curious mixture of some unfinished business from
earlier attempts at 'reform', some rearrangement masquerading as radical reform,
and a certain amount of the 'genuine article'.

The new Conservatives and police pay

As for much of his future plans, David Cameron set out his stall for his police
programme early in his leadership. In his Dalston Youth Project speech of January 2006 he stated clearly his intentions. Police chiefs needed to be able to manage 'workforces which are professional, flexible and incentivised to do their
job—fighting crime. That meant modernization.' Because the police did a difficult and dangerous job they would 'remain well rewarded', but 'reforms' would

be needed 'to equip the police to meet today's challenges'. In its generalities the programme he outlined was pretty vague and relatively uncontentious. There would be 'flexibility for pay and conditions'; a pension scheme designed so that 'people can join and leave at the right time and at the right level'; improved means to sack underperforming officers through 'modern employment contracts'; reduction in the number of officers on restricted duties; and, finally, limiting the number of part-time officers. On the potentially controversial matters of levels of basic remuneration, pay uplift, and what kind of pensions officers might receive, he was, unsurprisingly, silent, but astute observers would have noted what he did not say. There was no commitment to continue the Edmund-Davies pay formula or the final salary pension scheme.[1]

Cameron and his senior policy advisers might have reasonably assumed that changing, much less abolishing, index-linked pay uplift and the final salary police pension scheme might be fraught with danger. The police had what looked like a gold-plated pensions scheme, which recognized that much police work required a physical fitness that could not be guaranteed to last long past an individual's fiftieth year. From 1987 to 2006 the Police Pension Scheme (PPS) operated on the basis of an individual officer's eligibility for a full pension of two-thirds final salary after thirty years' service. For that the individual contributed 11 per cent of salary, a substantial amount for any sector of employment and certainly higher than comparisons with the military, nurses, teaching, or the civil service. Even so, the cost of police pensions was still estimated to be too high to be sustainable in the long term, and so in 2006 new regulations were introduced for officers joining after their introduction. The rate of contribution was reduced to 9.5 per cent but the length of service extended to thirty-five years before a full pension of half final salary was obtainable. Some analysts, however, believed that even that was unsustainable.[2]

Pensions were, however, 'a slow-burn' issue. Of more immediate relevance to officers and policy-makers alike was police pay. Since 1978 basic police pay had been largely 'parked' as a contentious issue because of the Edmund-Davies pay formula. This had been introduced to placate a massively demoralized workforce in the late 1970s, itself a result of the adverse effect of high inflation on police pay and the example of workers in other sectors gaining inflation-proof pay increases through strike action. Talk of strike action was enough to prompt Labour Home Secretary Merlyn Rees to institute the Edmund-Davies pay review and the creation of the face-saving average pay index formula. Whether the police would have pressed for a right to strike if Rees had toughed it out will never be known, but it was probably unlikely.

---

[1] 'David Cameron's speech on police reform', guardian.co.uk, 16 January 2006 (<http://www.guardian.co.uk/politics/2006/jan/16/conservatives.ukcrime1> [accessed 25 April 2012]).

[2] E Boyd, *Police Officer Pensions: Affordability of Current Schemes* (Policy Exchange policy briefing, <http://www.policyexchange.org.uk/images/publications/police%20officer%20pensions%20-%20feb%202012.pdf> [accessed 17 December 2012]).

The formula, brought in to address particular circumstances at a moment in time, determined police pay for more than thirty years. In the years that followed the formula protected the police from government cuts, although it only gave the police an annual increment based on an average of comparative pay settlements. It meant the police never led in terms of pay, but never lagged either. Edmund-Davies effectively neutralized pay as a cause of dispute between police and government, although this did not stop the Home Office seeking to modify the basis of the comparison from time to time in order to decrease the calculation of the average. The most serious and contentious attempt at a general change in police pay and conditions occurred in 1992–3 with the Sheehy Inquiry. Conservative Home Secretary Kenneth Clarke had formally instituted the inquiry in the full enthusiasm of the prevailing personnel management philosophy of the day. Sheehy's underlying principle was that pay should be related to skills, experience, role, and performance, and calculated according to a complicated pay matrix. Additionally, the number of ranks was to be reduced, and fixed term appointments introduced for all ranks, performance being a critical factor in re-engagement. Local negotiations would replace much currently determined by national police regulations, and pension entitlement would not be reached until forty years' service or age 60. Sheehy did not recommend abandoning an annual uplift by means of an index, merely that a lower index would be used.

It was too much to take in one go, and provoked a near-frenzied reaction amongst junior ranks and a more measured rejection by several chief officers. A new Home Secretary, Michael Howard, favoured a more incremental approach, and the most radical and contentious elements, including the pay matrix, dispensing with police regulations, and pension change, were left for another day. It was Labour Home Secretary David Blunkett who picked up the torch thrown aside by John Major's Conservative government. In *Policing a New Century* in 2001, amongst a plethora of other 'reforms', performance- and skill-based pay was forced upon a highly reluctant Federation as part of a general pay deal which preserved the Edmund-Davies principle.[3] There remained much unfinished business, but the Home Office displayed impressive resilience and patience, and was prepared to wait for more favourable circumstances, including new personnel in the top ministerial jobs.

Those circumstances occurred in 2006–7, which resulted in a bitter dispute, redolent of Sheehy, between the Labour Home Secretary Jacqui Smith and the Police Federation. Smith won to the extent that there was an incremental adjustment downwards in the index used, but caused anger in not backdating the settlement by some three months to make allowance for the completion of the arbitration process. The decision seemed petty and caused much anger amongst the Federated ranks, resulting in a mass protest through Whitehall and talk of agitating for the right to strike. But the public mood was not with the police and

---

[3] T Brain, *A History of Policing in England and Wales* (OUP, Oxford, 2010), 223–7 and 316 and Sir P Sheehy, *Inquiry into Police Responsibilities & Rewards*, vol 1 (HMSO, London, 1993), *passim*.

the deal was disconsolately accepted. The following year the Home Office got its act together in good time, instituting a pay review under Sir Clive Booth, which produced a modified, and to the staff side less generous, pay index. In 2008, with general economic recession threatening, the staff side sensibly agreed to a three-year pay deal, based on 2.5 per cent a year uplift, which expired on 31 August 2011, just over one year into the Coalition's term in office.[4] By then, however, police pay became subject to the general requirements of macroeconomic policy, and, once the existing three-year settlement deal expired, was frozen in common with the remainder of the public sector in the autumn of 2012.[5]

The Coalition

The prevailing economic circumstances of 2010 might have dictated that there would be a public sector pay freeze (and police representatives did not demur that the police had to be part of such general arrangements), but it was clear that the new government would have on principle challenged the prevailing assumptions around police pay. It was a subject, as we have seen, that David Cameron addressed in his Dalston Youth Project speech, but detail was left for another occasion. Nick Herbert's Police Reform Taskforce 2007 report *Policing for the People* expanded on some of the themes. The underlying assumption of the narrative presented in the section titled 'A professional workforce' was that in order to meet 'today's challenges' the workforce needed to be 'highly professional' with 'multiple skills'.[6] The inference was that the current workforce was not, the reason being that 'current workforce practices hold the police back'. The evidence for this came from within the police service itself, in fact from an ACPO report, 'ACPO vision for workforce modernisation: the missing component of police reform'. This asserted: 'There is a wealth of evidence from previous reports that despite the excellence of the majority of individual officers and staff, the police workforce model is in many respects obsolete with inefficient and restrictive practices causing waste and suppressing latent capacity.'[7] What was needed was a new 'workforce model' which would 'enhance the ability of the police chiefs to manage their workforce', giving them 'flexibility and discretion to innovate and ensure their organisation can meet local needs'. Individual officer pay would be based on recognition of 'skills and performance'. Ideas included a shift allowance, payment for team rather than individual performance, and payment for

---

[4] House of Commons, *Police Pay—Booth Review* (2008–11 pay deal) (<http://www.parliament.uk/briefing-papers/SN04139.pdf> [accessed 20 December 2012]), *passim* (cited as *Booth*).

[5] L Peacock, 'Pay freeze won't kick in until September 2011 for nearly 1m public sector workers', *The Telegraph*, 23 June 2010 (<http://www.telegraph.co.uk/finance/jobs/7850089/Pay-freeze-wont-kick-in-until-September-2011-for-nearly-1m-public-sector-workers.html> [accessed 20 December 2012]).

[6] Police Reform Taskforce (sic), *Policing for the People: Interim Report of the Police Reform Taskforce* (Conservative Party, London, 2007), 109–28.

[7] Quoted in Police Reform Taskforce, *Policing for the People*, 109.

specific skills accreditation. Overtime would remain but only for cancelled rest days or bank holiday working.

Overall pay would be set in a new context. New, but still unspecified, procedures would make it easier to dismiss poorly performing officers, but there would in any case be a fundamental change to the basic terms of engagement for officers. Instead of enjoying secure tenure of employment officers would be engaged on 'modern employment contracts', although this did not mean extending fixed term appointments to junior ranks. The flexible approach to pay scales would enable individuals to join at higher levels of pay and rank appropriate to their skills, qualifications, and experience. The principle of the 'omnicompetent' officer was no longer seen as sustainable given the complexity of modern policing. Increased in-service mandatory training would be introduced to enhance professionalism, specific fast-tracking for graduates would be reintroduced, while to enhance leadership direct entry at senior and chief officer rank would be reintroduced.[8] Leadership training would be mandatory and officers trained in a police-specific leadership doctrine, which the authors correctly assessed was currently lacking.

There would also be pension reform, but while there was no precision as to what was on offer, the generalities went further than what David Cameron had said in his Dalston speech. It seemed that a more flexible, officer-friendly pension scheme was to be developed, but reading between the lines it was more likely that officers would have to work longer for their full benefits, or alternatively leave earlier but have payment deferred.

> Even if an officer would be better off leaving the force, they have a huge incentive to stay for the full 30 years in order to get their full pension. Similarly, a good officer who has reached 30 years of service and still has much to offer the force, has little financial incentive to stay on. There is concern that many senior officers in their fifties who could still offer many years of service are retiring after 30 years. People need to be able to leave and join the force at the right time and a more staggered pension scheme would facilitate this. Our final report will evaluate attempts to make the police pension system less rigid and propose any necessary further reform.[9]

None of the ideas for pay, pensions, and conditions of service contained in *Policing for the People* were new. To some extent they had featured in earlier publications, such as the *Operational Policing Review*, or failed attempts at change, such as Sheehy. The proposed programme was, however, significant because it grew intellectually from Cameron's first principles as stated at Dalston, and was likely to form the basis of what the Conservatives would do if elected. The basics were

---

[8] Before the Second World War the 'Trenchard Scheme' (named after its founder, Hugh, First Viscount Trenchard, Metropolitan Commission 1931–5) had operated in the Metropolitan Police as a direct entry scheme at inspector level. In the face of indifference from the Home Office and opposition from the Police Federation it was abandoned after the end of the war.

[9] Police Reform Taskforce, *Policing for the People*, 111.

all there three years in advance of the election. Given the hostility that previous attempts at change had stirred up, observers might have concluded that the confident opposition leadership anticipated a similar reaction to their own proposal but nevertheless were prepared to see it off.

The Winsor Review

By accident or design there was never to be another report from the Taskforce, so there was much unfinished business at the time of the May 2010 general election. There was nothing specific about police pay in the Conservative manifesto, although there was a general reference to addressing 'the growing disparity between public sector pensions and private sector pensions, while protecting accrued rights'.[10] However, the full Coalition Agreement committed the new government to 'a full review of the terms and conditions for police employment', together with a general review of public service pensions.[11] The Home Secretary wasted little time in getting things in motion and on 1 October 2010 she appointed solicitor and former rail regulator Tom Winsor to conduct the review. That an outsider had been appointed was not surprising, as that had been the pattern with Desborough (1919), Oaksey (1949), Edmund-Davies (1978), and Sheehy (1992–3), but it was not strictly necessary, as David Blunkett had demonstrated in 2001–2. An independent review would, however, add weight to the recommendations. The key, from the Home Secretary's perspective, was to get the right people in place to conduct the review. Tom Winsor was thus a sound choice. He had previously been involved in the detail of rail privatization and water regulation, in which he had demonstrated considerable resilience. He was, therefore, unlikely to be intimidated by any of the parties involved in the review process. He was supported by former West Midlands chief constable Sir Edward Crew, who while in office had favoured finding easier means of disposing of poorly performing officers, and Professor Richard Disney, a pensions and NHS sector pay expert with impeccable academic credentials.[12] Significantly, he had recent relevant experience as a member of the NHS Pay Review Body, enough to have seen what had and what had not worked in the implementation of the 'Agenda for Change' programme, all valuable experience for his new task.

The review worked within terms of reference set by the Home Secretary. It might be argued that they pointed the reviewers in the broad direction of the conclusions and recommendations of *Policing for the People*. The terms of reference, set out in a user-friendly website, were how to:

- use remuneration and conditions of service to maximise officer and staff deployment to frontline roles where their powers and skills are required

---

[10] Conservative Manifesto 2010, 23.   [11] *Coalition Programme for Government*, 13 and 26.
[12] Richard Francis Disney, *Curriculum Vitae* (<http://www.ifs.org.uk/staff/cv_disney.pdf> [accessed 27 December 2012]).

- provide remuneration and conditions of service that are fair to and reasonable for both the public taxpayer and police officers and staff
- enable modern management practices in line with practices elsewhere in the public sector

In reaching its conclusions, the website continued, the review was required to 'have regard to' such factors as 'the tough economic conditions and unprecedented public sector deficit, and the consequent government's spending review'; 'the government's policy on pay and pensions'; comparisons with 'other workforces'; 'wider government objectives for police reform'; and the recently announced separate review by Lord Hutton into public service pensions. The review's authors were also required to recognize the particular frontline role and nature of the 'office of constable' in British policing, including the lack of a right to strike. Because of the 'urgency' of the matters in question they were to report by February 2011. In reaching their conclusions they consulted widely, including with staff and employer representative organizations.[13]

Winsor 1

In the event, Winsor missed his deadline by a few days, Part 1 of his report being published in March 2011. The reviewers had diligently discharged their responsibilities. In regard to pay comparisons, Professor Disney pointed out that, despite the lack of formally required educational qualifications for the role, police constables were better paid than paramedics, junior military ranks, and even veterinary surgeons, and better paid than average workers in most regions except London and the South East. Wastage rates (a significant factor behind Edmund-Davies) were very low. The review found that 'two in every five' Federated officers did not work unsocial hours yet they were paid the same, which was considered 'unfair'. The effective veto that a local branch of the Federation held on variable shift arrangements was unjustified. Overtime was necessary to retain flexibility, and the principle of reasonable compensation for time worked in unforeseen circumstances justified, but the review was less convinced about the justification for all of the enhanced rates of compensation. Interestingly, given the preferences stated in David Cameron's Dalston speech and Policing for the People, the review found no evidence that a limited amount of outside employment by police officers was causing any particular problem and recommended no change to the existing arrangements.

Of most significance was the conclusion that the current system of pay progression based on time spent in the rank was 'no longer sustainable', while there was a strong case for immediate suspension of annual increments during the current economic crisis. It found, furthermore, that the current limited element of

---

[13] *Independent Review of Police officers' & Staff Remuneration & Conditions*, 'About Tom Winsor and his role' (<http://review.police.uk/about-tom-winsor/terms-of-reference/> [accessed 21 December 2012]).

performance- and skill-related payments 'had not worked as it was intended', in essence because officers should not be rewarded for doing the job they were in any case supposed to do. However, conclusions relating to the various bonuses were more equivocal. Some element of bonuses, including team bonuses, 'for exceptional actions' was justifiable but not Special Priority Payments which were found to be of no discernible value. However, rewarding qualified specialists in investigation, firearms, public order, and neighbourhood policing was acceptable, and should be through an 'Expertise and Professional Accreditation Allowance'. Surprisingly, the review concluded that the procedures for dismissing poorly performing officers were sound; they just needed better management. The review was, however, equivocal on the issue of compulsory redundancy, partly on the grounds of losing officers' valuable experience and partly because of legal complexities relating to the office of constable. It favoured instead a system of career breaks, not significantly different from Sheehy's fixed term regime for all ranks.

The specific recommendations flowed logically from these general conclusions. There would be an unsocial hours allowance but only for those officers that worked them; the Federation veto over local shift variations would be removed; overtime payments would be reduced; officers could still take a second job but there would be improved guidance; progression through the pay scales would be suspended for two years, as would the current system of performance-related pay; the pay system for deputies and chiefs would remain the same but assistant chief constables (ACCs) would be remunerated according to the weight of their responsibilities; bonuses for superintending ranks would be suspended for two years, but chief constables could continue to make *ex gratia* payments of up to £500 to officers engaged in 'outstandingly demanding, unpleasant, or important work'; an 'Expertise and Professional Accreditation Allowance' was to be introduced, although only as a transition measure until 'longer-term arrangements' were developed; and, a voluntary 'exit' scheme, based on the civil service scheme, should be developed for the police. There would also be amendments to a range of allowances.[14]

There was a mixed reaction to the publication of Part 1. ACPO was broadly supportive, in particular welcoming the suspension of chief officer bonuses. The Federation's response, however, signalled something of the bitterness to come. Paul McKeever, Federation chairman, warned that it amounted to a '15–20 per cent' reduction in officers' pay, with worse to come on pensions. He concluded: 'officers and their families are paying the price for the failure of the Home Secretary to safeguard policing from the 20 per cent cut on the service imposed by the Treasury. We have to work around the law. We do not have a right to strike. We are being bullied at the moment.' The Metropolitan Federation chairman, Peter

---

[14] T Winsor, *Independent Review of Police officers' & Staff Remuneration & Conditions*, Part 1 (Independent Review of Police Officer and Staff Remuneration and Conditions, London, March 2012), *passim*, cited as *Winsor 1*.

Smyth, went further: 'When officers have deciphered the report's opaque language and realise the reality of the massive cuts to the police pay budget, they will be dismayed and very angry.'[15]

Reviewing the range of recommendations in Part 1 it is clear that much of the focus was very much about saving money in the short term, hence the recommendations concerning suspension of annual pay progression and bonuses. However, there was a fundamental repositioning towards rewarding shift workers and those who qualified for specialist work. Winsor estimated that there would be significant first-year costs but benefits would occur thereafter producing net savings of £485 million over three years up to 2013–14. Crucially, however, to realize these savings it would be necessary to implement the full programme by September 2011. In reality this was all but impossible given the complex police negotiating and arbitration machinery. In any case these savings might mitigate some of the worst effects of the CSR 2010 spending cuts but would not eliminate their need. Nor would they have more than a marginal impact on the various projected personnel losses that were required as these had assumed already that pay would be flatlining.

Predictably little progress was made in the negotiations which followed and in September the outstanding issues were referred to the Police Negotiating Board (PNB). With publication of Part 2 of the review still pending the Police Arbitration Tribunal (PAT) published its determination on Part 1 in January 2012. The rulings were broadly in favour of the Home Secretary and the *Winsor* recommendations, although there were some minor concessions over overtime, 'Competence Related Threshold Payments', and the full effect of the two-year suspension of annual increments, exempting officers on the first three increments. The determination on the Expertise and Accreditation Allowance was delayed until the publication of Part 2, the timing of which had slipped from the summer of 2011 to the spring of 2012.[16] On the whole it was a success for the Home Secretary, the few concessions made being hardly material.[17] What was of materiality, given the overall state of police finances, was the delay in realizing the cost benefits contingent upon the review's implementation.

What had not helped the reaction to the publication of *Winsor 1* was its near simultaneous timing with the publication of the final report of the review into public pensions chaired by former Labour minister Lord Hutton. It broadly recommended replacing final salary with career average schemes (less of a disadvantage for rank-and-file members than for those who rose through the ranks) and that the retirement age for public services should be the same as the state pension

---

[15] BBC News, 'Police pay review: politicians and groups react', 8 March 2011 (<http://www.bbc.co.uk/news/uk-12679445> [accessed 22 December 2012]).

[16] Police Arbitration Tribunal, *Decision of the Police Arbitration Tribunal: Winsor Part 1*, January 2012 (<https://www.gov.uk/government/uploads/system/uploads/attachment_data/file/143830/pat-decision.pdf> [accessed 4 July 2013]).

[17] BBC News, 'Police pay deal: Teresa May accents £150m-a-year compromise' (<http://www.guardian.co.uk/uk/2012/jan/30/police-pay-deal-theresa-may> [accessed 22 December 2012]).

age (which would rise from the current 65). There would be an exception for 'uniformed services', which included the police, for whom the retirement age would be 60. This was a substantial increase from the current 55 but, it was argued, reflected increased life expectancy and the general ability of retired members of uniformed services to pick up good jobs after leaving their service. There would be protection of accrued rights for existing members of the schemes, but that did not mean that their future benefits were protected. It was recognized that there would need to be some flexibility and customization for each segment of the public sector, so no single scheme was recommended and the detail of the application of the scheme to the police was left to *Winsor 2*.[18] However, it was already clear that for the majority of serving and future members of the police pension scheme that it would mean working longer for reduced benefits.

Winsor 2

Part 2 of the Winsor Report (*Winsor 2*), published in March 2012, was far more fundamental than Part 1 in the changes it proposed.[19] *Winsor 2* recognized that there was a special or 'X-factor' element to policing that made it distinctive from other professions, but it equally recognized that there were comparable professions and that a monetary value could be attached to it. By various means that value was established at 8 per cent of a constable's pay, but as not everyone worked in a frontline role, not everyone merited that payment. In fact Winsor found that there was no real link between 'contribution' and pay, and there ought to be. It accepted that there should remain a pay scale through which officers should progress but the scale itself should have fewer grades (seven compared to ten). Reaching the top of the scale should be attained more quickly but subject to satisfactory progress measured by skills, qualification, and experience assessments. The rationale was that this was a fairer system, and it was difficult to argue that it was not. However, a shortened pay scale might mean that officers who qualified would progress to the top grade more quickly but they would earn less in total over the duration of that progression. There would also be a significantly lower starting point (by £4,259) for officers who joined either without a basic qualification in policing skills obtained by unpaid training under force schemes before joining, or previous experience as a special constable or PCSO. The top point of the scale was to remain the same at £36,519, but the reduction of pay grades amounted to a cumulative pay cut over seven years for individual officers of £14,910 even if suitably qualified on joining. The

---

[18] Independent Public Service Commission, *Pensions Commission Final Report*, March 2011 (<http://www.cdn.hm-treasury.gov.uk/hutton_final_100311.pdf> [accessed 22 December 2012]), 4, 13, 14, 103, and 111, cited as *Hutton.*

[19] The following summary is taken from T Winsor, *Independent Review of Police officers' & Staff Remuneration & Conditions, Final Report*, vols 1 and 2 (Independent Review of Police Officer and Staff Remuneration and Conditions, London, 2012), *passim*, cited as *Winsor 2* (NB page numbers are continuous between volumes 1 and 2 of the final report).

scheme would apply to new and serving officers but be gradually introduced between 2013 and 2016. However, the problems for officers, both serving and future, were not quite over, because significant changes were recommended to police pensions, applying in detail the broad recommendations of *Hutton*. The normal police pension age would be 60, but those who left before their sixtieth birthday would have to wait till the general state retirement age, whatever that might in the future be, before accessing their police pension. There was also to be a regional pay element, with some discretion for chief constables to link this to individual performance. In essence, officers based in London would earn most, followed by the South East and Midlands, with those in the remainder of the country earning least, a calculation based on the average earning potential for the area.

The effect of *Winsor 2* on individual officers was mixed. Experienced officers in specified frontline roles would be better off in terms of salary, but lose in terms of pension. Those in non-specified frontline roles would lose out across the board. Officers in the South would gain over officers in the Midlands and North. *Winsor 2* did not try to hide this (in fact, that would not have been what the commissioning politicians would have wanted). *Winsor 2* estimated net cumulative savings of £741 million by 2017–18, assuming an implementation date in 2012. There were broadly similar recommendations for civilian staff, although here the local pay element was to be even more aggressively applied, with individual forces paying 'no more than is required to recruit and retain individuals of the requisite quality'. Chief constables' salaries would continue to be based on the size of their forces, but ACC salaries would be weighted according to their responsibilities.

Winsor 2 followed *Booth* in recommending the abolition of the Police Negotiating Board on the grounds that it was over-cumbersome and had, in recent years, failed to resolve some of the critical issues of difference between the official and staff sides, necessitating more recourse to the weighty and time-consuming Police Arbitration Tribunal before the Home Secretary made a determination. *Booth* in 2007 had recommended that the PNB be replaced by a pay review body, the standard practice for other public services, and chief officers' salary be addressed by the Senior Salaries Review Body (SSRB), but the political realities of the time suggested delaying the resolution of both issues. For Winsor the time had now come to settle both. These might seem somewhat arcane issues, but pay review bodies, and especially the SSRB, gave the relevant secretary of state more discretion in determining the outcome of any proceedings.

Winsor 2 was not just about pay. Recruiting standards, evidenced by the absence of formal educational qualifications and the under-representation of graduates, were found wanting, as was leadership training and development. In a phrase that it is difficult to imagine being found in a report during Labour's period in office, *Winsor 2* concluded that the police were drawn 'from too narrow a stratum of society, and formal intellectual attainment has played too little a part in recruitment'. *Winsor 2* did not recommend going down the all-graduate professional route, but did recommend a 'Level 3' (A level equivalent) or 'a police qualification which is recognised by the sector skills council', although previous service as special constable or PCSO would count.

Flaws were found in the current 'Higher Potential Development Scheme' (HPDS), not the least of which were that progress to higher ranks was not fast enough nor the minimum level of promotion guaranteed. *Winsor 2* recommended a series of measures, not radical in the wider context of professional management development, but radical in policing where the Federation, and until recently the Home Office and ACPO, placed primacy on initial experience as a constable over potential for early junior managerial rank. In line with the expectations of *Policing for the People*, *Winsor 2* recommended improving the internal accelerated promotion scheme as well as opening up the service to direct entry at inspector, superintendent, and chief officer, the latter including amending regulations to permit transfer from other 'common law' jurisdictions, which would certainly permit direct entry by those with US police experience. To support the new leadership paths the 'Police College' at Bramshill was to be reinstated, with specialist police leadership featuring as a major component of courses. External observers have been surprised that police leadership did not already feature as such a component.

Before concluding, there was a range of important miscellaneous recommendations concerning fitness tests (in the process implying that too many officers were unfit and some obese—a headline gift for the media), reducing those on recuperative duties, and compulsory severance, although unusually for such schemes *Winsor 2* saw this as being linked to performance. Compensation would be based on the Civil Service scheme.

Winsor's original remit was to find remuneration and conditions of service which were 'fair and reasonable', but crucially not just for officers but for 'the taxpayer' as well. It might well be argued that the package he delivered met that test. To a great extent *Winsor 1* and *2* completed and updated the two previous attempts at structural change in police pay (*Sheehy* and *Booth*). Two of the critical elements of *Sheehy* were a pay matrix which reflected individual specialisms and qualifications, and fixed term appointments for all ranks. *Winsor* modified these by recommending a more effectively enforced poor performance regime, contribution-related payments, the opportunity to leave before pensionable age, and a severance scheme. *Booth* had recommended abolishing PNB and replacing it with a pay review body, and placing chief officer pay into the senior salary review body. *Winsor* simply reiterated these recommendations.

Nevertheless, it might be argued that *Winsor* still represented a good deal for the police given the prevailing economic circumstances and the general determination of the Conservatives, and to a lesser extent their Liberal Democrat partners, to reduce the scale of the public sector wage bill. There can be no doubt that the reports were well researched, and it would be difficult to gainsay the findings of such an eminent expert as Professor Disney. It might be possible to critique elements of Disney's pay comparisons (were police officers strictly comparable to firefighters, nurses, soldiers, and teachers?), but only by doing so in detail and probably in a way which would not engage the public's imagination or sympathy. The *Winsor* recommendations were also in line with much else which had happened or was happening across the public sector. In many respects it resembled a police-specific version of the NHS 'Agenda for Change', especially regarding pay grades reflecting qualifications and role, and regional pay (essentially with Greater London at its centre and then spreading out in layers). However, Agenda for Change when introduced between 2003 and 2009 had cost, not saved, money because of the effects of annual pay uplifts, annual pay increments, and pension. *Winsor*, being introduced in a time of pay freezes and pension restructuring, would not be subject to the same constraints. Nevertheless, it still might be argued that the police would still fare slightly better than workers in other sectors, even if the proposals might prove complex to administer and restrict organizational freedom to develop individual officers through important but non-operational jobs.

In terms of pay *Winsor* might have been essentially updating *Sheehy* and *Booth*, but in one respect it was significantly more radical, and that was in its recommendations concerning police leadership. *Winsor* did not simply recommend direct entry at senior officer level, radical enough for the Federation, but direct entry at three levels which would in a few years radically alter police leadership culture and reduce career opportunities for constables. *Winsor* recommended direct entry at the three management grades—junior (inspector), middle (superintendent), and strategic (chief officer). This offered the possibility of significantly changing the cultural perspective of senior officers within a very few years. For most of the period since the end of the Second World War, no matter how much they had distanced themselves from the most junior ranks of the service by subsequent promotion and training, all senior officers had started as constables and could to varying degrees empathize with the views, concerns, and experiences of the junior ranks. If the *Winsor* recommendations on direct entry were accepted, in future fewer would have that background and experience. It must be assumed that this change of culture had been foreseen and was welcomed by the report's authors. Given the Conservative Party's opinion of police leadership in general and a series of recent mistakes, misjudgements, and scandals involving chief officers (the enforced resignation of two Metropolitan commissioners, a finding of guilt in a misconduct hearing for a chief constable, the sacking of another for corruption, and the whole of the uncertainty created by the phone hacking scandal) it could be assumed that there would only be a limited degree of public and political support for the current single-point-of-entry system. Nevertheless, direct entry at junior, middle, and senior ranks offered the possibility of a less distinctively police-orientated and experienced officer cadre.

There was, however, risk associated with the direct-entry recommendations. This lay not so much with direct entry at inspector level, for these officers would still receive basic frontline experience as part of their training and would then have the opportunity to build up more experience in junior managerial ranks before being exposed to the demands of middle and senior rank. The risk was also diminished at chief constable rank, where experienced professionals would be available to provide relevant advice. The greater risk lay at the superintending ranks, which were essentially operational and technical, and where there would be less experience from other ranks to provide support.

Reaction

For the staff associations, constructing effective opposition to *Winsor* was difficult. With unemployment hovering around 2.5 million and many sectors suffering from reductions in pay, job security, and pension benefits there would be little public sympathy for an esoteric defence of what might seem a privileged pay position. Furthermore, there was no indication that recruiting would suffer in the short to medium term. The combined effect of these factors meant that Mrs May was in a far stronger position to drive a hard bargain with the police than either Clarke or Howard had been in 1992–3, or Blunkett in 2002. It was clearly a good time to apply the maxim of never wasting a crisis.[20]

But none of this meant that *Winsor* would be accepted without criticism, not to say anger and resentment, by many police officers. In essence it was always Winsor's remit to save money,[21] and no matter how the research and recommendations were presented most officers were going to be worse off once the package of measures were taken together with increased pension contributions and deferred benefits. Security of tenure was also threatened through the introduction of severance procedures. But it was not just the monetary and material issues that caused damage. *Winsor* had effectively attempted to measure the monetary value of the difficult and dangerous job that most officers undertook for most or even all of their careers. *Winsor*, or more strictly Professor Disney, assessed that element, the 'X-factor', to be just 8 per cent of a constable's salary. The only justification for providing the police with a better-than-average pay scheme was that they did something very special; now *Winsor* said they were just 8 per cent special. *Winsor* amounted to a substantial moral devaluation of the worth of police work, an implication not lost on most officers.

The police reaction to the publication of *Winsor 2* was along predictable lines. Sir Peter Fahy for ACPO was generally positive, welcoming the underlying principle of recognizing through pay an officer's experience and contribution.[22] Derek Barnett for the Superintendents' Association expressed concern that it

---

[20] Stamford economist Paul Romer is attributed with the most direct form of the maxim: 'A crisis is a terrible thing to waste.' Quoted in M Barber, *Instruction to Deliver: Tony Blair, Public Services and the Challenge of Achieving Targets* (Politico, London, 2007), 149.

[21] See 'About Tom Winsor and his role', n 13.

[22] ACPO, 'Peter Fahy—Winsor part two', 30 March 2012 (<http://www.acpo.police.uk/ThePoli ceChiefsBlog/201203PeterFahyBlog.aspx> [accessed 28 December 2012]).

would further erode morale but did not reject the report outright.[23] The Police Federation, however, was unequivocal in its condemnation. Chairman Paul McKeever, aware of the cumulative effect of cuts, privatization, and constant criticism, express or implied, summarized:

> Police officers have had enough of the constant state of uncertainty and the deliberate, sustained attack on them by this government. They want to get on with the job they joined to do, serving their communities, and they expect the support of government. Instead they find themselves contending with cuts to pay and conditions of service, increased stress and pressures, falling numbers of police officers, low morale and the privatisation of essential police functions. Despite a growing list of demands and the reality of the cuts, they are doing their very best, but they know the government cuts are jeopardising public safety and the quality of service they are able to provide. The service cannot take anymore; enough is enough.[24]

Despite that language, McKeever was in fact a moderating force, for the reaction from many within the Federated ranks appeared to be wholly negative, whether it was in respect of pay and pensions or direct entry. Resentment and anger boiled over as officers felt they were being taken advantage of because they could not strike. It was not without precedent for home secretaries to receive a sullen welcome at Police Federation conferences, but when Mrs May appeared at the May 2012 conference, the mutual hostility was evident. Mrs May told her audience to 'stop pretending' they were being 'picked on'. Most sat and listened in silence, but when one told her she was 'a disgrace' many others responded with cheering and stamping of feet. She left to shouts of 'resign'.[25] It might have all made the delegates feel better but it probably did no more than confirm Mrs May in her thoughts that her brand of reform was not only necessary but also long overdue.

The Federation's decision to ballot members on the right to strike was hastily made, but then it baulked, delaying the vote itself until early 2013.[26] This would allow the police negotiating machinery to complete its intricate processes but it weakened the Federation's bargaining position. If that outcome was disadvantageous, as was likely, the Federation would have little alternative but to pressure

---

[23] D Barnett, quoted in Police Federation of England and Wales, 'Review on police pay and conditions could "dismantle" the British police service', 15 March 2012 (<http://www.polfed.org/ mediacenter/mag_update_review_police_pay_conditions_could_dismantle_police_150312.asp> [accessed 28 December 2012]).

[24] Police Federation of England and Wales, 'Chairman's reaction to Winsor Part 2. How much more are we expected to take?', 15 March 2012 (<http://www.polfed.org/mediacenter/ B9FBE13BE5004BBC93C9AAEDA8E1AD6B.asp.asp> [accessed 28 December 2012]).

[25] *The Telegraph*, 16 May 2012 (<http://www.telegraph.co.uk/news/uknews/law-and-order/ 9270791/Theresa-May-barracked-by-Police-Federation-as-she-defends-reforms.html> [accessed 30 December 2012]).

[26] Thames Valley Police Federation, 'Thames talk: industrial rights vote—month long ballot in 2013', 20 November 2012 (<http://www.thamestalk.co.uk/?p=344> [accessed 28 December 2012]).

the government to introduce amending legislation to grant officers the right to strike, which would in turn be resisted by the government. That outcome would simply reveal to all how powerless the Federation was in the face of a government determined not to give way. What could the Federation do in response to such determination? It could hardly proceed with a strike, as that would be unlawful and have potentially disastrous consequences for good order in the country, which in turn could wreck public support for policing.

Such a rational appreciation of the general situation did not, however, prevent resentment building up; resentment, furthermore, which neither the Home Office nor the government in general did anything to assuage. The Federation organized a march on Parliament in May, characterized by politeness and good order, but while the turnout of 30,000 was impressive it made no impact on the government and elicited little public sympathy beyond the most general. The most a spokesperson for the Prime Minister would say was that, 'We think the reductions in spending on the police are challenging but manageable and that the police will still have the resources that they need to do the important work that they do.'[27] More grist was added to the mill when the Home Secretary appointed Tom Winsor as chief HMI in succession to the retiring Sir Denis O'Connor, making him the first non-police officer to be appointed to the post. It was another example of the changing 'police landscape', as it was expected that in future ministers could get operational advice when needed from the new police professional body, leaving the Inspectorate free to pursue its public championing role, but it was a provocative appointment, seemingly confirming the low esteem in which ministers held current police leadership. It was also a public vote of confidence in Tom Winsor personally by the Home Sectary. Further, he would be in prime position to oversee the implementation of his reports' recommendations.[28]

In terms of formal process, the *Winsor* recommendations had to be referred to and considered by the formal elements of the police negotiating machinery, principally the PNB and the Police Advisory Board. The recommendations concerning leadership would be subject to a longer consultation period, but as the employer responsible for the scheme the Home Secretary could be more specific in determining the direction of travel when it came to pensions, and the scheme which she asked the PNB to formally consider would be a Career Average Scheme based on employee contributions of 13.7 per cent, substantially higher than the 9.5 per cent being paid by the members of the New Police Pension Scheme after 2006 or the 11 per cent by those on the old Police Pensions Scheme. Those on the old scheme aged 45 or over and with less than ten years before current pension eligibility would be provided with transitional protection, and while

---

[27] guardian.co.uk, 10 May 2012 (<http://www.guarvdian.co.uk/uk/2012/may/10/police-officers-march-cuts> [accessed 28 December 2012]).

[28] guardian.co.uk, 8 June 2012 (<http://www.guardian.co.uk/commentisfree/2012/jun/08/tom-winsor-nomination-battle-police-tories> [accessed 28 December 2012]).

this was of value to officers with long service it probably reflected the legal requirement to act reasonably, fairly, and proportionately.[29]

'Plebgate'

With the police negotiating machinery poring over *Winsor* there was little to prevent a powder keg of negativity building up within the police throughout the summer of 2012. That exploded in mid-September when, on the 18th, two female officers were shot dead in a suburb of Greater Manchester when attending a routine call to deal with a suspected break-in. An armed man, already wanted in respect of an earlier gun and grenade attack in Manchester, ambushed them. It seemed at least one of the officers had attempted to use her taser before being ruthlessly gunned down. Federation chairman Paul McKeever, as well as expressing his sorrow and sympathy for family and colleagues, pointed to the evident moral of the incident: 'This tragedy makes us all stop and reflect on the very real dangers police officers face every day serving their local communities.'[30] The Home Secretary and Prime Minister also expressed sympathy.[31] There is no doubt that both were being sincere, but within less than twenty-four hours these sentiments seemed to ring hollow when a seemingly trivial incident caused an outpouring of rage, the destruction, at least in the short term, of a parliamentary career, and ensured that the mistrust between the police and the Conservative Party did not simply endure but magnified in the remaining months of 2012 and into 2013.

The incident occurred at about 7.30 pm on Wednesday 19 September when recently appointed chief whip Andrew Mitchell MP was cycling out of Downing Street after a meeting and was declined egress through the main gates into Whitehall by the police officers on duty. What happened next became the subject of intense dispute, but according to a leaked police log an altercation took place between Mr Mitchell and the officers in which the chief whip was alleged to have sworn at the officers and allegedly called them 'plebs'. By allegedly dubious means, the supposed elements of the incident were in the public domain and the subject of much controversy, especially coming as it did the day after two female officers had been shot dead in Greater Manchester. Mr Mitchell denied using the word 'plebs' but admitted to swearing at the officers and apologized to them. It was not enough. The story soon left the realms of a specific if disagreeable incident

---

[29] Letter from Home Secretary to Independent Chair of PNB, 27 March 2012 (<http://www.polfed.org/Letter_HS_to_John_Randall_Pensions_270312.pdf> [accessed 29 December 2012]).

[30] *The Telegraph*, 18 September 2012 (<http://www.telegraph.co.uk/news/uknews/crime/9550417/Two-female-police-officers-shot-dead-in-Manchester-as-man-arrested.html> [accessed 29 December 2012]).

[31] guardian.co.uk, 18 September 2012 (<http://www.guardian.co.uk/uk/2012/sep/18/woman-police-officer-killed-manchester> [accessed 29 December 2012]).

between an MP and two officers and entered the realms of high politics. The alleged comments seemed to typify how many officers believed the Conservatives thought of them, even if that amounted to a large generalization. Paul McKeever did not mince his words:

> It is hard to fathom how someone who holds the police in such contempt could be allowed to hold a public office. Mr Mitchell's half-hearted apology for the comments made whilst leaving Downing Street will do little to build bridges with the police who feel they have once again been treated with a lack of respect and civility by members of this government.[32]

Nevertheless, after a few days the story died down when the Prime Minister announced that he did not expect his whip to resign. However, it reignited just before the Conservative Party conference, which the chief whip felt unable to attend. Conservative backbenchers seemed suddenly disapproving of the man who was supposed to impose discipline on them. London Mayor Boris Johnson, perhaps conscious that he had some responsibility for the officers on duty in Downing Street, on dubious legal grounds said that those who swear at police officers should expect to be arrested. A clear-the-air meeting between Mr Mitchell and local Federation representatives in his Sutton Coldfield constituency failed to do just that, although Mr Mitchell later disputed their account.[33] The net result, with the Labour opposition wading in, was that Mr Mitchell lost the support of both Conservative backbenchers and the Prime Minister and he resigned on 19 October.[34]

It was a notable scalp but it did neither the Police Federation in particular nor the police service in general much good, even in the short term. Ministers accused the Police Federation of taking advantage of the situation for their own purposes, although this was denied.[35] The events, however, did not deflect the government from its path over *Winsor*. Part 1 recommendations had already been approved in April (including the unsocial hours element, reductions in overtime compensation, a two-year suspension of annual pay increments, and a freeze on competency-related payments).[36] The Federation in July had registered a formal 'failure to agree' on

[32] *The Telegraph*, 21 September 2012 (<http://www.telegraph.co.uk/news/politics/9557632/Andrew-Mitchell-should-resign-over-police-rant-says-head-of-police-federation.html> [accessed 28 December 2012]).

[33] guardian.co.uk, 4 October 2012 (<http://www.guardian.co.uk/politics/2011/oct/04/boris-johnson-people-swearing-police-arrested> [accessed 28 December 2012] and 12 October 2012 <http://www.guardian.co.uk/politics/2012/oct/12/andrew-mitchell-meets-police-federation> [accessed 28 December 2012]).

[34] *The Telegraph*, 19 October 2012 (<http://www.telegraph.co.uk/news/politics/9621695/Andrew-Mitchell-resignation-How-a-trivial-row-over-a-gate-ended-a-20-year-frontbench-career.html> [accessed 28 December 2012]).

[35] *The Telegraph*, 14 October 2012 (<http://www.telegraph.co.uk/news/politics/9607550/Andrew-Mitchell-row-ministers-accuse-Police-Federation-of-stoking-furore-over-pleb-comments.html> [accessed 28 December 2012]).

[36] Home Office Circular 010/2012 (<http://www.homeoffice.gov.uk/about-us/corporate-publications-strategy/home-office-circulars/circulars-2012/010-2012/> [accessed 28 December 2012]).

Part 2 and these were referred to the Police Arbitration Tribunal, which was deliberating as the 'Plebgate' events played out.[37] PAT announced its decision on 6 December. PAT upheld the Home Office submission on the big issues at stake; the new police pay scale with its lower starting point and its reduced number of increments. It also agreed on the principle of ending Competency Related Threshold Payments (although these were to be phased out between 2013 and 2016 rather than abruptly ending in April 2013) and regional pay. The introduction of the Expertise and Professional Allowance was accepted in principle but delayed in implementation until the College of Policing devised an appropriate scheme. There would be no immediate introduction of compulsory redundancy, but this too was only delayed pending further negotiations.

The Police Federation gave a balanced reaction, regretting the drop in salary for recruits but welcoming the delay on any decision concerning compulsory redundancy.[38] It was just about the only reaction possible. In practical terms there was not much immediate effect on serving officers, who, in a separate development, would at least now begin to benefit from the slight easing on public sector pay, receiving a 1 per cent uplift for the next two years. While the new scale represented a substantial drop for unqualified recruits, it was moderated for those who had a basic policing qualification or previous experience as a special constable or PCSO, as many would. Furthermore, it was somewhat academic as most forces were not recruiting at all because of the ongoing effect of grant and budget cuts. Fears that the starting salary might not be sufficiently attractive were therefore hardly a strong bargaining counter. However, the delay in considering compulsory severance meant that that the Federation had been effectively wrong-footed. The ballot on strike action was going ahead early in 2013, yet discussion on severance was delayed until the summer, preventing a concentration of resentment.

However, before the end of the year the Federation was further wrong-footed by another development in what had become known as 'Plebgate'. Andrew Mitchell might have resigned but doubt about the whole police account and media story grew when it emerged that a supposed public witness was in fact an off-duty Diplomatic Protection Squad officer, while released security CCTV pictures seemed to record only one member of the public present at the time of the incident, who, far from being shocked, seemed disinterested in proceedings. Mr Mitchell claimed he was the victim of a 'stitch up'; an officer and a member of the public were arrested as an internal investigation was launched; the Commissioner, Sir Bernard Hogan-Howe, appeared to give qualified backing to the two officers involved in the original incident, which only brought criticism from Mr Mitchell's supporters and some sections of the media, now backing away from what appeared to be a potentially over-hasty rush to

---

[37] C Caswell, 'Arbitration Tribunal Convenes for Winsor II', Police Oracle, 18 October 2012 (<http://www.policeoracle.com/news/Staff+Association+News/2012/Oct/18/Arbitration-Tribunal-Convenes-For-Winsor-II_56669.html> [accessed 28 December 2012]).

[38] Police Federation, 'Police officers starting salary slashed and possibility of redundancy still hangs in the air, following announcement', 6 December 2012 (<http://www.polfed.org/PR_Fed_Resp_PAT_Award_061212.pdf> [accessed 28 December 2012]).

judgement against the former chief whip in September and October.[39] Federation chairman Paul McKeever went on leave pending retirement early in 2013, but the role of the Federation came under such scrutiny that it voluntarily initiated an internal investigation into the way it had handled the affair. Later the Federation representatives whom Mr Mitchell met in October at his Sutton Coldfield constituency offices were also subject to investigation. Former Police and Justice Minister Nick Herbert quickly published an article in which he argued that 'Plebgate' was symptomatic of a wider problem of police corruption, which while not 'endemic' was neither 'an aberration'. He concluded: 'The extent of wrongdoing should not be exaggerated, but the cancer must be cut out before it spreads.'[40]

Whatever the rights or wrongs of the Plebgate affair (and the CCTV images, if not the identity of the alleged independent witnesses, had been known to Downing Street insiders almost since the original incident in September) the continuation of the incident and attendant fallout ensured that 2012 finished with police–government relations at a significant, if not quite all-time, low; maybe not as bad as matters had reached in the last years of the Callaghan government and immediately prior to the introduction of Edmund-Davies, but not far short. The traditional Christmas message from the Home Secretary rang hollow to many officers. As the *Guardian* reported:

> 'She says we're the best police force in the world; we do a good job,' said one recipient. 'Nobody in my station has had a good word to say about it. They would have preferred she didn't say anything'.
>
> 'I've seen people reading it and angry that she's got the gall to send out a Christmas message,' said the sergeant, who works for a provincial force. 'It's so two-faced. She says this, yet with the other hand they are taking it all away.'[41]

Was anyone worried that matters had reached such as pass? It needed a gesture of conciliation from someone; some leadership. But there was still a lot to play for with the ballot hanging over the whole of police–government relations and with Mr Mitchell fighting to resurrect his political career. Nevertheless, a senior Conservative MP did make something of an effort. On Christmas Eve Conservative Vice-Chairman Michael Fabricant offered the view that it was time to draw a conclusion to the whole affair. Neither side came out of the affair 'smelling of roses', but, significantly, he declined to give Mr Mitchell unequivocal backing. He went on, 'I suspect the truth is 6 of one and half a dozen of the

---

[39] guardian.co.uk, 23 December 2012 (<http://www.guardian.co.uk/politics/2012/dec/23/plebgate-andrew-mitchell-police-stitch-up> [accessed 28 December 2012]); BBC News, '"Plebgate": Met Police vows "ruthless" search for truth', 23 December 2012 (<http://www.bbc.co.uk/news/uk-20829901> [accessed 28 December 2012]).

[40] N Herbert, 'Britain's police must reform or lose respect and trust', *The Observer*, 22 December 2012 (<http://www.guardian.co.uk/commentisfree/2012/dec/22/police-reform-or-lose-respect> [accessed 28 December 2012]).

[41] S Morris, V Dodd, and C Davies, 'Theresa May's Christmas message stokes ire of police', guardian.co.uk, 21 December 2012 (<http://www.guardian.co.uk/uk/2012/dec/21/theresa-mays-christmas-message-police> [accessed 28 December 2012]).

other.'[42] It was not much of a gesture, and as the statement came out in a Twitter exchange possibly not too much could be read into it, but it was the closest yet to an attempt to improve the deteriorating relationship between the police and government. There was much riding on the outcome of the Metropolitan Police investigation into the whole affair, which was far from complete even in July 2013. By then a total of eight arrests had been made of police officers and associates in connection with unauthorized leaks to the press.[43]

The pay scale issue came to an end early in 2013 with a whimper, not a bang. On 15 January the Home Secretary announced that she accepted the PAT ruling, and although this left other *Winsor* issues, such as compulsory redundancies, to be resolved later, it amounted to a significant victory for the Home Secretary.[44] The Police Federation meekly accepted the ruling, ruefully noting that at least the Home Secretary had followed the PAT route, as she was always likely to, and as the outcome was binding on the Federation, this amounted to no consolation whatsoever. It was a subdued outcome, made all the more so with the news three days later that Paul McKeever, the about-to-retire Federation chairman, had died suddenly.[45] The result of the strike ballot in March presented no leverage either. Only 42 per cent of the Federation's membership voted, and while 81 per cent of the turnout voted in favour of gaining the right to strike the Federation leadership acknowledged this did not provide a sufficient mandate to take the matter further.[46]

Summation and prognosis

Three years into the supposed lifetime of the Coalition government the Conservative element could reflect that it had, to a very significant degree, accomplished what it had sought to do in opposition in respect of police pay, pensions, conditions of service, and leadership. It was, furthermore, very much a realization of David Cameron's personal vision as set out in his Dalston Youth Project speech six years previously. *Winsor* appeared to have succeeded where *Sheehy*, *Policing a New Century*, and *Booth* had not. Additionally, it had gone far further than any of them in respect of police leadership, and it was likely that this would

[42] J Meikle, 'Tory vice-chairman weighs in on Plebgate row', guardian.co.uk, 24 December 2012 (<http://www.guardian.co.uk/politics/2012/dec/24/tory-vice-chairman-plebgate?intcmp=239> [accessed 28 December 2012]).

[43] M Crick, 'Two more Plebgate arrests—now eight in total', 3 July 2013 (<http://www.blogs. channel4.com/michael-crick-on-politics/two-more-plebgate-arrests-now-eight-in-total/2680> [accessed 5 July 2013]).

[44] A Travis, 'Theresa May approves radical overhaul of police pay and conditions', *The Guardian*, 15 January 2013 (<http://www.guardian.co.uk/2013/jan/15/theresa-may-police-pay-conditions> [accessed 20 January 2013]).

[45] S Laville, 'Police Federation chairman Paul McKeever dies', *The Guardian*, 18 January 2013 (<http://www.guardian.co.uk/uk/2013/jan/18/police-federation-paul-mckeever-dies> [accessed 20 January 2013]).

[46] A Travis, 'Police fail to vote for right to strike', guardian.co.uk, 4 March 2013 (<http://www. guardian.co.uk/uk/2013/mar/04/police-vote-against-right-to-strike> [accessed 19 April 2013]).

be reordered, with a substantial import of direct entrants at junior, middle, and senior management ranks, and with all future officers above the rank of sergeant trained in a what the re-established Police College would deem to be the appropriate leadership philosophy. The cost of police pay and pensions would be cut in the short, medium, and long terms, although that outcome was facilitated by the general economic crisis and what was happening to rewards in the public sector as a whole. The replacement of the PNB (a matter settled by the spring of 2013), tilted the decisions on pay decisively in the Home Secretary's favour.[47]

There were, however, prices to pay, and these were in terms of morale and good will. Throughout the autumn of 2012, I met several experienced and previously highly motivated officers who, fed up with cuts, station closures, and staff losses, wished now only for retirement. A survey of the Metropolitan Police found that only 0.1 per cent of officers thought that the Coalition offered them 'a great deal of support'. Ministers acknowledged that morale was bound to suffer, but were prepared to simply tough it out. For Police Minister Damian Green the service was simply going through a 'bad period', but 'more importantly still, you ask "how is that organisation doing its job?"'. And crime is down 10 per cent over the last two years.'[48]

Green was almost certainly right in his expectation. For at the heart of *Winsor* was simply a hard but accurate calculation: the package would leave most officers, current and future, worse off in terms of pay, pensions, conditions of service, and prospects, but this was a price that could be paid. Recruiting was unlikely to be affected in the short term as there was so little of it and there was still an obvious pool of people wanting police careers, while by the time it picked up again it was unlikely that potential competitor employments would offer anything much better. Morale might suffer, goodwill might evaporate, but the government could reasonably calculate that osmosis would succeed where conviction did not, with most police personnel just keeping their heads down and doing their job, and if that really tailed off with a few individuals then the possibility of losing contribution recognition payments or an early exit through compulsory severance would be sufficient to clarify most minds. Strike action was an empty threat, while any general failure in performance could simply be passed over to local Police and Crime Commissioners, who in turn could simply pass it on to their chiefs, who were themselves less secure in their posts thanks to the constitutional changes of the Police Reform and Social Responsibility Act.

---

[47] J McDermott, 'Home secretary vows that the new pay body will be fair—but staff associations remain concerned', Police Oracle, 26 April 2013 (<http://www.policeoracle.com/news/HR%2C+Personnel+and+Staff+Development/2013/Apr/26/PNB-abolition-New-pay-body-will-be-fair_64268.html> [accessed 27 April 2013]).

[48] C Moreton, 'Police morale is plummeting, says Lord Stevens', *The Telegraph*, 3 November 2012 (<http://www.telegraph.co.uk/news/uknews/law-and-order/9653552/Police-morale-is-plummeting-says-Lord-Stevens.html>), and R Mason, 'Low morale in the police is "inevitable" after cuts, policing minister says', *The Telegraph*, 5 November 2012 (<http://www.telegraph.co.uk/news/uknews/defence/9655200/Low-morale-in-the-police-is-inevitable-after-cuts-policing-minister-says.html> [both accessed 29 December 2012]).

7

The new police landscape

Organization

Introduction

While the focus of the Coalition's police policies has understandably been on its plans for changing governance and for pay and conditions of service, it also had far-reaching plans to change the national organization of policing in England and Wales. These developments have not been the centre of public, media, or even parliamentary attention, and might be considered of interest to only 'insiders' or professionals, but they have the potential to affect not only national security but also the delivery of local services.

Once again it is necessary to set aside developments in Scotland and Northern Ireland where the devolved governments have responsibility for policing. The differences in policing between the constituent countries of the United Kingdom were by 2013 becoming more marked; the Scottish Government establishing a single national police force, Northern Ireland retaining its now-distinctive tripartite governance structure, and the Westminster Government adopting police governance by PCCs for England and Wales.

Developments in national policing before the Coalition

It is perhaps surprising to reflect that until the beginning of the 1990s there had been many examples of formal inter-force collaboration. The 1960–2 Royal Commission had recognized the need for national police organizations and what would later be termed 'cross-border' capability. The subsequent Police Act 1964 provided for central services and for collaborative agreements between forces, and even gave the Home Secretary authority to initiate them if required, a fact often conveniently overlooked by some succeeding home secretaries who may have found it useful to pass the blame for lack of collaboration back to chief constables and police authorities.[1] Consequently, from the 1960s to the 1990s there were regional crime squads (latterly with regional 'drugs wings'), regional fingerprint bureaux, regional criminal records offices, regional training at initial, junior management, and specialist levels, and, throughout the Cold War era, arrangements for regional civil defence and war planning. Additionally there were regional Home Office forensic laboratories and radio workshops. There were also examples of voluntary purchasing consortia and outsourcing arrangements between forces and local authorities for such services as payroll and legal. At the national level the Home Office provided higher level training, principally at the Police College (latterly the Police Staff College), Bramshill, and a range of other 'Common Police Services'. For all practical purposes the Metropolitan Police acted as what would be later known as a 'lead force' for counter terrorism and international engagement.

Much of this structure was to be deconstructed in the 1990s because of essentially opposing pressures. Individual forces became more efficient while improved technology made feasible national arrangements for such activities as fingerprints and criminal records. Supported by the Audit Commission, the Conservatives in the 1990s preferred to encourage privatization, outsourcing, and local arrangements, while at the same time replacing regional intelligence and crime squads with the National Criminal Intelligence Service (NCIS) in 1992 and the National Crime Squad (NCS) in 1998.[2] Rather than adopt potentially controversial formal structures, in 1989 Conservative Home Secretary Douglas Hurd encouraged ACPO to informally adopt a national coordinating role between the forty-three forces, a policy pursued by all home secretaries until Theresa May's appointment in 2010. Somewhat belatedly, in 1996 the Police Information Technology Organisation (PITO) was created to coordinate police information technology, although it lacked sufficient power to do more than encourage greater collaboration between forces.

From 1997 Labour was less inhibited about pursuing national solutions. As far back as 1983 elements within the party had favoured hiving off the national functions performed by the Metropolitan Police (including the national lead on Irish-related terrorism and international liaison) into a 'National Police Agency'.[3] As we have seen in Chapter 1, Labour when in office (1997–2010) created a whole series of central institutions, matched by an increase in central funding. It was this growth in central power and funding that would give grist to the Conservative mill that Labour was pursuing too much centralization at the expense of

---

[1] Police Act 1964, ss 13 and 41–3.

[2] Although the National Crime Squad commenced operations in 1998, ie under Labour, it had been planned by the Conservatives.

[3] GLC Police Committee Support Unit, *passim.*

local policing. It was even less certain whether all this centralization represented value for money.

Antecedents of Conservative thinking on collaboration and national policing

As with so much else, the antecedents of Coalition national policing policy are to be found in the Conservatives' intellectual realignment initiated by David Cameron. That national policing issues were at the front of Mr Cameron's mind when he became leader is illustrated by his setting up a 'national and international security' review group under former diplomat Dame Pauline Neville-Jones to review the options even before he made his Dalston Youth Project speech on 16 January 2006. The group's terms of reference were to 'investigate the structure of policing in the UK, including reform to bring local policing closer to local populations and to provide a fully effective force or forces to deal with regional, national, and international policing challenges, including international terrorism.'[4] Consequently, little was said in the January 2006 speech about the national or cross-border dimensions of policing. Mr Cameron was a little, but only a little, more forthcoming in his Police Foundation lecture of July 2006. There 'fighting serious crime and terrorism' were lumped together, and there was a little hint of the outcome of the Neville-Jones review: 'If we conclude that it's necessary to create a new national agency to lead that fight [against terrorism] we will. But we mustn't make the mistakes of the USA where there is a deep chasm between local police departments and the Federal agencies like the FBI.'[5] Setting aside whether Mr Cameron's assessment of the US scene amounted to a challengeable generalization,[6] the hint was that a new kind of national police organization, at least in respect of terrorism, was within Conservative thinking as early as 2006, even if this was to be set in the context of maximum devolution of power and authority to local political officials.

In the event, when the Neville-Jones review was published in early 2007 there was plenty for a future Conservative government to contemplate in terms of the UK's preparedness for national security, notably setting up a third force to deal with terrorism and national emergencies, but little specifically for

---

[4] Conservativehome, 'Cameron announces "national and international security" policy group' (<http://conservativehome.blogs.com/torydiary/2006/01/cameron_announc.html> [accessed 4 January 2012]).

[5] D Cameron, 'Police Foundation Lecture', 10 July 2006 (<http://www.police-foundation.org.uk/uploads/holding/johnharris/jhml2006.pdf> [accessed 4 January 2012]).

[6] In 2005 the US Department of Justice Audit Division assessed relations with local police departments as having 'improved over the last few years', at least suggesting that something needed to improve but that by 2006 there may not have been a 'chasm' (US Department of Justice Office of the Auditor General Audit Division, *The External Effects of the Federal Bureau of Investigation's Reprioritization Efforts* (<http://www.justice.gov/oig/reports/FBI/a0537/final.pdf> [accessed 4 January 2012]), xv.

the police.[7] Surprisingly, Dame Pauline had set aside part of her original remit and left the policing aspects of national security to Nick Herbert's Police Reform Taskforce.[8] However, Nick Herbert's team had once again been given a little help from the highly influential think tank Policy Exchange.

Although the focus of Policy Exchange's 2003 report *Going Local* had been the re-municipalization of England and Wales's police forces and increased local political control, it had also made recommendations concerning national and cross-border functions. The report recommended that police functions

> with a national or international dimension (eg counter-terrorism, royal, and government protection), should be transferred from the Metropolitan Police to a 'National Crime Agency', whose chief officer should report to the Home Secretary. The agency should incorporate the existing National Crime Squad and National Criminal Intelligence Service.[9]

The agency was to cooperate with HMIC in combating corruption. Regarding other national functions the report recommended a twin-track approach:

> Assets currently belonging to individual police forces which are not integral to individual forces' local functions (eg police training colleges, forensic laboratories etc) should be transferred to a National Police Holding Body administered by a board appointed by the Home Office. Within five years, the National Police Holding Body should dispose of all assets by selling them to local authorities, floating them off as self-financing stand-alone institutions or shutting them down. Experience of residual bodies from the 1980s suggests that this could be accomplished with relative ease.[10]

There was to be more from Policy Exchange. In 2006 at the height of the debate over the Labour government's police force amalgamation scheme, Policy Exchange published a provocative report entitled *Size Isn't Everything* in which not only were the central principles, evidence, and argument for fewer strategic forces effectively demolished, but a radically alternative model of policing was proposed. The principal author was once again Barry Loveday, and once again assisted by Anna Reid, with research by Jacqueline Riozzi. The report did not simply oppose the reduction in the number of forces but went in the opposite direction, arguing for splitting up the forty-three into an increased number of smaller forces, ideally about the size of a sustainable BCU and, wherever practicable, coterminous with a unitary local authority, which would provide political governance. It was, however, recognized that smaller forces might not be self-sufficient in terms of capability to investigate serious crimes and an additional

---

[7] BBC News, 26 July 2006, 'Tories ponder major crisis force' (<http://news.bbc.co.uk/1/hi/uk_politics/6916773.stm> [accessed 4 January 2012]).

[8] National and International Security Policy Group, *An Unquiet World* (<http://www.conservatives.com/pdf/securityreportfinal.pdf> [accessed 4 January 2012]), 3.

[9] B Loveday and A Reid, *Going Local: Who should Run Britain's Police?* (Policy Exchange, London, 2003), 60.

[10] Loveday and Reid, *Going Local*, 61.

dimension was needed to address cross-border crime. The government would therefore 'allow' the smaller, essentially municipal forces 'voluntarily to feder-ate where necessary, extend the remit of national policing agencies and/or re-establish Regional Serious [sic] Crime Squads, devolve more responsibilities to Basic Command Units, and make them genuinely accountable to local commu-nities.' Such confederation would extend not only to major crime and cross-border investigation, but also to alliances to achieve economies of scale in IT, purchasing, and fleet management.[11] The problem with this approach was that it essentially ignored the problem that the financial flaws attached to the Labour amalgamation plan extended to most forms of voluntary collaboration schemes. However, this was less important than it providing another apparent intellectual justification for the developing trends in contemporary Conservative philoso-phy. The arguments contained in *Size Isn't Everything* seemed to promise the elixir of having small forces subject to local political control coexisting with the capa-bility to combat higher levels of serious crime and achieve financial efficiencies. Above all, it was an intellectually cogent alternative to Labour's centralizing agenda.

Consequently, even as Labour was constructing its elaborate and extensive central policing structures, there was a growing intellectual argument for alterna-tives even by the time Cameron's Police Reform Taskforce produced its 2007 report. This concluded that the 'regional' forces proposed by Labour in 2005–6 would be 'too far removed from the public, and ultimately lead to centralisation and a loss of local accountability.' Instead it proposed two alternatives. Either 'effective leadership from the centre' would drive greater collaboration between the forty-three forces, or 'approximately forty-three forces' (there might be evo-lution to more, smaller forces) focusing on local crime supported from above by a 'new Serious Crime Force'. The latter would deal with not only 'serious and organised crime' but also 'major' crime which fell outside the local forces' capa-bility and capacity. Flying high with the momentum of its own intellectualism, the Taskforce also thought this 'Force' might, by retaining a 'large pool of officers' on stand-by, deal with 'civil contingencies and major public order incidents'. All cross-border crime and organized criminality would be dealt with by the national force, though the question was left open whether counter terrorism would be incorporated within the Force or remain to be allocated to a separate 'counter-terrorist force or agency'.[12]

There were several impracticalities with the idea of a single national force deal-ing with not only cross-border crimes, but also major crimes (presumably such as murders, serious sexual offences, and complex frauds beyond the capacity and capability of the newly constituted smaller forces), not the least of which were

---

[11] B Loveday, assisted by A Reid and J Rozzi, *Size isn't Everything: Restructuring Policing in England and Wales* (Policy Exchange, London, 2006), *passim*.
[12] Police Reform Taskforce, *Policing for the People: Interim Report of the Police Reform Taskforce* (Conservative Party, London, 2007), 105–8.

the costs associated with establishing such a unit and what to do with the officers allocated to civil contingencies and major public order incidents when these were not occurring, which was most of the time; but there was a superficial attractiveness about this layered approach to reconciling the simultaneous demands of local, cross-border, and national policing requirements. The Taskforce report was also light on solutions around central coordination of police IT. However, the important feature of the Taskforce's options for serious, organized, and cross-border crime lay not in their detail but in the key conclusion that there would remain a need for central operational police agencies, if ones that would be subtly different, and set in a different context, from those currently in place and under development by Labour.

As with much else in the Taskforce's report, further detail and resolution of critical questions remained for a projected further report which in the event never appeared. There was instead some help from another right-wing think tank, 'Reform'. This was significant because of its close connections with Shadow Police Reform Minister Nick Herbert, who had been one of its founders. Reform's 2009 report *A New Force* reinforced the existing argument for smaller forces, and accused Labour of uncoordinated and inefficient national funding, leaving too much national leadership to the unaccountable ACPO. Chief constables were seen as meddling in national areas which were not their primary concern, and not focusing enough on local operations, which were. Significantly for the future, and on the basis of limited evidence, SOCA was dismissed as 'a white elephant', being frequently described as 'ineffective'. It plainly did not like the national institutions that Labour had created but eschewed creating alternative ones of its own. Instead it recommended a new national lead for the Metropolitan Police, not only replacing SOCA but also providing the national lead on IT, communications, uniform, equipment, human resources, and training.[13] It was an eccentric solution, given the Metropolitan's recent dubious track record of success, but this was less important than the weight it added to the building case against the existing national institutions of ACPO, NPIA, and SOCA. This added some intellectualism to the growing feeling amongst many Conservatives that many in police senior leadership were too close to Labour and that ACPO, as their representative organization, needed taking down a peg or two. New Shadow Home Secretary Chris Grayling summed up the general mood not long after taking up post in September 2009: 'No particular representative organisation should have a privileged position. You talk to everybody but you listen with a sceptical ear.'[14] It did not bode well for the future relationship between the Conservatives and ACPO, and was not to change when Theresa May rather than Grayling became Home Secretary.

---

13 D Bassett, A Haldenby, L Thraves, and E Truss, *A New Force* (Reform, London, 2009), *passim*.

14 J Oliver, 'Tories will rein in new Labour police', timesonline, 12 September 2009 (<http://www.timesonline.co.uk/tol/news/politics/article5581736.ece> [accessed 12 September 2009]). See Chapter 3, p. 64.

Policing in the 21st Century and national policing

The 2010 Conservative manifesto focused on local policing issues and governance, and there were only indications of what changes might happen to national policing. There would be a national border force, 'part of a refocused Serious and Organised Crime Agency'; the government would 'work with forces to strengthen arrangements to deal with serious crime and other cross-border challenges', and 'extend collaboration between forces to deliver better value for money.'[15] It was not quite the extensive programme of the Police Reform Taskforce, Policy Exchange, or Reform, but the sum total was that the Conservatives intended to make significant changes if elected.

This meant that several areas of national policy had to be rapidly developed after the election. Some detail was provided in the white paper *Policing in the 21st Century*, published just twelve weeks after the 2010 election. Although styled 'a white paper', and therefore theoretically open to a measure of consultation, it was highly didactic in style and in reality sought only views on implementation, not the principles at stake. The government wanted to see a 'golden thread' of policing run from the local to the national, and believed it had found the way to provide this. It would preserve local policing, eschewing mergers to create strategic forces, but it would simultaneously expect significantly more collaboration between forces to secure better value for money and effectiveness. This collaboration would include 'back office' as well as cross-border operations, and would be driven not by chief constables but the new PCCs. Public scrutiny, in keeping with the general new Conservative commitment to provide more detailed local information about services in general to the public, through HMIC databases would ensure that progress would be made. Force collaboration was to be enhanced by simplified national arrangements, which in practice meant time was to be called on both SOCA and the NPIA, and, to a large extent, ACPO. A new 'National Crime Agency' would replace SOCA but also encompass the hitherto stand-alone Child Exploitation and Online Protection Centre (CEOP) and, it was suggested, elements of the UK Border Agency. Some other national elements, such as the Police National Information and Co-ordination Centre (PNICC), in presumably a nod towards the Police Reform Taskforce's idea of the wider remit of its 'Serious Crime Force', would come under the auspices of the NCA. 'Robust' governance was promised.[16]

Policing in the 21st Century accepted that the NPIA had 'done much to bring about welcome changes to policing', especially effecting increased collaboration and some economies of scale, but this was not enough to save it. It was considered that this was 'the right time to phase out the NPIA, reviewing its role and how this translates into a streamlined national landscape.' There was even a target date—spring 2012. What there was not was any clear idea about what

---

[15] Conservative Manifesto 2010, 68.
[16] Home Office, *Policing in the 21st Century: Reconnecting Police and the People, passim.*

would remain as national functions and how they would be administered. As for ACPO the language was opaque, but something would change. ACPO would provide 'a leading role in leadership development, including some training programmes', and advice to the Home Secretary and PCCs, but its role in strategy would be diminished. In future, 'strategic policy will be set locally by Police and Crime Commissioners and nationally by the Government.'

Running parallel to the *Policing in the 21st Century* consultation process was a review initiated by the Home Secretary on police leadership and training by the current head of the NPIA Peter Neyroud. Amongst its purposes was to answer questions about how to reposition ACPO in the new landscape and how 'the NPIA leadership functions can be transpositioned [sic] effectively'. It was not invited to consider whether such transposition was necessary. Neyroud concluded that a new 'Professional Body' was needed, which would 'simplify the burgeoning national standards for policing, picking the really important ones and jettisoning what has become a welter of unnecessary and bureaucratic guidance'. This was a curious conclusion for the head of the organization that bore a major responsibility for that 'welter of unnecessary and bureaucratic guidance'. ACPO's functions would be merged with the new organization, but would also engage police officers and civilian staff from outside the chief officer ranks. Chief Constables' Council would remain, to provide advice to chief constables and ministers. On training and leadership there would be a 'Police Initial Qualification' for new officers and a new 'qualification framework for managers'. The key organizational recommendation, however, related to the creation of the new 'Professional Body' which would undertake several functions of ACPO and the NPIA, and even some detailed functions of HMIC and the Home Office respecting the appointment and development of chief officers. Neyroud did not exaggerate when he concluded: 'The creation of the Professional Body allows the phasing out of a complex and convoluted governance structure of the overseeing police leadership and training that has evolved over the last 100 years.' He envisaged that the new body would be established by charter, although this was not an essential feature of his recommendations.[17]

Developing the new landscape

The new landscape took some time to develop. Various announcements were made throughout 2011 and 2012. A 'Strategic Policing Requirement', a late inclusion following the white paper consultation process, would set out the government's

---

[17] P Neyroud, *Review of Police Leadership and Training*, vol 1 (<http://www.homeoffice.gov.uk/publications/consultations/rev-police-leadership-training/report?view=Binary> [accessed 11 January 2013]), 10–14, and vol 2 (<http://www.homeoffice.gov.uk/publications/consultations/rev-police-leadership-training/appendices?view=Binary> [accessed 12 January 2013]), 199–201. The idea of a chartered institute of policing was not new. The author can recall much talk of this initiative at the time of the *Operational Policing Review* 1989–90.

view of the various national threats and policies to which PCCs and chief constables should 'have regard'. Much was expected of it, not least by ACPO, but it sat uneasily alongside the Coalition's prevailing localism.[18] It took over two years to produce, a surprisingly long time given that its contents were to prove so unremarkable. It categorized two tiers of risk, but identified only four national risks— terrorism (tier one), organized crime (tier two), large-scale public order beyond the ability of a single force to cope with (not tiered), and 'a large-scale cyber incident' (not tiered). PCCs and chief constables were theoretically required to ensure that they understood the risks in their areas, were prepared to collaborate where necessary, and had the 'capacity and capability' to meet what was expected of them. PCCs and chief constables were enjoined to ensure 'consistency' when it came to procurement of equipment and their ability to interact with other forces.[19] The Strategic Policing Requirement amounted to a useful reminder to any local PCC who simply saw the policing requirement beginning and ending at the borders of their force, and it could be used by a chief constable who felt it necessary to remind his or her PCC that there was more to policing than neighbourhood patrols and dealing with anti-social behaviour. It was also recognition by the government that there was more to policing than the merely local. It was, however, light on detail and specifics, and when it came to priorities added little insight beyond the immediately obvious. Whether it would add any value on issues of consistency of equipment and tactics, which most, but not all, forces were capable of achieving without external assistance, would remain to be seen.

Under the overarching Strategic Policing Requirement there was much rearrangement and retitling. Out would go the NPIA; in would come the College of Policing and a new police ICT (Information and Communications Technology) company. Out would go SOCA; in would come the National Crime Agency. ACPO would remain, but its principal function of making national policy through the medium of its committees, or 'business areas', would be assumed by the College of Policing. Within the overarching structure there would be much realignment of functions.

The College of Policing

The NPIA was to be wound down by December 2012 and largely replaced by the College of Policing, but for an institution only created in 2007 and allegedly obsolescent by 2010 the NPIA proved remarkably difficult to displace. *Going Local* had envisaged that some functions could simply be dispensed with, but this did not prove possible in the short term at least. After Peter Neyroud had retired as NPIA chief executive in December 2010, his deputy Nick Gargan took over as

---

[18] Home Affairs Committee, 'New landscape of policing', examination of witnesses, 10 May 2011 (<http://www.publications.parliament.uk/pa/cm201012/cmselect/cmhaff/939/11051002.html> [accessed 16 January 2013]).

[19] Home Office, *The strategic policing requirement* (Home Office, London, 2012), *passim*.

acting head with the unenviable job of winding the organization up while not disrupting service. He fulfilled his task in an exemplary fashion, for it was no mean feat. The NPIA website listed thirty-one 'main products' or 'services' and eighty-four 'sub products' or 'services' that were to continue to function, with thirty-nine (including such essential systems as the Police National Computer (PNC), the National Firearms Licensing Management System, Automatic Number Plate Recognition, and the National Identification Services (fingerprints, etc)) destined for the Home Office to administer directly. The remainder was split between the new professional body (including all higher training and national selection processes) and SOCA (including the Specialist Crime Operations Centre and Serious Crime Analysis) prior to its own migration to the National Crime Agency. There was one institution which, however, was to cease. In December 2012 the Home Office decided to sell the Bramshill site, the iconic home since 1960 of national police leadership training. The Home Office had concluded it was uneconomic, but this was also a highly symbolic break with the historical past.[20] Henceforth, national and international training would be delivered in more prosaic surroundings.

The new professional body was to be called the 'College of Policing', being an unimaginative and unnecessary distension of 'Police College', the name for the institution that provided national leadership training from 1947 to 1978. It would have responsibility for 'training, standards, and leadership', but these terms would be interpreted liberally. The focus of the College's work would be leadership training but with renewed emphasis on engaging with other academic institutions, particularly universities and the private sector. That the College had a remit for higher training, promoting operational excellence, and working with universities and other institutions to deliver Winsor's expectations concerning a distinctive style of British police leadership was hardly contentious, indeed it was welcome and long overdue. That its primary medium was evidence-based policing, or, more prosaically, 'what works', was perhaps of slightly more concern, as, for purists, it might be argued this could inhibit innovation.

However, the College of Policing's training remit was of less significance than the constitutional change its creation masked. The College was to assume responsibility for national policy-making, hitherto jointly held between ACPO and the NPIA. Responsibility for ACPO's 'business areas', the powerful committees in which policy was developed before approval by Chief Constables' Council, would transfer to the College of Policing, under the authority of its 'Chief Executive', a new national post. ACPO's senior managing body, its 'cabinet', was also to transfer to the College's 'Professional Committee', although it was not to assume responsibility for national mutual aid coordination. The chief executive's precise constitutional role in national policy-making was yet to be determined. Who

---

[20] Police Oracle, 'Bramshill Sale "Disappointing"—ACPO', 14 December 2012 (<http://www.policeoracle.com/news/HR,+Personnel+and+Staff+Development/2012/Dec/14/Bramshill-Sale-Disappointing---ACPO_59086.html> [accessed 12 January 2013]).

the post holder would be was settled in October 2012, when the Home Secretary appointed Alex Marshall, the chief constable of Hampshire, to the post. Interestingly, this appointment preceded the necessary legislation being passed by Parliament. The chief executive would operate within a governance arrangement that had been suggested by Policy Exchange's 2003 *Going Local*, that is it would become a company limited by guarantee, with the fifteen-person board 'chaired by someone independent of policing' and the remainder comprising representative PCCs, 'non-police representatives', as well as representatives from the police staff associations, of which ACPO would be but one, even if it was to have three members compared to the Federation's one.[21]

All this represented a considerable downgrade for ACPO, which had been responsible for national policy-making since given the task by Douglas Hurd in 1990. This arrangement had neatly sidestepped the issue of who was in charge in the absence of a national police force and saved the government the bother of passing complicated and potentially controversial legislation. By voluntarily agreeing policies in Chief Constables' Council the legal notion of direction and control of forces resting with individual chief constables was retained. Under the new arrangements ACPO would simply be one of the stakeholders in the College, while Chief Constables' Council would continue in existence but instead of being ACPO's ultimate policy-making body in future its purpose would now be to implement the decisions made by the College's business areas.[22] It also left ACPO with a financial problem, as much of its funding depended on it fulfilling the national policy-making and coordination roles.[23] Quite where accountability for the business areas and their work would lie was not clear, except that it would not be with ACPO. In theory, individual chief constables could still opt out of policies, but the balance of power within the broader governance of policing had tilted decisively away from the collective leadership of ACPO. ACPO would now simply be one of the stakeholders in the new College, a clear realization of Chris Grayling's dictum that a future Conservative government would give the association no precedence over other representative bodies and individuals.

---

21 Home Office, *College of Policing* (<http://www.homeoffice.gov.uk/police/college-of-policing/> [accessed 20 January 2013]; [HM Government], *New Landscape of Policing: the Government Response to the Fourteenth Report of the Home Affairs Committee Session 2010–12*, HC 939 (<http://www.official-documents.gov.uk/document/cm82/8223/8223.pdf> [accessed 11 January 2013]), *passim*; and, Police Oracle, 'College of Policing: clarity needed on governance' (<http://www.policeoracle.com/news/Police+Performance/2013/Jan/17/College-Of-Policing-Clarity-Needed-On-Governance_60117.html> [accessed 20 January 2013]).

22 Home Office, 'Home secretary outlines plans for new police professional body', 15 December 2011 (<http://www.homeoffice.gov.uk/media-centre/press-releases/police-professional-body> [accessed 13 January 2013]); Home Office, *College of Policing* (<http://www.homeoffice.gov.uk/police/college-of-policing/> [accessed 20 January 2013] and HM Government, *Response to fourteenth report* (n 20), *passim*.

23 C Caswell, 'In focus: Politics, policing and the future of ACPO', Police Oracle, 25 February 2013 (<http://www.policeoracle.com/news/Police+Performance/2013/Feb/25/In-Focus-Politics,-Policing-And-The-Future-Of-ACPO_61330.html> [accessed 6 March 2013]).

The *Neyroud Report* had set out to change the 'complex and convoluted governance structure' of policing; whether the creation of the new College, with its extensive remit and unusual governance had succeeded in clarifying or simplifying it was another matter. It certainly allowed for the phasing out of ACPO as the police service's principal internal policy-making body and gave other 'stakeholders', principally the other staff associations and the PCCs, a greater influence over polices that chief constables would have to implement and be responsible for. Whether this amounted to an improvement was debatable. Furthermore, devising such a radical change might be argued as being beyond Neyroud's original terms of reference, but he certainly answered the question 'if not ACPO then who would provide some uniformity of policy?' A cynical view might be to assume that the body of opinion that had been developed by the think tanks, the Taskforce, and shadow ministerial and latterly ministerial statements, had plainly signalled that the writing was on the wall for ACPO even before Neyroud commenced his review. Some institution needed to make national policy and if that were not to be ACPO then it would have to be something else; the College fitted the bill. There were problems, however; it would be no more democratically accountable than ACPO, and although the Coalition had promised, and claimed to have delivered, a 'bonfire of the quangos', illustrating the Conservatives' distaste and disapproval of these unaccountable bodies, in the governance of the new College it looked like that is exactly what it had created.[24]

Police Information and Communication Technology

The new landscape for police ICT proved equally difficult to fit into the new landscape. The *Operational Policing Review* in 1990 had recommended that the forty-three forces collaborate in a single ICT organization to develop and implement new technology for the service in order to ensure economies of scale and uniformity of systems and platforms. Hitherto ICT had been dealt with in a hybrid fashion, with some large systems, such as PNC, being developed and owned nationally, while with more local systems forces developed their own systems at their own pace and according to their financial circumstances. With respect to the latter, the Home Office was loath to impose any central control, and, as in the case of automatic fingerprint technology and radio communications, sometimes lagged behind the enthusiasm of forces either individually or collectively to make progress. The belated creation of PITO in 1996 meant that forces of necessity had pursued their own in-house systems and that there was therefore a plethora of legacy systems and investments already in existence. It was relatively easy to agree on common operating standards; much harder to agree common systems.

---

[24] '114 public bodies axed in "bonfire of the quangos"', *The Telegraph*, 29 December 2012 (<http://www.telegraph.co.uk/news/politics/9770441/114-public-bodies-axed-in-bonfire-of-the-quangos.html> [accessed 13 January 2013]).

As is often the case, however, it was easier to dwell on the failings rather than the successes, and, as a Home Office review demonstrated in 2005, there was actually an impressive record of developing and implementing new national systems in what was, after all, a devolved constitutional structure and highly dynamic operating environment.[25] Dissatisfied with this performance, however, in its latter years the Labour government imposed on the service and PITO an ambitious target to achieve complete convergence of all forty-three forces' ICT systems by 2015. This was to be delivered through the Information Systems Improvement Strategy (ISIS), which the NPIA inherited when it assumed responsibility for PITO.[26]

Policing for the People argued that police ICT was too fragmented, even with ISIS. However, somewhat confusingly, the idea of imposing a centrally funded and controlled mechanism of the forty-three forces proved too much at odds with new Conservative ideology. Instead the Conservatives looked north of the border and liked what they saw in Scotland, where the eight forces had come together to produce a common strategy and database.[27] Seemingly beset by the same hesitation that had inhibited previous attempts to impose a central programme, ultimately the Taskforce fell short of a precise recommendation, for the reality was that this was constitutionally and practically a difficult area. When in power the Conservatives backed a centralized structure and fell back on the existing ISIS strategy. They could not, however, simply leave PITO to remain as before, so a new organization, variously called 'NewCo' or 'PitCo', was created. It too would be a 'public company', but not 'a centrally funded body'. Instead it would be 'owned and run by those police forces which voluntarily buy in to the organisation', although the Home Office would also be 'an "owner" of the company'.[28] Chief constables were originally to figure prominently in the company, but in keeping with the Home Office view that they should be operationally rather than strategically focused, they faded from the picture as the PCCs gained ascendency. It was an ingenious and intellectually satisfying way of reconciling localism with central direction, common systems, and economies of scale.

It may have been ingenious and intellectually satisfying, but was it sufficiently different from PITO and would it deliver? It was different in its constitution, as a limited company with PCCs in the majority, but it was still to be a voluntary organization, the success of which might not be measured on the success of its products but on the political preferences of its board members. In theory forces could go on the open market to buy their systems, so PitCo's products would

---

[25] Home Office, *The Report of the Review of the Police Information and Technology Organisation* (PITO) (Home Office, London, 2005), 23–4.

[26] NPIA, Information System Improvement Strategy (ISIS) (<http://www.npia.police.uk/en/docs/ISIS_briefing_Jul11-final_(2).pdf> [accessed 13 January 2013]).

[27] Police Reform Taskforce, *Policing for the People*, 99.

[28] Public Accounts Committee, 'Central procurement and the new policing landscape' (<http://www.publications.parliament.uk/pa/cm201213/cmselect/cmpubacc/129/12907.htm> [accessed 13 January 2013]).

have to be the best and financially viable; not easy given that ICT existed in the same economic climate as all other aspects of policing, and while there was a great belief that more and better ICT would relieve the pressure on the frontline, there was no absolute evidence that it would.[29] In any case, some of the available money would have to be spent on simply upgrading existing systems, such as replacing the major incident system, HOLMES 2 with HOLMES 3. Besides, there was much else for police ICT to keep up with—digitalization, speech recognition, integrated databases, biometric identification, the use of secure 'cloud' technology, and the further roll-out of mobile data, in which ministers had overwhelming faith as a police time saver but for which the evidence was equivocal.[30] However, it is clear that those involved in the current transition and ISIS programmes are determined to make a difference this time.[31] What is less clear is if there is enough momentum and money in the system to achieve the desired outcome.

The National Crime Agency

Similar issues of principle affected the creation of the NCA, only here the questions were not simply in terms of policy but also operations. *Policing in the 21st Century* expected quite a lot from the new organization—more enforcement against organized criminals but 'at reduced cost', improving intelligence, and, crucially, 'effective national tasking and coordination of police assets'.[32] How might more effective tasking and coordination be achieved in a police constitutional structure in which direction and control of the principal assets, the resources of the forty-three forces, were under the direction and control of individual chief constables who might by convention and goodwill agree to be tasked and coordinated from central agencies but could opt out if necessary? In June 2011 the Home Secretary gave the clearest indication of how that conundrum, which had been the crux of all attempts to provide national direction, control, and coordination since the creation of the 'New Police' in the early to mid-nineteenth century, and to which Neyroud had claimed to find the solution, would be resolved. It was also an indication of the increasing confidence of the Coalition to see through its policing agenda. The answer, set out in *The National*

---

[29] N Herbert, 'Speech to City Forum [sic]', 25 January 2011 <(http://www.homeoffice.gov.uk/media-centre/speeches/city-forum> [accessed 13 January 2013]).

[30] Herbert , Speech to City Forum. For a criticism of the use of police mobile data see National Audit Office, 'Mobile technology in policing' (<http://www.nao.org.uk/publications/1012/mobile_technology_in_policing.aspx> [accessed 13 January 2013]). For a contrary view see 'Evaluating the use of mobile data in the police', *Wireless*, 13 July 2012 (<http://www.wireless-mag.com/Features/21823/Evaluating_the_use_of_mobile_data_in_the_police_.aspx> [accessed 13 January 2013]).

[31] I am grateful to ACC Tony Dawson for his insight into many aspects of the developing police ICT strategy and programme. He is not, however, responsible for the opinions expressed here, which are my own.

[32] Home Office, *Policing in the 21st Century*, 29.

Crime Agency: a Plan for the Creation of a National Crime-Fighting Capacity, was to provide the agency with sufficient legal powers to 'undertake tasking and coordination of police and other law enforcement agencies to ensure networks of organised criminals are disrupted and prevented from operating.'[33] The plan went further in creating a network of regional units available for tasking by the head of the NCA. The plan was not specific about how these regional units would be created, but by 2011 all police regions possessed regional intelligence and operational units, effectively recreating through voluntary collaboration the regional crime squads that had existed before the creation of the National Crime Squad in 1998. The plan itself was supported by a new organized crime strategy, with, in keeping with the underlying philosophy of the government's principal members, emphasis on 'prevention and self-protection' alongside 'more enforcement activity'.[34] Without waiting for the necessary legislation to be presented much less passed by Parliament, the Home Secretary appointed Keith Bristow, the chief constable of Warwickshire, as the first 'Director General' (not, it will be noted, 'Chief Constable') of the nascent National Crime Agency in October 2011.[35]

The government eventually gave legislative teeth to the new arrangements in the Crime and Courts Bill 2012, abolishing SOCA and creating the NCA. The strategic priorities of the agency were to be determined by the Home Secretary, to which the Director General must, in the familiar phrase, 'have regard'. The bill, however, made it plain that the agency's purpose was to secure 'that efficient and effective activities to combat organised crime and serious crime are carried out (whether by the NCA, other law enforcement agencies, or other persons).' The bill went further in specification: chief officers of the UK (not just England and Wales) or any other person in 'a UK law enforcement agency' 'may perform a task if the Director General requests the person to perform it'. The legislation stopped short of requiring chief constables to carry out a direction from the Director General, but it had gone further than any other legislation is limiting the parameters of a chief constable's 'direction and control' powers. A chief constable would have to have a pretty good reason for declining a request, especially as in his region would be a regional crime unit the sole purpose of which was to deal with organized and serious crime (subtly, no longer 'serious and organised crime').[36]

With the ability of the Home Secretary to set priorities for the NCA, the ability of the Director General to make requests which would be difficult to deny, and the existence of regional units perhaps only now notionally under the direction

---

[33] Home Office, *The National Crime Agency: A Plan for the Creation of a National Crime-Fighting Capability* (Home Office, London, 2011), 5.

[34] Home Office, *Local to Global: Reducing the Risk from Organized Crime* (<http://www.home-office.gov.uk/publications/crime/organised-crime-strategy?view=Binary> [accessed 15 January 2013]), 14.

[35] BBC News, 'UK National Crime Agency head to be Keith Bristow', 10 October 2011 (<http://www.bbc.co.uk/news/uk-15241052> [accessed 20 January 2013]).

[36] Crime and Courts Bill 2012, clauses 1–4.

and control of local chief constables, the government had succeeded in creating the 'golden thread' it wanted to see extending from the international to the local. When it came to organized and serious crimes, the Coalition had taken steps to give to itself legislative powers and resources on a new scale, which exceeded even that of its predecessor. The problem that the new arrangements faced, however, was that despite the high expectations of legislative empowerment it suffered from the same problem besetting all contemporary policing—declining resources. In 2009–10 SOCA's budget was £425 million. By 2012–13 it was £394 million, a decline of 7 per cent, perhaps not as bad as that of the forty-three forces, but enough given the expectations placed upon the new organization, more so when it was considered that at the beginning of 2013 the budget for the NCA had not been declared.[37]

Given the enthusiasm to provide central direction and authority with serious and organized crime it is perhaps curious that the government did not make similar arrangements when it came to counter terrorism. Instead the non-statutory conventions continued to apply, with the Metropolitan Police securing the overwhelming share of the national resources and the commissioner, through the Assistant Commissioner Specialist Operations as chair of the ACPO Counter Terrorism Business Area, retaining a de facto national operational lead. At a regional level the larger forces, located in conurbations, possessed regional operational counter terrorism units, while the more rural regions made do with counter terrorism intelligence units. The only justification for continuing with the arrangements was that they seemed to work, as evidenced by the few terrorist incidents that occurred after the 7 July 2005 attacks. However, such pragmatism had not been sufficient rationale for retaining other elements of the status quo. It can only be assumed that the political effort involved in creating a national counter terrorism command, answerable to the Home Secretary, outweighed the government's desire to rationalize and, at least in respect of serious and organized crime, command and coordinate.

Collaboration

The government not only sought to ensure greater coordination between forces through the structures contained within the new police landscape; it intended to deliver increased financial efficiency and operational effectiveness through degrees of formal collaboration. It was a strategic intention inherited from the previous Labour government. Before 2005 Labour had recognized that forces collaborated across a range of services and functions, but O'Connor's *Closing the Gap* report essentially concluded that these ad hoc arrangements were not delivering enough efficiency or effectiveness. It went further, concluding that collaboration could

---

[37] Home Office, *Departmental Report 2009*, and SOCA, *Annual Plan 2012/13* (<http://www.soca. gov.uk/about-soca/.../372-soca-annual-plan-201213.pdf> [accessed 15 January 2013]), 8.

never deliver enough efficiency or effectiveness, and that a new policing structure was required, which was fewer but larger 'strategic forces'. Home Secretary Charles Clarke adopted the recommendation and embarked on a forced merger programme in 2005–6, but, as we have seen, the scheme collapsed because of internal weaknesses, particularly relating to finance. However, the Home Office could not leave well alone, so when Home Office Minister Tony McNulty wrote to forces announcing that the mergers were off he added a rejoinder that instead there would have to be more collaboration.[38] HMIC duly followed up with inspection activity, and in 2009, unsurprisingly, concluded that there was insufficient collaboration.[39]

The report, however, failed to recognize that there was nothing intrinsically efficient or effective about collaboration. Each collaboration scheme had to work on its own terms. A further report in 2012 found that 'progress' had, nevertheless, been made and that there were 543 projects either planned or in operation. Of those 381 were between forces, 116 between forces and other public sector partners, and thirty-four with the private sector. Collaboration was expected to deliver 11 per cent of the savings calculated to be required as a consequence of government cuts. The report also found, however, that there was too much variation between forces and that the greatest opportunity for savings through collaboration lay in 'sharing support functions' (ie 'back office'). But even the enthusiasts in HMIC recognized there were limitations to what collaboration could deliver:

> It is important to note that there is a limit to the amount of change that the Service can sustain while still delivering core business. The key aim must therefore be for forces and the Service to understand the benefits and risks attached to the range of options for increasing efficiency, and to make an informed and manageable set of choices in the best interests of the public.[40]

The issue that was not addressed was that of accountability. In theory the single elected individual, the PCC, was to be accountable for the delivery of services in their area, but in reality accountability was diluted, even obfuscated, in collaboration schemes, especially where there was more than one partner, and where those partners were from the private sector. The savings, furthermore, while useful in the context of increasing government cuts, were not sufficient in themselves to bridge the funding gap by some significant degree.

Force structures

The government did not attempt to dictate to forces what internal structures they should adopt. The Police Act 1964 specified a two-tier structure of divisions

---

[38] T Brain, *A History of Policing in England and Wales* (OUP, Oxford, 2010), 373.

[39] HMIC, Press release, #001/2009—Police forces must work together in the public interest (<http://www.hmic.gov.uk/news/releases-2009/release-001-2009/> [accessed 16 January 2013]).

[40] HMIC, Increasing efficiency in the police service (<http://www.hmic.gov.uk/media/increasing-efficiency-in-the-police-service.pdf> [accessed 16 January 2013]), 9.

and sub-divisions, with a headquarters structure superimposed upon that. That structure was good in achieving stability and internal control, but tended to administrative inefficiency. Developments spearheaded in Northamptonshire in the early 1980s cut out the divisional tier and concentrated resources on increasingly self-resilient BCUs, which streamlined decision-making and stripped out administrative overheads. Devolving resources from headquarters and de-layering management was current across both public and private sectors in the 1990s and became a key principle of what was known as 'New Public Management'. By the end of the 1990s HMIC and the Audit Commission encouraged then cajoled all forces, regardless of size, geography, and local political circumstances, to adopt the BCU structure, and most did. The improvements made were hard to quantify but there were perceptible improvements in partnership working as BCU boundaries became coterminous with local authority boundaries at district or unitary level. However, there was a tendency to unnecessarily duplicate functions, which became even more apparent as technology improved in the 2000s. By the end of the 2000s forces, by then already under financial pressure, began to experiment with structures that maintained local operational units for neighbourhood and response policing, but which allowed for more variation in terms of investigation and administrative support. By 2012 an internal survey by the Superintendents' Association found that sixteen out of the forty-three forces had abandoned the pure BCU structure for some localized hybrid, and eight of the remainder had ether reduced the number of BCUs or were planning a review of structure.[41] In essence the survey revealed that by the end of 2012 there was no longer a uniform structure of policing below the force level.

Summation and prognosis

The broad outlines of the new police organization are traceable, as with much else, to the work of the right-of-centre think tank Policy Exchange. In 2003 *Going Local* proposed a highly devolved police structure situated alongside a limited range of national agencies. This strain of thinking was, however, far less well developed than the new localism which supported the drive to create PCCs, and this plainly showed in the length of time it took to move beyond bright ideas to presentable policies. *Going Local* envisaged three outcomes for national institutions—selling them off to local authorities, 'floating' them as stand-alone companies, or shutting them down, a process to be completed within five years. It has not yet worked out like that, nor is likely to do so. However, there has been a substantial move in that general direction, with both the College of Policing and 'PitCo' becoming 'stand-alone' companies outside direct Home Office control, although still within its influence. This is entirely pragmatic. The functions of

---

[41] I am grateful to Chief Superintendent Irene Curtis of the Police Superintendents' Association of England and Wales for providing me with details of the survey.

the College and PitCo are simply too important to be dealt with in the same way as any other commercial company. The exception to the stand-alone approach has, for equally pragmatic reasons, been the NCA, which as an operational unit must remain within direct Home Office governance.

One outcome has been apparent through all three approaches to governance: ACPO has been downgraded from its previous position of eminence to being simply one of a group of internal stakeholders, and one certainly subordinate to the new PCCs. For the time being, the President of ACPO, Sir Hugh Orde, would retain a degree of influence and status by virtue of his personality and experience, but this is likely to wilt as the years progress under his successors, not least because chief constables themselves will change in terms of status and experience. They are likely to hold their posts for shorter periods, be subordinate locally to their PCCs, and increasingly come from backgrounds external to the police service. This will mean, incrementally but inevitably, their views are likely to command less authority, maybe even less respect. Chief constables will still retain several important vehicles by which to influence policy, including their seats on various boards of governance, the lead role several will have in the business areas, and the collective voice of Chief Constables' Council; but their voice will have become dispersed amongst these various mediums, and again is likely to command less authority. ACPO as an institution is likely to continue, but it will be increasingly hard to justify the level of finance it receives from its funding bodies—the PCCs collectively and the Home Office—as its national policy-making role diminishes. It is difficult not to conclude that its glory days have passed. Conversely, the statuses of the College of Policing and its Chief Executive are likely to increase.

There is no doubt that the Coalition had achieved by the mid-point of its projected (first?) term in office a high degree of structural reorganization. In addition to the College replacing the NPIA, the NCA will replace SOCA and 'PitCo' will become a stand-alone organization. However, the real question is not so much has a 'new landscape' been created—it has—but will the reconfigured elements work, and will they add value to the sum of policing?

In answer to the first part of the question, the reconfigured elements will almost certainly work in a technical sense. The reason for having some surety about this is simply because they are not significantly different from the organizations they replace to have any real danger of failing. It is really difficult to conclude other than that there has been a great deal of change, if not exactly for change's sake, then at least for the sake of presentational politics. The Conservatives could not be seen simply to inherit Labour's structure uncritically and get on with the job. There had to be change, even if it only amounted to rearranging and renaming. The NCA appears to be little more than a reconfigured SOCA. Including the Serious Fraud Office within its remit might have added cohesiveness and specialist capacity, but this is not happening. For no obvious reason, the opportunity has again been missed to create a national counter terrorism agency of similar status and remit to the NCA. Further, the evidence that Labour's structures were failing is scant to non-existent. This is not to say that they would not have benefitted from serious scrutiny and adjustment, but there was no attempt to do either. The need for reconfiguration was simply assumed. There was a general feeling that the NPIA had become too 'baggy', but that hardly amounts to a catalogue of failure, and in any case if bagginess was a genuine problem it could have been addressed by internal restructuring and adjustment, and perhaps even by simply dropping the redundant term 'Improvement' from its title.[42] None of its functions have been dispensed with in the short term; they have simply been dispersed between the College, the NCA, and the Home Office. The Home Office has no notably successful track record in operational administration, but there is no reason to assume that the management of each of the transferred segments will not be able to continue to function as before. The elements transferred to the NCA may unnecessarily broaden its remit, but equally there may be opportunities for managerial synergies.

The College of Policing will have a reduced administrative and operational mandate compared to the NPIA, but it will have acquired a new constitutional remit. The College of Policing is as much about constitutional change as it is about improvements to training. As for police ICT, this had existed outside a larger parent body before and could do so again. The challenges police ICT faces do not relate to organization but rather to deciding whether all forty-three forces should or even can be coerced into procurement unity. There has been plenty of opportunity to force this on the service, but the Home Office has always baulked. Why? Probably because the record of government ICT procurement in other sectors has been weak and it has no desire for any failures in police ICT to be traced to its door in the same way failures in defence and health ICT have been laid at the door of its respective government departments. 'PitCo' will have no more authority to impose unity on police ICT procurement than its predecessors; in fact it appears to have less. The change in governance, with PCCs possessing the lead role in ownership is of uncertain benefit, which is another way of saying it might work for the better or it might not. There are encouraging signs that progress is being made in positioning the service to meet the benefits and challenges of the next developments in the ICT environment, but that has little to do with the new arrangements.

The second part of the question of whether the new arrangements will add real value is far harder to answer. Can simply reconfiguring make that much difference? The government clearly thinks so, but as no business cases have been presented with definable benefits identified, how would anyone know? The government is likely to claim that less money has been spent on the new institutions compared to the old but that is a simply a consequence of budget cuts consequent upon CSR 2010 and the 2012 Autumn Statement. The reality is that all of the new and reconfigured institutions of the new landscape, except for

---

[42] Editor, 'Home Office addresses Fed Conference on new Police professional Body, Constabulary, 15 May 2012 (<http://www.constabulary.org.uk/2012/05/15/home-office-addresses-fed-conference-on-new-police-professional-body/> [accessed 20 January 2013]).

counter terrorism, will have to function with less financial resources, although the impact of this will be hard to track, as like-for-like comparisons will be difficult to make. On the other hand, despite its lack of depth the Strategic Policing Requirement is likely to be of some benefit, if only to remind PCCs that there are problems and issues beyond their local boundaries which require their active cooperation to address. The NCA, furthermore, will have two advantages over its predecessor; first the Director General will possess more power to direct local resources (a constitutional change that has excited remarkably little parliamentary interest, much less protest); second, having a new regional network to direct, although in theory the network's parts remain the property of the constituent regional forces. However, these are not benefits intrinsic to the nature of the NCA. The power to direct chief constables could have been given to the Director General of SOCA, while the regional units are not new in concept for they are simply a return to regional crime squads that were precipitately abolished to facilitate the creation of the National Crime Squad. They are also staffed from the constituent forces within each ACPO region and do not, therefore, represent a step change in capacity. This reconfiguration might make a difference, but it is difficult not to conclude that the scale of the serious and organized crime problem is beyond the scope of the resources arrayed against it.

At a local level, the trend to restructure forces in order to adapt to declining financial resources and fewer personnel is likely to continue as cuts deepen beyond 2015. Restructuring is a rational response to changes in resources, while changes in management practice and technology have made changes to the BCU structure a logical development. This has not passed without adverse comment from Policy Exchange; in a late-2012 pamphlet it argued for additional crime-prevention officers and maintenance of the BCU structure.[43] Neither is likely given the scale of the cuts required by CSR 2010 and the 2012 Autumn Statement. What seems equally unlikely, given the Coalition's preferences, Labour's experience, the doubtful business case, and the absence of sufficient set-up funds is that ACPO's argument for fewer 'strategic' forces will be accepted, so the regional arrangements for dealing with 'level 2' cross-border crime are likely to remain as the best fit available.

The reality is that much will be expected from NCA, the College, and PitCo, but they are all likely to be under-resourced for the tasks in hand. Yet these reconfigured bodies will have to meet those expectations in a demanding operating environment, and it is to that which this study now turns.

43 E Boyd and D Skelton, *Policing 2020* (Policy Exchange, London, 2012), 10–11.

8

The policing environment

Politics, society, and economics, and their implications for policing

Introduction

If there is a new policing landscape it is reasonable to ask the question, 'What will be the environment in which it is to operate?' It seems to be a question that has excited the Coalition less than determining what the structure ought to be, regardless of future circumstances. Theirs has been a deterministic approach, which assumes that beneficial outcomes will naturally follow their political and organizational initiatives. This might prove to be the case, but the changes are occurring, so it seems, with minimum regard to the operating environment. The Coalition is in control of its political initiatives; it is not in control of all the economic and social factors which may determine the success of those initiatives. It is the purpose of this chapter to identify those principal trends and developments and consider their general impact for policing. Their more detailed operational implications will be considered in the chapter following.

Society

The early results of the 2011 census reveal a seismic shift in the demographics of England and Wales. The population in 2011 stood at 56.1 million, a growth of 3.7 million since 2001, and at 7.1 per cent the largest growth spurt since official records began in 1801. The reasons were a combination of increased net immigration (2 million), longer life expectancy, and increased fertility. The most common birthplaces for people born outside the UK were India, Poland, Pakistan, and the Irish Republic. All of the regions grew, but the greatest growth was in London and the South East. Ethnically the population remained overwhelmingly white at 86 per cent, but this represented a substantial change from the 2001 census when 91 per cent were recorded as white. London was the most ethnically diverse region, with only 45 per cent of its residents described as 'white British'. The country had also become measurably less Christian, indeed, less religious, with a 12 per cent reduction since 2001 in those describing themselves as Christian while those classifying themselves as of 'no religion' grew by 10 per cent.[1]

To a degree, the police service had changed its ethnic and gender diversity, but arguably insufficiently to keep pace with the developments around it. By 2012, 27 per cent of officers were female, an increase of ten percentage points since 2000, but, despite several years of so-called 'family friendly' policies, by January 2013 there were only five female chief constables and cuts in overall police numbers greatly reduced future promotion opportunities.[2] There had been two minority ethnic officers of chief constable or equivalent rank but by September 2012 both had retired.[3] Also, while in 2009 the Equalities and Human Rights Commission had, after several years of sustained training and equality initiatives, lifted the 1999 Macpherson Report's assessment that the police service as a whole was 'institutionally racist', the minority ethnic recruiting target set in that report was missed.[4] More problematically, that target itself had been overtaken by the population changes marked by the 2011 census.

In keeping with its principles, while retaining a commitment to promote equality the new Coalition dispensed with specific measurable equality targets.[5] This, however, caused a problem for Sir Peter Fahy, chief constable of Greater Manchester and head of ACPO's 'workforce development' business area, who argued that the police needed some help to become more ethnically representative. His argument was a nuanced one, since it appeared that he was not calling for 'positive discrimination', but for some kind of wider interpretation of employment law when making selection decisions. Quite what he had in mind was less clear, but whatever it was it did not receive much sympathy from Police Minister

---

[1] Office for National Statistics (ONS), 2011 Census—population and household estimates for England and Wales, March 2011 (<http://www.ons.gov.uk/ons/dcp171778_270487.pdf> [accessed 21 January 2013]) and ONS, 2011 Census: key statistics for England and Wales, March 2011 (<http://www.ons.gov.uk/ons/dcp171778_290685.pdf> [accessed 21 January 2013]).

[2] Home Office, *Police Service Strength, England and Wales, 31 March 2012* (<http://www.homeoffice. gov.uk/publications/science-research-statistics/research-statistics/police-research/hosb0912/ hosb0912?view=Binary> [accessed 21 January 2013]) and House of Commons Library, *Police service strength, 10 September 2012* (Standard Note SN00634, <http://www.parliament.uk/briefing-papers/ SN00634> [accessed 21 January 2013]), and Home Office, *Assessment of women in the police service* (<http://library.npia.police.uk/docs/homeoffice/assessment-women-police-service.pdf> [accessed 22 January 2013]), 6.

[3] Standard Note SN00634, 3, and L Tickle, 'Female chiefs: what's holding them up?', Guardian Professional, 3 April 2012 (<http://www.guardian.co.uk/public-leaders-network/2012/apr/03/ female-police-chiefs-holding-up> [accessed 22 January 2013]).

[4] See T Brain, *A History of Policing in England and Wales* (OUP, Oxford, 2010), 406.

[5] *Coalition Programme for Government*, 18 and HM Government, *The Equality Strategy—Building a Fairer Britain* (<http://www.homeoffice.gov.uk/publications/equalities/equality-strategy-publications/ equality-strategy/equality-strategy?view=Binary> [accessed 22 January 2013]), 6–10.

Damian Green. He agreed that there needed to be much more improvement, but saw this as entirely a problem for the police.[6]

There also remained the continuing problem of stop and search. A 2010 Equality and Human Rights Commission report criticized the police for continued disproportionality in terms of the number of stops and searches conducted on ethnic minority people, finding that people from ethnic minorities were six times more likely to be stopped and searched than whites. The report concluded that despite sufficient good practice guidance there remained evidence of 'racist attitudes, stereotyping and discrimination . . . among a number of police officers', of which the most besetting was 'stereotyping'. The commission threatened 'enforcement action' against a small number of forces whose figures were deemed excessively disproportionate, although by 2013 none had been taken.[7]

Stop and search disproportionality was, however, a problem that belied a simple solution. A human rights judgment required the government to amend section 44 of the Terrorism Act 2000, and numbers conducted under that power subsequently declined. However, searches conducted under the principal powers (section 1 of PACE, and under section 60 of the Criminal Justice and Public Order Act 1994) continued to increase, and in 2010–11, 27 per cent of all stops and searches were conducted on black people or Asian people, a clear and continuing disproportionality.[8] A further complication was that the Metropolitan Police conducted substantially more searches than any other force, even allowing for its significantly larger population. Despite the increased use of stop and search, however, there was no clear evidence that it was actually effective in reducing crime.[9]

The underlying problem with seeking some kind of stop and search proportionality between ethnic groups is that section 1 of PACE requires reasonable grounds for a search to take place. It is not, therefore, possible to conduct stops and searches on grounds of simple proportionality. It seems that the majority of the public backs the use of the police stop and search powers.[10] Yet despite this

---

[6] S Laville, 'Call for new law to force police to tackle diversity at top', *The Guardian*, 27 January 2013 (<http://www.guardian.co.uk/uk/2013/jan/27/law-police-diversity> [accessed 30 January 2013]) and Granada, 'Police chief calls for more diversity in recruitment', 28 January 2013 (<http://www.itv.com/news/granada/2013-01-28/chief-calls-for-more-black-and-ethnic-minority-officers/> [accessed 2 February 2013]).

[7] Equality and Human Rights Commission, *Stop and Think: A Critical Review of the Use of Stop and Search Powers in England and Wales* (<http://www.equalityhumanrights.com/uploaded_files/raceinbritain/ehrc_stop_and_search_report.pdf> [accessed 22 January 2013]), 5, 12, 32, 57, and 62–3. That no enforcement action was taken may have been a result Professor Marian Fitzgerald's work with Thames Valley Police which demonstrated uncertainty concerning the original finding of disproportionality.

[8] Home Office, Stop and Search Statistics—Financial Year 2010/11 (<http://www.homeoffice.gov.uk/publications/science-research-statistics/research-statistics/police-research/immigration-tabs-q4-2011/stops-searches-1011-tabs?view=Binary> [accessed 23 January 2013]).

[9] BBC News, 'Met police stop and search powers "not effective"', 25 January 2010 (<http://news.bbc.co.uk/1/hi/england/london/8479124.stm> [accessed 23 January 2013]).

[10] For example see, Police Foundation, 'Stop and search', The Briefing, March 2012 (<http://www.police-foundation.org.uk/uploads/catalogerfiles/stop-and-search/stop_and_search_briefing.pdf> [accessed 23 January 2013]).

the issue remains one that can damage police efforts to increase confidence among minority ethnic communities. In January 2013 Stephen Lawrence's brother Stuart formally complained about the twenty-five times that he had been stopped by the police in recent years.[11] In the twentieth year since the murder of Stephen Lawrence it was an embarrassment the Metropolitan Police and the service in general did not need.

That the police service will need to adapt to first a continuing growth in the total population and one of increasing diversity and complexity over the next decade or more seems inevitable.[12] How successfully that happens, however, is not entirely dependent upon the police but requires a response from the totality of government. Nevertheless, the police service is constantly at the point of interface between government and society, where the consequences of mistakes, in policy or tactics, are at the most obvious and fraught. The failure to judge the consequences of action which is inappropriate in the circumstances can have catastrophic consequences, as the 'trigger' incidents that have precipitated urban disorder from the 'Swamp' tactics in Brixton in 1981 to the shooting of Mark Duggan in 2011 so dramatically illustrate. The service must necessarily continue to pursue policies which sensitize officers to their actions and which ensure that the service itself is realistically representative of the population as whole. This has not been and will not be easy, but the service is likely to find it more difficult to achieve as officer numbers continue to decline then stabilize. Put simply, the service cannot become significantly more representative if it is not recruiting to any significant degree; a situation that is likely to prevail beyond 2015. The qualification and promotion policies recommended in the *Winsor* reports, no matter how potentially beneficial in other respects, may also serve to have a negative effect in terms of inclusion and diversity.

Another aspect of social change with implications for policing has been the growing economic inequality of the British population. The 'Gini Coefficient', the standard measure of income inequality, stood at 0.26 for much of the 1960s and 70s. By 2010–11 it stood at 0.34.[13] Moreover, the inequality was not evenly distributed. Thus greatest extremes of both wealth and poverty concentrated, unsurprisingly, in Greater London. The greatest concentration of wealth is found in London and the South East in general, while the lowest incomes are found in the North East, North West, the Midlands, and Wales.[14] Unemployment, a reasonable indicator of wealth, well-being, and confidence, reached a cyclical low at 1.42 million in August 2005, from whence it gradually crept up until it accelerated

---

[11] BBC News, 'Stephen Lawrence's brother begins race case against Met', 9 January 2013 (<http://www.bbc.co.uk/news/uk-england-london-20958573> [accessed 23 January 2013]).

[12] BBC News, 'UK population "to rise to 71.6 million"', 21 October 2009 (<http://news.bbc.co.uk/1/hi/uk/8318010.stm> [accessed 23 January 2013]).

[13] J Cribb, R Joyce, and D Phillips, *Living Standards, Poverty and Inequality in the UK: 2012* (Institute for Fiscal Studies, London, 2012 <http://www.ifs.org.uk/comms/comm124.pdf> [accessed 1 February 2013]).

[14] The Poverty Site, United Kingdom Income Inequalities (<http://www.poverty.org.uk/09/index.shtml> [accessed 1 February 2013]).

after the onset of the recession in 2008, reaching a peak of 2.68 million in November 2011. Even so, by November 2012 it was plateauing at 2.49 million. As with other aspects of economic distribution, the effects were not felt evenly, with the young and otherwise socially and educationally disadvantaged suffering disproportionately. Regionally, the highest concentrations of unemployment were found in the already economically disadvantaged South Wales, Midlands, North West, and North East. As with other forms of wealth distribution, extremes were to be found in London, while in the South East and South West unemployment was below the national average.[15]

Lastly, there is the social and economic pressure which will be created by the ageing population. Over the next twenty-five years the proportion of the population aged over 65 is expected to rise to 22 per cent. The Coalition has responded by raising the general pension eligibility age, but even this may not be sufficient as the decades pass.[16]

In sum, by the middle of the second decade of the twenty-first century, British society has undergone and is still undergoing a period of rapid social and demographic change, and is doing so at a time of economic recession, the effects of which are felt disproportionately in social, demographic, ethnic, and regional terms.

The economy and public finances

As will be discussed further later, there is small prospect of a change of government before 2015. It follows that there will be little prospect of anything other than incremental change to economic and public spending policies. Besides, the forces at play are bigger than those within the control or influence of any government. With economic growth 'flatlining', despite technically avoiding by a narrow margin a 'triple dip' recession in the first quarter of 2013, there was little possibility that the Coalition would change its economic policy, despite pressure from such disparate sources as Goldman Sachs and the TUC, to do so.[17] The 2013

---

[15] BBC Economy Tracker: Unemployment, 17 April 2013 (<http://www.bbc.co.uk/news/ 10604117> [accessed 19 April 2013]); Datablog, *The Guardian* (<http://www.guardian.co.uk/ news/datablog/2010/nov/17/unemployment-and-employment-statistics-economics> [accessed 19 April 2013]); and TUC, 'Young black men have experienced sharpest unemployment rise since 2010', 16 October 2012 (<http://www.tuc.org.uk/economy/tuc-21533-f0.cfm> [accessed 19 April 2013]).

[16] K Dunnell, The changing demographic picture of the UK: National Statistician's annual article on the population (<http://www.ons.gov.uk/ons/rel/population-trends/no--130--winter-2007/ the-changing-demographic-picture-of-the-uk.pdf> [accessed 25 January 2013]).

[17] J Moulds, 'UK GDP shrank by 0.3% in fourth quarter', guardian.co.uk. 25 January 2013 (<http://www.guardian.co.uk/business/2013/jan/25/uk-gdp-crunch-time-osborne> [accessed 25 January 2013]) and Transcript BBC News 24 broadcast, 11.07 am, 25 January 2013 (<http:// www.youtube.com/watch?v=NGULLBk_HzU&feature=youtube_gdata> [accessed 25 January 2013]) and BBC News, 'UK economy avoids triple-dip recession', 25 April 2013 (<http://www.bbc. co.uk/news/business-22290407> [accessed 25 April 2013]).

budget confirmed that, despite the downgrading of the UK's 'AAA' international credit rating, there would be no fundamental change to the Coalition's economic policy except some funding for infrastructure projects.[18]

Whatever was to happen to the general economy, for the public services the funding prospects looked bleak. With the failure of the economy to regenerate, the Chancellor of the Exchequer instituted a general cut in public expenditure in addition to that required by CSR 2010. The 2012 Treasury Autumn Statement imposed new cuts of £6.6 billion, to take effect in the 2013–14 financial year. The Home Office was set to lose £250 million over two years but the police, along with local government, were shielded from the cuts for 2013–14, although they would impact in 2014–15.[19] If the police service received the full effects of a 2 per cent cut in budget using estimates similar to other departments, and using 2011–12 figures (the latest then available) as the baseline, the effect on the police would be to lose in the region of £173 million, or the equivalent of some 3,300 FTEs in addition to those consequent upon CSR 2010, taking numbers back to March 2004.[20]

However, the 2012 Autumn Statement was no more than a precursor to the 2013 spending review. This was set in the context of the economy continuing to 'flatline' and only narrowly missing an unprecedented 'triple dip recession'. Of necessity the Chancellor's forecasts for eliminating the structural deficit were extended beyond 2015, but while spending reviews normally set spending plans for three years, the 2013 review covered only 2015–16, a procedure to allow the post-2015 election government maximum room for fiscal manoeuvre.

The Spending Review 2013 delivered cuts in total departmental spending of 2.3 per cent on top of those required by CSR 2010 and the Autumn Statement. However, intelligence, health, and overseas aid were absolutely protected from cuts (growing by 3.4, 0.1, and 1.1 per cent respectively), while education was relatively well protected by losing only 1.0 per cent.[21] It was expected that the Home Office and the police might come off relatively well too when it became clear that Mrs May had reached an early agreement with the Treasury over the amount to be cut from her departmental budget.[22] However, this proved not to be the case, with the Home Office budget being cut by 6.1 per cent, better than local government

---

[18] BBC News, 'Fitch downgrades UK credit rating to AA+', 19 April 2013 (<http://www.bbc.co.uk/news/business-22219382> [accessed 20 April 2013]) and G Topham, 'Budget 2013: chancellor pledges extra £3bn for infrastructure projects', *The Guardian*, 20 March 2013 (<http://www.guardian.co.uk/uk/2013/mar/20/budget-2013-infrastructure-projects-pledge> [accessed 5 April 2013]).

[19] HM Treasury, *Autumn Statement 2012* (TSO, London, 2012), 57, and HM Treasury, *Budget 2013* (TSO, London, 2013), 27.

[20] Cipfa Police Actuals 2003–4 and 2011–12 and HM Treasury, *Autumn Statement 2012 Policy Decisions Table* (<https://www.gov.uk/government/publications/autumn-statement-2012-policy-decisions-table/autumn-statement-2012-policy-decisions-table> [accessed 6 July 2013]).

[21] HM Treasury, *Spending Round 2013* (<https://www.gov.uk/government/uploads/system/uploads/attachment_data/file/209036/spending-round-2013-complete.pdf> [accessed 6 July 2013]), 10.

[22] BBC News, 14 June 2013, 'Spending Review: Home Office agrees cuts with Osborne' (<http://www.bbc.co.uk/news/uk-politics-22904306> [accessed 6 July 2013]).

at 10 per cent, but less well not only than the protected departments but also defence (–1.9 per cent), Business, Innovation and Skills (–5.9 per cent) and, significantly, the Law Officers Departments (–5 per cent). In political terms it might be argued this was a small return given that she had seen off the Police Federation to deliver the *Winsor* recommendations and was still able to boast continuing falls in crime and rising confidence. In fact, these successes might have worked against her and the police, because it seemed demonstrable that the police could take the cuts yet still deliver the outcomes. Of course, a more detailed scrutiny of the timings would reveal that the continuing fall in crime and the rise in confidence had occurred before the full effects of the cuts were being felt.

In his Commons speech at least Chancellor Osborne said the police would not be cut by the same amount as the Home Office as a whole. That proved to be the case, with the police budget being cut by 4.9 per cent, although that still amounted to £269 million in 2015–16.[23] This would amount to a further 3,340 FTEs at the 2011–12 rate, taking numbers below the 2004 threshold.

The problem for the police, and for other public services, is that 2015–16 does not look like being the end of the cuts. Looking beyond 2015–16 the independent and respected Institute for Fiscal Studies forecast extreme difficulties for the unprotected departments, with cuts building to 16 per cent in 'real' terms by 2017–18, 'or cuts of nearly a third since 2010'. It considered such an outcome 'inconceivable', and concluded the Chancellor would have to increase cuts to welfare or raise taxes.[24]

Assuming the IFS forecasts to be accurate that would mean an additional £1.4 billion to be found from the police, Home Office and Communities, and Local Government and Welsh Government grants by 2017–18. The average cost of FTE police personnel—police officers, and civilians—was £51,760 in 2011–12.[25] This baseline calculation means that between 2015–16 and 2017–18, 27,000 FTE police posts would have to be lost in addition to those already lost or forecast to be lost.[26] This would mean that by March 2018 somewhere in the region of 64,000 FTEs would have been lost since the Coalition came into office. In effect the whole of the growth engineered under Labour would have been more than negated by taking overall numbers back close to what they were in 1989. This figure might seem incredible until it is taken into account that some 26,000 FTE, officers and civilians, or over 10 per cent of the workforce, had been lost between 2010 and 2012 as a direct consequence of spending cuts by the Home Office, the CLG, and police authorities.[27] Policing was in a very difficult place in 1989, as it was

---

[23] J McDermott, 'Policing budget cut by "almost five per cent"', 26 June 2013 (<http://www.policeoracle.com/news/Police+Finance/2013/Jun/26/Policing-budget-cut-by-almost-five-per-cent_67283.html> [accessed 6 July 2013]).

[24] IFS, Autumn Statement 2012: Introductory Remarks (P Johnson (author), <http://www.ifs.org.uk/publications/6485> [accessed 2 February 2013]), 2–3.

[25] Cipfa Police Actuals 2011–12.

[26] Cipfa Police Actuals 2011–12, see Chapter 4, p. 85.

[27] Cipfa Police Actuals 2009–10 and 2011–12; author's extrapolations.

emerging from arguably its most trying decade in its history. Would policy-makers allow numbers to sink to such levels? Considering its track record, it is doubtful that the Home Office is modelling such scenarios, as the department has shown an inclination to rigorously engage in effective financial modelling in the past. There is therefore a high risk that, unless there is a vigorous economic recovery, a change in government fiscal policy, or a revision of protected spending, police numbers will fall incrementally until historically low numbers are reached.

Clearly it is possible for the police service to continue to function at these levels, for these are still higher, if marginally so, than the levels of the 1990s or earlier, but there are some significant qualifications. First, it was the growth in officers and PCSOs that made possible the kind of neighbourhood policing prescribed from the centre by Labour. It is therefore unlikely that this intense kind of proactive, problem-solving neighbourhood policing can be consistently sustained into the future. This will mean a converse refocus on response and investigation, even if these are locally based.[28] By 2012 HMIC had already recognized that neighbourhood policing had been diluted.[29] There might be a further decline in neighbourhood policing resources should the Home Secretary choose to favour national policing institutions, notably the College of Policing and the National Crime Agency, over resources distributed to the forty-three forces.

Second, legal and procedural changes have made policing, in hard to quantify ways, a more labour-intense activity. The Conservatives had hoped to release additional police potential by cutting bureaucracy, and the 2013 spending review did promise more money for creating a common digital platform for the police and the CPS, although with it would come more responsibility in the form of the police prosecuting 'volume, low level motoring offences'.[30] The problem for the police looking forward was that with cuts on the scale of the 2010 and 2013 spending reviews, and the prospect of more to come post 2015, efficiencies through cutting bureaucracy, once viewed as a benefit to increase productivity, would become essential in order to simply mitigate cuts in basic service levels to the public.

Third, the expectation that 2014–15 would prove to be the end of the cuts, and therefore permit a period of stabilization within the service is very unlikely to occur. It will, therefore, be necessary for police leaders (including PCCs) to sustain morale through a prolonged period of confidence-sapping staff losses. However, as a result of the *Winsor* recommendations (see Chapter 6) the professional police leadership will itself be going through a period of fluctuation as it absorbs new senior officers from external organizations. The effect of this is simply unpredictable.

---

[28] See for example Mayor of London Office for Policing and Crime, Police and Crime plan 2013–2017 Consultation Draft (<http://www.london.gov.uk/sites/default/files/Draft%20Police%20and%20Crime%20Plan%202013-2016%20CONSULTATION%20DRAFT%20FINAL_0.pdf> [accessed 19 April 2013]).

[29] HMIC, *Policing in Austerity: One Year On* (<http://www.hmic.gov.uk/media[force]> [accessed 31 October 2012]), 3.

[30] HM Treasury, *Spending Round 2013*, 42.

There may, however, be some mitigating factors. First, there are the savings the government expects to make through cutting bureaucracy. However, in the first years of the Coalition there is little quantifiable evidence of these cuts. For a flagship policy there has been remarkably little publicity about the effect of the cuts. It took a Freedom of Information Act request to the Home Office to elicit a response that it no longer retains central data by which calculations of personnel savings can be assessed, and while it expects that the 'package of policies' introduced 'could see up to 4.5 million hours of police time saved across all forces every year—the equivalent of over 2,100 back on the beat', the inference clearly is that those savings had not yet been realized.[31] Furthermore, even if the cuts in bureaucracy are effective, they will deliver only the 'equivalent' of 2,100 officers; the losses in actual numbers will still have to be borne, and they do not fully compensate for the likely losses, even at the lower end of the projections. Given the importance attached in policy and practical terms of reducing bureaucracy it is, perhaps, surprising that the Home Office has not attached more definitive means of measuring progress in attaining this end. (See Chapter 4, p. 89.)

Second, the council tax precept set by PCCs might offer some mitigation. There is some evidence that a small number of council tax increases occurred in police authorities in 2012–13 despite the offer of the Council Tax Freeze grant for the CLG. The expected council tax total began to approach £3.3 billion as the CSR 2010 estimated. For 2013–14 twenty-eight of the forty-one PCCs set council tax increases of between 1 and 4 per cent, and one, South Wales, set an increase of 7 per cent. However, twelve set zero increases, and although this meant, at least in England, qualifying for the CLG Council Tax Freeze Grant, it also meant that their base budgets did not grow, leaving them exposed if the Council Tax Freeze Grant should itself freeze at some point in the future.[32] The 2013 spending review confirmed that the freeze grant would continue to be available, but only for 2014–15 and 2015–16, leaving open the possibility that it would end in a post-2015 election spending review.[33] However, incremental council tax increases are not of sufficient scale to avoid most of the cuts in personnel; they can only mitigate them. To replace the £1.4 billion grant loss, a similar amount of council tax would require a collective 44 per cent increase over four years—a little over 14 per cent a year—which is simply an unrealistic expectation. Even if all PCCs increased council tax precept near to the maximum permissible in England without provoking a referendum, this would amount to a little under 12 per cent in three years, or the equivalent of approximately 8,600 FTEs. It would still mean that over 55,000 FTE posts would have been lost since 2010.

[31] Conservatives, Reduction in crime shows police reform is working (<http://www.conservatives.com/News/News_stories/2013/01/Reduction_in_crime_shows_police_reform_is_working.aspx> [accessed 18 April 2013]).

[32] Association of Police and Crime Commissioners, Precept and Crime Plan (<http://www.apccs.police.uk/fileUploads/homepage-adverts/Police_Precepts_Announcements_27.02.13.pdf> [accessed 6 March 2013]).

[33] HM Treasury, *Spending Round 2013*, 10.

Third, the precise number of FTEs likely to be lost will vary according to the mix of police officers and civilian staff. Because police officers are on average more expensive than civilian staff, the total numbers lost will reduce slightly if more officers are lost than civilians. Conversely, the number will increase if more civilian posts are lost. Additionally, there may be some savings to accrue as a result of *Winsor*, although these would probably be marginal given that the principal savings Winsor identified were in pay progression through the police salary scale. If forces continued to lose rather than recruit staff then there would simply be fewer officers to which this would apply, certainly in the short term. Furthermore, savings to police officer pay would not affect civilian staff pay. Similarly cuts could be made to non-staff budgets, such as equipment, buildings, and vehicles, but as these combined only amount to 19–20 per cent of the annual police revenue spend these would similarly be of only marginal effect. On the other hand, even marginal inflationary pay increases during this period would mean that the scale of personnel cuts would necessarily be greater.

Fourth, there is the increase in numbers of special constables, which have risen from 15,500 in March 2010 to 19,159 in September 2012. The special constabulary is in effect the 'Big Society' in action, with volunteers coming forward to police their community, and while not yet the equivalent of fully trained police personnel, they might yet become so under new force training schemes. There are, however, three qualifications to this increase. First, many may have joined the special constabulary in the hope of joining the regular force in the fullness of time, a prospect likely to prove distant for many. Second, while the September 2012 figure is an increase on the March 2010 figure, it represents a decrease on the March 2012 level of 20,352, possibly indicating that enthusiasm for joining the special constabulary may have peaked. Third, even the March 2012 figure was similar to that of 1995, suggesting that long-term fluctuations in police numbers may be directly associated with recruiting prospects.[34] Lastly, special constables are volunteers and, no matter how enthusiastic or competent, do not work the equivalent of the forty-hours-a-week duty performed by regular officers.

The Home Office might also hope that 'Street Watch' schemes would compensate for some of the loss of police neighbourhood capacity. These comprise local volunteers who actively patrol under local police supervision. The Home Office provided some schemes with set-up grants.[35] However, by mid 2013 it was not clear the extent to which schemes had been set up, evaluated, or sustained. Moreover, the idea was not new, several schemes having been attempted in the 1990s under Michael Howard's auspices, and using the generic title 'patrolling with a purpose'. After an initial flurry of activity in these schemes, enthusiasm from the volunteers appeared to wane to the point that the relaunch was necessary in 2012.[36]

---

[34] Home Office, *Police service strength, 10 September 2012*, 11.

[35] eg *LutonOnSunday* News, 'Funding for Street Watch scheme', 27 February 2012 (<http://www.luton-dunstable.co.uk/News/Funding-for-Street-Watch-scheme-27022012.htm> [accessed 21 April 2013]).

[36] See Brain, 236.

Would Labour, if elected in 2015, implement significantly different policies? They might in the long term, but in a speech on 3 June 2013 Shadow Chancellor Ed Balls indicated that there would be no early relief for public spending with Labour intending to stick with the Coalition spending plans, at least for 2015–16.[37] If the economy did not pick up, there would be every reason to suppose that there might even be further cuts for the duration of the next Parliament, whatever party, or combination of parties, might be in power.

Politics and the constitution

Will Labour be in power after 2015 to have the chance of implementing any policy change, economic or other? At the mid-point of the Coalition's projected five-year span in office the probability was that it would survive until the date the election was due in May 2015, and this despite occasional high-profile disagreements between the Coalition partners. The leadership of both parties remained committed to the Coalition principle and mutual self-interest suggested that an early poll would serve neither party well. The Liberal Democrat victory in the Eastleigh by-election, held in March 2013 following the conviction for perjury and resignation of the Liberal Democrat MP and former Cabinet minister Chris Huhne, suggested that the Labour opposition had not yet been able to turn its national opinion poll lead into votes when it counted. However, it equally suggested that the Conservatives, some of whose vote leached away to UKIP, could not beat the Liberal Democrats where they had a strong local organization, although it seems they were helped by Labour fielding a weak candidate.[38]

By March 2013 the polling arithmetic suggested a Labour victory at the next general election, possibly with an 84-seat majority.[39] Equally, earlier polls had suggested that Labour's lead might not be sustainable if the economy picked up.[40] The problem for the Coalition was that by mid-spring 2013 it had not picked up and was showing only limited signs of doing so in the future. The Conservatives also had to overcome the inbuilt disadvantage the current constituency boundaries gave them, and having fallen out with their Liberal Democrat partners over Lords reform there was no possibility of the situation being rectified before the

---

[37] E Balls, 'Striking the Right Balance for the British Economy', 3 June 2013 (<http://www.labour.org.uk/striking-the-right-balance-for-the-british-economy> [accessed 6 July 2013]).

[38] Lord Ashcroft, 'Here's why Eastleigh voted the way it did', [no date] (<http://conservative-home.blogs.com/platform/2013/03/lord-ashcroft-heres-why-eastleigh-voted-the-way-it-did.html> [accessed 20 April 2013]).

[39] J Legge, 'Labour will win 2015 general election, says Ashcroft poll', *The Independent*, 9 March 2013 (<http://www.independent.co.uk/news/uk/politics/labour-will-win-2015-general-election-says-ashcroft-poll-8527617.html> [accessed 20 April 2013]).

[40] P Wintour, 'Labour's poll lead may not last if economy improves', *The Guardian*, 11 February 2013 (<http://www.guardian.co.uk/politics/2013/feb/11/labour-poll-lead-ec>) and T Helm, 'Ed Miller band "not winning over Tory voters as Blair did" —poll', *The Observer*, 3 February 2013 (<http://www.guardian.co.uk/politics/2013/feb/03/ed-miliband-not-winning-tory-voters> [both accessed 16 February 2013]).

next election. Labour's problem, however, was its leader, Ed Miliband, who at the same time as his party led the polls was failing to convince voters that he was prime ministerial material.[41] There is, furthermore, the inclination amongst many in the electorate to moderate their intentions as a general election approaches, which would tend to assist the Conservatives and Liberal Democrats.

So an outright Labour victory is, therefore, possible but not certain. Should Labour fail to gain an outright majority, would the Liberal Democrats form a coalition with a minority Labour administration? Such an outcome might have been possible in the eighteenth or even nineteenth centuries, but might seem cynical to early twenty-first-century electorates. However, a Labour minority government would have to find a working majority from somewhere and the Liberal Democrats would be the likely source. By mid 2013 any of the possible outcomes seemed as likely as any of the others.

There were, however, even larger political forces in play that might also prove of significance for policing. The continued existence of the United Kingdom itself could not be guaranteed beyond the Scottish independence referendum in autumn 2014. The likelihood was that the Scottish electorate would reject independence, but that could not be guaranteed. In theory that should have little direct impact on policing in England and Wales, as, while there was cooperation, the Scottish forces always operated separately, a tendency enforced by separate legal systems and the decision by the nationalist-dominated Scottish Government to establish a single Scottish force in April 2013. ACPO and ACPO Scotland (ACPOS) are similarly separate but provide a vehicle for cross-border cooperation. Police cooperation and coordination, however, appeared a relatively neglected field in the preparation for the referendum.

Whatever the outcome of the referendum, what will be of interest to observers will be the functioning mechanics of the new Scottish single force. The Scottish Government has chosen a constitutional structure which places some distance between the Minister of Justice—the minister responsible—and the police, by creating a police board. However, the board is not constitutionally independent in the same way as is a PCC in England or Wales. The Edinburgh and Westminster governments have diametrically opposed views on the constitutional position of policing; the former centralist, and the latter devolutionist. It will also be interesting to see whether the single chief constable can exercise effective leadership and community contact over his disparate domain, and whether the anticipated synergies will deliver the benefits, principally financial, hesitatingly forecast. It may be expected that this, like PCCs south of the border, is too important a political experiment to be allowed to fail. Equally, it underlines that such are the different courses being pursued by the Scottish and Westminster governments in so many policy fields, of which policing is but a noticeable example, that it is not

---

[41] PA/Huffington Post, 'Ed Milliband not ready to be prime minister say three in four voters', *Huffington Post*, 18 April 2013 (<http://www.huffingtonpost.co.uk/2013/04/18/ed-miliband-prime-minister_n_3109720.html?utm_hp_ref=uk> [accessed 20 April 2013]).

necessary for there to be Scottish independence for there to be a de facto break-up of the Union.

Another 'big' political question in play is the future of the UK's relationship with, or within, the European Union (EU). In January 2013 the Prime Minister made a long-anticipated speech setting out his way forward on the question of the continued UK presence within the EU, aware of some antipathy to continued union within his own ranks and of growing support in the electorate for UKIP at the expense of his rather than the opposition parties. His argument was nuanced: there would be a referendum on continued membership, but the question would only be put after there had been an opportunity for the EU to change by becoming more flexible, with greater powers for national governments, or, failing that process and outcome, for the UK to formally renegotiate its position within the Union. The 2015 Conservative election manifesto would offer the electorate an 'in-out' referendum on the basis of the renegotiated settlement.[42] This might prove a high-risk strategy for the Prime Minister because while the head of the British electorate might favour continued union, the heart might not, even on the basis of a renegotiated settlement. Even the threat of this might have a destabilizing and dislocating effect on the UK economy.

However, there was a police-specific issue arising from the reappraisal of the UK's relationship with the EU. Law, order, and policing had barely been afterthoughts to the Maastricht Treaty, and while the UK became a leading constituent country of 'Europol', it remained aloof from the cross-border police cooperation created for the twenty-six members of the Schengen Agreement (signed in 1985). This had proved less of a problem than might have been the case because of specific treaty cooperation between the British and French for the policing of the Channel Tunnel, and because repatriation of suspects fleeing to other jurisdictions had been greatly facilitated by the European Arrest Warrant (EAW). The EAW differed from previous extradition arrangements (which required specific country-by-country treaties) by removing the requirement for the offender to be suspected of a broadly similar offence in both the countries involved. Under the EAW it was only necessary for the individual to be suspected of an offence in the country of origin. The arrangements even allowed for trials *in absentia*. Without formally arguing for the UK's withdrawal from the EAW system, in October 2012 the Home Secretary made it clear that it would be amongst the package of powers considered for repatriation. Curiously, she offered the prospect of opting back into the EAW after renegotiation. It all seemed unnecessary, but had to be seen in the context of some Conservative MPs being dissatisfied with the prospect of British nationals being extradited under the warrant and tried in other jurisdictions with only the minimum of due process here.[43] It was yet

---

[42] D Cameron, 'David Cameron speech: UK and the EU', BBC News, 23 January 2013 (<http://www.bbc.co.uk/news/uk-politics-21160684> [accessed 6 February 2013]).

[43] BBC News, 'Theresa May tells MPs UK Government wants EU law opt-out', 15 October 2012 (<http://www.bbc.co.uk/news/uk-politics-19944072> [accessed 6 February 2013]).

another area of divergence between ACPO and the Conservatives. ACPO accepted that there was a need for reform of the system, in particular to avoid lengthy delays awaiting trial, but that this reform should be sought from within rather than after opting out. On balance, ACPO argued it was 'cost-efficient' and 'relatively simple and easy to operate'.[44] A full European opt-out would inevitably have inhibited international pan-European cooperation against terrorism and serious and organized crime. In the end the Home Secretary reluctantly accepted retaining the EAW and several other EU criminal justice measures.

The Conservative element of the Coalition has also shown some enthusiasm for curtailing the current degree of independence of the judiciary and, thereby, eroding the 'separation of powers' within the unwritten UK constitution. John Tate in *What's Right Now?*, as part of his general essay on 'Democratic renewal, national identity and social justice', asserted that judges were 'unaccountable', the hint being that they should be under increased democratic (or perhaps political) control.[45] No doubt some Conservatives have again looked across the Atlantic where most judicial appointments are politicized. In Britain the independence of the judiciary, through a largely depoliticized appointment process, has been a feature of the limited and largely informal separation of powers established after the Revolution Settlement of 1688–9. The Conservatives, however, have moved cautiously in this most sensitive of policy areas. No plans were forthcoming in the 2010 manifesto, but that did not stop the Prime Minister moving surreptitiously in that direction. Kenneth Clarke might not have practised for a long time before his appointment as Justice Secretary and Lord Chancellor in 2010, but he was at least a barrister. His replacement in the 2012 Cabinet reshuffle with Chris Grayling, who had no previous professional legal experience, was seen as incremental politicization. Theresa May's criticism of judges for ignoring 'parliament's wishes' by refusing to deport foreign criminals because of their right to family life under article 8 of the European Convention on Human Rights was also interpreted as a political intervention, if not actual interference.[46]

These issues of high constitutional politics might not at first sight seem an issue of direct concern to policing, and many officers might notionally like judges to be subject to more practical and populist influence, but it bode ill for any who were concerned about the independence of the law from direct political influence. Was the logical conclusion of this process to be overt political appointments to the judiciary, and would it stop only at the most senior appointments,

---

[44] House of Lords, European Union Committee: Justice, Institutions and Consumer Protection Sub-committee—*UK's 2014 Opt-out Decision ('Protocol 36')* —written evidence (<http://www.parliament.uk/documents/lords-committees/eu-sub-com-f/Protocol36OptOut/VolofevidenceP36asat110113.pdf> [accessed 6 February 2013]) , and BBC News, 'Theresa May says UK to keep European Arrest Warrant', 9 July 2013 (<http://www.bbc.co.uk/news/uk-politics-23224306> [accessed 6 August 2013]).

[45] J Tate, *What's Right Now: Conservative Essays on the Role of Civil Society, Markets and the State* (Social Market Foundation, London, 2005), 63.

[46] BBC News, 'Theresa May criticises judges for "ignoring" deportation law', 17 February 2013 (<http://www.bbc.co.uk/news/uk-21489072> [accessed 17 February 2013]).

or would it eventually include junior judicial appointments, even the appointment of local chief Crown Prosecutors? This might seem politically attractive but what would be the longer term implications for public respect for the judiciary and the rule of law?

The final 'big' political question is the future of politics itself. General election turnouts have been in steady decline since 1970, although the 2010 turnout, at 65 per cent, was an improvement on the 61 per cent in 2005, the lowest since 1945.[47] The turnout for local elections in 2012 was 31 per cent, while that of the European elections in 2009 was 35 per cent. Even the high-profile and intensely contested London mayoral election of 2012 was only 37 per cent. The PCC election average of November was comfortably the lowest at 15 per cent.[48] What does this trend signify and what does it mean for the future of democracy in the United Kingdom? If, as seems likely, it signifies a general disillusionment on the part of the electorate with politics, politicians, and political institutions, then this portends a bleak future for democratic politics in the UK.[49] The Conservatives had recognized the phenomenon as part of the UK's 'broken politics' and the sum of its policies was intended to reverse the disengagement. PCCs were meant to be a flagship example of electoral re-engagement. The problem was that it did not work, and there is little evidence that re-engagement is occurring. If the disengagement continues then the danger will be that those who become sufficiently disengaged to the point of disaffection will not seek to re-engage through political means but through direct action. This is not a new phenomenon in British political history; there are many examples of disengagement leading to direct action, but the phenomenon has been particularly marked since the 1980s. Examples include the Greenham Common anti-cruise missile protest, the Miners' Strike, and a variety of environmental and animal rights protests and actions. The Occupy Movement was an extensive recent example.

The implications for the police are direct if political direct action replaces democratic engagement. The police will be placed on the frontline to protect a political system of declining legitimacy, in a not dissimilar way to the position it was in for significant periods of the nineteenth century. Much is sometimes made of the police lacking, or suffering some form of decline in, legitimacy. Less is made of the declining legitimacy of the national and local polities of which policing is but a part. Besides, in public esteem, and despite the vicissitudes of negative news stories and political opprobrium in late 2012, when it came to a poll of public trust in professions, the police heavily outscored politicians. In February 2013, 65 per cent of those asked said they trusted the police to tell them the truth; only

---

[47] UK Political Info, 'General election turnout 1945–2010' (<http://www.ukpolitical.info/Turnout45. htm> [accessed 16 February 2013]).

[48] Datablog, 'UK election historic turnouts since 1918', guardian.co.uk (<http://www.guardian. co.uk/news/datablog/2012/nov/16/uk-election-turnouts-historic> [accessed 16 February 2013]).

[49] In February 2013 only 18 per cent of those polled trusted politicians to tell them the truth, compared to 24 per cent for estate agents and 65 per cent for the police. Ipsos-MORI, Trust Poll—Topline Results (<http://www.ipsos-mori.com/Assets/Docs/Polls/Feb2013_Trust_Topline.PDF> [accessed 16 February 2013]).

18 per cent said they would 'generally' trust politicians.[50] Furthermore, based on a turnout of only 15 per cent it could not convincingly be claimed that PCCs had taken a decisive step in restoring confidence in policing even assuming that such confidence was in need of restoration.

The police, the law, and competing freedoms

In their last years in opposition the Conservatives developed an impressive legal reform programme. It was not, however, of the kind that came to characterize Labour's period in office. It was not, therefore, an extensive programme of micro-legislation, with offences and intrusions into personal life proliferating as the government sought to legislate its way out of social problems. The Conservatives intended the opposite.[51] For them, Labour's massive legislative programme was yet another example of the encroachment of the state and it was therefore another programme that required the antidote of new Conservatism. It was, furthermore, part of their wider programme of constitutional and political change; rolling back the state, and redistributing power from Europe and Westminster to the people. The specifics of the programme, by the time it emerged in the 2010 Conservative manifesto, were significant. The Human Rights Act 1998 would be replaced with a 'UK Bill of Rights', surveillance powers curtailed, freedom of speech reasserted, and legislation enacted to 'make sure that our DNA database is used primarily to store information about those who are guilty of committing crimes rather than those who are innocent.'[52]

The Liberal Democrats held similar philosophical views about restricting the encroachment of the state on personal freedoms, and agreed about upholding principle freedoms such as free speech, but differed in some of detail, particularly over the HRA, which they were committed to upholding.[53] The Coalition agreements, therefore, perforce contained compromises, but what emerged still amounted to an extensive programme. There would be a 'Freedom Bill'; ID cards, if introduced by Labour, would be scrapped; 'the protections of the Scottish model for the DNA database' would be adopted; the 'rights to non-violent protest' would be restored; safeguards would be introduced to prevent the 'misuse of anti-terrorism legislation'; finally, a commission would be established to 'investigate the creation of a British Bill of Rights' incorporating the European Convention on Human Rights.[54]

---

[50] Ipsos-MORI, Trust polling, February 2013 (<http://www.ipsos-mori.com/Assets/Docs/Polls/Feb2013_Trust_Charts.pdf> [accessed 20 April 2013]).

[51] See for example, J Norman, 'Renewing the conversation', in *What's Right Now*, 166–74 and D Grieve and E Laing, *Reversing the Rise of the Surveillance State: 11 Measures to Protect Personal Privacy and Hold Government to Account* (The Conservative Party, London, 2009 <http://www.conservatives.com/News/News_stories/2009/09/~/media/Files/Policy%20Documents/Surveillance%20State.ashx> [accessed 10 February 2013]), *passim.*

[52] Conservative Manifesto 2010, 79–80.

[53] Liberal Democrat Manifesto 2010, 93–5.

[54] *Coalition Programme for Government* (Cabinet Office, London, 2010), 11.

Given its scope, the Coalition moved rapidly to address most of these issues through the Protection of Freedoms Act, given its Royal assent on 1 May 2012. In addition to measures to introduce codes of practice for surveillance cameras and officials' powers of entry, outlawing wheel-clamping on private land, it also introduced restrictions on searches under the Terrorism Act 2000, limited detention before charge for suspected terrorism offences from twenty-eight to fourteen days, and introduced limitations to DNA retention.[55]

Given the continuing threat to the UK from internal and external terrorists, principally but not exclusively associated with the global jihadist movement, reducing the period of detention without charge might have proved controversial, with strong opposition from the police and security agencies.[56] There was every reason to suppose that ACPO might oppose the reduction given that its leadership had conspicuously supported the Labour government's somewhat clumsy, and ultimately unsuccessful attempt to extend the period of pre-charge detention from fourteen to ninety days.[57] However, that opposition did not emerge, partly because ACPO's influence on government had palpably declined, but also because the police and the Security Service had proved adept at preventing or disrupting terrorist attacks on the UK since 2005, thereby negating the need for extended periods of detention. No one had been detained under the terrorism legislation for more than fourteen days without charge, although this might have been attributable to the ability of the police to use charges under alternative legislation to secure extended periods of detention to enable investigation of terrorism offences.[58]

ACPO did put up more resistance to restrictions on DNA retention, but this was insufficient to persuade the government of the merits of their case. In opposition the Conservatives had concluded that the indefinite retention of DNA 'profiles' for suspects never charged with a criminal offence was a fundamental injustice, a principle supported, ironically, by a European Court of Human Rights judgment (*S and Marper v United Kingdom*, 2008).[59] Both the Conservative and Liberal

---

[55] parliament.uk, 'Protection of Freedoms Act 2012' (<http://www.services.parliament.uk/bills/2010-12/protectionoffreedoms.html> [accessed 9 February 2013]).

[56] The threat of an attack on the UK was, for example, still assessed as 'substantial' in early 2013. Home Office, Current threat level (<http://www.homeoffice.gov.uk/counter-terrorism/current-threat-level/> [accessed 9 February 2013]).

[57] Brain, 361.

[58] Security Service MI5, 'Terrorist plots in the UK' (<https://www.mi5.gov.uk/home/the-threats/terrorism/international-terrorism/international-terrorism-and-the-uk/terrorist-plots-in-the-uk.html> [accessed 9 February 2013]); Home Office, 'Arrests and outcomes' (<http://www.homeoffice.gov.uk/publications/science-research-statistics/research-statistics/counter-terrorism-statistics/police-powers-terror-act-q2-2012/arrests-outcomes-q2-2012> [accessed 9 February 2013]); and, HM Government, Review of Counter-Terrorism and security powers: findings and recommendations (<http://www.homeoffice.gov.uk/publications/counter-terrorism/review-of-ct-security-powers/review-findings-and-rec?view=Binary> [accessed 9 February 2013]), 7.

[59] D Grieve and E Laing, *Reversing the Rise of the Surveillance State: 11 Measures to Protect Personal Privacy and Hold Government to Account* (The Conservative Party, London, 2009 <http://www.conservatives.com/News/News_stories/2009/09/~/media/Files/Policy%20Documents/Surveillance%20State.ashx> [accessed 10 February 2013]), 9.

Democrat 2010 manifestos included commitments to restrict DNA detention, and it was, therefore, unsurprising that it emerged as a commitment in the Coalition Programme. This was reflected, at least to a degree, in the Protection of Freedoms Act 2012, although the legislation was insufficient to satisfy prominent civil liberty groups.[60] In essence this meant that the DNA and fingerprint profiles of persons arrested but not convicted of one or more of a range of relevant serious offences (principally violence, sexual, and burglary offences), would be destroyed after three years. Parliament had listened to but had not been convinced by evidence from ACPO that the number of offences detected as a result of this change would probably be cut by about 1,000, with some of that number inevitably relating to serious offences.[61]

This might not have sounded much of a decrease in detections, but the problem was that the statistics used to mount a counter-argument was based on weak evidence. The National DNA Database, established by a Conservative government in 1995, held over six million records and was the largest in the world, but the number of detections attributed to DNA in 2008–9 was only 32,209, or just over 2 per cent of all offences detected that year, a number itself falling, a trend explained by the overall fall in crime. The arguments about the effectiveness of DNA did not, in any case, revolve solely around the retention of DNA profiles created for persons not convicted, as some of the most successful examples of cases resolved by DNA had been the result of matching crime scene DNA against a suspect (for example the conviction of the Ipswich prostitute murderer, Steven Wright, in 2008).[62] The proportion of offences detected through fingerprint matching was marginally superior to those from DNA, but not decisively so.[63] The new protections were consequently introduced in the Protection of Freedoms Act 2012, although the measures were only slowly implemented through 2013, possibly because of the difficulties of disentangling and destroying legacy records, possibly because it might not be possible to separate out in all cases those records of persons not convicted of an offence from those merely arrested. The operational consequences of the measure are, to all practical purposes, impossible to predict. There simply is not enough statistical evidence. On balance, as ACPO asserted, 'some' serious offences might go undetected. It would be the price to be paid for increased freedoms.

---

[60] Protection of Freedoms Act 2012, s. 1 and Big Brother Watch, *The National DNA Database* (<http://www.bigbrotherwatch.org.uk/files/DNA_REPORT_June2012.pdf> [accessed 9 February 2013]), 11.

[61] House of Commons, Public Bill Committee, Protection of Freedoms Bill, 22 March 2011 (<http://www.publications.parliament.uk/pa/cm201011/cmpublic/protection/110322/am/110322s01.htm> [accessed 10 February 2013]).

[62] See House of Lords, 'Supplementary letter from Dr Helen Wallace, Director, GeneWatch UK', Surveillance: Citizens and the state—Constitution Committee (<http://www.publications.parliament.uk/pa/ld200809/ldselect/ldconst/18/8013007.htm> [accessed 10 February 2013]).

[63] Nuffield Council on Bioethics, 'Chapter 4—Criminal investigation' (<http://www.nuffield-bioethics.org/sites/default/files/files/Bioinformation%20Chapter%204%20-%20Criminal%20investigation.pdf> [accessed 10 February 2013]), 4.

More problematical for the Coalition was its position over the HRA. Despite their differences the Coalition partners agreed to establish a commission to review the Act and make recommendations. The greatest intellectual problem lay with the Conservatives, who were hoping simultaneously to repatriate British freedoms from European jurisdiction, reassert those freedoms in the face of curtailment under Labour, but also emphasize individual obligations as well as collective freedoms. The Liberal Democrats simply pledged themselves to 'protecting the Human Rights Act'.[64] The Coalition Programme commitment to establish an investigating commission was, therefore, a pragmatic way forward in 2010. However, it was only to delay the public realization of the fundamental differences between the two parties. The Commission's report was published in December 2012 and revealed the complexities of the argument and the strong differences of opinion between those who gave evidence and amongst the commissioners themselves. In the end a majority of the commissioners concluded that 'on balance, there was a strong argument in favour of a UK Bill of Rights'. Two of the commissioners, however, disagreed and thought that progression of the question should await the outcome of the Scottish independence referendum and the deliberations of a 'Constitutional Convention', and, moreover, that the case for a bill had not been made.[65] Thereafter, the arguments became increasingly subtle, with it by no means being certain in the minds of even those members of the Commission who thought there was an argument in favour of a Bill of Rights that it automatically followed that the UK would withdraw from the European Convention on Human Rights, although it would mean that the latter would no longer have status as the primary authority on human rights law in the UK.[66] Furthermore, a UK Bill of Rights did not mean abandoning human rights in UK law, it simply meant transferring the status as primary authority from European Convention to UK law. The language might be different, but the principles would remain the same. It might even prove more complex to interpret than the existing European Convention.[67] The lukewarm majority recommendation in favour of a Bill of Rights was not exactly what the assertive Justice Secretary Chris Grayling was looking for, and so it was hardly surprising that while officially welcoming the Commission's report, in practice he accepted that further progress in replacing the HRA was not possible in coalition and must await an outright Conservative majority.[68] In practice this meant no substantive change until at least 2015.

[64] Conservative Manifesto 2010, 79–80 and Liberal Democrat Manifesto 2010, 94.

[65] Commission on a Bill of Rights, *A UK Bill of Rights? The Choice Before Us*, vol 1 (Members of the Commission on a Bill of Rights, 2012, <http://www.justice.gov.uk/downloads/about/cbr/uk-bill-rights-vol-1.pdf> [accessed 10 February 2013]), 28–32.

[66] Commission on a Bill of Rights, *A UK Bill of Rights?*, 187.

[67] Commission on a Bill of Rights, *A UK Bill of Rights?*, 192–215.

[68] I Hardman, 'Chris Grayling wants a robust response to the European Court, but will he get his way?', *The Spectator*, 18 December 2012 (<http://www.blogs.spectator.co.uk/coffeehouse/2012/12/how-radical-can-the-conservatives-be-on-the-european-court/> [accessed 10 February 2013]).

What would replacing the HRA with a UK Bill of Rights mean in practical terms for policing? As with the introduction of the HRA, it would certainly mean an extensive re-training programme. There would be changes in detail, language, and interpretation to deal with. Instead, therefore, of every pre-planned police operation having somewhere in its text 'Human Rights Act implications' there, presumably, would be 'Bill of Rights implications', with much the same considerations being taken into account. There would continue to be mistakes; as with the HRA, the parameters of the legislation would continue to be tested in operational circumstances, although the final court of jurisdiction would be the UK Supreme Court, not the European Court of Human Rights. Mostly the police will interpret the intricacies of the legislation correctly, sometimes they will not.

Whether the law comes in the form of the HRA or a new UK Bill of Rights, the police will still have to contend with the competing, not to say the sometimes conflicting, demands of maintaining order while complying with the principles of statutorily enshrined rights. The policing of demonstrations with either the threat of disorder or its manifestation, such as the protest against the Iraq War in 2003 outside RAF Fairford, Gloucestershire; the G20 protests in London in April 2009; student protests in December 2010; and the Occupy Movement's occupation of the area in front of St Paul's Cathedral between October 2011 and February 2012 all serve to exemplify the difficulties the police have in striking the right balance between permitting 'peaceful protest', as is the protestors' right under English law, and allowing other legitimate activities, such as trade and commerce, to continue. The irony is that there is no right to 'peaceful protest' in the European Convention on Human Rights, or the HRA. Articles 10 and 11 respectively allow for freedom of expression and freedom of association. It is English judges who have combined the two articles in practice and asserted that they amount effectively to a new right, that of 'peaceful protest'.

In the case of the Gloucestershire protest the police turned back protestors making their way to the RAF base to demonstrate against American bombers lawfully using the base for offensive operations against Iraq. In holding them in coaches and escorting them back to London, the police were found to have breached their human rights of freedom of expression and assembly.[69] In the case of the G20 protests, in which a bystander, Ian Tomlinson, died after being pushed to the ground by a police officer, there was much criticism that the police, whose command feared massive disruption to the central London business areas, over-reacted, a conclusion with which HMIC partially agreed in its 2011 report *Policing Public Order*. In the case of the student protests of December 2010 the police were essentially criticized for under-reacting and allowing the protests to develop into

---

[69] BBC News, 'RAF Fairford protestors win legal battle against police', 8 February 2013 (<http://www.bbc.co.uk/news/uk-england-gloucestershire-21382889> [accessed 10 February 2013]).

a full-scale riot.[70] In the case of the Occupy Movement's prolonged demonstration the police looked on, along with City of London and cathedral authorities, uncertain what to do about protestors who were palpably peaceful but who had succeeded, at least for some days, in closing St Paul's, a national place of worship and a major City tourist attraction. Their right to peaceful protest was certainly respected but it took four months before a court order was obtained to evict the protestors and another six weeks before it was enforced. Aside from some scuffles the eviction took place peacefully, but the episode illustrated collective official inertia in the face of the enshrined rights.[71]

The police have adapted to the new circumstances and the 'kettling' tactic (corralling protestors until the likelihood of violent disorder had passed) was deemed to be lawful by the European Court of Human Rights as the best of the options available to police in difficult circumstances.[72] But even this tactic required good intelligence, advance planning (as *Policing Public Order* recognized), and overwhelming police numbers to enforce. The evidence of the 1980s is that the police will, after experience gained through trial and error, eventually adapt to the prevailing circumstances of disorder, but the evidence is that it is taking longer to do so in the era of the HRA.

Summation and prognosis

Modern policing since its inception in 1829 has always been at the fulcrum of social, political, economic, and legal change. In times of rapid collective change, such as those of the last decades of the twentieth and first decades of the twenty-first centuries it is hardly surprising that the police find it difficult to cope. What might be surprising is that it has done so relatively well. It has confronted its demons, fronted them out and moved on. The problems are that the police will normally be behind the curve, and it is not normally in control of the wider political agenda even if wishes to move faster.

The reality is that the period since 2001, as evidenced by the 2011 census, has been a period of remarkable social change, probably as great as any in recent history. The police have either adapted or sought to adapt. The essential problem has been that it has not adapted fast enough. It is not alone in that. Furthermore,

---

[70] HMIC, *Policing Public Order: An Overview and Review of Progress Against the Recommendations of Adapting to Protest and Nurturing the British Model of Policing* (HMIC, London, 2011) *passim* and, for example, G Rayner, C Hope, and R Edwards, 'Millbank tuition fee protests: "embarrassed" Metropolitan police caught out by student riots', *The Telegraph*, 11 November 2010 (<http://www.telegraph.co.uk/news/uknews/law-and-order/8124770/Millbank-tuition-fee-protests-embarrassed-Metropolitan-Police-caught-out-by-student-riots.html> [accessed 10 February 2013]).

[71] T Burgis, 'Authorities clear St Paul's Occupy camp', ft.com.uk, 28 February 2012 (<http://www.ft.com/cms/s/0/3b89ef38-61ab-11e1-94fa-00144feabdc0.html#axzz2KWcMYeLS> [accessed 10 February 2013]).

[72] BBC News, 'European Court says "kettling" tactics in 2001 lawful', 15 March 2010 (<http://www.bbc.co.uk/news/uk-17378700> [accessed 10 February 2013]).

it has had recently to adapt when its material resources have been placed under enormous strain, as have other welfare and caring agencies, because of the deep and enduring consequences of economic recession. In mid 2013 there remained little prospect of rapid and sustainable economic growth, which might lead to a reinjection of resources into public services in general and the police in particular. In fact the portents were in the opposite direction, with reductions in public spending extending well into the next parliament and with no prospect of the police being considered a special case. This means that the likelihood is that somewhere in the region of over 60,000 FTE posts will be lost between 2010 and 2018, effectively reversing the growth under Labour. This will not mean a collapse of all forms of effective policing but it is likely to severely limit its scope and lead to a prolonged period of poor morale. There has been, at best, limited evidence that government changes, including the *Winsor* pay policies and the limited cuts so far extant in bureaucracy, have had any significant mitigating effect, despite some claims to the contrary. On the other hand, the police will have to continue to address the effects of the decline in engagement in national and local politics and the commensurate rise in forms of direct action. The police might yet also have to address the adverse consequences of economic decline in terms of crime and disorder, and it is to that possibility that this study will now turn.

9

Operational policing

Crime, anti-social behaviour, disorder, and confidence

Introduction

While such factors as the political imperatives, social trends, economic factors, and organizational developments shape the service provided by the police, arguably what counts for the majority of the public is a belief that they can trust the police to help them when needed and that they contribute to a safe and calm social environment in which to live. In practice the public seek help from the police over a wide range of issues. A 2011 Government Statistical Service study revealed that while 4.3 million (25 per cent) calls related to 'notifiable crime' and 3.5 million (20 per cent) to anti-social behaviour, 9.5 million (55 per cent) related to 'other incidents'.[1] This complexity is not something which appeals to political policy-makers. For Michael Howard the main job of the police was to 'catch criminals'. It was a simplification too far, but Blair for Labour still sought to focus more specifically on 'crime and disorder'. There is, however, a point to this political condensing of the police role, and that is when the public are *asked* what they want from the police they tend to focus on the crime and disorder functions.[2] In February 2013 the regular Ipsos MORI poll of what are 'the most important issues facing Britain today', 'Crime/Law&Order/Violence/Vandalism' ranked fourth in a list of thirty-two issues, coming below only the economy, the

---

[1] Government Statistical Service, *National Statistician's Review of Crime Statistics: England and Wales* June 2011 (<http://www.statisticsauthority.gov.uk/national-statistician/ns-reports—reviews-and-guidance/national-statistician-s-reviews/national-statistician-s-review-of-crime-statistics.html> [accessed 7 July 2013]).

[2] eg *Operational Policing Review*, sections 4 and 5, 6–7. Joint Consultative Committee, *The Operational Policing Review* (Joint Consultative Committee, Surbiton, 1990).

NHS, and immigration.[3] It had been even higher before the economic crisis of 2007–8. It was this seeming political imperative the Conservatives sought to address in their 2010 election manifesto, and was further reflected in the Coalition's early white paper *Policing in the 21st Century*. However, in both these documents there was a recognition that 'crime' meant something more than what was recorded as crime by the police, or even that recognized in crime surveys. Mrs May sought to identify this nuance in her introduction to *Policing in the 21st Century*. The police were 'charged with keeping people safe; cutting crime and anti-social behaviour.'[4] The problem with this approach is that it creates a fundamental mismatch between what politicians and, to an extent, the people say they want, and what in practice the people demand of the police on a daily basis. For example, it seems that in many areas the police necessarily have to address the public-facing issues of mental health, but this is not an issue likely to feature on any political or public list of police priorities.[5]

But what exactly does 'keeping people safe; cutting crime and anti-social behaviour' amount to? In her introduction to *Policing in the 21st Century* the Home Secretary appears to place herself and her government in a direct line of succession to Sir Robert Peel in insisting that the 'mission' of the police is 'preventing crime and disorder'. However, she adds a very twenty-first-century nuance to that mission. For her, 'disorder' now includes 'anti-social behaviour'.[6] It is at least open to debate whether Sir Robert Peel would have accepted such a sweeping definition, but even in the twenty-first century it causes some interpretive problems. Is anti-social behaviour (ASB) really the same as disorder? Contemporarily the Home Office necessarily has adopted a wide definition of what constitutes 'anti-social behaviour'. It is 'any aggressive, intimidating, or destructive activity that damages or destroys another person's quality of life'.[7] That it remains a priority for the Coalition is evidenced by the presentation for consultation in December 2012 of the 'Draft Anti-Social Behaviour Bill', in effect a set of replacements for Labour's own anti-social behaviour measures (notably the Anti-social Behaviour Order or 'ASBO') which had been deemed over-bureaucratic by the Conservatives when in opposition.[8] That 'disorder' has a far more serious dimension was, however, vividly illustrated by the August 2011 riots.

---

[3] Ipsos MORI, Issues Index: 2007 onwards (<http://www.ipsos-mori.com/researchpublications/researcharchive/2905/Issues-Index-2012-onwards.aspx?view=wid> [accessed 20 April 2013]). Cf HMIC, *Demanding Times: the Front Line and Police Visibility* (<http://www.hmic.gov.uk/media/demanding-times-062011.pdf> [accessed 20 April 2013]), 32–5.

[4] Home Office, *Policing in the 21st Century*, 4.

[5] BBC News, 'Police deal with more mental health calls, says chief', 5 March 2013 (<http://www.bbc.co.uk/news/uk-england-manchester-21672348> [accessed 21 April 2013]) and Police Oracle, 'PCC moots plans for 24/7 mental health response teams to work in collaboration with officers', [no date] (<http://touch.policeoracle.com/news/article.html?id=63452> [accessed 21 April 2013]).

[6] Home Office, *Policing in the 21st Century*, 3.

[7] Home Office, *Antisocial Behaviour* (<http://www.homeoffice.gov.uk/crime/anti-social-behaviour/> [accessed 7 March 2013]).

[8] Home Secretary, Draft Anti-Social Behaviour Bill, December 2012 (<http://www.homeoffice.gov.uk/publications/about-us/consultations/community-remedy-consultation/draft-antisocial-behaviour-bill?view=Binary> [accessed 7 March 2013]).

By consciously linking her government's policing policy with Sir Robert Peel, Mrs May has invited comparison with other aspects of the so-called 'Peelian Principles'. Modern scholarship may suggest that Peel probably never stated them in the form they have been traditionally presented but over time they came to embody Peel's policing philosophy and, by osmosis, have come to be regarded as the founding principles of policing in a liberal democracy.[9] At their heart is the principle that the police in a democracy can only function with the support of the people, and for that consent to be present the public must have confidence that police will discharge their responsibilities under the rule of law, fairly, and with respect.[10] In sum 'confidence' is a central principle in democratic policing and consequently there inevitably must be more to assessing the effectiveness of policing in a democracy than simply 'cutting crime', even in the modern extended form favoured by the Home Secretary.

So this chapter will consider the prospects for the police service's core mission to reduce crime, disorder, and anti-social behaviour, and the extent to which public confidence will support the service in its endeavours.

Crime

Recorded crime was at a very low level until the First World War after which crime rose on average at 5½ per cent a year. The rate accelerated in the 1970s through the 1980s, and only began to decrease from the mid 1990s.[11] Crime rates attracted little media or political attention until after the Conservatives made policing an electoral issue in 1979, since when it has routinely featured in both national and local media coverage. Much attention focused on police recorded crime statistics (PRCS), until recently the responsibility of the Home Office but since 2012 that of the Office for National Statistics (ONS). However, it has long been recognized that PRCS did not provide a full picture of crime as, for a variety of reasons, not everyone who experiences crime reports it to the police, so since 1981 these have been supplemented with increasing frequency by figures from the British Crime Survey, renamed in 2012 the Crime Survey for England and Wales (BCS/CSEW). However, even the BCS/CSEW probably under-records crime because of limitations to the scope of the survey sample.[12] However, while individually both have limitations, taken together PRCS and BCS/CSEW provide a reasonably comprehensive picture of what is happening to the trends in crime.[13]

---

[9] See S Lentz and R Chaires, 'The invention of Peel's principles: a study of policing "textbook" history', *Journal of Justice* 35 (2007), 69–79.

[10] The Peelian Principles as generally understood are detailed in the Appendix.

[11] Home Office, Historical crime data 1898 to 2001/2.

[12] By limiting the types of crime recorded and the time frame for reporting victimization, and those surveyed to householders and, until recently, those aged above 16.

[13] ONS, Trends in Crime—A short story 2011/12 (<http://www.ons.gov.uk/ons/rel/crime-stats/crime-statistics/period-ending-march-2012/trends-in-crime—a-short-story.html> [accessed 23 April 2013]), 6.

A recent Office for National Statistics study broke down crime trends since 1981 into four distinct periods.

1. 1981–95—a sustained period of steeply rising crime in all categories. A more detailed examination reveals notable increases in property crime, especially vehicle crime and burglary. PRCS crime began to register decreases from 1993 onwards.
2. 1995–2004/5—sharply falling BCS/CSEW crime, but gradually rising PRCS crime principally attributable to the introduction of new 'counting rules' by the Home Office, and especially after the introduction of the NCRS in 2002–3.
3. 2005/6–9/10—a more gradual downward trend in BCS/CSEW crime, with occasional annual fluctuations. After the NCRS embedded the downward trend in PRCS continued.
4. 2009/10 to date—the downward trend in BCS/CSEW crime has 'flattened out', but the downward trend in PRCS has continued producing, even allowing for NCRS, a twenty-year low point in both PRCS and CSEW crime.

The question is what has caused, or more precisely what combination of factors has caused these fluctuations over time? There has often been an assumed link between crime and unemployment, with the former Justice Secretary Kenneth Clarke saying as much in December 2011. Researchers tend to suggest that the relationship with this and other factors is more complex, even unknown, and furthermore a predictive model is all but impossible to create.[14] However, while this may be sound social science there needs to be some explanation advanced for what has happened to crime and disorder, and what might, therefore, happen in the future. One way is to look at the major social and policy events and trends which occurred in the four crime trend periods identified by the ONS, advance some explanations, and consider how these explanations might be applied to future trends.

The graph at Figure 9.1 illustrates the trends in crime, unemployment, prison population, and police full-time equivalent personnel (officers and civilian FTE) since 1981. For practical presentational purposes the prison population and police FTE figures have been multiplied by 100, otherwise their numbers (measured in thousands) would be too small to register in comparison with crime and unemployment (measured in millions). The graph illustrates that initially there is some correlation between rising unemployment and rising crime, and then between generally improving employment, rising police numbers, and prison population, and decreasing unemployment and lower levels of crime. The trends are broad rather than exact, as should be expected in dealing with social

---

[14] B Glaze, 'Crime could rise, admits Clarke', Press Association, 13 December 2011 (<http://mediapoint.press.net/article.jsp?id=8040561> [accessed 13 December 2011]). In contrast see S Field quoted in R Harries, 'Modelling and predicting recorded property crime trends in England and Wales—a retrospective', *International Journal of Forecasting*, 19 (2003), 565.

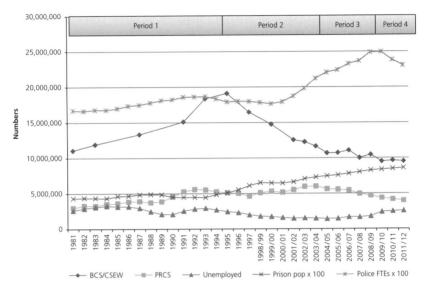

Figure 9.1: Crime, unemployment, prison population, and police FTEs 1981–2011/12
Home Office Recorded Crime and Cipfa Police Actuals[15]

rather than scientific factors, and also allowing for inexact data sets (eg crime figures since 1998–9 being recorded on a financial year basis rather than, as for unemployment statistics, recorded by calendar year) and changes in compilation criteria (eg new Home Office counting rules from 2002). Even allowing for these qualifications the correlation between increasing police numbers and prison population and falling BCS/CSEW crime is particularly striking.

A more detailed analysis of each of the ONS periods also offers further explanation of the factors that may have influenced crime, both BCS/CSEW and PRCS.

Period 1: 1981–95—sustained increase

During this first period unemployment peaked at an annual average of 3.3 million in 1984, but, after a brief period of decrease, a second recession saw unemployment reach 2.7 million in 1993. Unemployment averaged 2.7 million for the period. The prison population increased by 18 per cent over the period, but there was considerable fluctuation, and at the end of the period the population decreased from an interim peak at 48,000 in 1989 and was deliberately allowed to fall to 44,500 in 1993 before a conscious change in policy (the Criminal Justice Act 1993 and the 'prison works' policy) saw the population rise to 51,000 at the end of the period. The prison population averaged 46,000 for the entire period. Over the same period all police personnel (FTEs) increased by 17,900, or 11 per cent, averaging 175,800 for the period. Recorded crime increased by 72 per cent, and BCS/CSEW by 73 per cent.

---

[15] NB BCS/CSEW was not produced annually until 2001–2.

Although there were episodes of deep recession, over the period as a whole there was general growth in GDP, practically demonstrated by increased availability of consumer goods and home ownership. There was, however, growing economic inequality as measured by the Gini Coefficient. This combination of recession and growth, increasing general wealth, and specific inequalities provided the socio-economic environment in which crime increased exponentially, especially property crimes such as car crime (notably theft of car radios/stereos) and burglary (notably recently available domestic video-recording machines (VHS)). Despite increasing GDP the economic transition from large production industries like coal and steel to service and consumer businesses created high and prolonged unemployment, which was sustained, with a short period of relief, into the 1990s. Although difficult to measure, there was a growing consciousness of marginalized groups and the loosening of informal social controls, together with increased alcohol and drug use, particularly as the cost of the former decreased in real term value. There were also bouts of severe inner-city rioting.

This was a period of considerable change in policing, with the introduction of PACE and the CPS in 1985, as well as drives to improve 'effectiveness, efficiency, and economy' through increased civilianization, privatization, and internal restructuring. The end of the period saw the initiation of 'Police Reform', focusing on performance monitoring, objectives, and targets. Situational crime prevention, initially rudimentary, was improving by the end of the period but was still fragmentary rather than strategic. The criminal justice system was largely left to look after itself, with multiple cautions for juveniles common until 1994.

In summary, the combined effects of a more stable socio-economic environment, improved police and crime prevention techniques, more police numbers, and an increased prison population, backed up with a more assertive sentencing regime were only being fully felt at the end of the first period, which was otherwise characterized by extremes of socio-economic transition and tension, incremental increases in police resources, and inconsistent prison and sentencing policies. Police and prison population numbers were, however, relatively stable for much of the period, both declining slightly towards the end.

Period 2: 1995–2004/5—rapid decrease

At the start of this period unemployment stood at 2.4 million in 1995 but decreased to 1.4 million in 2004–5, and averaged 1.8 million. The prison population rapidly increased to reach 75,000 by 2004, an increase of 46 per cent. Police FTE personnel increased by 37,000 to reach 220,500, an increase of 20 per cent, although numbers dipped at the start of the period, and it was not until the Labour second term that growth acceleration occurred.[16] Recorded crime fell by 11 per cent between 1995 and 1997, but then rose by 31 per cent between 1997 and 2003/4, before marginally decreasing by 2004/5. There were, however,

---

[16] See Chapter 4, Figure 4.1.

significant changes to Home Office counting rules, which brought more categories of criminal activity within official statistics and which made strict comparisons with previous years very difficult, but which clearly had the effect of reversing the earlier downward trend. In contrast BCS/CSEW crime *fell* by 44 per cent.

Economic growth was sustained and matched with a fall in unemployment. There was also a change in the demographic, with a slight fall in the 15–24 year age range. Economic inequality continued to increase, but more slowly than in the 1980s. Illicit consumer preferences changed, with the illegal markets for car radios and VHS recorders apparently sated and a growing preference for new goods of choice, notably mobile phones. Adopting a 'broken windows' approach, crime and disorder were explicitly joined together, with a view to reducing both. Crime prevention and community safety partnerships between the police and local authorities became strategic and mandatory; personal and situational security (including vehicle security) became more sophisticated and more widely used. The use of multiple cautions ended to be replaced by an elaborate range of interventions, including ASBOs, Criminal Anti-social Behaviour Orders (CRASBOs), and Drug Treatment and Testing Orders. The growth in the prison population accelerated particularly after the Crime Sentences Act 1997 (a Conservative measure retained by Labour), the Crime and Disorder Act 1998, and the Sexual Offences Act 2003. There was evidence that illicit drug use declined in this period, possibly attesting to the value of the various education and intervention measures that had been introduced.

In summary, the combined effects of new initiatives, a substantial increase in criminal justice, and especially police resources, an acceleration in the rate of increase in the prison population, combined with sustained periods of lower unemployment, and increased, if unevenly distributed prosperity, all coincided with this period of rapidly decreasing BCS/CSEW crime and, at the very end of the period, the beginning of a new downward trend in PRCS crime.

Period 3: 2005/6–9/10—slower decrease

During the third period unemployment rose to 2.4 million by 2009–10, though this was the result of a sharp rise at the end of the period due to the effects of the banking crisis extending to a full recession. Only a year before the first of the recent recessions, unemployment stood at 1.8 million and even allowing for a sharp rise in 2009–10 averaged only 1.7 million for the period. The prison population increased by 13 per cent over the period, and averaged 80,000. The growth in police numbers continued until 2010, when combined officer and civilian numbers peaked at 240,000. There was evidence of continued decline in illegal drug use.[17] Stability characterized the broader socio-economic environment,

---

[17] Datablog, 'Drug use in England and Wales: is it under control?' (<http://www.guardian.co.uk/news/datablog/2012/jul/26/drug-use-england-wales-2011-12> [accessed 11 March 2013]) and 'Drug use in England and Wales—find out which are the most popular and human use of them' (<http://www.guardian.co.uk/news/datablog/2012/sep/28/drug-use-age-popular-cannabis> [accessed 24 March 2013]).

with the adverse effects of the recession being felt only at the very end of the period with unemployment increasing. There was some levelling out in inequality as measured by the Gini Coefficient, while the effects of the recession only began to be felt from 2008–9 onwards. As the NCRS bedded down, recorded crime fell by 22 per cent, while BCS/CSEW crime fell by 11 per cent.

Period 4: 2009/10 to date—flattening out

During the final period, with the full effects of a 'double-dip' recession being felt, unemployment reached 2.6 million in 2011–12 and averaged 2.5 million for the period. The prison population reached 86,507 in September 2012 and averaged 85,700 for the period. However, by March 2013 the population had marginally declined from that peak to reach 84,505, appearing to reflect the Coalition's preferences for a smaller prison population and the use of alternative methods of punishment and rehabilitation. It would remain to be seen if the trend would continue under the new Justice Secretary Chris Grayling, for despite high rhetoric about not artificially reducing the prison population, the numbers fell between September 2012, just before he was appointed, and March 2013.[18] Police FTEs had decreased to 213,000, a decline of 27,000, or 11 per cent, in three years. Between 2009–10 and 2011–12 the annual rate of reduction slowed and BCS/CSEW crime flatlined at an average of 9.5 million. At the very end of the period, however, the year-on-year January-to-December reduction accelerated again to fall to 8.9 million BCS/CSEW (–5 per cent) and 3.7 million PRCS (–8 per cent).[19]

Overview

Although the links between crime and unemployment, between crime and police numbers, and between crime and the prison population are disputed,[20] the trends across the four periods identified by the ONS suggest that there are links. Certainly the recent stabilization in BSC/CSEW crime from 2009–10 to 2011–12 coincided with (a) a prolonged economic recession and high unemployment; (b) a decrease in police resources; and, (c) a levelling out in the prison population.

---

[18] cf J Slack, 'Chris Grayling gets tough: New Justice Secretary ditches Ken Clare's plan to cut jail numbers', MailOnline, 19 September 2012 (<http://www.dailymail.co.uk/news/article-2205062/Chris-Grayling-gets-tough-New-Justice-Secretary-ditches-Ken-Clarkes-plan-cut-jail-numbers.html> [accessed 21 April 2013] with GOV.UK, Prison population, Population bulletins—weekly 28 September 2012 and weekly 8 March 2013 (<http://www.gov.uk/government/publications/prison-population-figures> [accessed 21 April 2013]).

[19] ONS, 'Crime in England and Wales, year ending December 2012' (<http://www.ons.gov.uk/ons/rel/crime-stats/crime-statistics/period-ending-december-2012/stb-crime-in-england-and-wales—year-ending-december-2012.html> [accessed 25 April 2013]), and Home Office, Police Workforce, England and Wales, 31 March 2013 (<https://www.gov.uk/government/publications/police-workforce-england-and-wales-31-march-2013/police-workforce-england-and-wales-31-march-2013> [accessed 6 August 2013]).

[20] eg BBC News, 'Ken Clarke says imprisonment not linked to crime fall', 11 June 2011 (<http://www.bbc.co.uk/news/10624171> [accessed 21 April 2013]).

On the other hand, BCS/CSEW crime did not rise in this period, while PRCS continued to decrease. The BCS/CSEW and PRCS for the period January to December 2012 revealed a continuing decrease. The decrease in violent crime was accentuated in media coverage although the decrease occurred in most categories of crime, with the notable exception of theft from the person. Explanations for the decline in violent crime included: the UK and the world becoming more culturally averse to violence; changes to police practices; an aging population; decreasing alcohol consumption; the rise in real wages due to the minimum wage; the absence of lead in paint and petrol from the 1970s which in turn removed the potential to harm the brains of infants; and the increase in legal abortions since the 1970s.[21] Former Metropolitan Police Commissioner Lord Blair, agreeing with the cultural change hypothesis, asserted that police numbers did not count, but equally offered the value of neighbourhood policing, evidence-based policing, targeted patrol, and increased police interventions in domestic violence, some of which, it might be argued, are dependent on police being available in sufficient numbers to be implemented as tactics. Professor Marian Fitzgerald questioned whether the decrease was as significant as it seemed at first sight because of continuing limitations of both crime survey and police crime statistics, but also observed that crimes of alcohol-related violence could be expected to decline in a period of recession as many people had simply less to spend on alcohol-based recreation.[22]

It is only possible to hypothesize about why crime began to decline in period 2, continued in period 3, began to flatten out in period 4, and then experienced an accentuated decline in crime in 2012. The graph in Figure 9.1, however, illustrates that from the mid 1990s there occurred a coalescence of factors that *may together* have had a cumulative effect on reducing crime. These include a rising then sustained high prison population; a long-term trend in the increase of police numbers; and, until 2010, a generally low level of unemployment, at least compared to the 1980s and early 1990s. To this list might be added the increased range of non-custodial judicial and social interventions created by the Labour government 1997–2010 ('tough on crime, tough on the causes of crime', including ASBOs, CRASBOs, and DTTOs). Included in this list of new interventions should be the Integrated Offender Management Programme and its offshoot, the Priority and Prolific Offender Programme (PPOP), which seemed to have some beneficial effect in inhibiting reoffending.[23] Even here there is a link with the

[21] See UK Peace Index, *Exploring the Fabric of Peace in the UK from 2003 to 2012* (<http://www.visionofhumanity.org/wp-content/uploads/2013/04/UK-Peace-Index-2013-IEP-Report.pdf> [accessed 27 April 2013]), 8–9, G Monbiot, 'Yes, lead poisoning could really be a cause of violent crime', *The Guardian*, 7 January 2013 (<http://www.guardian.co.uk/commentisfree/2013/jan/07/violent-crime-lead-poisoning-british-export> [accessed 27 April 2013]) and J Donohue III and S Levitt, 'The impact of legalized abortion on crime', *Quarterly Journal of Economics*, vol CXVI, May 2001, issue 2 (<http://pricetheory.uchicago.edu/levitt/Papers/DonohueLevittTheImpactOfLegalized2001.pdf> [accessed 27 April 2013]).

[22] *Today*, BBC Radio 4, 24 April 2013 (BBC iPlayer [accessed 27 April 2013]).

[23] Ministry of Justice, *Prolific and Other Priority Offender Program—5 Years On: Maximizing the Impact* (Home Office, 2009 <https://www.gov.uk/government/uploads/system/uploads/attachment_data/file/118035/PPO-5-years-on.pdf> [accessed 28 April 2013]), 10.

high prison population because, self-evidently, it is necessary to be convicted and receive a custodial sentenced to be eligible for the post-release PPOP. Policing also became more sophisticated (eg 'intelligence-led policing'), over all of the periods, but especially in periods 2, 3, and 4. In this hypothesis there is no single 'magic bullet'; no one factor predominates, rather all have combined in unquantifiable ways to create a prevailing social environment in which crime falls.

An additional tactical and time-specific cause for the accentuated fall in crime from January to December 2012 was the continuing effect into 2012 of imprisonment and other interventions following the 2011 riots.[24] This cannot be quantified, but neither can it be discounted amongst the hypotheses developing to explain the phenomenon. Nor can under-recording by the police be entirely discounted, at least in having some accentuating or exaggerating effect on the decrease. The investigations into general under-recording of crime in Kent and the under-recording of some rape crimes in the Metropolitan Police, and the assertion from the Cleveland Police Federation chairman that officers are under pressure to under-record to meet targets, mean that the concerns voiced by the Office for National Statistics that police recording practices are exaggerating the fall in crime cannot easily be set aside, despite precise rules governing recording practice and intensive auditing systems.[25] However, while this might explain an exaggeration in police figures, it would not account either for all of the fall in recorded crime or the decrease in BCS/CSEW crime.[26]

The link between a high prison population and falling crime is perhaps controversial, given that reoffending appeared to reach a high level in 2011, although despite media coverage official figures revealed that over time numbers had marginally declined.[27] The answer may be that a high prison population is

---

[24] O Bowcott, 'Riots led to 1,400 imprisoned or held on remand, figures show', guardian.co.uk, 28 June 2012 (<http://www.guardian.co.uk/uk/2012/jun/28/riots-prison-figures> [accessed 27 April 2013]).

[25] N Morris, 'Fall in crime rates may have been exaggerated because of pressure not to record lower-level offences', *The Independent*, 24 January 2013 (<http://www.independent.co.uk/news/uk/crime/fall-in-crime-rates-may-have-been-exaggerated-because-of-pressure-on-police-not-to-record-lowerlevel-offences-8464692.html> [accessed 27 April 2013]), J Wills, 'Police officers under "massive pressure" nit to record crime', thenorthernecho.co.uk, 25 January 2013 (<http://www.thenorthernecho.co.uk/news/10184223.Police_officers_under__massive_pressure__not_to_record_crime/> [accessed 27 April 2013]), and V Dodd, 'Rape victim "pressured by police to drop claim against man who later killed"', guardian.co.uk, 26 February 2013 (<http://www.guardian.co.uk/uk/2013/feb/26/rape-victims-police-allegations> [accessed 27 April 2013]).

[26] See M Cox, 'Kent Police defends high rate of "no crime" records', kentnews.co.uk, 3 February 2012 (<http://www.kentnews.co.uk/news/kent_police_defends_high_rate_of_no_crime_records_1_1196744> [accessed 1 April 2013]); Kent Police and Crime Commissioner, 'Investigation launched into police crime figures' (<https://www.kent-pcc.gov.uk/accountability/commissioner-to-investigate-po.html> [accessed 1 April 2013]); and, V Dodd, 'Rape victim "pressured by police to drop claim against man who later killed"', guardian.co.uk, 26 February 2013 (<http://www.guardian.co.uk/uk/2013/feb/26/rape-victims-police-allegations> [accessed 1 April 2013]).

[27] Contrast BBC News, 'Reoffending rates reach record level', 24 May 2012 (<http://www.bbc.co.uk/news/uk-18188610> [accessed 28 April 2013]) with Ministry of Justice, *Proven Re-offending Statistics Quarterly Bulletin July 2010 to June 2011, England and Wales* (<http://www.gov.uk/government/uploads/system/uploads/attachment_data/file/192631/proven-reoffending-jul-10-jun-11.pdf> [accessed 7 July 2013]), 7.

representative of successful police investigation activity and the two taken together suppress and disrupt criminal activity, thereby becoming one of the factors that contributes to falling crime. The alternative hypothesis is that falling crime and the rising prison population are mere coincidences, which is possible but unlikely. A factor that may be important is the number of suspected offenders remanded in custody before criminal proceedings begin, which would certainly have a disruptive and suppressant effect on the criminal activity of those who have committed offences, even if they are released after later court proceedings. These numbers have increased between 2007 and 2011.[28] Even these measures cannot be treated in isolation but alongside the criminal justice interventions created between 1997 and 2010, including the active management of offenders on bail, Integrated Offender Management, and the Priority and Prolific Offender Management Programme. In this hypothesis the key gateway factor comprises police detections, which themselves arise from effective investigations. Research by Civitas suggests a link between increased police detections and decreasing crime rates.[29]

There is, then, no certain explanation for the decrease in crime. It is, therefore, necessary to hypothesize. Is the reduction in recorded crime since the mid 1990s explained not by one single factor, or even a small number of primary factors, but by the coalescence of a number of factors, no one of which predominates but which cumulatively, over a sustained number of years (twenty-plus), have brought about a continuing fall in crime? If that is the case, the question becomes, 'How sustainable will the coalescence of those factors be for the future?' That question will be explored at the end of this chapter, and taken in the context of what might happen to anti-social behaviour and more extreme disorder.

Anti-social behaviour

The Home Office definition for anti-social behaviour is understandably wide, and includes 'any aggressive, intimidating, or destructive activity that damages or destroys another person's quality of life'. Despite this broad definition and despite public perceptions to the contrary, incidents of ASB recorded by the police have also been decreasing in recent years. In 2007/8 there were 3.9 million recorded incidents; in 2011/12 there were 2.7 million, a 30 per cent drop in five years.[30] This might seem an excessive decrease, yet it is supported by a corresponding trend in PRCS and CSEW crimes of criminal damage or vandalism.[31]

---

[28] Ministry of Justice, Criminal Justice statistics: quarterly update to December 2011 (Ministry of Justice statistics bulletin, 24 May 2012 <http://www.gov.uk/government/uploads/system/uploads/attachment_data/file/162610/criminal-justice-stats-dec-2011.pdf.pdf> [accessed 28 April 2013]).

[29] S Bandyopadhyay, *Acquisitive Crime: Imprisonment, Detection and Social Factors* (<http://www.civitas.org.uk/crime/crimeanalysis2012.pdf> [accessed 27 April 2013]), 3.

[30] ONS, Crime in England & Wales Quarterly First Release to March 2012—police force area tables (<http://www.ons.gov.uk/ons/dcp171778_273169.pdf> [accessed 7 July 2013]).

[31] ONS, Trends in crime, 7, and ONS, Crime in England & Wales 2012.

A plausible explanation is that much anti-social behaviour and damage are essentially neighbourhood crimes, and therefore susceptible to the problem-solving, personnel-intensive neighbourhood policing developed in the early 2000s and sustained by the substantial increase in police numbers, including both police officers and PCSOs. The question, as the 2010s progress, is the degree to which those reductions can be sustained as neighbourhood police numbers, or more specifically those neighbourhood-based officers allowed to engage in proactive problem solving, as opposed to response and investigative policing, decline as the spending cuts continue to bite.[32]

Aligned to the availability of neighbourhood policing resources is the use of ASBOs and CRASBOs since 1999. After a hesitant start, the use of these orders by police and local authorities (necessarily required to work in partnership) increased, peaking at 4,122 issued in 2005, although this moderated to 1,414 in 2011.[33] There was both a measurable and perceived decline in anti-social behaviour following their introduction, although it was not clear that this was attributable to the orders. A National Audit Office study suggested that a range of other, less formal interventions might have contributed, while the breach rate for ASBOs was slightly over 50 per cent.[34] This uncertainty gave the Conservatives in opposition the chance to claim that ASBOs were 'blunt instruments that often fail their purpose of deterring people from committing more crime', and promise to introduce more practical and instant measures 'without criminalising young people unnecessarily'.[35] In government a white paper published in May 2012 sought to deliver on this promise by a combination of measures that would allow frontline professionals more discretion and 'common sense', including restorative approaches, and simplified formal procedures, the key to which would be 'Acceptable Behaviour Contracts'. To ensure that communities would not be forgotten or run around from agency to agency, a 'community trigger' would be introduced. In keeping with the Coalition's philosophy, and particularly its Conservative element, the government would not 'spell out in legislation exactly how local areas should implement the trigger. Instead, relevant authorities . . . will be required to decide and publish the thresholds, criteria, process . . . and reporting mechanism they intend to use locally.'[36]

---

[32] See Chapter 8, p. 168.

[33] Home Office, Anti-Social Behaviour Order Statistics—England and Wales 2011 (<http://www.homeoffice.gov.uk/publications/science-research-statistics/research-statistics/crime-research/asbo-stats-england-wales-2011/> [accessed 12 March 2013]).

[34] National Audit Office, *The Home Office: Tackling Anti-Social Behaviour* (TSO, London, 2006), 6–7.

[35] Conservative Manifesto 2010, 56.

[36] Home Office, *Putting Victims First: More Effective Responses to Anti-social Behavior* (Home Office, 2012 <http://www.official-documents.gov.uk/document/cm83/8367/8367.pdf> [accessed 12 March 2013]), 18.

The white paper also reflected the Coalition's preferences for reduced bureaucracy, intending to simplify the existing range of orders and injunctions from nineteen to just six and speed up the implementation of remedies for ASB. In a more radical step, the process by landlords to evict 'nightmare neighbours' would be speeded up where there was an anti-social, aggravating element involved.[37] A draft Anti-Social Behaviour Bill was presented to Parliament in December 2012. The chief features were a reduction in the number and variety of orders, the most significant of which was the replacement of ASBOs with 'Criminal Behaviour Orders' and 'Community Protection Notices'. The localism principle meant that communities and individuals would be able to initiate action to resolve anti-social behaviour through the 'community trigger' mechanism. PCCs would be given a key role in community consultation on community sanctions, although, interestingly, chief constables would be required to agree with sanctions that are 'achievable and realistic', such as 'community work options and certain types of courses'. Offenders would not, however, be obliged to carry out the penalty proposed, but if they did refuse the CPS would consider prosecution.[38] Pledges in the white paper to deal with the causes of anti-social behaviour, however, received something of a setback when plans for a minimum pricing for alcohol appeared to be dropped by the Coalition.[39]

The draft bill represented an amalgam of radical change (community triggers, PCC 'menu' of sanctions, and community-based restorations and reparations), together with at best a consolidation and simplification of existing anti-social behaviour control measures, or, it might be argued, repackaging. However, the bill did demonstrate that while striking a politically different pose, the Coalition intended to continue to reflect the high concern that the public attached to addressing anti-social behaviour. There was no reason to think that the measures would make it more difficult for the police to deal with anti-social behaviour and might, with the emphasis on community reparations and restorations, improve public confidence. At least the evidence of restorative and reparative action should be available locally. However, it would, at first sight, appear to give a new role to the police in actually implementing community options and sanctions, a role at a time when the resources available to neighbourhood policing were diminishing. Furthermore, given that recorded incidents of ASB had been reducing in recent years it might be possible to argue that the measures proposed in the draft bill are no more than a predetermined solution in search of a social problem. It might even be an attempt to thwart further attempts to cut the police budget. In any case, the government appears to have no urgency, as the bill will not become an Act of Parliament before 2015.

---

[37] *Putting Victims First*, 25.   [38] Draft Anti-Social Behaviour Bill.

[39] BBC News, 'Anti-social behavior victim's "pick punishments"', 13 December 2012 (<http://www.bbc.co.uk/news/uk-politics-20709393> [accessed 12 March 2013]), and 'Minimum alcohol pricing plan "may be dropped"', 12 March 2013 (<http://www.bbc.co.uk/news/uk-politics-21760806> [accessed 12 March 2013]).

Disorder

The first years of the Coalition government were marked by exceptional episodes of serious disorder. These commenced with the student protests of November 2010, extended into more complex economic, social, and political protests through the winter of 2010 and into the spring of 2011. In August 2011 there was widespread rioting and looting across much of England and Wales. In global terms, these were not isolated episodes but possibly part of wider imprecise movements of protests against the prevailing economic and political status quos.

The 1980s had seen in Britain a series of urban riots, starting in the St Paul's district of Bristol in April 1980, extending through the summer of 1981 and climaxing in the Broadwater Farm riot of October 1985, when PC Keith Blakelock was murdered. The urban disorders of the early to mid 1980s coincided with rising unemployment, a trend accentuated amongst young black communities of the inner cities. Further outbreaks of rioting occurred in the early 1990s in out-of-town estates such as Blackbird Leys in Oxford, Hartcliffe in Bristol, and Marsh Farm in Luton. Racial tension added to economic deprivation produced riots in Bradford, and in the early 2000s in Oldham, Leeds, and Burnley. However, since then, although unemployment remained disproportionately high in these areas, a series of measures to improve police–minority ethnic relations, social amelioration in deprived areas, and neighbourhood policing may have combined to ensure that riots did not recur to any significant degree for the remainder of the 2000s. The return of rioting in the 2010s therefore broke the prevailing trend of relative mass social tranquillity.

The British disorders of 2010–11 occurred against an international background. In late 2008 the Greek government had commenced a programme of fiscal retrenchment in response to its burgeoning debt crisis. This coincided in December with the shooting by police of a 15-year-old student in Athens. Protest demonstrations extended into riots in which petrol bombs were thrown at the police. More demonstrations and rioting occurred in other parts of Greece and then across Europe. Students were at the heart of many of them, including an assault on the Greek embassy in London. January 2009 also saw international demonstrations against Israeli action in Gaza, several of which, including the one in London, extended into violence. May Day 2009 saw riots in Greece, Turkey, Russia, France, and Austria. Britain, which had generally proved historically immune to the attraction of 1 May as anything other than a somewhat drab bank holiday and as yet largely shielded from the worsening effects of the global recession, remained aloof. That changed in November 2010 when students began to protest against planned Coalition cuts to education in general and an increase in the tuition fees cap. The National Union of Students and the University and College Union organized the official protests. However, there were splinter elements, surreptitiously organized by student activist groups, using syndicalist methods and linked by the 1960s left-wing

'Situationist' movement, that planned to escalate the peaceful demonstration into violent protest.[40]

The police had planned for a peaceful demonstration, and, as was usual, the organizers had cooperated in good faith in the arrangements. Neither the organizers nor the police were prepared for the breakaway violence, the most serious episode of which occurred at the Conservative Party HQ in Millbank Tower. The police were outnumbered and were unable to prevent a group occupying the roof. One student threw a fire extinguisher off the roof, which had it connected with anyone below would almost certainly have killed them. It was a moment of individual madness that seemed to sum up the collective urge to extend protest into violent direct action. More violent protests and occupations followed, including on 9 December protests against the education vote taking place that day in Parliament. The police responded with 'kettling' tactics, but these were unable, indeed ill-suited, to counter the breakaway tactics of many fringe protest groups, including one which attacked the car taking the Prince of Wales and the Duchess of Cornwall to an evening engagement in Regent Street.

The episode seemed to emphasize how little the police understood the motives and tactics of the 'Situationists' and fellow travellers such as 'Horizontalists' and anarchists like 'Black Bloc'. Small in number, esoteric in political belief, and defying generalization, these and similar groups exploited peaceful and organized mass protest. The cell structure, supported by mobile phone technology, was ideally suited to latching on to and exploiting mainstream protests to confound police kettling tactics. The more the police concentrated and contained the main demonstration the more opportunity there was for breakaway groups to attack symbols of global capitalism, such as the Christmas tree in Trafalgar Square, the National Gallery, Top Shop, The Ritz and, most spectacularly, Fortnum and Mason. But almost anything might be attacked and damaged, and certainly the police were an easy symbol of authority at which to throw bricks and bottles. Following the damage caused by splinter groups from an otherwise peaceful TUC-organized protest against spending cuts in March 2011, Metropolitan Police Commander Bob Broadhurst understandably described the assaults and damage as 'mindless vandalism'.[41] That might have been true for some protestors, but not all. The police had been confronted with a new phenomenon of mobile, fragmented, but ultimately organized protest, and had responded using largely static and already outmoded tactics. The lessons would be learnt, but not quickly enough.

The protests and violence achieved nothing in terms of changing government policy. The spending cuts went through; the tuition fee cap was raised. This might have earned the Coalition credit amongst its supporters but it appeared to those

---

[40] P Mason, *Why It's Kicking Off Everywhere: The New Global Revolutions* (Verso, London, 2012), 46.

[41] BBC News, 'TUC condemns post-rally violence in central London', 27 March 2011 (<http://www.bbc.co.uk/news/uk-12873191> [accessed 25 March 2013]).

disadvantaged by government plans that it was not listening. The student protest movement petered out as many potential demonstrators may have been deterred by approaching exams and the way extremists had hijacked peaceful protest. Their revolutionary ardour may also have been cooled by the knowledge that Edward Woollard, the student who had thrown the fire extinguisher from the Millbank Tower roof, had received a thirty-two-month jail sentence.[42] However, there were worrying signs that might have been registered had police community intelligence and tension-indicator processes been working as they should. Student protestors might have grabbed the headlines in the autumn and winter of 2010–11 but present in their number were a more socio-economically eclectic number from schools and further education colleges of the less fashionable housing estates; just the class being more than averagely disadvantaged by the deepening recession and widening inequality as measured by the Gini Coefficient.[43] The failure of the autumn–winter organized demonstrations to achieve any change in political policy ensured that there was plenty of discontent left over for the summer of 2011.

In identifying the causes of historical events historians have little difficulty in tracking long-term or background causes from those which precipitate the final event. One historian, the late Lawrence Stone, constructed a brilliant analytical framework to explain the origins of 'The English Revolution 1529–1642'. He distinguished between 'Preconditions'—the social, economic, and political factors that made the revolution possible; 'Precipitants'—how these factors combined into the general events which hastened the final crisis and cataclysm; and 'Triggers'—those specific events which turn probability into certainty.[44] The same framework can be applied to the August 2011 riots.

There were a number of significant preconditions—high unemployment, disproportionately affecting the young and already disadvantaged economic regions; increasing inequality; lack of a political voice amongst existing relatively deprived and excluded groups; the ineffectiveness of the 2010–11 protests; and the knowledge variously gained in the use of mobile phones and social media to achieve rapid horizontal communication. There was also the 'Operation Trident' effect. This was the Metropolitan Police unit which targeted gun and gang crime. In theory it was ethnically neutral and had community support, but in practice it necessarily focused on Afro-Caribbean drug gangs and, albeit if unintentionally, stigmatized the black community.[45] To that might be added the continuing disproportionality in stops and searches of black and Asian people, and while this was lower in Haringey, where the August rioting was to start, than the Metropolitan

---

[42] C Davies, 'Student protester who threw fire extinguisher from roof jailed', guardian.co.uk, 11 January 2011 (<http://www.guardian.co.uk/education/2011/jan/11/student-fire-extinguisher-protests-jailed> [accessed 25 March 2013]).

[43] Mason, *Why It's Kicking Off Everywhere*, 49.

[44] L Stone, *The Causes of the English Revolution 1529–1642* (Routledge and Paul, London, 1972), 58–145.

[45] *Jamaica Times*, 27 March 2013 (<http://www.jamaicatimesuk.com/index.php/news/item/108-operation-trident-successful-unit-or-dismal-failure> [accessed 21 April 2013]).

Police Service (MPS) average, there was nevertheless disproportionality and additionally there had been a recent surge in searches under section 60 of the Criminal Justice and Public Order Act.[46] The precipitants were essentially local. Despite there having been much progress in police–community relations since the riots of October 1985, when PC Blakelock was murdered, there remained unresolved tensions in the Tottenham area of north London.[47] Then on 4 August an Operation Trident unit intercepted a local black man, Mark Duggan, who had been under their surveillance and who, by some accounts, was involved in the local drug and gang scene. In somewhat confusing circumstances, a police officer shot and killed him, the officer involved stating that he believed Duggan to have been carrying a shotgun. Although the officer claimed to have seen the gun wrapped in a sock (a standard concealment technique) before firing the shot, after the event it was never found. Nevertheless, in February 2013 Kevin Hutchinson-Foster was convicted of supplying Duggan with the weapon and sentenced to eleven years' imprisonment.[48] However, despite official findings to the contrary,[49] some members of the local and wider black communities saw this event as simply the most recent in a series of unexplained, or inadequately explained, deaths of black and minority ethnic people involving the police.[50] Suspicion was increased when, in confusing circumstances, there was a delay in the Metropolitan Police informing Duggan's family of his death.[51] That tension was high was indicated by warnings from community to police leaders on the morning of 6 April that a riot was possible.[52]

---

[46] EHRC, *Stop and Think*, 88, and North London Citizens, Citizens; Inquiry into the Tottenham Riots (<http://www.citizensuk.org/wp-content/uploads/2012/02/Citizens-Inquiry-into-the-Tottenham-Riots-REPORT.pdf> [accessed 29 March 2013]), *passim*, and Metropolitan Police, Stops and searches monitoring mechanism, July 2011, Haringey (<http://www.met.police.uk/foi/pdfs/priorities_and_how_we_are_doing/borough/haringey_stop_and_search_monitoring_report_july_2011.pdf> [accessed 19 April 2013]).

[47] D Lammy, 'Tottenham Riot: The lesson of Broadwater Farm', *The Guardian*, 7 August 2011 (<http://www.guardian.co.uk/commentisfree/2011/aug/07/tottenham-riot-broadwater-farm> [accessed 25 March 2013]).

[48] D Williams, 'Shooting inquiry: Answers to the key questions behind the man who was gunned down by police triggering the riots', MailOnline, 9 August 2011 (<http://www.dailymail.co.uk/news/article-2023951/Mark-Duggan-shooting-inquiry-Answers-key-questions-triggered-Tottenham-riots.html> [accessed 25 March 2013]), and Press Association, 'Man who gave gun to Mark Duggan jailed for 11 years', guardian.co.uk, 26 February 2013 (<http://www.guardian.co.uk/uk/2013/feb/26/man-gave-gun-mark-duggan> [accessed 25 March 2013]).

[49] IPCC, Deaths during or following police contact: statistics for England and Wales 2011/12 (<http://www.ipcc.gov.uk/en/Pages/reports_polcustody.aspx> [accessed 21 April 2013]).

[50] See for example S Jones, 'Musician Smiley Culture dies during police raid on Surrey home', *The Guardian*, 15 March 2011 (<http://www.guardian.co.uk/music/2011/mar/15/smiley-culture-dies-police-raid> [accessed 25 March 2013]) and A Higgins, 'Guardian: The ignored London riots context—deaths in police custody, 0 convictions', Philosophers Stone (<http://philosophersstone.co.uk/wordpress/2011/08/guardian-the-ignored-london-riots-context-333-deaths-in-police-custody-0-convictions/> [accessed 25 March 2013]).

[51] V Dodd and D Taylor, 'Police apologise to Mark Duggan's family for not telling them of his death', *The Guardian*, 29 February 2012 (<http://www.guardian.co.uk/uk/2012/feb/29/police-apologise-mark-duggan-death> [accessed 21 April 2013]).

[52] R Reicher and S Scott, *Mad Mobs and Englishmen? Myths and Realities of the 2011 Riots* (Constable and Robinson, London, 2011), e-book loc 1041.

The 'trigger' cause for the most serious rioting of the modern era, outstripping in scale even the worst of the 1980s riots, was a demonstration organized, with the MPS's knowledge, outside Tottenham police station on Saturday evening to demand answers about Mark Duggan's death. A crowd of about 120 gathered and representatives sought to engage with a senior officer. Police, not initially in riot gear, were deployed outside the station to marshal the protest. A chief inspector began negotiations but he was deemed insufficiently senior and the referral of the shooting to the IPCC inhibited further communication. Lack of communication by the MPS, no matter how justified, was a critical factor in the build-up of frustration and tension. Protestors also saw deployment of the police in riot gear as a significant escalation, although the police saw it as a reasonable response to the gathering crowd. Missiles had already been thrown at 6.52 pm but had petered out. However, once the representatives left the Tottenham police station area at 8.26 pm more serious missile throwing started and two police cars were set on fire. Eyewitnesses claim that it was an attempt by the police to either disperse the crowd or at least push it further away from Tottenham police station, in which a young girl was possibly pushed over and struck by the police, that was the actual 'trigger' event which sparked the disorder.[53] Police support units were available, but following this 'trigger' event rioting quickly escalated, and although the MPS put into operation its prearranged public disorder plan it was insufficient to meet the scale consequent upon the rapid escalation. Rioting spread across the Haringey Borough where the Tottenham station was situated, and 'intense disorder and criminality' continued through the night. The next day it spread to other north London boroughs and on day three to south London and thence to many parts of England and Wales. Looting accompanied much of the rioting and five associated fatalities occurred. Given the indiscriminate nature of much of the arson it could easily have been more.

At this point it is necessary to distinguish between the 'trigger' for the riots and their 'dynamics'; what caused them to spread and take on the nature that they did. The trigger was related to the events outside Tottenham police station, and this caused the police to escalate their response. This in turn gave the rioters initial cause for further anger against the police. Violence begat coercive response and the escalation began. But what may have started as an anti-police riot may have become something more class conscious by the time it reached Croydon and other areas where relative affluence and relative deprivation sat uneasily alongside each other.[54] From protest the rioting quickly turned to uninhibited destruction and then looting, a course that allowed the government to cite criminality and greed as the causes. So they were, but *after* the Tottenham trigger. Much of what followed was to do with the dynamics of riots, seen over the centuries, in which once the normal, essentially informal constraints of society are

---

[53] Reicher and Scott, *Mad Mobs and Englishmen?*, loc 1018, 1041, and 1060.
[54] Reicher and Scott, *Mad Mobs and Englishmen?*, loc 1337.

removed and the anonymity of the crowd asserts itself, the instincts of the mob take over and unbridled violence follows. It is the traditional dynamism of 'the mob', the *mobile vulgus* of history. Disillusionment with society, disengagement, and deprivation, relative or absolute, may have played their part in creating the preconditions for rioting in seats of disorder far from Haringey, but once the rioting started, and once it became apparent through the frequent live broadcasts of the twenty-four-hour news media that the police were hanging back, unrestrained hedonism could assert itself. Criminality, greed, and stealing to order, could escalate. There was a palpable sense amongst some of those involved that they ought to get their 'slice of the action' and if they did not they were somehow missing out. Historically riots, without assertive political leadership, run out of steam. The 2011 riots were different because mobile phones and social media could provide horizontal, informal intelligence and direction. As one young rioter sent in text: 'What ever ends [area] your from put your ballys [balaclavas] on link up and cause havic [sic], just rob everything. Police can't stop it.'[55] As the final report of the Riots Communities and Victims Panel laconically concluded:

> Lack of confidence in the police response to the initial riots encouraged people to test reactions in other areas. Most of the riots began with some trouble in retail areas with a critical mass of individuals and groups converging on an area. Rioters believed they would be able to loot and damage without being challenged. In the hardest-hit areas they were correct.[56]

The riots petered out after Tuesday 9 August, due to a combination of exhaustion and, as police mobilization gathered momentum, eventual containment.[57] Police tactics from the start had seemed to focus on containment rather than arrest and resolution, a situation probably dictated by the rapid fluidity of the rioting, the inability to concentrate sufficient numbers at critical locations, simple lack of numbers in comparison to the scale of the rioting, and horizontal communication through social media, features that had not been evident even in the worst days of the 1980s riots. Many officers subsequently felt that the difficulties they

---

[55] Quoted in D Matthews, 'Out of the ashes by David Lammy—review', *The Guardian*, 9 December 2011 (<http://www.theguardian.com/books/2011/dec/09/out-ashes-riots-david-lammy-review-matthews> [accessed 29 March 2013]).

[56] Riots Communities and Victims Panel, *After the Riots: The Final Report of the Riots Communities and Victims Panel* (Riots Communities and Victims Panel, London, 2012 <http://webarchive.nationalarchives.gov.uk/20121003195935/http:/riotspanel.independent.gov.uk/wp-content/uploads/2012/03/Riots-Panel-Final-Report1.pdf> [accessed 29 March 2013]), 22.

[57] Riots Communities and Victims Panel, *5 Days in August: An Interim Report on the 2011 English Riots* (<http://webarchive.nationalarchives.gov.uk/20121003195935/ http://www.riotspanel. independent.gov.uk/wp-content/uploads/2012/04/Interim-report-5-Days-in-August.pdf> [accessed 25 March 2013]) and Metropolitan Police Service, *4 Days in August: Strategic Review into the Disorder of August 2011* (final report, March 2012 <http://content.met.police.uk/cs/Satellite? blobcol=urldata&blobheadername1=Content-Type&blobheadername2=Content-Disposition& blobheadervalue1=application%2Fpdf&blobheadervalue2=inline%3B+filename%3D%22145% 2F595%2Fco553-114DaysInAugust.pdf%22&blobkey=id&blobtable=MungoBlobs&blobwhere= 1283551523589&ssbinary=true> [accessed 25 March 2013]).

faced in getting to grips with situations unprecedented in terms of scale and fluidity had not been recognized.[58]

The official inquiry into the riots provided an interim report with commendable speed. It identified no single cause but found an inescapable link with deprivation, exclusion, under-achievement, and disillusionment.

> There appears to be a link between deprivation and rioting. Our unique analysis shows that 70% of those brought before the courts were living in the 30% most deprived postcodes in the country. Although many deprived areas did not riot, of the 66 areas that experienced riots, 30 were in the top 25% most deprived areas in England. Job Seekers Allowance Claimant Rates are 1.5 percentage points higher among 16–24-year-olds in riot areas (7.5%) than non riot areas (6%).[59]

Criminality, and rioters' previous criminal histories, were assessed to have played a significant part in the motivation of many of them, but,

> these were not just 'the usual suspects'. A third of under-18s seen by the courts had not committed a previous offence. We know that the great majority of these youths were not considered 'at risk' of offending by local area Youth Offending Teams. This suggests that a significant number of these young people made bad decisions after getting caught up in the moment.
>
> The fact that many people abused society's moral and legal codes when the opportunity arose paints a disturbing picture. Most disturbing to us was a widespread feeling that some rioters had no hope and nothing to lose.[60]

The report warned that the riots might happen again.[61] To avoid that outcome a wide series of amelioration measures were proposed, but nearly two years after the events of August 2011 unemployment was not significantly lower, especially among young people in general and those young people already disadvantaged. Nor was there any evidence that the sense of detachment and disillusionment detected by the inquiry team had significantly abated. The government did launch the 'Troubled families' initiative, before the final report of the riot inquiry, targeting the 120,000 'most troubled' families in Britain, and backed by £448 million. However, despite the quality of the interventions, the results were uncertain, and while the sum of money invested sounded impressive it in fact amounted to no more than £3,733 per family, and it did not address the wider economic and social causes that underpinned the 2011 unrest.[62] In his personal assessment of the government's

---

[58] P Lewis and T Newburn, 'Reading the riots study revels police fears over further unrest', *The Guardian*, 1 July 2012 (<http://www.guardian.co.uk/uk/2012/jul/01/reading-the-riots-police-fears> [accessed 26 March 2013]).

[59] Riots Communities and Victims Panel, *5 Days in August*, 9.

[60] Riots Communities and Victims Panel, *5 Days in August*, 10–11.

[61] Riots Communities and Victims Panel, *5 Days in August*, 5.

[62] N Robertson, '"Real danger" Manchester could return to devastating scenes of 2011 riots, according to former probation chief', mancunianmatters, 7 March 2013 (<http://mancunianmatters.co.uk/content/07039134-real-danger-manchester-could-return-devastating-scenes-2011-riots-according-former> [accessed 26 March 2013]) and BBC News, 'Helping the most troubled families in Britain', 22 January 2013 (<http://www.bbc.co.uk/news/magazine-21122132> [accessed 26 March 2013]).

post-riot policy response Tottenham Labour MP David Lammy calculated that just eleven of the sixty-three recommendations made by the riot panel had been followed through.[63] In effect almost two years on most of the 'preconditions' still existed. All that would be needed would be a series of events to create the 'precipitants' and one specific incident to provide the 'trigger'. Therefore, if rioting on the scale of August 2011 is to be avoided in the future it is likely to be largely down to good local policing and effective avoidance interventions as tension builds, and effective suppression tactics once it starts. The problems are that, as has been observed before, neighbourhood policing—that part of policing most useful in obtaining community intelligence and most useful in providing early avoidance interventions—is likely to be that part of policing most adversely affected by personnel cuts.

Confidence

Peel understood that in a democracy, even the limited one of the early nineteenth century, the police could not rule by force alone. For him, and for most of his successors, both as home secretaries and prime ministers, recourse to force was to be the last not first resort, and even then only in a limited, proportional form. That fundamental premise has not changed in twenty-first-century Britain. Even if politicians and the police wanted to do things differently, and there is nothing to suggest that the majority of either group does, there are simply insufficient police to rely upon arbitrary coercion. So for most of the time the police do their job on the basis of an intangible mixture of public trust, confidence, and respect in their authority. This is the true meaning of 'policing by consent'. As Mike Hough and others have summarized:

> Trust in policing is needed partly because this results in public cooperation with justice, but more importantly because public trust in justice builds institutional legitimacy and thus public compliance with the law and commitment to the rule of law.[64]

Trust, confidence, and respect are intangible qualities. If that intangibility is ever seriously questioned, as it was to an unprecedented scale in August 2011, then normal policing becomes impossible. Maintenance of public trust and confidence is not therefore simply some measure of the 'feel-good factor' in policing, or even some kind of popularity test for politicians and their policies. It is an essential tool of the job and a precious asset. If confidence and respect in the

---

[63] V Dodd, '2011 riots inquiry recommendations ignored by government, says Lammy', *The Guardian*, 29 March 2013 (<http://www.guardian.co.uk/uk/2013/mar/29/2011-riots-panel-proposals-unimplemented> [accessed 29 March 2913]) and Riots Communities and Victims Panel, *Final Report*, 120–31.

[64] M Hough, J Jackson, B Bradford, A Myhill, and P Quinton, 'Procedural justice, trust, and institutional legitimacy', *Policing*, vol 4, issue 3, August 2010, 203.

police are important, the questions are, 'What are their state under the Coalition, and what are their prospects?'

The evidence available to answer the first question is equivocal. In 2011–12, 62 per cent of people in a representative sample survey by the Home Office considered that their local police were doing a 'good/excellent job', an increase from the 2010–11 total of 59 per cent.[65] This was despite some events and headlines of 2011–12 which might have been thought to have dented general confidence in the police. These included fallout from the phone hacking investigation, the failure to initially grip the response to the 2011 riots, and the removal, resignation, or investigation of several senior officers in various controversial circumstances. Despite these potentially negative influences the Ipsos MORI veracity index for February 2013 showed that 65 per cent of those asked would trust the police to tell the truth compared to 63 per cent in the 2011 survey.[66] Victim satisfaction also illustrated a general satisfaction with the way the police dealt with them, and again the trend of recent years was for improvement, even if incrementally. There was, however, much variation between forces, ranging from 51 per cent in Derbyshire to 69 per cent in Dorset and Hertfordshire. The victim survey also illustrated a general satisfaction with the way the police dealt with them, and again the trend of recent years was for improvement, even if incrementally.

However, looking forward from mid 2013 there might be other factors which would negatively affect public confidence. First, there was that 51 per cent to 69 per cent variation in individual force performance. Second, there were several national events in 2013 which might have a negative impact on general public opinion, potentially the most significant of which would be findings from the new investigation and inquest into the 1989 Hillsborough tragedy. Although both strictly relate to the forces involved in the original incident and investigation (South Yorkshire and the West Midlands) there might be wider negative fallout. Then the 'Plebgate' affair revealed alleged inappropriate disclosures to the media, although an internal MPS investigation report, itself allegedly leaked to the press, apparently found that none of the officers directly involved had lied.[67]

---

[65] ONS, Crime in England and Wales Quarterly First Release to March 2012—police force area tables (<http://www.ons.gov.uk/ons/rel/crime-stats/crime-statistics/period-ending-march-2012/stb-crime-stats-end-march-2012.html> [accessed 29 March 2013]) and Home Office, Crime in England and Wales 2010/11: Police Force Area tables (<http://www.homeoffice.gov.uk/publications/science-research-statistics/research-statistics/crime-research/hosb1011/hosb1011-pfatabs?view=Binary> [accessed 29 March 2013]).

[66] Ipsos MORI, Veracity Index 2011 and Trust polling February 2013 (<http://www.ipsos-mori.com/Assets/Docs/Polls/Feb2013_Trust_Charts.pdf>, and <http://www.ipsos-mori.com/Assets/Docs/Polls/Feb2013_Trust_Charts.pdf> [accessed 21 April 2013]).

[67] S Laville, '"Plebgate"' file passed to prosecutors contains no evidence that police lied', The Guardian, 28 March 2013 (<http://www.guardian.co.uk/politics/2013/mar/28/lebgate-file-contains-no-evidence-that-police-lied> [accessed 29 March 2013]) and BBC News, 'Cleveland Police Chief Constable Sean Price suspended', 3 August 2011 (<http://www.bbc.co.uk/news/uk-england-tees-14386361> [accessed 29 March 2013]).

This elicited a formal complaint from Mr Mitchell. The investigation into historical child abuse, centred mainly on the late Jimmy Savile, revealed instances of past police indifference to allegations of child sex abuse, and while there had been substantial procedural and cultural changes in the meantime it was another potential negative influence on the public estimation of the police.[68] There were also further damaging allegations concerning a Metropolitan Police undercover operation in 1993 to find 'dirt' on the bereaved family of the murdered Stephen Lawrence.[69] That many of these events and revelations were historical and subject to ongoing investigations or inquiries would not necessarily be decisive in determining contemporary media or public opinion. However, the consequences were not only felt in terms of public confidence. The associated negative media coverage plus cuts in numbers, increasing workload, the *Winsor* recommendations, and the seeming indifference of government ministers, all combined to lower morale, according to some, to dangerous levels.

However, the most serious threat to confidence is the further decline in neighbourhood policing. Police numbers have fallen and are set to fall further. The evidence emerging was that neighbourhood policing would suffer in the process. HMIC in its 2012 report *Policing in Austerity: One Year On* found that the size of the 'frontline' was shrinking and that the distinction between 'local response, investigation, and community teams' was becoming blurred.[70] This might mean that while the numbers of officers and staff allocated to neighbourhoods might look protected, in reality they would be performing a broader range of tasks, including response, detracting from their ability to do proactive community police work. This might prove a successful formula, but it might not. Hence, the decline in neighbourhood resources represents a risk to public confidence, however it is measured. Set against this the introduction of the 'Single Non-Emergency' public contact number between March 2011 and June 2012, although technically successful and generally well received, might prove small compensation in terms of public confidence.[71]

---

[68] J Halliday, 'Police could have stopped Jimmy Savile in the 1960s, says official report', *The Guardian*, 12 March 2013 (<http://www.guardian.co.uk/media/2013/mar/12/jimmy-savile-metropolitan-police> [accessed 29 March 2013]), C Moreton, 'Police morale is plummeting, says Lord Stevens', *The Telegraph* (<http://www.telegraph.co.uk/news/uknews/law-and-order/9653552/Police-morale-is-plummeting-says-Lord-Stevens.html> [accessed 29 March 2013]), and The Police Foundation, 'Police morale is a real issue' (<http://www.police-foundation.org.uk/news/55/15/Police-morale-is-a-real-issue> [accessed 29 March 2013]).

[69] R Evans and P Lewis, 'Police "smear" campaign targeted Stephen Lawrence's friends and family', 24 June 2013 (<http://www.guardian.co.uk/uk/2013/jun/23/stephen-lawrence-undercover-police-smears> [accessed 7 July 2013]).

[70] HMIC, *Policing in Austerity: One Year On*, 4–7.

[71] Home Office, *Research Report 66 – Rolling Out the Police Single Non-Emergency Number (101): Research into the Public's and Practitioners' Views* (<https://www.gov.uk/government/uploads/system/uploads/attachment_data/file/115835/horr66-report.pdf> [accessed 8 July 2013]).

Prognosis for crime, anti-social behaviour, disorder, and confidence

In March 2013 as a precursor to the spending review Chief Secretary to the Treasury, Danny Alexander, asked departments to look at further cuts in their budgets of up to 10 per cent. In the case of the police he provided a rationale. An article in the *Guardian* observed that the Home Office would be 'under pressure to reduce police numbers further on the basis that crime is falling.'[72] It may be assumed that this was not random speculation on the part of the journalist author but the consequence of a briefing (not, presumably, a 'leak') that he had received. That the police did not in the end face such cuts is not the point. It was consistent with all that had gone before under the Coalition, both in terms of public funding policy and its attitude towards the police. What was unusual on this occasion was the justification. It was not that the police were over-resourced and inefficient, and therefore could take the cut because reducing bureaucracy would unleash hidden potential. It was instead that crime was falling. Presumably that is how the Treasury saw it, in which case it revealed a worryingly superficial reading of the operational environment, current and future, for two principal reasons.

First, as we have seen, crime and anti-social behaviour represents less than half of the calls the police receive from the public, and that 'general welfare' represents a substantial part of the work done by the police on a daily basis.[73] Second, the coalescence of factors that led to the sustained fall in crime since the mid 1990s might begin to dissipate or weaken, in which case would crime and anti-social behaviour begin to increase? The accentuated fall in crime registered in 2012 cannot be attributed yet to the success of Coalition policing and criminal justice policies simply because, save principally for the introduction PCCs and the reduction in police officer numbers, most of these measures had only been planned, not implemented. It is likely that the BCS/CSEW and PRCS fall in crime and disorder remains attributable to the coalescence of factors identified previously. If police numbers fall further, or the prison population significantly decreases; if the new criminal justice measures fail to be effective, or simply take a long time to embed; if unemployment remained at 2.5 million; if relative or absolute deprivation increased; would crime continue to decrease, or would the trend reverse? There must be at least a risk that it would. The 2013 UK Peace Index Report, which otherwise optimistically reported on the decline in violent crime, noted that the greatest risk of violent crime existed in the areas of greatest deprivation and poverty.[74] It might be countered that despite the decrease in police officer numbers since 2010 there had been no reverse in the crime and disorder trend, but it might be that numbers were still sufficiently high in 2012 to maintain the

---

[72] P Wintour, 'Whitehall may have to find £3bn of extra spending cuts', *The Guardian*, 27 March 2013 (<http://www.guardian.co.uk/politics/2013/mar/27/whitehall-3bn-extra-spending-cuts> [accessed 29 March 2013]).
[73] See Chapter 9, p.184.   [74] UK Peace Index Report 2013, 38.

principal police services of response, investigation, and proactive neighbour-hood patrol. Would that continue to be the case if numbers fell further, as they seemed set to do?

Another risk would be a decrease in the prison population. By early 2013 the prison population had decreased from its peak the previous autumn but was still high. Former Justice Secretary Kenneth Clarke expressed the prevailing view when he said that imprisonment was 'a costly and ineffectual approach that fails to turn criminals into law-abiding citizens'.[75] However, while prison might generally reform criminal behaviour, especially for those detained for short sentences, the clear statistical link between a high prison population and decreasing crime, as illustrated in Figure 9.1, still required an explanation. Equally, there was a risk that significantly rather than incrementally decreasing the prison population would constitute a risk to maintaining the decrease in crime. Would the decrease in police numbers have a negative effect on detec-tions, which are the gateway to non-custodial interventions? Again, it was a risk. Associated with this risk is the decline in successful police investigations, consequent upon the decrease in police numbers, which lead to active inter-ventions to deter and disrupt criminal behaviour. Some of these interventions are custodial, some are not, but all would be at risk. As noted previously, per-haps some of the most successful interventions are remands in custody, which would be equally at risk.

The weakening of the numbers available for proactive, dedicated neighbour-hood policing also increases the risk to a reverse in the decrease in levels of anti-social behaviour. There were, of course, downsides to Labour's ASB measures, including bureaucracy and the criminalization of nuisance, but the Coalition's new interventions will be untried, and while in the longer term they may prove as effective as the previous measures, in the shorter term there is a risk that they will prove less effective in inhibiting anti-social behaviour. It is simply another risk to register, as is the disillusionment registered in the Riot Panel's report.

Besides, the nature of crime itself is changing, in ways which are not necessar-ily susceptible to measurement in PRCS or even BCS/CSEW.[76] For example, cyber crime, or its attempt, is now almost a daily experience for anyone with email or online banking. The phone hacking and sexual abuse scandals illustrate that the police must become more involved in intensive investigations of private behav-iour which a few years previously would not have been thought the business of the public police. The police now investigate race crimes, hate crimes, sex crimes, minor assaults, and harassments to a higher degree than was the case before the 2000s. In 2001–2 the police recorded 650,330 crimes of violence; in the year end-ing September 2011–12 the police recorded 739,651. There were 49,581 sexual

---

[75] Quoted in Bandyopadhyay, *Acquisitive crime* (n 29), 1.

[76] 'Down these not-so-mean streets', *The Economist*, 20 April 2013 (<http://www.economist.com/news/britain/21576437-better-policing-only-one-reason-why-despite-persistent-economic-slump-and-high-youth> [accessed 27 April 2013]).

crimes recorded in 2001–2 compared to 51,814 in 2011–12.[77] While these are declining from the peak they reached in the mid 2000s they are still higher than they were in the 1990s. Assaults and sexual crimes are resource intensive to investigate properly. An example of how resource intensive is demonstrated in the words of a Metropolitan Police detective writing to the *Guardian* in February 2013.

> I am officer on the case for five separate incidents of GBH. These are not my only crimes; they are just the most serious. Despite their importance, I am constantly distracted from being able to provide the victims with a proper service because the workload is so crushingly high. Since 1 January, more than 3,000 crimes had been reported in our borough. There are 30 offices in my unit, each with an average of 15–20 serious crimes to investigate . . . Victims get poor service, crimes are not solved, offenders go free, and police officers' mental and physical health suffers from the pressure that is applied to us.[78]

Furthermore, hate and cyber crimes require specialist resources to investigate them; the type of squads that are being disbanded and merged with generalist neighbourhood policing units. Nor are most forces sufficiently equipped to handle local forms of organized crime such as people trafficking and racketeering; crimes which are likely to fall below the radar of a National Crime Agency which is already under-resourced to deal with the existing national scale of serious and organized crime.

There then remains the threat of renewed disorder similar in scale to that of August 2011. At best most, and arguably all, the preconditions for the 2011 riots remain. That there have not been repetitions is attributable to absence of the precipitants and triggers, even the persistent cold and wet weather that predominated through much of 2012 into 2013. If riots returned would the police be better able to tackle them? The initial flurry of post-riot interest in new equipment such as water cannon rapidly abated and the equipment available to officers remains much as it was in 2011. The problem then was not equipment but principally intelligence, numbers, concentration at critical points, and a willingness to use forward suppressant tactics rather than containment. Baton rounds were available (and had been since the 1980s) but not used, and there seemed unwillingness, albeit an understandable one, to commit officers into situations where they might be isolated and overwhelmed. The thought of what befell PC Keith Blakelock was a desperate example of what might happen if officers misjudged a situation in the confusion, darkness, and violence.[79] If numbers and the ability to concentrate them were issues in 2011 there seems to be no reason why they would not be again in the immediate future. The chances of

---

[77] Home Office, Historical crime data 1898 to 2001/2 and ONS, Crime in England and Wales, year ending September 2012 (<http://www.ons.gov.uk/ons/dcp171778_296191.pdf> [accessed 22 April 2013]), 21.

[78] Quoted in *The Week*, 9 February 2013, 25.

[79] See G Slovo, *The Riots from Spoken Evidence* (Oberon Books, London, 2011).

avoidance would, however, be diminished because of the decline in neighbour-hood policing.

Predicting human behaviour is an uncertain activity. Humans behave and interact as they do, sometimes predictably and often not. There can, therefore, be no certainty with predicting human behaviour. It is only possible to look at the evidence, identify the patterns, and assess what might happen. On that basis, the prognosis is that the improvement seen in recent years in the experience for most people of crime and anti-social behaviour will abate during an extended period of economic recession and declining police resources, the latter most keenly felt at the neighbourhood level. The underlying social and economic causes of the 2011 riots by the mid-point of 2013 remained unaddressed with the consequent likelihood that a recurrence, at least at a local level, would be avoided by the continuing absence of 'precipitant' and 'trigger' factors, the avoidance of which would be aided by the maintenance of strong, proactive neighbourhood polic-ing, the very aspect of policing which HMIC identified as being at risk even as early as mid 2012.[80]

---

[80] HMIC, *Policing in Austerity: One Year On*, 36–7.

10

A future for policing?

The Conservatives' vision

It was one of the underlying premises of this book that in 2010 David Cameron's government had embarked upon a programme of revolutionary change for the police service in England and Wales. By mid 2013 all of the critical foundations of that programme were in place—PCCs, fundamental changes to pay, pensions and conditions of service, the near elimination of national targets, and a fundamental shift from national to local funding, albeit during a period of general financial cuts. New national institutions have been created, even if this amounted in practice to reorganization rather than radical restructuring. The professional element of police leadership has been subordinated to the political, while the process of outsourcing has diluted the professional element of the workforce. Cuts meant that the service was smaller and would get smaller still, but this is seen by the Coalition as a beneficial adjunct, even a prerequisite to increased efficiency and effectiveness.

At the point two years from when the next general election was due the government could claim a high degree of success in implanting its programme. It could even claim political success, retaining a substantial lead on crime and anti-social behaviour over Labour.[1] In its favour it could also claim the continued decline of recorded crime and anti-social behaviour, and the absence of a repeat of the disturbances of 2010–11. That such a claim was premature, by reason of timing if for no other, is immaterial to the government's political case for 'reform'. However, the reality was that in mid 2013 the Coalition's police programme had reached a critical stage, as it moved first from intention to implementation, and then to outcome.

If the programme is successful in terms of outcome, what will the police service look like? First, it will be consciously more political. The Coalition has

---

[1] Ipsos MORI, *Best Party on Key Issues: Crime/Law & Order* (<http://www.ipsos-mori.com/researchpublications/researcharchive/poll.aspx?oItemID=29> [accessed 21 April 2013]).

deliberately deconstructed the chief check against politicization—the tripartite system, where Home Secretary, chief constables, and local politicians held each other in balance. This has been replaced by a more linear structure, with chief constables more, if not entirely, subordinate to the PCC. This is not, however, seen by the Coalition as a negative outcome. One of the main points of the 'Big Society' is to reconnect the people to politics and thence to beneficial community outcomes. The crucial element for the Coalition is that this reconnection will be principally, although not exclusively, to local, not national, politics. It follows that the local leadership of the service provided by chief constables will also risk becoming, over time, more politicized. This does not necessarily mean that chief constables will have to be overtly of the same party as the incumbent PCC (although that development cannot be entirely ruled out), but it is likely to mean that many future chief constable appointments will be associated with the appointing PCC, and to gain the appointment chiefs will have to have a similar political worldview to that of the PCC and to be able to make some kind of personal connection with the appointing PCC. The problem with this process is that it will mean that a new PCC, even one of the same political view as their predecessor, is likely to want to make their own chief constable appointment, and PCCs will have the power to make that kind of change.

Second, police leadership is likely, at least to some degree, to be less professional. Again, this is not seen as a disadvantage, rather the reverse, as it is more than plain that the current Conservative leadership has little confidence in the current professional police leadership. The new leadership will be less professional by virtue of the short tenure and consequent high turnover of chief constables and the *Winsor* recommendations will ensure that an increasing proportion will be appointed from outside the service. This will be supplemented by the appointment of superintendents from outside the service. The appointment of graduates at inspector level will not have a similar effect as they will spend most of their career in the police service and may be the backbone of the chief officer cadre, but that is probably fifteen to twenty years hence. The conscious sidelining of ACPO will weaken the professional element still further. The epitome of this de-professionalization has been the appointment of Tom Winsor as chief HMI. This process of de-professionalization will also see the balance of local strategic leadership switch from chief constables to the office of the PCC, whose members will become the driving force behind the police and crime plans and budgets, as chief constables become personally more operationally and managerially focused. Again, the enthusiasts of this latest version of 'police reform' will see this as a positive, not negative, development.

Third, the focus of the police will become more local. This will be achieved through several strands including the slashing of central targets and protocols and the stimulus provided to local policing through the direct availability of local crime and disorder information, the sensitivity to local issues provided by PCCs and neighbourhood meetings, and the introduction of trigger mechanisms contained in the Anti-Social Behaviour Bill. The absence of a central doctrine on the subject meant that by early 2013 internal force structures were already becoming more bespoke to local circumstances. Slashing centrally set objectives and targets will support localism. Police localism will be supported by more rationally structured national arrangements, stemming from the coordination provided by the Strategic Policing Requirement through the National Crime Agency and the College of Policing's constitutional remit. The forty-three-force structure will remain for the foreseeable future, centrally driven amalgamations being a philosophical anathema to the Coalition. This would not prevent individual partner forces seeking voluntary amalgamations but, as there would be no central financial support to assist with the set-up costs, few forces and their PCCs, unless in financial *extremis*, are likely to initiate the option. Conversely, collaboration between forces will be positively encouraged and more schemes can be expected. The oversight body, HMIC, too will become less professionally orientated and more a champion of the public consumer of policing services.[2] A more local service is intended to generate higher levels of public confidence.

Fourth, the police will become more economic, effective, and efficient. Although inferred rather than explicitly stated, a key enabler will be the continuing reductions in resources and personnel, albeit the result of forced economies, which will require the police to become more efficient and hence more effective. By early 2013 the Conservatives claimed that the strategy was already working, evidenced by the continuing fall in crime. Massive reductions in bureaucracy will deliver '4.5 million police hours' the 'equivalent of 2,100 officers back on the streets'.[3] Reduced Home Office funding for local police will require more local funding, increasing the beneficial effects of localism as PCCs seek greater value for money and in turn are held to increased local scrutiny and accountability. The scale of required economies will require forces to increase outsourcing to the private sector, which will induce greater efficiencies simply by virtue of involving the private sector, which is *ipso facto* seen as more efficient than the public sector. Community reparations for anti-social behaviour and outsourced rehabilitative programmes would be both more economic and more effective than high levels of incarceration or the range of intervention orders which proliferated under Labour. In this worldview decline in resources becomes a positive advantage.

Finally, the *Winsor* reforms to pay, pensions, and conditions of service are intended to support a more efficient and effective workforce by abandoning bureaucratic hindrances such as bonus payments, by improving recruit qualifications, by incentivizing frontline working, and by placing pensions on a sustainable basis. As it is presumably anticipated that few frontline officers will remain in service until their mid 60s, it will follow that the workforce that remains will

---

[2] HMIC, 'Our role' (<http://www.hmic.gov.uk/about-us/what-we-do/> [accessed 7 April 2013]).

[3] Conservatives, 'Reduction in crime shows police reform is working', 24 January 2013 (<http://www.conservatives.com/News/News_stories/2013/01/Reduction_in_crime_shows_police_reform_is_working.aspx> [accessed 7 April 2013]).

be younger and more energized. By standing firm, the influence of the Police Federation has been substantially weakened, in the process enhancing the political standing of Theresa May to the point where she has become a credible alternative Conservative leader to David Cameron.[4]

What will be the outcome in terms of social benefit of this combination of policy initiatives? It will be even lower levels of crime and disorder, effective measures against serious and organized crime, and continued effectiveness against international and domestic terrorism. As for internal morale, once those officers and staff entrenched in the old system have passed from the service by one means or another the current episode of poor and lowering morale will be replaced by a revitalized workforce.

Risk

That is the vision, but what are the problems that may inhibit it being realized?

First, it must be acknowledged that there is a risk that the programme will not be achieved either in whole or in part. The first part of that risk stems simply from this being a huge business change programme, and any business change programme runs the risk of partial or complete failure. The generally accepted figure is that only 30 per cent of change programmes are successful, and this is despite years of developing practice in securing successful change management. Common causes cited are distraction by all elements of the workforce, but particularly management, and failure to change 'employee attitudes and management behaviour'.[5] The recent track record of change management in British public services is variable. The NHS has been subject to almost constant change-management since the 1970s as management and political fashions change, with the only common assumption for each phase of change being that the previous change did not work. Defence is similarly subject to frequent review but here the driving force is normally finance and the government, whatever its political persuasion, can normally rely on the positive attitude of those military personnel that are left after any redundancy programme. The police service probably has one of the better track records of coping with change, but that may be because since the 'big bang' restructuring of the 1970s it has generally been incremental and, arguably, based on the bedrock of job security for the core workforce, ie police officers. The problems with such an approach, from the perspective of impatient ministers whose tenure of office can often be markedly less than the duration of a single parliament, is that the process is slow, tends to yield

---

[4] N Watt, 'Theresa May eyes Tory leadership as a "realist"', *The Guardian*, 10 March 2013 (<http://www.guardian.co.uk/politics/2013/mar/10/theresa-may-eyes-conservative-leadership-realist> [accessed 7 April 2013]).

[5] S Keller and C Aiken, *The Inconvenient Truth About Change Management* (<http://www.mckinsey.com/App_Media/Reports/Financial_Services/The_Inconvenient_Truth_About_Change_Management.pdf> [accessed 7 April 2013]).

cumulative rather than dramatic results, and does not change workforce attitudes—indeed, it relies on its tacit consent. Hence David Cameron's view that the
police are the last unreformed public service.

Due to its very nature, the police service relies on the enthusiasm and effectiveness of its frontline workforce, who work with very low levels of direct supervision. That is one of the reasons why they must be individually well qualified for
their job and well motivated. *Winsor* addressed the first part of that requirement
by seeking to raise entry educational standards. The problem is that by doing so
it has either deliberately or accidentally impugned the educational standards of
existing frontline officers. Furthermore, the majority of those frontline officers
currently serving will have their pay, pensions, and conditions of service adversely
affected by many of the remainder of the *Winsor* reforms. These reforms may be
a rational response to the human resource and financial circumstances of the
service in the early twenty-first century, but they have not been presented in a
way calculated to win the hearts and minds of the existing workforce. Nor has
there been much attempt to do so in general terms. That officers feel exposed and
neglected by the current political leadership is amply evidenced by their poor
morale.[6] That the workforce may realistically not have voted for the right to
strike is a hollow victory because police officers intuitively do not want to strike.
The measure of poor morale is that the ballot took place at all. The Home Office
is therefore already at risk of failing in its change management programme by not
making the necessary investment in convincing the workforce that fundamental
change is in its best interests. A primary risk is that job security, which has under-
laid previous change programmes, will almost certainly be removed as the *Winsor* report implementation gathers momentum. Supporters of change might
point to the relatively smooth implementation of the single Scottish force, but
serving police officers in Scotland have not been subject to the same degree of
change to their pay and conditions as have their counterparts in England and
Wales. Finally, in keeping with the government's fundamental philosophy,
there will be no central oversight and direction of the change programme. Each
force will be left to its own devices. This almost certainly means that there will
be a bell curve of implementation and outcome, ranging from some excellent
examples to some near failures through a middle mass of satisfactory but no better. HMIC inspections will highlight successes and failures; the former barely
registering, and the latter reinforcing poor internal morale. The government
can, however, rely on the individual police officer's sense of duty not to let the
public down. That, however, is hardly a recipe for moving the programme from
the 70 per cent failure category to that of 30 per cent success.

The changing nature of police leadership must also be registered as a risk. There
has already been a substantial change in police leadership at the very top, the

---

[6] C Moreton, 'Police morale is plummeting, says Lord Stevens', *The Telegraph*, 3 November 2012
(<http://www.telegraph.co.uk/news/uknews/law-and-order/9653552/Police-morale-is-plummeting-
says-Lord-Stevens.html> [accessed 7 April 2013]).

result of some enforced change and the natural consequence of retirement. The new appointments have come from the traditional internal career path, and will do so until the *Winsor* report recommendations are given official sanction. Once that occurs the probability is that several will be from outside the traditional cadre, including the Metropolitan Police Commissioner. That brings operational as well as managerial risk. Chief constables, and equivalent, are not simply general managerial posts; they do have specific operational and legal roles. A relevant professional background is likely to be an advantage in making these operational and legal decisions. Even though technically experienced assistants and staff officers will support these leaders, ultimately the decision will have to be made by a single responsible individual. This does not mean that all external appointments will fail, or that all internal appointments will succeed. Two Civil Nuclear Constabulary chief constables in succession have been appointed from non-Home Office force backgrounds without disadvantage, although it might be argued that the range of responsibility in operational and community terms is more limited compared to Home Office forces. Equally, there have been several instances of failure in police leadership evident in officers from a traditional career background. Nevertheless, a switch from a wholly police professional senior leadership cadre to one of mixed experience contains elements of high risk.

Another risk is the negative aspects of politicization through PCCs. In April 2013 the Kent PCC came under heavy criticism for appointing a 'youth police and crime commissioner' on a £15,000-a-year salary. In a harsh lesson for them both in the realities of modern political life, it soon emerged that the youth PCC had posted potentially 'racist and anti-gay' tweets. The local Conservative MP immediately criticized the independent PCC Ann Barnes for making the appointment in the first place, and the high-profile chair of the Home Affairs Committee, Keith Vaz, called on the 17-year-old youth PCC to resign. Twenty-four hours later she had resigned in tears.[7] In the aftermath of the November 2012 elections several PCCs were criticized for appointing expensive deputies.[8] Although there has been little post-election assessment of effectiveness there is some evidence that individual PCCs have made little impact, positive or negative, in their areas. The 15 per cent November 2012 turnout was hardly evidence that their existence was filling the presumed democratic deficit, but the excuse that this was an untried process was tenable to some degree. It will not be so in 2016. A similarly low turnout would seriously shake credibility in the system, and there is no reason to suppose that it will be different second time around.

---

[7] BBC News, 'Kent youth PPC Paris Brown urged to resign over tweets', 8 April 2013 (<http://www.bbc.co.uk/news/uk-england-kent-22070354> [accessed 8 April 2013]) and BBC News, 'Paris Brown: Kent youth PCC resigns after Twitter row', 9 April 2013 (<http://www.bbc.co.uk/news/uk-england-22083032> [accessed 9 April 2013]).

[8] See Chapter 5 and A Travis, 'Police and crime commissioners accused of power grab', guardian.co.uk, 6 December 2012 (<http://www.guardian.co.uk/uk/2012/dec/06/police-commissioners-accused-of-power-grab> [accessed 9 April 2013]).

Further risks are associated with the operating environment. The claim that Coalition reforms are working as evidenced by the continuing decline in crime and disorder is at best premature, principally because by early 2013, when the claim was made, there had simply been insufficient time for the measures introduced by the Coalition to have had effect. A more likely explanation is that the momentum created by the combination of positive factors that had produced the long-term decline in recorded crime that existed before the Coalition's election in 2010 was continuing through 2012 into 2013. The risk was that in the future this combination might weaken and dissipate, with high unemployment, continuing inequality, rapidly declining police numbers, and a small but measurable decrease in the prison population. Perhaps each of those factors can be countered. The economy may pick up and unemployment decrease; the improving economy may lessen inequality; increasing police efficiency might compensate for decreasing numbers; new community-based punishments and rehabilitative measures might similarly compensate for the decrease in the prison population. There is a further complication in the form of the changing nature of crime, in particular the increasing awareness of sexual crimes and the rise of new crimes such as cyber crime, all of which are complicated and resource intensive to investigate. Each of these negative factors represents a risk, and together they equate to high risk.

Similarly, the risk remains that there will be, at some point, a return of the disorders of 2011. In Chapter 9 it was observed that by mid 2013 the preconditions which gave rise to the August 2011 riots remained. That does not equate to an inevitability of their recurrence unless a set of precipitants is present followed by a trigger cause. Avoidance of precipitants will rely on the availability of good community policing and good community intelligence, both of which will be weakened by the decrease in police numbers consequent upon existing spending plans and those that are likely post CSR 2013. The scale of the 2011 riots was exceptional, and this alone may make a return of a similar extent unlikely, but that means that even a lesser extent of disorder could still be relatively serious, particularly in local terms. Again, the return of serious disorder unless there is some mitigation of the likely combination of negative social, economic, and policing factors is high risk. The police are also likely to have to face disorder arising from political and environmental protest. After an initial burst of activity associated with student protest, education cuts, and globalization, there has been an abatement of activity in 2012 and early 2013. However, new causes, both national and local, could regenerate activity.

The Coalition intends its creation of the National Crime Agency to increase national effectiveness in combating serious and organized crime. The actual degree of change from SOCA to NCA, however, is incremental rather than radical, so while the NCA is in itself unlikely to have any negative impact, it is unlikely to have a significant benefit either. Such benefits as there may be are likely to be derived from new leadership, new focus, and, perhaps, a greater empathy between officers in the forty-three forces and personnel in the NCA, but this will be intangible. What might make a difference is the injection of additional resources, and this seems unlikely. The reality is the national effort against serious and organized crime will remain under-resourced.

The potential for terrorist attack remains, notwithstanding the success the police and security agencies have had since 2005 in detecting and disrupting them. However, the fundamental issues that have given rise to the threat, notably the international jihadist movement, remain, while the ability of individuals outside any formal terrorist structure to launch a one-off attack was demonstrated by the murder of an off-duty soldier at Woolwich in May 2013. The continuing threat is therefore a continuing risk with low probability but high consequence. The effectiveness of the police and security agencies is therefore critical in avoiding a new attack. The question is, therefore, whether the existing diffuse structural arrangements represent the optimum? The government does not appear to think so, as in early 2013 it was still considering placing national police counter-terrorist policing within the remit of the NCA. There is a case for rationalizing counter-terrorist policing in a single national organization. If serious and organized crime policing merits a national organization it is difficult to see why counter terrorism does not. The refined question is therefore does subsuming counter terrorism policing within the NCA with its already wide brief, represent the optimum arrangement? A national counter terrorism police organization distinct from the NCA would ensure that counter terrorism would be the primary focus of its leadership and governance. It would also ensure accountability in terms of governance and clarity in terms of available resources. An NCA responsible for both serious and organized crime and counter terrorism would permit obfuscation of resource allocation, and facilitate future under-resourcing. Future counter terrorism arrangements unfit for purpose is therefore another high risk.

The final high risk is the continuing decline in police resources. By early 2013 the police service was already substantially smaller, by some 26,000 FTEs, than that which the Coalition inherited in 2010. So far there has been no serious dislocation of service to the public, although the indications are that there is downsizing in neighbourhood policing. One of the reasons why this had had so little adverse impact by 2013 is that the service had barely begun to absorb the final increases made under Labour, so their immediate loss passed without much notice. That will not be the case in future as further losses will have to be absorbed. The combined effect of the 2012 Treasury Autumn Statement and the 2013 spending review suggests a loss of at least 37,000 FTEs by the end of the Parliament. If the cuts continue into the next Parliament, as seems likely, then the loss could be as great as 64,000 FTEs, taking numbers back to those last seen in 1989.

Clearly the police service can still function at the 1989 level of FTEs, but there remain high risk factors. First, investigations and procedures are complex and increasingly resource intensive. Coalition cuts in bureaucracy are hard to evidence and even harder to link with savings in FTEs. However, even the Coalition's best estimate is that cuts in bureaucracy will save only the equivalent of 2,100 FTEs. Second, the cuts will fall principally in neighbourhood policing. Third, the drip-feed loss of personnel is debilitating in terms of morale. Fourth, the continuing loss of personnel will mean an asymmetrical personnel profile in most, if not all, forces, disproportionately skewed towards middle and senior service officers and staff. In effect a generation of new recruits will be lost. This is unhealthy in organizational terms. It also represents a collective mass of individual disappointments for young people who otherwise would have found a career in policing. Fifth, even at the higher levels of personnel the police in 2011 was only just able to contain the serious disorder of August that year. Finally, it seems that high police numbers was at least one of the factors that contributed to falling crime and rising confidence.

The counter-vision—the nightmare

In most change programmes the theory is that there is short-term pain but long-term gain, at least for those who survive the process. For those who do not, there is at least the offer of a decent financial settlement and the prospect, in a buoyant economy, of reasonable re-employment. The resettlement programme for the transition from the Royal Ulster Constabulary to the Police Service of Northern Ireland is perhaps a classic example of facilitated change. For those currently serving in the police forces of England and Wales there is no such prospect in sight. It might very well in the long term be much better, but that long term is very long indeed. What is happening to the police service is arguably a compression of what is happening to UK society as a whole. There may or may not be an alternative, but that is small comfort to those at the wrong end of the economic curve.

The Coalition has a vision for policing which will see it radically altered in the space of a few years. The theory is that it will be a uniform change for the better. The likelihood is that not all of what it changes will be successful or beneficial. If the risks outlined previously are realized, or at least not sufficiently mitigated, then the service will be not only smaller, but also demoralized and inconsistently led. The College of Policing, despite its success in training, fails as the alternative to ACPO's collective leadership. Such long-term planning as there is will be subverted to the short-term political needs of largely transient elected local officials. Cuts in bureaucracy remain largely superficial and make little or no difference to working practices, although deft political handling enables the Home Office to pass the blame for this down to chief constables or PCCs. Those benefits, efficiencies, goals, or targets that are achieved are inadequately measured and do not provide sufficient compensation for the losses in personnel. Increased privatization may prove more effective, efficient, or economic than in-house alternatives, while at the same time obfuscating accountability. A similar outcome is registered for intra-force collaboration.

As the number of police professionals fall, and the number of volunteers fail to compensate; as the economy fails to recover and unemployment remains relatively high; and as the prison population falls without being compensated by effective community restorative regimes, so crime and disorder rises. The degree to which it rises is to all practical purposes impossible to calculate, although it is probably not in the annual double-digit terms of the 1980s. Given prospective changes to the way crime is officially recorded, the key indicator is likely to be the Crime Survey for England and Wales. However registered, crime will still be a relatively remote experience for most people, but those who are victims of the crimes which primarily feature in police and crime survey statistics will be principally drawn from the already deprived and disadvantaged. Conversely, crimes which affect businesses, corporations, and the general economy—frauds, cyber crime, money laundering—will remain largely undetected because of the unavailability of specialist police investigative resources. Despite the successes of recent years, a terrorist 'spectacular' remains a possibility. A negative coalescence of precipitant factors is more likely than not to occur in the next few years, heightening the likelihood of serious disorder, even if not on the extensive scale of 2011.

Would it be different under Labour?

Not least amongst the difficulties in estimating what it would be like under a future Labour government is the almost total absence of policy statements by the Labour opposition. Shadow Home Secretary Yvette Cooper has been able to criticize the Coalition's agenda, particularly over the decline in police numbers, increased privatization, and PCCs.[9] However, as with much else in its policy development, by the middle of 2013 Labour had failed to present a coherent, consistent, and extensive alternative narrative, much less vision. This is partly because Shadow Chancellor Ed Balls has made it clear that a future Labour government would, at least initially, stick to the Coalition spending plans announced in the 2013 spending review, but it is also because Labour has effectively outsourced the development of its new policing policy to an external body, the Independent Police Commission under the chairmanship of Lord Stevens.

The review was commissioned in September 2011 with the remit to 'examine the roles and responsibilities of the police service in England and Wales in the twenty-first century. In so doing [it] will examine the application of the Peelian Principles of policing for the twenty-first century, including reducing crime and increasing community confidence.'[10] It is not the purpose of the Independent

---

[9] 'Yvette Cooper's speech in full', politics.co.uk, 3 October 2012 (<http://www.politics.co.uk/comment-analysis/2012/10/03/yvette-cooper-speech-in-full> [accessed 10 April 2013]).

[10] Independent Police Commission, Home (<http://independentpolicecommission.org.uk> [accessed 10 April 2013]). I declare 'an interest' at this point. I was invited to be a member of the Independent Commission but resigned in April 2012 over the issue of restrictions on my ability to comment freely on contemporary policing matters.

Commission to write Labour's policing policy, and the party remains notionally free to receive or reject the final report. Even if it accepts the final report it remains free to develop its own detailed policing policies. However, it would be a public relations difficulty if it developed distinctively different policies.

The advantage for Labour of using the Independent Commission is that it has effectively created its own policing think tank, performing a role similar to that performed by Policy Exchange and Cchange for the Conservatives while in opposition. Labour in 2013 was in a similar position to the Conservatives in 1997–2005. It had been in opposition after having been in power for a long time; had run out of ideas by the time it was ejected from office, and by the mid-point of the parliament was still in need of fresh ideas to generate distinctive but effective policies. The problem was that with the Independent Commission not having delivered its report by April 2013 Labour was not leaving itself much time to absorb the Independent Commission's report, respond, and then develop those distinctive policies in time for them to take root in public perception before the next general election, notionally due in May 2015. It will have the added disadvantage of probably inheriting an economic situation little improved from the one it had left behind in 2010. Certainly it would lack much manoeuvring room in terms of public spending.

What could Labour do? It had opposed PCCs but had done reasonably well in the first PCC elections; nevertheless, it will have to have a policy on governance in place for the 2015 manifesto. To maintain the new status quo, given its opposition to PCCs, would leave it open to charges of hypocrisy or, at best, lack of imagination. So the likelihood is that it will develop the idea of a fully elected commission, with a single lead figure as 'Commissioner' fulfilling a role not dissimilar to an elected mayor in a local authority.

Labour will not be under great pressure to alter the new national arrangements and will probably let these run, although it could gain some useful allies in chief officers if it restored some of ACPO's lost status. It will not need to reintroduce the centralist, bureaucratic tendencies of the Blair–Brown years. It could trim the effects of the *Winsor* recommendations by overturning those relating to direct entry at middle and senior ranks, and win some popularity by slightly lowering the new retirement age, but it is likely to want to keep most in place to give it the kind of flexibility that erstwhile Home Secretary David Blunkett had sought but not entirely achieved when Labour had last been in office. The most difficult issue it will have to tackle, however, is funding. If there is the glimmer of general economic growth it might be able to introduce the opposite of the 2010 emergency budget and inject some funding into beleaguered government public service departments but broadly stick with the principles of CSR 2013 until established in government. But it will still not have much room to manoeuvre if it wishes to retain 'AAA' status from those credit agencies which still give the UK that rating. Furthermore, it will be under immense political pressure from its own supporters to lessen the impact of Coalition changes to the welfare system, which it is likely to prioritize along with health and education, restricting opportunities to increase police funding. The strongest pressure to increase central funding will come from those sections of communities most affected by any increase in crime, but even then it will be necessary for crime and disorder to replace the economy as the driving force in opinion polls. A simple solution may be to accept the losses in numbers up to 2015, then stabilize central police funding but allow local funding to rise through the council tax by raising the threshold for triggering a referendum. It will, however, be several years before a Labour government would have the confidence much less the financial base to start significantly increasing police numbers. It is likely to be at least a generation before the near quarter of a million police personnel of 2010 is restored, and probably not even then.

In short, Labour will have its freedom to manoeuvre in police policy matters restricted by its lack of preparation before the 2015 general election, the continued under-performance of the economy, the pressure to deliver on other commitments, and the fact that even as soon as 2015 some of the Coalition police 'reforms' will have become embedded.

Is there an alternative?

At the end of the 1980s the police service was facing a difficult time. The Conservative government under Margaret Thatcher had to a great extent transformed the country but had done so at the price of either causing or at least not sufficiently mitigating social and economic divisions. The police had been caught in the middle but had for many opposed to the government become indelibly linked with the government of the day; in popular parlance 'Maggie's Army'. However, as social unrest and crime had risen inexorably through the decade, the government preferred to identify police inefficiency as a primary cause rather than the effect of its own policies. The answer was a heavy dose of 'New Public Management'—quantifiable targets, objectives, privatization, outsourcing, and, if Mrs Thatcher had had her way, new leadership provided by former army officers. In the face of this challenge and as an antidote to the perceived decline in public confidence, the collective leadership of the police service—ACPO, the Superintendents' Association, and the Police Federation—came together, recognized the problem, and determined to do something about it. It commissioned the OPR, which produced thirty-six recommendations, arguably the most important of which was the Statement of Common Purpose and Values, which in turn led to the Quality of Service initiative. It did not entirely prevent the imposition of the New Public Management agenda, although it may have been a factor in deflecting, at least for the time being, the de-professionalization of police leadership. What it crucially achieved was to provide a distinct alternative police-centred narrative to the one being developed by the government.

In 2013 there is no new OPR, no alternative professional narrative. By 2013 it was probably too late to develop one. The right time to have developed one was before 2010, but that would have run the risk of appearing too political by siding with one or other of the parties. After the Coalition had formed, to have presented an alternative police programme would have risked alienating those in power, but it would probably have resulted in no more damage than that which has occurred and is occurring. As it is, there is no alternative professional programme to balance the overtly political one of the Coalition or to influence a potential Labour government after 2015. The boat has been well and truly missed.

If such an alternative had been developed what might it have included? A narrative for the 2010s might have included a new statement of common purpose and values, or at least an emphatic restatement. The Peelian Principles could have been revamped to re-emphasize the importance of distancing the police from direct party political influence. A case could have been made for a sustainable establishment of FTEs sufficient to maintain the primary purposes of investigation, response, and community patrol. The service should have been energizing the slashing of bureaucracy rather than responding to external pressure. The facts should have been laid bare concerning under-resourcing of the investigation of serious and organized crime and exposure to new crimes, particularly cyber crime and people-trafficking. ACPO should have abandoned its anachronistic preference for mergers and had the value of individual forces restated, rather than continuing to undermine public confidence in them by favouring either mergers or enhanced levels of collaboration. The Federation needed to meet the pressure for changes to pay and conditions halfway, and ACPO should have unequivocally argued for direct entry at inspector level. The service should also have embraced a single counter terrorism police organization. The sum might not have deflected the Coalition from its programme, but it would at least have presented a credible plan to argue against and to give confidence to those who lead, those who are led, and those who receive policing services.

A cautionary tale

No organization can stand still, and the police service is no exception, but the Coalition had embarked upon a high-risk, all-or-nothing change programme, when history suggests a more evolutionary approach would have been more valid. Politically that would not be acceptable as the Coalition, and particularly the Conservative element, must demonstrate that, like so much else in government and the public services, the police service is broken and they know how to fix it. The change process itself runs a risk of failure, but in reality it is unlikely that it will fail completely; there is simply too much professionalism and loyalty to the public in the police service for that to happen. Also, there is no reason to suppose that much of the change will not 'work' in some fashion. But the programme has to do more than just 'work'. The result must be demonstrably more successful than what it is replacing, and this may be hard to do. The Coalition is likely to point to the completion of its change programme, such as creating the NCA or

College of Policing, as evidence of success, but in reality that is only the beginning of the measurement of success. In business terms it is necessary to demonstrate what added value the change has brought and, in the absence of measurable success criteria, that is likely to prove too difficult. Conversely, it will be equally hard to demonstrate that the change programme has failed.

What will count for most people will be that they experience less crime and disorder, and feel safe. By mid 2013 the evidence was that the Coalition is getting away with it. Fewer police personnel but lower recorded crime and no repeat of the 2011 riots. But continuing cuts and inequality suggest that fortune will have to continue to favour the Coalition for that run to continue. The irony is that it might be a post 2015 Labour, or at least Labour-led government that reaps the consequences, one way or the other.

Forecasting is a tricky matter. There are decisions to be made, events to occur that will alter the assumptions upon which this book has been based, and the trends will develop differently, for better or worse. But risk can be identified, and identifying it is the ultimate purpose of this book. It is therefore a 'cautionary tale'; a description of what *might* be. But if authors cannot predict the future, neither can politicians and policy-makers, much as they might like to think they can. The reality is that in 2010 the Coalition, and principally its Conservative element, embarked upon a massive experiment in policing, the outcome of which is, at best, uncertain.

Appendix
The 'Peelian Principles'

The accepted nine so-called 'Peelian Principles' of policing are normally listed as:

1. The basic mission for which the police exist is to prevent crime and disorder.
2. The ability of the police to perform their duties is dependent upon public approval of police actions.
3. Police must secure the willing co-operation of the public in voluntary observance of the law to be able to secure and maintain the respect of the public.
4. The degree of co-operation of the public that can be secured diminishes proportionately to the necessity of the use of physical force.
5. Police seek and preserve public favour not by catering to public opinion but by constantly demonstrating absolute impartial service to the law.
6. Police use physical force to the extent necessary to secure observance of the law or to restore order only when the exercise of persuasion, advice and warning is found to be insufficient.
7. Police, at all times, should maintain a relationship with the public that gives reality to the historic tradition that the police are the public and the public are the police; the police being only members of the public who are paid to give full-time attention to duties which are incumbent on every citizen in the interests of community welfare and existence.
8. Police should always direct their action strictly towards their functions and never appear to usurp the powers of the judiciary.
9. The test of police efficiency is the absence of crime and disorder, not the visible evidence of police action in dealing with it.

Source: ACPO, 'What do the Police do?' (<http://www.acpo.police.uk/documents/reports/2012/201210PolicingintheUKFinal.pdf> [accessed 8 March 2013]).

Bibliography

Books, essays, pamphlets, papers, and theses

Baker, K, *The Turbulent Years: My Life in Politics* (Faber and Faber, London, 1993)

Bale, T, *The Conservative Party: From Thatcher to Cameron* (Polity Press, Cambridge, 2010)

Barber, M, *Instruction to deliver: Tony Blair, Public Services and the Challenge of Achieving Targets* (Politico, London, 2007)

Blunkett, D, *The Blunkett Tapes: My Life in the Bear Pit* (Bloomsbury Publishing, London, 2006)

Brain, T, *A History of Policing in England and Wales* (OUP, Oxford, 2010)

Briscoe, S, *Britain in Numbers: The Essential Statistics* (Politico, London, 2005)

Comfort, N, (ed), *The Politics Book: A Lexicon of Political Facts from Abu Ghraib to Zippergate* (Politico, London, 2005)

Concise Oxford English Dictionary (12th edn, OUP, Oxford, 2011)

Copperfield, D (pseud S Davidson), *Wasting Police Time* (Monday Books, Cheltenham, revised 2007)

De Tocqueville, A, *The Ancien Regime and the French Revolution* (translated S Gilbert, Fontana, London, 1971)

Elliott, F and Hanning, J, *Cameron: The Rise of the New Conservative* (Harper Perennial, London, 2009)

Fukayama, F, *The End of History and the Last Man* (Penguin Books, London, 1992)

Kelling, G and Coles, C, *Fixing Broken Windows* (Free Press, New York, 1996)

Kennedy, P, *The Rise and Fall of the Great Powers* (Fontana Press, London, 1989)

Lee, S and Beech, M (eds), *The Cameron–Clegg Government: Coalition Politics in an Age of Austerity* (Palgrave Macmillan, Basingstoke, 2010)

Mason, P, *Why it's Kicking Off Everywhere: The New Global Revolutions* (Verso, London, 2012)

Newburn, T and Neyroud, P (eds), *Dictionary of Policing* (Willan, Cullompton, 2008)

Norman, J, *The Big Society: The Anatomy of the New Politics* (University of Buckingham Press, Buckingham, 2010)

Phillips, C, Jacobson, J, Prime, R, Carter, M, and Considine, M, *Crime and Disorder Reduction Partnerships: Round One Progress* (Home Office Police Research Series Paper 151, London, 2002)

Reicher, R and Scott, S, *Mad Mobs and Englishmen? Myths and Realities of the 2011 Riots* (Constable and Robinson, London, 2011)

Reiner, R, *The Politics of the Police* (4th edn, OUP, Oxford, 2010)

Savage, S, *Police Reform: Forces for Change* (OUP, Oxford, 2007)

Seldon, A (ed), *Blair's Britain, 1997–2007* (Cambridge University Press, Cambridge, 2007)

Seldon, A, Snowdon, P, and Collings, A, *Blair Unbound* (Pocket Books, London, 2007)

Silvestri, A (ed), *Lessons for the Coalition: An End of Term Report on New Labour and Criminal Justice* (Centre for Crime and Justice Studies, London, 2011)

Stone, L, *The Causes of the English Revolution 1529–1642* (Routledge and Paul, London, 1972)

Tate, J (ed), *What's Right Now: Conservative Essays on the Role of Civil Society, Markets and the State* (Social Market Foundation, London, 2005)

Taylor, R, *Major* (Haus Publishing, London, 2006)

Worcester, R, Mortimore, R, Baines, P, and Gill, M, *Explaining Cameron's Coalition: An Analysis of the 2010 British General Election* (Biteback, London, 2011)

Articles

Ballinger, A, 'New Labour and responses to violence against women' in A Silvestri (ed), *Lessons for the Coalition* (Centre for Crime and Justice Studies, London, 2011)

Bennett, T and Lupton, R, 'A survey of the allocation and use of community constables in England and Wales', *British Journal of Criminology*, vol 32, no 2, Spring 1992

Brain, T, 'Accentuate the positive', *Policing Today*, September 2012

Bullock, K and Johnson, P, 'The Impact of the Human Rights Act 1998 on Policing in England and Wales', *British Journal of Criminology*, October 2009

Donohue III, J and Levitt, S, 'The impact of legalized abortion on crime', *Quarterly Journal of Economics*, vol CXVI, May 2001, issue 2 (<http://pricetheory.uchicago.edu/levitt/Papers/DonohueLevittTheImpactOfLegalized2001.pdf>, accessed 27 April 2013)

Harries, R, 'Modelling and predicting recorded property crime trends in England and Wales—a retrospective', *International Journal of Forecasting*, 19 (2003)

Higgins, A, 'Guardian: The ignored London riots context—deaths in police custody, 0 convictions', Philosophers Stone (<http://philosophers-stone.co.uk/wordpress/2011/08/guardian-the-ignored-london-riots-context-333-deaths-in-police-custody-0-convictions/>, accessed 25 March 2013)

Hough, M, Jackson, J, Bradford, B, Myhill, A, and Quinton, P, 'Procedural justice, trust, and institutional legitimacy', *Policing*, vol 4, issue 3, August 2010

Innes, M, 'The reassurance function', *Policing*, vol 1, no 2, 2007

Keller, S and Aiken, C, 'The inconvenient truth about change management' (<http://www.mckinsey.com/App_Media/Reports/Financial_Services/The_Inconvenient_Truth_About_Change_Management.pdf>, accessed 7 April 2013)

Lentz, S and Chaires, R, 'The invention of Peel's principles: a study of policing "textbook" history', *Journal of Justice* 35 (2007)

Simey, M, 'All dressed up and nowhere to go?', *Police*, August 1976

Solomon, E, 'New Labour and crime prevention in England and Wales: what worked?', *IPC Review*, vol 3, March 2009 (<http://www.sciencessociales.uottawa.ca/ipc/fra/documents/ipcr3solomon.pdf>, accessed 8 April 2013)

Official papers, reports, and briefings

ACPO, *ACPO Response to Policing in the 21st Century: Reconnecting Police and the Public* (<http://www.acpo.police.uk/documents/HO_Consultation_Response.pdf>, accessed 21 November 2012)

Association of Police and Crime Commissioners (APCC), 'Police and crime commissioners' (<http://www.apccs.police.uk/page/pcc-candidates>, accessed 30 November 2012)

Association of Police and Crime Commissioners (APCC), 'Precept and Crime Plan' (<http://www.apccs.police.uk/fileUploads/homepage-adverts/Police_Precepts_Announcements_27.02.13.pdf>, accessed 6 March 2013)

Association of Police and Crime Commissioners (APCC), 'What might police and crime commissioners do?' (<http://www.apccs.police.uk/fileUploads/PCC_election_results_2012/APCC_analysis_of_PCCs_priorities_201112.pdf>, accessed 30 November 2012)

Association of Police Authorities (APA), *Response to Policing in the 21st Century: Reconnecting the Police and the Public* (APA, London, 2001)

Berman, G, *Prison Population Statistics* (House of Commons Library, London, 2012)

Berry, J, *Reducing Bureaucracy in Policing: Final Report* (<http://www.homeoffice.gov.uk/publications/police/reducing-bureaucracy/reduce-bureaucracy-police?view=Binary>, accessed 4 August 2012)

Bradford, B, *Police Numbers and Crime Rates—A Rapid Evidence Review* (<http://www.hmic.gov.uk/media/police-numbers-and-crime-rates-rapid-evidence-review-20110721.pdf>, accessed 24 March 2013)

Chartered Institute of Public Finance and Accountancy (Cipfa), Police Actuals 1995–2011 (http://www.cipfastats.net/publicprotection/policeactuals/, accessed variously)

College of Policing, *Guidance for the Appointment of Chief Officers* (<http://www.acpo.police.uk/documents/reports/2012/201212guid-appt-chief-off-cop.pdf>, accessed 6 August 2013)

Commission on a Bill of Rights, *A UK Bill of Rights? The Choice Before Us*, vol 1 (Members of the Commission on a Bill of Rights, 2012 <http://www.justice.gov.uk/downloads/about/cbr/uk-bill-rights-vol-1.pdf>, accessed 10 February 2013)

Community Oriented Policing Services, *The Impact of the Economic Downturn on American Police Agencies* (US Department of Justice, Washington DC, 2011)

Conservatives, *Conservative and Liberal Democrat Coalition Negotiations: agreements reached 11 May 2010* (<http://www.conservatives.com/News/News_stories/2010/05/Coalition_Agreement_published.aspx>, accessed 21 September 2012), cited as Coalition Agreement

Crown Prosecution Service (CPS), *Justice For All* (<http://www.cps.gov.uk/publications/docs/jfawhitepaper.pdf>, accessed 12 April 2013)

Data.gov.uk, *Crime in England and Wales 2009/10* (<http://data.gov.uk/dataset/crime-in-england-and-wales-bcs>, accessed 8 April 2013)

Dunnell, K, *The Changing Demographic Picture of the UK: National Statistician's Annual Article on the Population* (<http://www.ons.gov.uk/ons/rel/population-trends/no--130--winter-2007/the-changing-demographic-picture-of-the-uk.pdf>, accessed 25 January 2013)

Equality and Human Rights Commission (EHRC), *Stop and Think: a Critical Review of the Use of Stop and Search Powers in England and Wales* (<http://www.equalityhumanrights.com/uploaded_files/raceinbritain/ehrc_stop_and_search_report.pdf>, accessed 22 January 2013)

Flanagan, Sir Ronnie, *The Review of Policing: Final Report* (Home Office, London, 2008)

GOV.UK, *Prison Population, Population Bulletins*—weekly 28 September 2012 and weekly 8 March 2013 (<https://www.gov.uk/government/publications/prison-population-figures>, accessed 21 April 2013)

Government Statistical Service, *National Statistician's Review of Crime Statistics: England and Wales June 2011* (<http://www.statisticsauthority.gov.uk/national-statistician/ns-reports—reviews-and-guidance/national-statistician-s-reviews/national-statistician-s-review-of-crime-statistics.html>, accessed 7 July 2013)

Hackney Borough Council, *A Ward Profile of Dalston* (<http://www.hackney.gov.uk/Assets/Dalston/dalston-ward-profile.pdf>, accessed 25 April 2012)

HM Government, *New Landscape of Policing: the Government Response to the Fourteenth Report of the Home Affairs Committee Session 2010–12*, HC 939 (<http://www.official-documents.gov.uk/document/cm82/8223/8223.pdf>, accessed 11 January 2013)

HM Government, *The Coalition: Our Programme for Government* (Cabinet Office, London, 2010), cited as *Coalition Programme for Government*

HM Government, *The Equality Strategy—Building a Fairer Britain* (<http://www.home-office.gov.uk/publications/equalities/equality-strategy-publications/equality-strategy/equality-strategy?view=Binary>, accessed 22 January 2013)

HM Government, *Review of Counter-Terrorism and Security Powers: Findings and Recommendations* (<http://www.homeoffice.gov.uk/publications/counter-terrorism/review-of-ct-security-powers/review-findings-and-rec?view=Binary>, accessed 9 February 2013)

HM Treasury, *Autumn Statement 2012* (TSO, Norwich, 2012)

HM Treasury, *Autumn Statement 2012, Policy Decisions Table* (<https://www.gov.uk/government/publications/autumn-statement-2012-policy-decisions-table/autumn-statement-2012-policy-decisions-table>, accessed 6 July 2013)

HM Treasury, *Budget 2010* (TSO, London, 2010)

HM Treasury, *Delivering a Step Change in Police Productivity* (<http://www.openeyecommunications.com/agencyreports/delivering-a-step-change-in-police-productivity/>, accessed 20 October 2012)

HM Treasury, *Spending Review 2010* (TSO, London, 2010)

HM Treasury, *Spending Round 2013* (<https://www.gov.uk/government/uploads/system/uploads/attachment_data/file/209036/spending-round-2013-complete.pdf>, accessed 6 July 2013)

HMIC, 'Our role' (<http://www.hmic.gov.uk/about-us/what-we-do/>, accessed 7 April 2013)

HMIC, *Adapting to Austerity: A Review of Police Force and Authority Preparedness for 2011/12–14/15 CSR period* (HMIC, London, 2011)

HMIC, *Annual Reports, 1967–91* (HMSO, London, 1967–91)

HMIC, *Demanding Times: The Front Line and Police Visibility* (<http://www.hmic.gov.uk/media/demanding-times-062011.pdf>, accessed 20 April 2013)

HMIC, *Increasing Efficiency in the Police Service* (<http://www.hmic.gov.uk/media/increasing-efficiency-in-the-police-service.pdf>, accessed 16 January 2013)

HMIC, *Increasing Efficiency in the Police Service: The Role of Collaboration* (HMIC, London, 2012)

HMIC, *Modernising the Police Service: A Thematic Inspection of Workforce Modernization—the Role, Management and Development of Police Staff in the police Service of England and Wales* (HMIC, London, 2004)

HMIC, *Policing in Austerity: One Year On* (<http://www.hmic.gov.uk/media[force]> accessed 31 October 2012)

HIMIC, *Policing in Austerity: Rising to the Challenge* (<http:// www.hmic.gov.uk/media/policing-in-austerity-rising-to-the-challenge.pdf>, accessed 18 July 2014)

HMIC, *Policing Public Order: An Overview and Review of Progress Against the Recommendations of Adapting to Protest and Nurturing the British Model of Policing* (HMIC, London, 2011)

HMIC, Press release, #001/2009—*Police Forces Must Work Together in the Public Interest* (<http://www.hmic.gov.uk/news/releases-2009/release-001-2009/>, accessed 16 January 2013)

Home Affairs Committee, *New Landscape of Policing', Examination of Witnesses*, 10 May 2011 (<http://www.publications.parliament.uk/pa/cm201012/cmselect/cmhaff/939/11051002.htm>, accessed 16 January 2013)

Home Affairs Committee, *Examination of Witnesses*, 11 October 2011 (<http://www.publications.parliament.uk/pa/cm201012/cmselect/cmhaff/1456/11101101.htm>, accessed 29 November 2012)

Home Affairs Committee, *Examination of Witnesses*, 30 November 2010 (<http://www.publications.parliament.uk/pa/cm201011/cmselect/cmhaff/645/10113002.htm>, accessed 29 November 2012)

Home Office, *A New Approach to Fighting Crime* (<http://www.homeoffice.gov.uk/publications/crime/new-approach-fighting-crime?view=Binary>, accessed 21 October 2012)

Home Office, 'Anti-social behaviour' (<http://www.homeoffice.gov.uk/crime/anti-social-behaviour/> accessed 7 March 2013)

Home Office, *Anti-Social Behaviour Order Statistics—England and Wales 2011* (<http://www.homeoffice.gov.uk/publications/science-research-statistics/research-statistics/crime-research/asbo-stats-england-wales-2011/>, accessed 12 March 2013)

Home Office, *Arrests and Outcomes* (<http://www.homeoffice.gov.uk/publications/science-research-statistics/research-statistics/counter-terrorism-statistics/police-powers-terror-act-q2-2012/arrests-outcomes-q2-2012>, accessed 9 February 2013)

Home Office, *Assessment of Women in the Police Service* (<http://library.npia.police.uk/docs/homeoffice/assessment-women-police-service.pdf>, accessed 22 January 2013)

Home Office, 'College of Policing' (<http://www.homeoffice.gov.uk/police/college-of-policing/>, accessed 20 January 2013)

Home Office, *Consultation on a Revised Framework for Recorded Crime Outcomes* (Home Office, 2012 <https://www.gov.uk/government/uploads/system/uploads/attachment_data/file/157794/crime-outcomes.pdf>, accessed 1 April 2013)

Home Office, *Crime in England and Wales 2010/11: Police Force Area Tables* (<http://www.homeoffice.gov.uk/publications/science-research-statistics/research-statistics/crime-research/hosb1011/hosb1011-pfatabs?view=Binary>, accessed 29 March 2013)

Home Office, *Departmental Report 2009* (TSO, London, 2009 <http://www.official-documents.gov.uk/document/cm75/7592/7592.pdf>, accessed 21 April 2013)

Home Office, 'Extent and trends in illicit drug use among adults aged 16 to 59' (<http://www.homeoffice.gov.uk/publications/science-research-statistics/research-statistics/crime-research/drugs-misuse-dec-1112/extent-adults>, accessed 4 August 2012)

Home Office, *Have You Got What it Takes?* (<http://www.homeoffice.gov.uk/publications/police/pcc/have-got-what-takes/got-what-it-takes?view=Binary>, accessed 30 November 2012)

Home Office, *Have You Got What it Takes? Working with the Reducing Bureaucracy Programme* (<https://www.gov.uk/government/uploads/system/uploads/attachment_data/file/117428/reducing-bureaucracy.pdf>, accessed 18 April 2013)

231

Home Office, 'Historical crime data: A summary of recorded crime from 1898 to 2001/2' (<http://www.homeoffice.gov.uk/publications/science-research-statistics/research-statistics/crime-research/historical-crime-data/>, accessed 8 March 2013)

Home Office, 'Home secretary outlines plans for new police professional body', 15 December 2011 (<http://www.homeoffice.gov.uk/media-centre/press-releases/police-professional-body>, accessed 13 January 2013)

Home Office, *Local to Global: Reducing the Risk from Organized Crime* (<http://www.homeoffice.gov.uk/publications/crime/organised-crime-strategy?view=Binary>, accessed 15 January 2013)

Home Office, *Neighbourhood Policing: Your Police; Your Community; Our Commitment* (Home Office Communications Directorate, London, 2005)

Home Office, *Police Reform: A Police Service for the Twenty-first Century* (HMSO, London, 1993)

Home Office, *Police Service Strength England and Wales, 31 March 2010* (<https://www.gov.uk/government/uploads/system/uploads/attachment_data/file/115745/hosb1410.pdf>, accessed 3 July 2013)

Home Office, *Police Service Strength, England and Wales, 31 March 2012* (<http://www.homeoffice.gov.uk/publications/science-research-statistics/research-statistics/police-research/hosb0912/hosb0912?view=Binary>, accessed 21 January 2013)

Home Office, *Police Service Strength England and Wales, 30 September 2012* (<https://www.gov.uk/government/uploads/system/uploads/attachment_data/file/143957/hosb0113.pdf>, accessed 3 July 2013)

Home Office, *Policing in the 21st Century* (TSO, London, 2010)

Home Office, *Policing in the 21st Century: Reconnecting Police and the People: Summary of Consultation Responses* (<http://www.homeoffice.gov.uk/publications/consultations/policing-21st-century/response-policing-21st?view=Binary>, accessed 22 November 2012)

Home Office, *Proposals for Revised Funding Allocations for Police Authorities in England and Wales 2010/11*, 27 May 2010 (<http.www.epolitix.com/>, accessed 30 May 2010)

Home Office, *Putting Victims First: More Effective Responses to Anti-social Behavior* (Home Office, 2012 <http://www.official-documents.gov.uk/document/cm83/8367/8367.pdf>, accessed 7 July 2013)

Home Office, *Recorded Crime Statistics, 1898 to 2001/2* (<https://www.gov.uk/government/publications/recorded-crime-statistics-1898-to-2001-02>, accessed 8 April 2013)

Home Office, *Research Report 66 – Rolling Out the Police Single Non-Emergency Number (101): Research into the Public's and Practitioners' Views* (<https://www.gov.uk/government/uploads/system/uploads/attachment_data/file/115835/horr66-report.pdf>, accessed 8 July 2013)

Home Office, *Review of Core and Ancillary Tasks* (HMSO, London, 1995)

Home Office, *Stop and Search Statistics—Financial Year 2010/11* (<http://www.homeoffice.gov.uk/publications/science-research-statistics/research-statistics/police-research/immigration-tabs-q4-2011/stops-searches-1011-tabs?view=Binary>, accessed 23 January 2013)

Home Office, *The Government's Crime Reduction Strategy* (Home Office Communications Directorate, London, 1999)

Home Office, *The National Crime Agency: A Plan for the Creation of a National Crime-Fighting Capability* (Home Office, London, 2011)

Home Office, *The National Policing Plan 2003–2006* (<http://webarchive.nationalarchives.gov.uk/20100413151441/http://police.homeoffice.gov.uk/publications/national-policing-plan/nat_police_plan022835.pdf?view=Binary>, accessed 29 July 2012)

Home Office, *The Report of the Review of the Police Information and Technology Organisation* (PITO) (Home Office, London, 2005)

Home Office, *The Strategic Policing Requirement* (Home Office, London, 2012)

Home Secretary, *Draft Anti-Social Behaviour Bill, December 2012* (<http://www.homeoffice.gov.uk/publications/about-us/consultations/community-remedy-consultation/draft-antisocial-behaviour-bill?view=Binary>, accessed 7 March 2013)

House of Commons, *Police Pay—Booth Review* (2008–2011 pay deal)

House of Commons, Public Bill Committee, *Protection of Freedoms Bill*, 22 March 2011 (<http://www.publications.parliament.uk/pa/cm201011/cmpublic/protection/110322/am/110322s01.htm>, accessed 10 February 2013)

House of Commons Library, *Labour Policy on Domestic Violence—1999–2010* (Standard note SN/HA/3989, 22 May 2010, Home Affairs section <http://www.parliament.uk/briefing-papers/SN03989.pdf>, accessed 30 June 2013)

House of Commons Library, *Police Service Strength*, 10 September 2012 (Standard Note SN00634 <http://www.parliament.uk/briefing-papers/SN00634>, accessed 21 January 2013)

House of Lords, European Union Committee: Justice, Institutions and Consumer Protection Sub-Committee—*UK's 2014 Opt-out Decision ('Protocol 36')*—written evidence (<http://www.parliament.uk/documents/lords-committees/eu-sub-com-f/Protocol36OptOut/VolofevidenceP36asat110113.pdf>, accessed 6 February 2013)

House of Lords, Supplementary letter from Dr Helen Wallace, Director, GeneWatch UK, *Surveillance: Citizens and the State*—Constitution Committee (<http://www.publications.parliament.uk/pa/ld200809/ldselect/ldconst/18/8013007.htm>, accessed 10 February 2013, <http://www.parliament.uk/briefing-papers/SN04139.pdf>, accessed 20 December 2012)

Independent Police Complaints Commission (IPCC), *Deaths During or Following Police Contact: Statistics for England and Wales 2011/12* (<http://www.ipcc.gov.uk/en/Pages/reports_polcustody.aspx>, accessed 21 April 2013)

Independent Public Service Commission, *Pensions Commission Final Report*, March 2011 (<http://cdn.hm-treasury.gov.uk/hutton_final_100311.pdf>, accessed 22 December 2012), cited as *Hutton*

Independent Review of Police Officer Staff Remuneration and Conditions, *Part 1 Report* (<http://review.police.uk/publications/945287?view=Binary>, accessed 21 April 2013), cited as *Winsor 1*

Independent Review of Police Officer Staff Remuneration and Conditions, *Final Report*, volumes 1 and 2 (<http://review.police.uk/publications/part-2-report/>, accessed 26 April 2012), cited as *Winsor 2*

Independent Review of Police Officers' & Staff Remuneration & Conditions, 'About Tom Winsor and his role' (<http://review.police.uk/about-tom-winsor/terms-of-reference/>, accessed 21 December 2012)

Joint Consultative Committee, *The Operational Policing Review* (Joint Consultative Committee, Surbiton, 1990)

Local Government Association (LGA), *Local Government Association Response to Policing Consultation Paper* (<http://centrallobby.politicshome.com/members/member-press/member-press-details/newsarticle/local-government-association-response-to-policing-consultation-paper///sites/local-government-association/>, accessed 22 November 2012)

Mayor of London Office for Policing and Crime, *Police and Crime Plan 2013–2017*, Consultation Draft (<http://www.london.gov.uk/sites/default/files/Draft%20Police%20and%20Crime%20Plan%202013-2016%20CONSULTATION%20DRAFT%20FINAL_0.pdf>, accessed 19 April 2013)

Metropolitan Police, 'Stops and searches monitoring mechanism', July 2011, Haringey (<http://www.met.police.uk/foi/pdfs/priorities_and_how_we_are_doing/borough/haringey_stop_and_search_monitoring_report_july_2011.pdf>, accessed 19 April 2013)

Metropolitan Police Service, *4 Days in August: Strategic Review into the Disorder of August 2011* (final report, March 2012 <http://content.met.police.uk/cs/Satellite?blobcol =urldata&blobheadername1=Content-Type&blobheadername2=Content-Disposit ion&blobheadervalue1=application%2Fpdf&blobheadervalue2=inline%3B+filena me%3D%22145%2F595%2Fco553-114DaysInAugust.pdf%22&blobkey=id&blobt able=MungoBlobs&blobwhere=1283551523589&ssbinary=true>, accessed 25 March 2013)

Ministry of Justice, *Criminal Justice statistics: Quarterly Update to December 2011* (Ministry of Justice statistics bulletin, 24 May 2012 <https://www.gov.uk/government/ uploads/system/uploads/attachment_data/file/162610/criminal-justice-stats-dec-2011.pdf.pdf>, accessed 28 April 2013)

Ministry of Justice, *Prolific and Other Priority Offender Program—5 Years on: Maximizing the Impact* (Home Office, 2009 <https://www.gov.uk/government/uploads/system/ uploads/attachment_data/file/118035/PPO-5-years-on.pdf>, accessed 28 April 2013)

Ministry of Justice, *Proven Re-offending Statistics Quarterly Bulletin July 2010 to June 2011, England and Wales* (<https://www.gov.uk/government/uploads/system/ uploads/attachment_data/file/192631/proven-reoffending-jul-10-jun-11.pdf>, accessed 7 July 2013)

National Audit Office, 'Mobile technology in policing' (<http://www.nao.org.uk/ publications/1012/mobile_technology_in_policing.aspx>, accessed 13 January 2013)

National Audit Office, *The Home Office: Tackling Anti-Social Behaviour* (TSO, London, 2006)

National Policing Improvement Agency (NPIA), Information System Improvement Strategy (ISIS) (<http://www.npia.police.uk/en/docs/ISIS_briefing_Jul11-final_(2). pdf>, accessed 13 January 2013)

Neyroud, P, *Review of Police Leadership and Training*, vols I and II (<http://www.home-office.gov.uk/publications/consultations/rev-police-leadership-training/ report?view=Binary>, accessed 12 January 2013)

Normington, D, *Reducing the Data Burden on Police Forces in England and Wales* (Home Office, London, 2009)

Office for National Statistics (ONS), *2011 Census: Key Statistics for England and Wales*, March 2011 (<http://www.ons.gov.uk/ons/dcp171778_290685.pdf>, accessed 21 January 2013)

Office for National Statistics (ONS), *2011 Census—population and household estimates for England and Wales*, March 2011 (<http://www.ons.gov.uk/ons/dcp171778_270487. pdf>, accessed 21 January 2013)

Office for National Statistics (ONS), *Crime in England and Wales Quarterly First Release to March 2012*—police force area tables (<http://www.ons.gov.uk/ons/rel/crime-stats/crime-statistics/period-ending-march-2012/stb-crime-stats-end-march-2012. html>, accessed 29 March 2013)

Office for National Statistics (ONS), *Trends in Crime—A Short Story 2011/12* (<http:// www.ons.gov.uk/ons/rel/crime-stats/crime-statistics/period-ending-march-2012/ trends-in-crime--a-short-story.html>, accessed 23 April 2013)

Office of Community Oriented Policing Services, *The Impact of the Economic Downturn on American Police Agencies* (US Department of Justice, Washington DC, 2011)

parliament.uk, 14 September 2011, *Police Reform and Social Responsibility Bill*, Commons amendments (<http://www.publications.parliament.uk/pa/ld201011/ldhansrd/text/ 110914-0002.htm>, accessed 29 November 2012)

Police Arbitration Tribunal, *Decision of the Police Arbitration Tribunal: Winsor Part 1* January 2012 (https://www.gov.uk/government/uploads/system/uploads/attachment _data/file/143830/pat-decision.pdf>, accessed 4 July 2013)

Police Leadership Development Board, Police Leadership Development Board, *Getting the Best Leaders to Take on the Most Demanding Challenges* (Home Office, London, 2004)

Public Accounts Committee, *Central Procurement and the New Policing Landscape* (<http://www.publications.parliament.uk/pa/cm201213/cmselect/cmpubacc/ 129/12907.htm>, accessed 13 January 2013)

Public Administration Select Committee, *The Big Society* (<http://www.publications. parliament.uk/pa/cm201012/cmselect/cmpubadm/902/90203.htm>, accessed 17 August 2012)

Riots Communities and Victims Panel, *5 days in August: An Interim Report on the 2011 English Riots* (<http://webarchive.nationalarchives.gov.uk/20121003195935/http:/ riotspanel.independent.gov.uk/wp-content/uploads/2012/04/Interim-report-5-Days-in-August.pdf>, accessed 25 March 2013)

Riots Communities and Victims Panel, *After the Riots: the Final Report of the Riots Communities and Victims Panel*, 2012 <http://webarchive.nationalarchives.gov.uk/ 20121003195935/ http:/riotspanel.independent.gov.uk/wp-content/uploads/2012/ 03/Riots-Panel-Final-Report1.pdf>, accessed 29 March 2013)

Security Service MI5, 'Terrorist plots in the UK' (<https://www.mi5.gov.uk/home/the-threats/terrorism/international-terrorism/international-terrorism-and-the-uk/ terrorist-plots-in-the-uk.html>, accessed 9 February 2013)

Serious and Organised Crime Agency (SOCA), *Annual Plan 2012/13* (<http://www. soca.gov.uk/about-soca/.../372-soca-annual-plan-201213.pdf>, accessed 15 January 2013)

Sheehy, Sir Patrick, *Inquiry into Police Responsibilities & Rewards*, vol I (HMSO, London, 1993)

Strickland, P, *Police Reform and Social Responsibility Bill—House of Lords Amendments* (House of Commons Library, Home Affairs Section, 8 September 2011 <http:// www.parliament.uk/briefing-papers/SN06063.pdf>, accessed 29 November 2012)

Tarling, R, Burrows, J, and Clarke, A, *Dalston Youth Project Part II: An Evaluation* (Home Office Research Study 232, Home Office Research, Development and Statistics Directorate, November 2001 <http://library.npia.police.uk/docs/hors/hors232. pdf>, accessed 25 April 2012)

US Department of Justice Office of the Auditor General Audit Division, *The External Effects of the Federal Bureau of Investigation's Reprioritization Efforts* (<http://www. justice.gov/oig/reports/FBI/a0537/final.pdf>, accessed 4 January 2012)

Welsh Government, *Programme for Government* (<http://wales.gov.uk/about/programme forgov/communities/keyactions?lang=en>, accessed 14 December 2012)

Winsor, T, *Independent Review of Police Officer and Staff Remuneration and Conditions*, Part 1 (Independent Review of Police Officer and Staff Remuneration and Conditions, London, March 2012), cited as *Winsor 1*

Winsor, T, *Independent Review of Police Officer and Staff Remuneration and Conditions*, *Final Report*, vols 1 and 2 (Independent Review of Police Officer and Staff Remuneration and Conditions, London, 2012), cited as *Winsor 2*

Non-governmental policy papers, reports, and briefings

Ashcroft, Lord, 'Here's why Eastleigh voted the way it did', [no date] (<http://conservativehome.blogs.com/platform/2013/03/lord-ashcroft-heres-why-eastleigh-voted-the-way-it-did.html>, accessed 20 April 2013)

Bandyopadhyay, S, *Acquisitive Crime: Imprisonment, Detection and Social Factors* (<http:// www.civitas.org.uk/crime/crimeanalysis2012.pdf>, accessed 27 April 2013)

Bassett, D, Haldenby, A, Thraves, L, and Truss, E, *A New Force* (Reform, London, 2009)

Big Brother Watch, *The National DNA Database* (<http://www.bigbrotherwatch.org. uk/files/DNA_REPORT_June2012.pdf>, accessed 9 February 2013)

Boyd, E, *Police Officer Pensions: Affordability of Current Schemes* (Policy Exchange policy briefing <http://www.policyexchange.org.uk/images/publications/police%20 officer%20pensions%20-%20feb%2012.pdf>, accessed 17 December 2012)

Boyd, E and Skelton, D, *Policing 2020* (Policy Exchange, London, 2012)

Cameron, D, *The Big Society*, 10 November 2009 (<http://www.conservatives.com/ news/speeches/2009/11/david_cameron_the_big_society.aspx>, accessed 16 August 2012)

Carswell, D, *Direct Democracy: Empowering People to Make their Own Decisions* (<http:// www.douglascarswell.com/downloads/upload12.pdf>, accessed 13 December 2012)

Conservative Party, *1979 Conservative Party General Election Manifesto* (<http://www. conservative-party.net/manifestos/1979/1979-conservative-manifesto.shtml>, accessed 6 September 2012)

Conservative Party, *1992 Conservative Party General Election Manifesto: The Best Future for Britain* (<http://www.conservativemanifesto.com/1992/1992-conservative-manifesto.shtml#law>, accessed 1 October 2012)

Conservative Party, *Are You Thinking what We're Thinking?* (<http://www.conservatives. com/pdf/manifesto-uk-2005.pdf>, accessed 21 August 2012)

Conservative Party, *Built to Last* (Conservative Party, London, 2006)

Conservative Party, *Built to Last: the Aims and Values of the Conservative Party* (<http:// www.conservatives.com/pdf/BuiltToLast-AimsandValues.pdf>, accessed 25 April 2012)

Conservative Party, *Control Shift: Returning Power to Local Communities* (Conservative Party, London, 2009)

Conservative Party, *Delivering Some of the Best Health in Europe: Outcomes not Targets* (Conservative Party, London, 2008)

Conservative Party, *Election Manifesto: Time for Common Sense* (<http://www.conservative-party.net/manifestos/2001/2001-conservative-manifesto.shtml>, accessed 16 September 2012)

Conservative Party, *Invitation to Join the Government of Britain* (<http://media. conservatives.s3.amazonaws.com/manifesto/cpmanifesto2010_lowres.pdf>, accessed 29 August 2012)

Conservative Party, *Prosperity with a Purpose* (<http://www.conservativemanifesto. com/1964/1964-conservative-manifesto.shtml>, accessed 4 September 2012)

Conservative Party, *Raising the Bar, Closing the Gap: An Action Plan for Schools to Raise Standards, Create More Good School Places and Make Opportunity More Equal* (Conservative Party, London, 2007)

Conservative Party, 'Reduction in crime shows police reform is working', 24 January 2013 (<http://www.conservatives.com/News/News_stories/2013/01/Reduction_in_crime_shows_police_reform_is_working.aspx>, accessed 7 April 2013)

Conservative Party, *Repair Plan for Social Reform: Plan for Change* (Conservative Party, London, 2009)

Conservativehome, 'Cameron announces "national and international security" policy group' (<http://conservativehome.blogs.com/torydiary/2006/01/cameron_announc. html>, accessed 4 January 2012)

Cribb, J, Joyce, R, and Phillips, D, *Living Standards, Poverty and Inequality in the UK: 2012* (Institute for Fiscal Studies, London, 2012 <http://www.ifs.org.uk/comms/ comm124.pdf>, accessed 1 February 2013)

Economic Competiveness Policy Group, *Freeing Britain to Compete: Equipping the UK for Globalisation* (Conservative Party, London, 2007)

Election Commission, Media briefing (<http://www.electoralcommission.org.uk/__ data/assets/pdf_file/0011/151769/PCC-Media-Briefing-Nov-2012-FINAL-2.pdf>, accessed 30 November 2012)

Garland, J and Terry, C, *How Not to Run an Election: The Police & Crime Commissioner Election* (<https://www.electoral-reform.org.uk/downloadfile.php?PublicationFile=268>, accessed 18 April 2013)

GLC Police Committee Support Unit, *A New Police Authority for London* (GLC, London, 1983)

Grieve, D and Laing, E, *Reversing the Rise of the Surveillance State: 11 Measures to Protect Personal Privacy and Hold Government to Account* (The Conservative Party, London, 2009 <http://www.conservatives.com/News/News_stories/2009/09/~/media/ Files/Policy%20Documents/Surveillance%20State.ashx>, accessed 10 February 2013)

Gyngell, K, *The Phoney War on Drugs* (Centre for Policy Studies, 2009 <http://www.cps. org.uk/files/reports/original/111026175647-thephoneywarondrugs.pdf>, accessed 8 April 2013)

Harris, Lord Toby, 'A tied vote means that the Government's Police Reform and Social Responsibility Bill will get Royal Assent tomorrow and become law' (<http://www. lordtobyharris.org.uk/2011/09/>, accessed 29 November 2012)

Independent Police Commission, Home (<http://www.independentpolicecommission.org.uk>, accessed 10 April 2013)

Institute for Fiscal Studies (IFS), *Autumn Statement 2012: Introductory Remarks* (P Johnson (author) <http://www.ifs.org.uk/publications/6485>, accessed 2 February 2013)

Institute for Fiscal Studies (IFS), *Election Briefing 2010 Summary* (<http://www.ifs.org.uk/election/ebn_summary.pdf>, accessed 23 April 2013)

Labour Party, *Partners Against Crime: Labour's Approach to Tackling Crime and Creating Safer Communities* (Labour Party, London, 1994)

Labour Party, *Labour Party General Election Manifesto: Ambitions for Britain*, 2001, (<http://www.labour-party.org.uk/manifestos/2001/2001-labour-manifesto.shtml>, accessed 28 July 2012)

Labour Party, New Labour Because Britain Deserves Better (<http://www.labour-party.org.uk/manifestos/1997/1997-labour-manifesto.shtml/>, accessed 18 July 2012)

Labour Party, *The Labour Party Manifesto 2010* (<http://www2.labour.org.uk/uploads/TheLabourPartyManifesto-2010.pdf>, accessed 11 October 2012)

Labour Party, *The Labour Way is the Better Way* (<http://www.labour-party.org.uk/manifestos/1979/1979-labour-manifesto.shtml>, accessed 6 September 2012)

Lewis, P and Newburn, T, 'Reading the riots study revels police fears over further unrest', *The Guardian*, 1 July 2012 (<http://www.guardian.co.uk/uk/2012/jul/01/reading-the-riots-police-fears>, accessed 26 March 2013)

Liberal Democrat Party, Manifesto 2010 (<http://network.libdems.org.uk/manifesto2010/libdem_manifesto_2010.pdf>, accessed 21 September 2012)

Liberal Democrat Party, Our Manifesto (<http://www.libdems.org.uk/our_manifesto.aspx>, accessed 30 August 2012)

Liberty, *Liberty's Response to the Home Office Consultation Policing in the 21st Century: Reconnecting Police and the People* (<http://www.liberty-human-rights.org.uk/pdfs/policy10/policing-in-the-21stc-reconnecting-the-people-and-the-police-sept-2010.pdf>, accessed 22 November 2012)

Loveday, B and Reid, A, *Going Local: Who should Run Britain's Police?* (Policy Exchange, London, 2003)

Loveday, B, assisted by Reid, A and Rozzi, J, *Size Isn't Everything: Restructuring Policing in England and Wales* (Policy Exchange, London, 2006)

National and International Security Policy Group, *An Unquiet World* (<http://www.conservatives.com/pdf/securityreportfinal.pdf>, accessed 4 January 2012)

Norman, J and Ganesh, J, *Compassionate Conservatism* [sic] (Policy Exchange, London, 2006)

North London Citizens, *Citizens' Inquiry into the Tottenham Riots* (<http://www.citizensuk.org/wp-content/uploads/2012/02/Citizens-Inquiry-into-the-Tottenham-Riots-REPORT.pdf>, accessed 29 March 2013)

Nuffield Council on Bioethics, 'Chapter 4—Criminal investigation' (<http://www.nuffieldbioethics.org/sites/default/files/files/Bioinformation%20Chapter%204%20-%20Criminal%20investigation.pdf>, accessed 10 February 2013)

Police Foundation, *Stop and Search (Briefing)*, March 2012 (<http://www.police-foundation.org.uk/uploads/catalogerfiles/stop-and-search/stop_and_search_briefing.pdf>, accessed 23 January 2013)

Police Reform Taskforce, *Policing for the People: Interim Report of the Police Reform Taskforce* (Conservative Party, London, 2007)

Poverty Site, United Kingdom Income Inequalities (<http://www.poverty.org.uk/09/index.shtml>, accessed 1 February 2013)

Prison Reform Trust, *Bromley Briefing Fact File, April 2006* (<http://www.prison reformtrust.org.uk>, accessed 23 July 2012)

Prison Reform Trust, *Prison Briefing, May 2010* (<http://www.prisonreformtrust.org. uk/uploads/documents/prisonbriefingsmall.pdf>, accessed 23 July 2012)

UK Peace Index, *Exploring the Fabric of Peace in the UK from 2003 to 2012* (<http://www. visionofhumanity.org/wp-content/uploads/2013/04/UK-Peace-Index-2013-IEP-Report.pdf>, accessed 27 April 2013), cited as UK Peace Index Report 2013

YouGov, 'UKpollingreport', 16 December 2012 (<http://ukpollingreport.co.uk>, accessed 16 December 2012)

Circulars, guidance, and ministerial and departmental statements

Home Office Circular 010/2012 (<http://www.homeoffice.gov.uk/about-us/corporate-publications-strategy/home-office-circulars/circulars-2012/010-2012/>, accessed 28 December 2012)

Acts of Parliament, Bills, Statutory instruments, statutory codes, regulations, etc

Crime and Courts Bill 2012

Crime and Disorder Act 1998

Criminal Justice and Public Order Act 1994

Draft Anti-Social Behaviour Bill 2012

Police Act 1964

Police Act 1996

Police and Magistrates' Courts Act 1994

Police Reform Act 2002

Police Reform and Social Responsibility Act 2011

Protection of Freedoms Act 2012

Regulation of Investigatory Powers Act 2000

Statutory Instruments, Police, England and Wales, The Policing Protocol Order 2011

Newspapers, magazines, and online news sites

bbc.co.uk

computerweekly.com

constabulary.org.uk

Daily Telegraph

express.co.uk

ft.com

Guardian iPad edition

theguardian.com/uk

huffingtonpost.co.uk

independent.co.uk

itv.com

jamaicatimesuk.com

Local Government Chronicle

LutonOnSunday
mancuniammatters.co.uk
marketoracle.co.uk
media.press.net
Police Review (cited as PR)
policeoracle.com
spectator.co.uk
telegraph.co.uk
thamestalk.co.uk
The Economist
The *Independent*
The *Sun*
The Times
The Week
thenorthernecho.co.uk
thesun.co.uk
timesonline.co.uk
wireless-mag.com

Other online sites

acpo.police.uk
bernardrix.com
blogs.channel4.com
choosemypcc.org.uk
Cipfastats.net
communities.gov.uk
conservatives.com
GOV.UK
government-news.co.uk
homeoffice.gov.uk
ifs.org.uk
Ipsos-mori.com
justice.gov.uk
LabourList.org
nationalarchives.gov.uk
parliament.uk
polfed.org
publicfinance.co.uk
rusi.org
theyworkforyou.com
touchstoneblog.org.uk
ucl.ac.uk/constitutional-unit
ukmediacentre.pwc.com
ukpolitical.info
ukpublicspending.co.uk
wales.gov.uk

Speeches

Balls, E, 'Striking the Right Balance for the British Economy', 3 June 2013 (<http://www. labour.org.uk/striking-the-right-balance-for-the-british-economy>, accessed 6 July 2013)

Blair, T, 'Modern policing for safer communities' (Police Foundation Lecture, 14 June 1994, Labour Party Campaigns and Communication Directorate, London)

Cameron, D, 'Balancing freedom and responsibility: a modern British bill of rights', quoted in House of Commons Library, Background proposals for a British bill of rights and duties (Standard Note SN/PC/04559, 3 February 2009 <http://www. parliament.uk/documents/commons/lib/research/briefings/snpc-04559.pdf>, accessed 31 August 2012)

Cameron, D, 'David Cameron's speech on police reform', guardian.co.uk, 16 January 2006 (<http://www.guardian.co.uk/politics/2006/jan/16/conservatives.ukcrime1>, accessed 25 April 2012)

Cameron, D, 'Fixing our broken society' speech, 7 July 2008 (<http://www.conservatives. com/News/Speeches/2008/07/David_Cameron_Fixing_our_Broken_Society.aspx>, accessed 31 August 2012)

Cameron, D, 'Full text: David Cameron's speech to the Conservative Party Conference 2005', guardian.co.uk, 4 October 2005 (<http://www.guardian.co.uk/politics/2005/ oct/04/conservatives2005.conservatives3>, accessed 25 April 2012)

Cameron, D, 'Police Foundation Lecture', 10 July 2006 (<http://www.police-foundation. org.uk/uploads/holding/johnharris/jhml2006.pdf>, accessed 4 January 2012)

Cameron, D, 'Speech to the LGA Conference', 2 July 2009 (<http://www.conservatives. com/News/Speeches/2009/07/David_Cameron_Speech_to_the_LGA_Conference. aspx>, accessed 28 August 2012)

Cameron, D, 'UK and the EU' speech, BBC News, 23 January 2013 (<http://www.bbc. co.uk/news/uk-politics-21160684>, accessed 6 February 2013)

Cooper, Y, 'Yvette Cooper's speech in full', politics.co.uk, 3 October 2012 (<http:// www.politics.co.uk/comment-analysis/2012/10/03/yvette-cooper-speech-in-full>, accessed 10 April 2013)

Herbert, N, 'Speech to City Forum [sic]', 25 January 2011 (<http://www.homeoffice. gov.uk/media-centre/speeches/city-forum>, accessed 13 January 2013)

Letwin, O, *The Neighbourly Society: Collected Speeches 2001–2003* (Centre for Policy Studies, London, 2003)

May, T, 'Home Secretary's speech on police bureaucracy', 9 May 2011 (<https://www. gov.uk/government/speeches/home-secretarys-speech-on-police-bureaucracy>, accessed 25 August 2013)

Osborne, G, 'Stopping Labour's tax rise on working people', 29 March 2010 (<http:// www.conservatives.com/News/Speeches/2010/03/George_Osborne_Stopping_ Labours_tax_rise_on_working_people.aspx>, accessed 29 August 2012)

Osborne, G, 'We will lead the economy out of crisis', 6 October 2009 (<http://www. conservatives.com/News/Speeches/2009/10/George_Osborne_We_will_lead_the_ economy_out_of_crisis.aspx>, accessed 29 August 2012)

Miscellaneous sources, notes, and correspondence

Slovo, G, *The Riots from Spoken Evidence* (Oberon Books, London, 2011)

Today, BBC Radio 4, 24 April 2013 (BBC iPlayer)

Index